A History of American Thought 1860–2000

This book is a comprehensive overview of the history of modern American thought and examines a wide range of modern thought and thinkers from 1860, when Charles Darwin's *Origin of Species* was published in the United States, to the end of the twentieth century.

The focus of this volume is on the destabilizing effects of modern challenges to notions of fixed order and absolute truths, and the contradictory consequences for philosophical, political, social, and aesthetic thought. The intellectual response to the unprecedented changes of this era produced visions of both liberation from the hierarchies of the past and new forms of control and constraint. One of the central contradictions in modern thought was between biological and cultural ideas of social, psychological, and moral order. This is the first work to provide an interpretive vision of the entire period under consideration. Topics covered include evolutionary thought, philosophical Pragmatism, ideas of race and gender, pluralism and cultural relativism, Cold War Liberalism, science and religion, feminist thought, evolutionary psychology, and the late twentieth-century Culture Wars. Thinkers from William James and Charlotte Perkins Gilman through Judith Butler and Cornel West are analyzed as historical figures.

This volume is an ideal resource for a general audience as well as undergraduate and graduate students in the field of American intellectual history.

Daniel Wickberg has taught intellectual history at the University of Texas at Dallas for over 25 years. His primary areas of research are the history of American social thought and historiography. He is the author of *The Senses of Humor: Self and Laughter in Modern America* (1998).

A History of American Thought 1860–2000
Thinking the Modern

Daniel Wickberg

Taylor & Francis Group

NEW YORK AND LONDON

Designed cover image: Boat on water, Neil Fox/Alamy Stock Photo

First published 2024
by Routledge
605 Third Avenue, New York, NY 10158

and by Routledge
4 Park Square, Milton Park, Abingdon, Oxon, OX14 4RN

Routledge is an imprint of the Taylor & Francis Group, an informa business

© 2024 Daniel Wickberg

The right of Daniel Wickberg to be identified as author of this work has been asserted in accordance with sections 77 and 78 of the Copyright, Designs and Patents Act 1988.

All rights reserved. No part of this book may be reprinted or reproduced or utilised in any form or by any electronic, mechanical, or other means, now known or hereafter invented, including photocopying and recording, or in any information storage or retrieval system, without permission in writing from the publishers.

Trademark notice: Product or corporate names may be trademarks or registered trademarks, and are used only for identification and explanation without intent to infringe.

Library of Congress Cataloging-in-Publication Data
Names: Wickberg, Daniel, 1960– author.
Title: A history of American thought 1860-2000: thinking the modern / Daniel Wickberg.
Other titles: Thinking the modern
Description: New York, NY: Routledge, 2024. | Includes bibliographical references and index.
Identifiers: LCCN 2023012699 (print) | LCCN 2023012700 (ebook) | ISBN 9780367638108 (hbk) | ISBN 9780367633110 (pbk) | ISBN 9781003120803 (ebk)
Classification: LCC E169.1 .W485 2024 (print) | LCC E169.1 (ebook) | DDC 973—dc23/eng/20230428
LC record available at https://lccn.loc.gov/2023012699
LC ebook record available at https://lccn.loc.gov/2023012700

ISBN: 978-0-367-63810-8 (hbk)
ISBN: 978-0-367-63311-0 (pbk)
ISBN: 978-1-003-12080-3 (ebk)

DOI: 10.4324/9781003120803

Typeset in Sabon
by codeMantra

For Susan and Eleanor

Contents

Preface ix
Acknowledgments xi

Introduction 1

PART I
American Modernisms: 1860–1919 15

1 Darwinism and the Evolutionary Sensibility 17

2 Pragmatism and Antifoundational Thought 34

3 The Research University, The Idea of Culture, and The Social Sciences 48

4 Progressivisms 64

5 Rethinking Woman and Man 80

PART II
The Contradictions of the Democratic Imagination: 1920–1962 99

6 Cultural Relativisms and Modern Hierarchies 101

7 Science as Culture: The Moral Order of Modernity 119

8 From Protestant Hegemony to Religious Pluralism 135

viii Contents

9   Pluralism and Cosmopolitanism   152

10 Self and Social Order in the Cold War World   169

PART III
Rethinking Modernisms: 1963–2000   197

11 Cultural Revolutions and Ruptures   199

12 The Social Construction of Everything   219

13 The Return of Nature   233

14 Gender and Sexuality   248

15 Culture Wars   265

Bibliographical Essay   283
Index   301

Preface

In the mid-twentieth century, it was common to have the kind of comprehensive historical synthesis this book seeks. But since the 1960s, the project of writing a coherent one volume interpretive account of the history of modern American thought has foundered on the seeming impossibility of integrating new research and new perspectives, the increasing specialization and fragmentation of the field, and a kind of methodological suspicion of every generalization for concealing a contradiction or complexity that demands further analysis. For many, the very idea of an overview is suspect as a form of reductionism. For others, the challenge of choosing what to include and what to leave out imposes a burden of its own, a sense that no one will be satisfied or uncritical of the choices made. For yet others, the diversity of the field yields no coherent form in which to order our understanding.

I came to write this book for two reasons. First, I thought it was long overdue. American intellectual history, the history of thought in the United States, has been in need of a revision, a reframing, and an accessible introduction. In particular, it seemed possible to link the characteristic forms of thought of the last third of the twentieth century with those that had gone before, and to revise older patterns of thinking and ideas in light of more recent ones. Second, I have been teaching courses on modern American thought for almost 30 years. In part I have been frustrated by the absence of a book that I might use in my classes, but more importantly, thinking about these ideas has been my life's work. I thought I had something to say, a distinctive approach to the subject matter, and a way of making sense of the disparate elements that make up modern thought and thinking. This book is an overview, but it also expresses a way of seeing the world. We think in terms of modernity ourselves. We can't help but see the ideas of modern thinkers through the lenses, categories, and sensibilities they have given us—or that we have taken from them.

I have made many choices to make the story I tell here a coherent and comprehensive one. I am certain that other historians would have made other choices. I have necessarily simplified bodies of thought and the conditions of their creation. Scholars specializing in the particular thinkers and topics I have covered here are likely to want more or to question my characterizations. I can only plead that the form here demands something different than specialization and detailed exploration. My hope is that my treatment inspires readers to dig more deeply into the particular topics explored here.

This book is written for many different readers: undergraduate students taking courses in American intellectual history; graduate students preparing for field exams; non-academic readers who are interested in understanding the development and transformation of the intellectual worlds we all live in, in one way or another. Some of the ideas I discuss are difficult to understand, but the larger pattern of which they are a part is equally important, so the book can be read profitably on a number of different levels.

Finally, just a note on the choice to use very limited endnotes. I have only used citations when I have provided direct quotations from primary sources, and I have done so in the interest of keeping the book length manageable. The bibliographic essay includes many of the secondary sources I have relied upon. The field of intellectual history is vast; I hope this book provides a gateway to understanding the conditions of what it has been and continues to be, to think in modern terms.

Acknowledgments

My thanks go to all the students I have taught in intellectual history courses over the years; they have shaped this book in ways both big and small. The classroom has been the testing ground for the conceptions that have guided me in thinking about the history of modern American thought. I am also grateful to my colleagues in the field, particularly those associated with the Society for U.S. Intellectual History. A special thanks to Andrew Hartman and Ray Haberski, who sustained SUSIH, and who reviewed a proposal for the book. My faculty writing group at the University of Texas at Dallas has been a source of support, criticism, and engagement. I couldn't ask for a better or more generous group of readers than Ashley Barnes, Erin Greer, Charles Hatfield, Annelise Heinz, Eric Schlereth, and Shilyh Warren. They read and provided helpful feedback and encouragement on some of the chapters here. Lilian Calles Barger read a draft of Chapter 14 and provided me with an unpublished paper of her own that helped me think about the issues in that chapter. My friends and colleagues at UTD, past and present, have provided a collegial space for thinking about the relationship between history, philosophy, and literature. In particular, I want to thank Michael Wilson, Theresa Towner, and Erin Smith for their kindness and friendship over the many years we have served in the trenches. My greatest debt is to my wife, Susan Evans-Wickberg, and my daughter, Eleanor Evans-Wickberg; they have provided me with the love and support that makes all other things possible. I have tried to provide some small thanks in the dedication of this volume. I wish I could say any errors are somebody else's, but they're all mine.

Introduction

Between the middle of the nineteenth century and the end of the twentieth century, peoples all over the world created a host of new ways of thinking about that world. We refer to these new ways of thinking as "modern," characterized by a consciousness of innovation, of the need for new ways of imagining knowledge, nature, society, human beings, morality, beliefs, and values. Whether promoting a vision of the new or reacting in opposition to it, modernists of all stripes could not help but engage the dynamic world they faced—a new economy defined by industrial production and market capitalism; a new encounter with peoples unlike themselves; the political fallout of an age of revolutions; an upending of the conditions and frame of religious belief. This book tells one part of the story of modern thought and its contradictions—that specific to the United States, a nation at the forefront of many of these changes. Because ideas and thoughts have no respect for national borders, this cannot be a story told in isolation from the larger transnational context. But the specific conditions of American life did create a kind of variant of modern thought that can be distinguished from those in other places. Not more optimistic, nor more moderate, nor more ideologically coercive, as some have suggested, but recognizable as a distinctive idiom nonetheless. Nor was there any degree of consensus among Americans—modern thought was not a body of doctrines subscribed to, a creed, a set of shared propositions. Rather, it consisted of various attempts by various people to grapple with a world unmoored from its foundations, a world made fluid. This is an intellectual history of those attempts.

As a preliminary, this introduction aims to do two things. First, it assumes that for many of its readers, the field of intellectual history is an unfamiliar thing, and so it seeks to explain what it is intellectual historians do, and what the distinctive features of the study of the intellectual dimension of the past might be. This discussion of method, concept, and focus is designed to orient readers to the kind of history they can expect to find here. Second, it seeks to outline the general argument and structure of the book and provide in a nutshell the main themes of the work. These two elements of the introduction will illuminate some of the choices I have made in this volume.

What Is Intellectual History?

The study of history encompasses all that human beings have done and said in the past. We conventionally divide that study into units organized by regions and periods, recognizing that the definitions we create are man-made, and not given in the nature of things. But beyond the categorization of history by time and place, we recognize that the activities that people engage in, and the structures they create, are varied and distinct. Hence, we create forms of historical study defined by the objects and activities of people in the past. In the nineteenth century, as the professional discipline of history was being created, it was commonly imaged that history was "past politics." This idea that the political activities and structures of human beings are the proper focus of the discipline of history leaves its residue in the present; the popular conception of history is that its main subject matter is politics. But over the course of the twentieth century, a vast array of new forms of historical study were created or remade: social history, economic history, cultural history, military history, religious history, history of the family, gender history, labor history, environmental history, among them. One of those new forms was something called "intellectual history." How we are to distinguish it from these other forms? What makes intellectual history a distinct kind of practice? What is it, exactly, that we are studying when we study intellectual history?

While it would seem obvious that any field of history must rest on a consensus among its practitioners, a shared set of definitions and principles, when we look closely at the practice of intellectual historians, we discover widely divergent objects and methods of study operating under a common disciplinary umbrella. For some, the proper object of intellectual history is the study of intellectuals—those men and women whose central identities involve thinking, formulating arguments, and critically assessing the world through the use of the power of thought. It is the practices of intellectuals—a specific social type with a specific social role—that appear central to intellectual history in this formulation. But, even here, there is little consensus on who qualifies as an intellectual. Others imagine that it is not intellectuals, but ideas that should be the object of our study. The ideas that people create have a history—they come into being and are developed under specific conditions, and it is the job of the intellectual historian to trace and explain those origins and developments through time and space, the influence of ideas as they are transmitted and shared; sometimes the people who promulgate these ideas are "intellectuals," but often they are not. Even here, however, it's not clear that all ideas are the objects of study, but perhaps only "generally held" ideas that speak to broad aspects of human experience. That is, technical ideas that are very specialized don't necessarily seem to fall under the purview of the intellectual historian. A third orientation of intellectual historians is to look not at individual ideas but at the products of intellectual activity defined as arguments, discourses, or shared intellectual practices. Instead of seeing ideas as having a distinct existence, these historians imagine that ideas are utterly dependent upon the arguments and purposes of those persons involved in persuading others. The concept of "discourse," slippery as it sometimes is, is a widely held one among historians. A fourth and related form of intellectual history involves a focus on specific disciplinary knowledge and concepts, which are often imagined as distinct and internal to small groups of specialists. The history of natural sciences, but also of disciplines such as sociology, psychology, and philosophy, for instance, often assume the institutional specificity of thinking within their domains. The history of psychological ideas, in this conception, consists of debates within the discipline of psychology and is minimally concerned with larger social, cultural, and intellectual contexts. Finally, some intellectual historians focus on intellectual "movements," shared intellectual dispositions defined by a collective set of concerns and sensibilities. Whenever we think of "isms," of one kind or another, we are generally talking about intellectual movements: Pragmatism, feminism, conservatism, Progressivism, and Marxism can all be understood as movements.

In addition to the range of potential objects of study by intellectual historians, there is the question of the boundaries between intellectual history and other forms. Does theology belong more appropriately to the study of religious history than to intellectual history? Are policy ideas and their implementation better understood under the umbrella of political history? When ideas become broadly held collective beliefs do they cease to be the concern of intellectual historians and become the concern of cultural historians? Should legal history—at least in its formulation of legal theories, principles, and modes of argument—be a branch of intellectual history? Some might imagine that since all other human activities involve ideas and thinking, we should give those other subfields proprietary interest in the forms of thinking relevant to the activities they study—that there is no general field of intellectual history that shares a common outlook, and that legal historians are better qualified to study legal thought, religious historians are better qualified to study religious thought than intellectual historians. Similarly, shouldn't we cede the study of the history of philosophy to philosophers, the study of the history of economic theory to economists, and the history of mathematics to mathematicians?

I think both the idea that there is no general object of intellectual history, and that disciplinary specialists are better qualified to write the history of their own disciplinary practices, are wrong. This book is premised on the idea that there is a common object for the study of intellectual history, and that the perspective of intellectual history illuminates its objects in ways that, say, narrower disciplinary histories, or studies of the thought of individual thinkers by philosophers, theorists, theologians, or political scientists, does not. Although there is no single way to be an intellectual historian, and the methods of practice are diverse, there is a shared sensibility among intellectual historians. That sensibility is composed of two central orientations: (1) A commitment to thinking historically and contextually, and (2) an approach that foregrounds thinking and thought as its central objects. To conceive of the process and product of intellectual activity as a historical object is to reject the notion that thinking is a purely rational and universal project of human intelligence, to be evaluated by transhistorical standards. Rather, intellectual history approaches thought as something contingent, dependent upon its particular historical contexts; it is concerned with the development, persistence, transformation, abandonment, repression, expression, and contradiction of thought in particular times and places. Intellectual history is a "big tent," with many different methodological and definitional differences within it, but it does have boundaries, and ultimately a shared outlook among its practitioners.

Intellectual history differs from the work of most practitioners who study the same texts and thinkers as intellectual historians do, but in related disciplines. Because historians are concerned with explaining how thought came into being and the directions it took, relative to particular contexts, they are less concerned with the question of the validity of ideas and arguments from the past than disciplinarians concerned with the same texts. For the historian, the questions of whether an argument is correct or not, whether the ideas have a logical flaw, or what improvement might be made on a particular argument, get in the way of understanding ideas in relationship to their multiple contexts. The question of whether an analysis made by a past actor is "right" tends to pull us away from the contexts and towards a transhistorical standard of evaluation. It is not that historians are or can be completely indifferent to truth claims, since they rely on some of their own in their own methodologies. But for the purpose of historical study, the question of the validity of a past idea is simply bracketed and held off as not relevant to the task of trying to understand how and why, and under what conditions, thought was constructed. Historians want to know "what is being said," "where did it come from," "where did it go," and "why," and not "is it true"? As one historian has said, intellectual historians operate under "the paradoxical working assumption that all ideas are false but important."[1] We can make judgments about the historical significance of thought without assessing the validity of it.

Take, for instance, one of the best-known claims by a twentieth-century thinker—W.E.B. DuBois's famous declaration in *The Souls of Black Folk* (1903) that African-Americans possess a "double consciousness." This is a complex idea, and DuBois seemed to mean more than one thing by it. But the intellectual historian is less concerned with whether this is an accurate description of the psychological makeup of Black Americans, and more concerned with how DuBois came to this idea and what he meant by it—the intellectual influences and sources he drew upon, the relationship to the particular conditions of race relations in the Progressive Era, the way his own situation as a Black intellectual was given expression in this idea. Such questions will lead us to the history of psychological thought in the late nineteenth century, and the role of one of DuBois's instructors at Harvard, William James, in shaping new conceptions of consciousness; DuBois's training in Germany and his exposure to the dialectical philosophy of the Hegelian tradition, with its own image of internal contradiction; the history of the idea of race; the development of African-American critiques of racial order in the context of an emerging movement for Civil Rights in which DuBois played a central role; the larger themes and goals of the text in which DuBois expressed this idea; the early DuBois's opposition to the economic and materialistic conceptions of values that he associated with one of the principle African-American leaders of the time, Booker T. Washington; whether the idea of "double consciousness" stood out as a central idea in the text at the moment of its publication and initial reception, or whether it was later generations of thinkers who read DuBois in a particular way that gave the concept its power and centrality. All of these are historical, contextual ways of framing the problem of understanding. Whether "double consciousness" is a valid description of the ways in which Black Americans see the world is an entirely separate question. Historians tend to believe that asking that latter question means that we are less likely to understand the idea as a historical entity; we become guilty of a kind of "presentism" by judging its validity by our own standards rather than situating it in relationship to its meaning in its own time and its influence in shaping other thinkers since. Unlike disciplinarians, who are inclined to see intellectual changes in terms of the context of the discipline (e.g. philosophical ideas as contextualized by the history of philosophical thought), intellectual historians draw on a wide array of different contexts—social, economic, political, institutional, and intellectual—to analyze the thought of the past.

The contextualizing sensibility of intellectual historians, however, is frequently balanced by the need to pay close attention to the specific form and content of texts and arguments. That is, most intellectual historians reject the notion that contextual analysis means avoiding the close reading of texts in favor of situating those texts in relationship to extratextual phenomena. This is a false choice, and since intellectual history is defined by its foregrounding of thought as a historical object, it means that historians simultaneously engage in close reading and contextualization. We might describe the general method of intellectual history as a tacking back and forth between intensive reading of sources—paying close attention to argument, form, language, perspective—and extensive reading of matters lying outside the individual text or corpus of work. The further we push into a text, the more we are drawn back outside of it, and the more we develop contexts, the more we are drawn back into the text; text and context are joined in any successful analysis of the historicity of thought and ideas. Intellectual historians do not believe in the autonomy of texts—their formalistic independence—but they also reject the idea that it is sufficient to see a text in terms of its general dispositions rather than its specific expression. Thought, for the intellectual historian, is not merely a reflection of some more significant or determinative context—it is the historical subject matter itself and demands close attention. But if we do not look outside of the intellectual sources, texts, and arguments, we fail to understand them historically. Mastering the skill of intensive and extensive reading conjoined is the challenging methodological goal of the intellectual historian.

Intellectual historians generally have a different interpretive relationship to sources than many other kinds of historians, since we tend to regard our sources as containers of thought rather than as containers of information. That is, all historians use primary sources to reconstruct the past, and various critical methods to assess those sources. But the intent of intellectual historians is to see their sources as texts which provide evidence of the thought of those who created them, rather than of some independent social, economic, or political reality. Many non-intellectual historians regard the critical treatment of sources as a way to remove the point of view or "bias" of their creator so as to document a reality that was observed and recorded by that creator. So, for instance, historians will frequently gather as many sources relevant to a particular event as they can, and check the accounts given by multiple authors against one another—what they are after is a characterization of the reality that was incidentally documented in the sources. What intellectual historians tend to be concerned with is not an independent reality, but the thinking that is intrinsic to the text, the point of view of the author being the thing that is documented. For intellectual historians, the documents they study are often the same things as the historical events they study. To remove the point of view of the author would be to remove the central object of study. For instance, the text of a work like William James's *Varieties of Religious Experience* (1902) is the object of study for an intellectual historian in the same way that, say, the election of 1896 might be the object of study for a political historian.

The political historian will use many different sources—personal diaries, newspaper articles, institutional records, etc.—to find out how the election of 1896 was conducted, what the aims and goals of politicians and voters might have been, what the outcomes of the election were for national politics. The sources are used to reconstruct an independent reality. But the intellectual historian sees the arguments, organization, and conceptual bearings of the *Varieties of Religious Experience* as being entirely encased in the text itself; our source leads us to the mind of its creator rather than to an event that exists independent of the thought of the document's creator. The documenting of thought is, in some large measure, the same thing as the document itself. We don't have a situation where documents are one order of reality, and "history" itself is another.

This, I think, is probably one of the hardest things to understand about the epistemology of the field of intellectual history. When we are contextualizing thought, we sometimes rely on sources that we use to establish a reality independent of the document; we don't tend to treat, say, documents containing biographical information as evidence of thought (although we might, since every document created by a person expresses thought in some sense). We don't tend to treat institutional records as if they were philosophical treatises. We are acting like most historians do in using records such as these to document independent events, conditions, and action. But when we turn to documents that we are considering in terms of their meaning and the thought they contain, we shift gears. We don't read Hannah Arendt's immigration records the same way we read *The Origins of Totalitarianism* (1951). The first we regard as most historians might; the second we look to as a document to be read for its expression of thinking, thought, and ideas. One way to conceptualize this difference is to say that some documents are sources, and others are texts. Some we use to establish an independent reality that provides contexts of particular kinds, others we approach through methods of close reading that have more in common with how literary scholars and philosophers approach texts.

While some sources lend themselves more to being regarded as texts, there is actually no clear and absolute line we can draw that says on one side we have texts, on the other we have documents establishing independent contexts. Unpublished personal letters, for instance, often contain biographical information as well as arguments and ideas. Even philosophical treatises and highly formal works of thought may contain contextual information. Tax records may establish independent facts about economic status, but they also are expressions of a philosophy of taxation—they are the products of human minds. The art of intellectual history is to find a way of reading and interpreting sources so as to establish the contingent meaning of thought in particular circumstances, and that requires that we make judgments about when it's appropriate to think of a source as a document of an independent reality, and when we might regard it as an expression of the thought contained in it. Since there is no rule for how we do this, and these judgments are often made tacitly rather than explicitly, there is no universal method of intellectual history. We are back to the earlier point: intellectual history is unified more by a sensibility and set of dispositions than it is by an explicit methodology.

One of the major divides between intellectual historians is one of scope, scale, and kinds of historical contexts. Many intellectual historians believe that we are on more solid ground when we localize contexts—that studying a particular time, place, institution or group of people provides a more concrete framework that makes their claims about the past more demonstrable and credible. Others believe that examining how ideas and thinking change over long periods of time and broad geographical units, and not only in a discrete times and places, provides a set of contexts that are illuminating about the meaning and role of specific ideas in modern thought—illumination that is obscured by focusing too narrowly. Each approach has benefits to recommend it. The approach associated with the term "History of Ideas," and its principal proponent Arthur Lovejoy, was dominant in the mid-twentieth century, but came under heavy criticism for making large sweeping claims about ideas over time, and for thinking about ideas in a way that critics referred to as "disembodied." Since the 1970s, more localized discourse studies, or works that invoke specific political, social, and economic contexts have been the norm. In the last decade, however, there has been a resurgence of interest in "long-range" intellectual history, and the history of ideas, partly to offset the kinds of fragmentation of the field produced by an abundance of localized and specialized studies, but also to remind historians that ideas do not appear merely as expressions of local contexts, but have long-range persistence—people are not free to think in wholly new ways, since they operate in the discursive and intellectual environment of inherited ideas. The current book seeks to balance these two orientations.

One of the major criticisms of intellectual history has been for its assumptions about which people are its proper object of study—who are the thinkers—and the exclusions that are built into those assumptions. In recent years, for instance, a new emphasis on African-American intellectual history, women's intellectual history, Asian-American intellectual history, and working-class intellectual history has sought to challenge the image of intellectual history as inherently biased toward educated and literate elites, who, in the American and European contexts, have been predominantly white, upper or middle class, and male. The result of these challenges has been not simply a more comprehensive model of inclusion, but also a redefinition of what counts as thought. Those who did not have the luxury of material and cultural support, sought different goals in their thinking, and found ways to express their ideas outside of the kinds of publication and authorized institutions that conferred prestige. For many historians, the very definition of "intellectual" had been inherently exclusionary. Intellectual historians' propensity to foreground philosophical thought, erudition, systematic and formal theories, and criticism was itself a foregrounding of a particular way of thinking, which some had equated with thinking in general. ==The challenge to intellectual history from the margins and the borderlands of thought drew thought that was engaged in more immediate and practical issues, thought that often did not share common assumptions, into the center of intellectual history.== Part of the issue here is that the term "intellectual" has been seen by many to be an honorific, rather than a merely descriptive, characterization. Intellectual historians are divided over this as well—some inevitably style themselves as intellectuals and look to past examples as models for the type. Others attach no specific praise or estimation to the category "intellectual," but use it to describe the general character of thought and thinking. The revival of intellectual history in the last two decades has fundamentally transformed the range of what counts as "intellectual" by bringing new perspectives and conceptions of thought in history.

One of the results has been that figures who were often viewed primarily as political and social leaders are now studied for their ideas and thought. The twentieth-century conception of "the intellectual" had tended to separate the intellectual from roles of political activity, and had imagined the intellectual as a kind of critic with no loyalties to political movements or governments (or other institutions, for that matter). Intellectuals had political positions and views of course, but they imagined themselves as something other than ideological advocates for their politics or simply partisan mouthpieces—they saw themselves as possessing a kind of autonomy and critical distance from power. Those who were too enmeshed in political movements, from this point of view, lacked the critical stance from which to construe arguments and extended analysis without being tied to strategy and tactics. Intellectuals of this kind did not imagine themselves as neutral or "objective," or having no commitments, but they did imagine themselves as too committed to truth to take dogmatic positions or be simply purveyors of ideologies. This is, of course, a very romanticized view of "the intellectual," and it belongs to a certain time and place, beginning in the late nineteenth century. The point of many of those seeking to transform the study of thought in more inclusive ways has been to suggest that the class position and privilege of the intellectual—the access to education, forms of publication, and recognition, for instance—is obscured by foregrounding thought and making its social and political origins disappear. Today, while historians shun reductionism—the idea that thought can be entirely explained by the social status of its creator—they are entirely conscious of the exclusions built

10 *Introduction*

into intellectual history, and have sought a remedy by redefining who counts as a thinker, and what counts as thought. This, too, has required a redefinition of sources—instead of looking for thought in philosophical arguments, journals of opinion, and well-developed formal arguments, some intellectual historians find in movement records, institutional documents, and notes of observed oratory, the presence of thought as an object of study. One historian has described her method as "free-range intellectual history," in search of thought wherever one might find it.[2]

The present volume aims to draw on the various approaches to intellectual history sketched here. Recognizing that intellectual history is a dynamic field of study, I seek to demonstrate its variety as well as its shared sensibility. The book is both synthetic and interpretive—it provides an overview of the subject, drawing on a rich secondary literature that has been created in the last 75 years. While it's important that the work is timely and relies on current and recent work in the field, the tendency of some historians to privilege current historiography at the expense of established and older work swings too far in the opposite direction. I am not neglectful of older works of history, which the reader will find illuminated and identified in the bibliographic essay. And although this is also an interpretive work—providing a distinct understanding of the patterns of intellectual development over the past century and a half—I will not be engaging in explicit historiographical discussion and identifying ongoing debates between historians; there simply is not room in a book of this length to do so. Historians make history, rather than just discovering it lying around, it is true. The reader must assume that I am doing something more in this book than simply presenting a factual record and a chronology. I am providing an interpretation.

The Interpretive Argument

The central interpretation that I advance in this book is one in which irony, contradiction, and unintended consequences are both the form and substance of modern thought. The thought that has been created since the mid-nineteenth century represents various attempts to navigate the possibilities of an epistemic, ontological, aesthetic, and moral order that consistently has emphasized both the power of critical intellect to remake the world, and the constraints of an increasingly complex, bureaucratic, technological, and highly organized world. Modernity has meant both new kinds of freedom and new determinisms; deracination and self-creation; conformity and critical intellect; secularism and renovated faith; nihilism and utopian possibility; subjectivism and science; progress and tradition. The tendency to think in terms of contrasts and contradictions is itself a pervasive feature of modern thought. So much of modern thought addresses central questions—if human beings have created their own worlds, both materially and intellectually, why do they find themselves in a condition of alienation and unfreedom? If the mind can be liberated by the process of demystification and destabilization of received truths, by embracing uncertainty and anti-dogmatic thought, why is the mind apparently enslaved by its own fictional categories? The underlying argument of this book is that the very conditions of possibility presented by modernity and modern thought were the instruments of new forms of limitation and control. The apparent battles between those who sought to maintain tradition and the received ways of the past, on the one hand, and those who promised a progressive overcoming of those received ways, on the other, were ultimately fought on the ground of the latter. The "authority of the past" was a modern category, both for those who sought to overcome it, and those who sought to reinstate it. The characteristically modern conflict was played out in the debates surrounding Darwinism in the mid-nineteenth century, the Culture Wars of the late twentieth century, the attempt to think in *and* against categories of race and gender, in the triumph of progressive cultural politics or the new synthesis of a modern conservative movement.

This work is organized around, in a sense, a Hegelian narrative. The philosophy crafted by G.W.F. Hegel in early nineteenth-century Germany has been undercut and dethroned in many ways, but its view of the logic of history unfolding through intellectual contradiction remains a powerful model, even for historians who don't imagine that they owe anything to Hegel at all. Hegel, of course, imagined a teleological history, one based on necessary progress toward an ultimate goal of universal freedom embodied in the State. But there is no teleology in the account I give here—history is a story of contingencies and we cannot extrapolate it into a foreordained future as both Hegel and Marx, following him, imagined. In fact, in part, the story of modernity is a story of loss of faith in a necessary order and an inevitably progressive vision of history—a destruction of the epistemic, ontological, and moral certainties that arose out of Enlightenment rationalism. But what remains of Hegel is a vision of history moving through the process of contradiction, of ideas containing and generating their opposites, of history not as a unilinear process of development, but as a dialectic process of continuity through opposition. The idea that ideas in history carry within themselves the seeds of their own destruction, that they are riven by internal contradictions, that they ironically produce unanticipated outcomes, that the apparent rejection of an idea is actually an expression of that idea in a new form: these are the Hegelian images I have drawn on to structure the tale of modern American thought found here. The story is neither a progressive tale of emancipation from the intellectual cages of the past, nor a tragic tale of alienation and loss of the firm structures of meaning inherited from the past. Rather, it is both at the same time.

This book contains 15 chapters organized into three sections. Although I follow a chronological structure, the reader will note that the topical chapters don't always fit neatly into chronological period. Nevertheless, by breaking the story into three rough periods, I aim to catch something of the dialectical logic of the history. The first section "American Modernisms: 1860–1919" seeks to articulate the novelty of a new set of approaches to reality associated with Darwinism, philosophical Pragmatism, the new professional social sciences, the political and cultural movement of Progressivism, and the redefinition of gender in the era between the Civil War and World War I. The second section, "The Contradictions of the Democratic Imagination: 1920–1962," sees some of the dominant orientations of the first wave of modernist thought both fulfilled and contradicted in the mid-twentieth century. The most significant turn during this era was away from the biological and evolutionary model informed by Darwinism, and toward the ideas of culture, pluralism, and the realm of human values imagined in both democratic and anti-democratic ways. The epistemic, cultural, and moral relativisms implicit in the modernisms of the first wave were both embraced and challenged by mid-century thinkers. The third section, "Rethinking Modernisms: 1963–2001," examines the foregrounding of ideas of rupture, fragmentation, and breakdown in the vision that mid-century modernist thinkers had put forward. It emphasizes the ways in which these images of disorder marched hand in hand with new understandings of the power of language, culture, and biology to provide a systematic determinism and ordering of the world. We might think of these three sections as providing the classic Hegelian order of thesis/antithesis/synthesis.

A comprehensive work like the present one recognizes that it cannot be inclusive of all the modes, schools, and figures of thinking over the chronological period it covers. Like all histories, it is inevitably selective. I could list dozens of important thinkers who do not appear, or appear only incidentally, in the following text. I have made choices to provide the best examples or indicators of the patterns of thought I aim to describe and analyze. Sometimes that means more detailed analysis of individual texts; sometimes it means making generalizations that I am sure some would quibble about. Obviously, other choices could have been made—I could have given greater attention to the pragmatic revival of the late twentieth century, to political ideas in the battle over Civil War and Reconstruction, to cultural pessimists like Henry Adams, to the sectarian in-fighting of the 1930s Old Left, to communitarian thinkers, to Talcott Parsons' mid-century sociological theory—the list goes on. Another historian would have made different choices, expressed different priorities. Nevertheless, I believe the general patterns of thought and its development portrayed here are a reasonably comprehensive and persuasive introduction to American thought, and changes in the specifics would not have substantially altered the force of the general argument that the book makes.

American intellectual history is a rich and important field of scholarship. It is my hope that this book brings the excitement, significance, and challenges of that field to a broader audience, that it lets us know that thought has a history that continues to shape the present, that we are always thinking in the categories that have been made available to us by thinkers in the past, even as we create new ideas under the pressure of current circumstances.

Notes

1 Laurence Veysey, "Intellectual History and the New Social History," in John Higham and Paul Conkin, eds., *New Directions in American Intellectual History* (Baltimore, MD: Johns Hopkins University Press, 1979), p. 4.
2 Sarah E. Igo, "Toward a Free-Range Intellectual History," in Joel Isaac, James T. Kloppenberg, Michael O'Brien, and Jennifer Ratner-Rosenhagen, eds., *The Worlds of American Intellectual History* (New York, NY: Oxford University Press, 2017), pp. 324–342.

Part I
American Modernisms
1860–1919

1 Darwinism and the Evolutionary Sensibility

In 1859, the British naturalist Charles Darwin published *On the Origin of Species*; in 1860 it made its way to the United States. On the one hand, this was a work based on long empirical study and an increasing body of scientific evidence in fields such as geology, zoology, and botany over the past century. On the other, it was a revolutionary work that contained within it entirely new ways of thinking about cosmology, a new understanding of human beings and their relationship to the natural world (although it had almost nothing directly or specifically to say about the origin of humans), and a new way of thinking about time, change, and continuity. The implications of Darwin's ideas were understood in multiple and conflicting ways in the second half of the nineteenth century, both by those who embraced them, and those who rejected them. While it would be an overstatement to say that Darwinism was the source of modernist thought in America, it is impossible to imagine the forms that scientific, social, and philosophical thought took in the decades following 1859 without the pervasive presence of Darwinian sensibilities. The world view of evolutionary naturalism that sprung from Darwin's thought moved the educated public, in diverse areas of thought, away from thinking in terms of fixed categories, universal essences, and firm boundaries. What Darwinism in its many instantiations provided was, in contrast, a world of fluid and mutable categories, adaptations to conditions, and order without design. Marx and Engels had famously declared in *The Communist Manifesto* (1848) that in the world created by the class-rule of the bourgeoisie, nothing was permanent, and "all that is solid melts into air." In the Darwinian vision, a world of permanent change came into being, but unlike the Marxist vision of history advancing to an ultimate utopian goal, it pictured nature as a process of open-ended evolution without a guiding hand. The solid world of fixed species in an ordered world of rational necessity, like the solid feudal inheritance that Marx imagined, was called into question.

Darwinism was truly revolutionary in the intellectual world in this sense—it transformed not just the way of looking at a particular phenomenon

DOI: 10.4324/9781003120803-3

but reordered the foundation of how to conceive of any phenomena. Its implications were not always apparent to those who engaged it as a mode of thought, either to apply it in new ways or to attempt to circumscribe and contain it. What exactly was Darwinism? That was itself up for dispute by those who would interpret Darwin's writings and their implications, as well as those who would get their Darwinist outlooks secondhand. Did Darwin imagine evolution as a progressive process, moving inevitably from lower to higher on a scale of existence, or was evolution an entirely contingent process in which accident, mutation, and circumstances were determinative? Did the mechanism of "natural selection" imply an intelligent agency behind the world, or did it strip the natural world of any intelligent or spiritual content? Was Darwinism compatible with theistic conceptions or inherently anti-theistic? Did Darwin draw the line between human civilization and the natural world in sharper terms, distinguishing one from the other, or did he provide a vision in which that distinction was collapsed? The Darwinian theory of evolution through natural selection could not be contained within a narrow sphere of natural history—it had implications for the larger questions of moral order, social good, religious truth, and knowledge itself.

Darwin's ideas, revolutionary as they were, did not come out of nowhere. The question of what was new in Darwinism and where Darwin was drawing from already existing thought is an important one. History is always a story of change within continuity. Darwin could not have developed the theory of evolution through natural selection without a set of intellectual and cultural preconditions that made it possible. As much as scientific change in this case touched on and reshaped the broader intellectual life of the late nineteenth century, the reverse was true as well—in spheres of understanding such as history, philosophy, and the proto-social science of political economy, in changes brought about by European expansionism, capitalist economic development, and in the attempts to square empirical accounts of nature with the scriptural authority of the Bible. Without the development of systems of taxonomy in the sciences of botany and zoology, without the puzzles raised and the debates over the meaning of the geological record, whatever accounts of nature that might have been produced in the mid-nineteenth century would not have looked anything like Darwin's account.

I will return to some of these earlier developments upon which Darwin's vision rested below, but first I want to spell out the ways in which Darwinism *did* represent novelty, the ways in which Darwinism *was* revolutionary. The idea of evolution, for instance, that nature is dynamic and not a fixed unchanging order, long preceded Darwin's writings, so the simple idea that the natural world has changed and developed in specific directions, including toward greater complexity, was very much already a product of debate in the early nineteenth century. The belief in evolution in learned circles was, it should be added, very much the minority position. But while ideas about evolution might challenge specific scriptural accounts of creation, what was novel about Darwin's theory is that it identified a specific, entirely naturalistic mechanism, as the driving force behind evolutionary process. Other theorists of evolution had, prior to Darwin, speculated that the evolutionary process was teleological and unilinear, moving always toward greater complexity. The late nineteenth century gave this theory the name "orthogenesis," (literally meaning creation in a straight or correct line); it implied a kind of metaphysical driving force innate to nature, and independent of circumstances and condition. It relied, therefore, on a notion of purpose and direction to nature. Darwin's theory of natural selection would dispense with orthogenetic accounts. The French zoologist Jean Baptiste-Lamarck in the early nineteenth century, synthesized an orthogenetic account with a mechanism for the heritability of acquired traits. The idea of the handing down to offspring of traits acquired by individuals through practice and experience (akin to how we might think of cultural and intellectual inheritance), and the loss of traits out of disuse, was a familiar idea and not specific to Lamarck, although it has come to be associated with him through its long use to illustrate an alternative to the mechanism of natural selection. This focus on acquired characteristics shared with natural selection the idea that the evolutionary process could be tied to increasing adaptability of organisms to circumstance and environment. Both orthogenetic accounts, and accounts that relied on the generational transmission of acquired characteristics, preserved a notion that evolution was a largely positive process, entirely consistent with divine purpose, and tied closely to more general ideas of progress.

While Darwin did not entirely reject the process of transmission of acquired characteristics, the principal mechanism for the evolutionary process as he imagined it was natural selection. In populations of organisms of the same species, there was natural diversity of traits, diversity produced in some sense by "accident"; nature "selected" those traits that were best suited for the survival of individuals to reproductive age. The gradual process of evolution over generations was based on the success particular individuals had in passing on characteristics that were better adapted to the environment. Those individuals who had characteristics that made them less likely to survive were thus less likely to reproduce. Nature "selected" through a process of elimination of less successful traits. What was novel here was the rejection of any telos, or goal, to the evolutionary process. The complexity of nature could be explained without any reference to purpose or "design." Darwinian theory was not so much an argument against theism, or the belief in the existence of God, as it was an argument that made theism unnecessary to an understanding of nature.

But, as the American botanist Asa Gray pointed out, this did not make it any different from virtually all scientific accounts, which didn't seek to challenge religious belief, but only to provide explanation based on empirical observation and naturalistic causes.

Darwin's theory was not unique in challenging Biblical accounts of nature. All evolutionary theories, or theories that allowed for something other than creation under the terms laid out in Genesis—that is, creation of the world and all its natural features fully developed in the course of a single week—did that. Advocates of "rational religion" or liberalizing Protestantism had, since the eighteenth century, gone in one of two directions—they had taken the path of "natural religion" and rejected the Bible as the ultimate source of authority in favor of empiricism and rational accounts of nature, or they had reinterpreted Genesis in ways that were non-literal. The Biblical account of creation if taken literally was inconsistent, for instance, with the knowledge gained from the geological record in terms of the age of the earth. It didn't take Darwin to push religious thinkers to an understanding that Biblical accounts of time and process should not be seen as competing or equivalent accounts of nature. The "days" of creation could be reinterpreted as "ages," happening over long periods of time rather than all at once; the ideas of Genesis could be seen as statements of spiritual priority, or read as symbolic, or mythic, rather than statements of empirical fact.

If Darwin provided a powerful novel understanding of evolution as a wholly naturalistic, non-teleological process, he did so in ways that also represented departures from earlier understandings. In the descriptive process of natural classification constructed by early modern European thinkers such as Linneaus and Cuvier, species were classified by structural similarities and differences, rather than by evolutionary relationship. In thinking of the taxonomy of flora and fauna, members of species were held to have essential characteristics and were distinct from one another, often in ways that were not clearly definable. They were grouped together by Linneaus, into, in increasing degree of generality, species, genus, family, order, class, phylum, and kingdom based on similarity of structure and function, rather than evolutionary relationship. The general position of naturalists was that species were fixed and based on lineal descent, that species were created distinct and remained so. Within biological species, there was diversity, which was recognized by the idea of "variety." Darwinism challenged the notion that "species" and "varieties" were different in kind—species, he held, began as varieties, and there was no essential distinction to be had between varieties and species. Variation, rather than being contained within the essentially sealed border of the species, was itself responsible for the possibility of evolution and creation of new species. The idea that taxonomic systems reflected a real fixed order in nature, merely a kind of description of that order, could, under Darwin, be sustained only with great difficulty. Rather, for Darwin, taxonomy provided a kind of temporary abstraction from a dynamic system in which relationships were in a constant state of flux based on reproducibility; today's variety could become the basis for tomorrow's species; today's species could become tomorrow's genera. Where previous generations had looked at nature and seen a bounded order, defined by types, in which inheritance meant simply the reproduction of the type, after Darwin careful readers might begin to see a world not of types, but of relationships unfolding in time, full of open possibilities.

The eighteenth and nineteenth centuries had given rise to new conceptions of history and time; evolutionary ideas were a part of this. As the social, political, economic, and intellectual order of modern Europe was the subject of observable change in the era of capitalist transformation of agriculture, industrial development, political and scientific revolution, so many thinkers began to see history as something more than a series of distinct and unrelated events in a world that largely remained the same. More centrally, the idea of progress was a relative novelty in terms of older conceptions of time, of cyclical rise and fall, of history as a record of the limitations and futility of human ambitions. Many modern thinkers confidently declared history to be a secular process of inevitable improvement in which the growth of knowledge, triumph over nature, material and moral improvement were not only observable but also inevitable. Belief in progress in the social and intellectual realm was often linked to notions of evolution in the realm of nature. The idea of progress was governed by rationality and human intent. But despite the mechanism of natural selection and the idea that there was a logic to evolution, Darwin placed a kind of randomness at the heart of the process, one that was not so easily squared with ideas of progress. While many would (and still do) associate evolution with progress, Darwinism revealed a more troubling vision—that nature and its processes were indifferent to the value system that emphasized the unity of moral and material improvement. The idea that natural selection required the existence of variation within species and that such variation occurred randomly and without purpose, meant that what appeared in nature was neither orderly nor necessary. Natural history acted through accident, contingency, circumstance, and situation, rather than as a result of an inherent drive for progress.

When the British social theorist Herbert Spencer, in the wake of *On the Origin of Species*, equated natural process with something he dubbed "the survival of the fittest," he was trying to tie natural evolution to a vision of progress. But his terminology revealed an ambiguity that could lead to opposed readings of Darwin. In the framework of natural selection, traits that aided survival were passed on to the next generation because those traits made the individuals more "fit." But "fit" was a relative concept, not an absolute one. To speak of "fitness" as an essential characteristic, as if one individual or species could be inherently more fit than another, missed one of the strong relativizing aspects of Darwinian thought. If a trait or a species was more fit for a particular environment or set of natural circumstances, it would be successful in contributing to the survival of that trait or species; but that very success would alter the environment in which organisms acted—for instance, predators that had success in capturing prey, might lead to the widespread destruction of prey species, and of the food supply to which the successful predators were best adapted. Fitness was a temporary condition, and as the environment changed (as it always did), yesterday's fitness could be tomorrow's weakness. The idea that somehow an ideal of fitness in some ultimate sense won out through the process of natural history implied, again, a kind of telos or goal waiting at the end of history. The "survival of the fittest" was not the survival of the best, only the best adapted to a temporary set of conditions. This didn't stop many converts to some version of Darwinism from equating fitness with evolutionary progress, and infusing it with a moral quality. Even a pessimist like Henry Adams, the disillusioned descendant of presidents John and John Quincy Adams, associated Darwinian evolution with progressive improvement, even as he argued against it as a reality.

In later works (*The Descent of Man, The Expression of Emotions in Man and Animals*), Darwin specifically addressed human beings as the product of the evolutionary process of natural selection—*On the Origin of Species* left the argument about human beings in nature implicit, rather than explicit. But, in fact, contemporaries did see the work in terms of its implications for the understanding of human beings. The idea that human beings did not occupy a distinct space based on an absolute distinction between humans and the animal world was a challenge to theistic accounts that had long emphasized the special creation of man as a being with a soul. Although the idea of human beings as part of nature was not new, until Darwinism nobody had developed a purely naturalistic account that provided a mechanism for demonstrating how human beings emerged and were potentially related to non-human relatives. The orthodox doctrine of the fixity of species allowed for a continuing belief that human beings had a special and distinctive character. The erosion of the boundary separating humans from the natural world was based on a foregrounding of biology, rather than an emphasis on the soul or consciousness, as the source of human identity. This put Darwinism very much in the line of increasingly well-known materialist accounts of human life. In the popular images of the history of Darwinism, this idea—that men were descended from apes— has often been accorded primacy of place. This was certainly an issue that engaged people in the long history of the reception of Darwinian ideas, but, as I am suggesting here, it was not the only issue, and the challenge to a notion of an ordered universe with fixed features and essential categories was possibly the more troubling implication for those who grappled with Darwinism.

One other source of tension with the equation of progress with evolution was the contradiction between the progressive vision of moral improvement and humanitarian ethics, on the one hand, and an understanding of the bloody and cruel ways in which the evolutionary mechanism operated, on the other. The struggle for existence was a central feature of Darwinian evolution. The idea that nature was "red in tooth and claw," that the way in which evolutionary development was produced was through systematic violent elimination of those too weak to live and reproduce, that nature was a Hobbesian war of all against all: these were ideas anathema to the Victorian humanitarian imagination. If progress was to be understood as a movement from a lower barbarian world of cruelty and torture to a higher civilized commitment to universal respect for the rights of individuals, for the various nineteenth-century reform efforts against cruelty and violence—campaigns against corporal punishment, animal vivisection, dueling, and penal reform—, then the idea that nature itself acted in ways that were neither benevolent nor humane, but used death, punishment, and pain as its instruments for progress, was difficult to accept. And this idea, of course, had theistic implications—the problem of the existence of evil, or theodicy, had a long history. Evil had to be justified as part of God's plan. What natural selection proposed was that a God who was potentially benevolent would put in place a system of nature in which cruelty and violence were necessary to its development. To accept the Darwinian naturalist account was either to question the existence of God or to accept a God of cruelty and violence.

While the sources of Darwin's idea were many and diverse, for our purposes, I want to suggest that we look beyond the world of natural history, geology, botany, and zoology for the intellectual contexts that informed Darwinian theory. Darwinism shaped social thought of the late nineteenth century, but it was also true that it was shaped by social thought. Darwin built his theory on a strong empirical foundation, based on the work of other scientists, but also on his own voyages. One of the consequences of the development of European expansionism and world travel during this era was an increasing recognition of the diversity of species, not only over time but also in relationship to geography. Darwin was able to observe the ways in which geographical separation created diversity of conditions, and as a consequence, diversity of species. The extent of the known world, of encountering types of flora and fauna that were unknown to previous generations of Europeans, raised questions about the adequacy of a fixed system of taxonomy of species. Increasing exploration of the geological record and the puzzles it presented about the age of the earth, the evidence for extinction of species, and the presence of aquatic fossils in mountainous regions called into question Biblically-based understandings of the earth, life, and creation.

And, yet, the idea of natural selection was indebted not just to these empirical observations, but to the "science" of political economy that had come into being in the late eighteenth century as an attempt to understand the nature of the distribution of wealth and the powers of productivity and commerce in new ways. British political economy, in particular, sought to portray the world of human interaction—of land, labor, and capital—as governed by natural laws. In works such as Adam Smith's *The Wealth of Nations* (1776), David Ricardo's *On the Principles of Political Economy and Taxation* (1817), and James Mill's *Elements of Political Economy* (1821), a vision of self-regulating economic activity based on governmental non-interference in the natural laws of markets was created—a vision of a laissez-faire economy without design. Darwin was heavily influenced by one of the important works in this school of what the British cultural critic Thomas Carlye referred to as "the dismal science": Thomas Malthus's *An Essay on the Principle of Population* (1798; 6th ed. 1826). Malthus argued that human population tends to grow geometrically, while the food supply is limited and grows only arithmetically. Population growth outstrips food supply, pushing wages to subsistence level, and leading to the checking of growth through reduced birth rates and higher mortality rates. Malthus's argument was deeply anti-utopian, imagining a world in which limitations in a competitive order meant that poverty, misery, disease, and death were in the natural order of things. Darwin would later comment that the idea of competition over scarce resources in an expanding population led him to the conclusion that variations that would promote survival would be preserved, and variations that did not would be eliminated. In *On the Origin of Species* he wrote "this is the doctrine of Malthus, applied with manifold force to the animal and vegetable kingdoms."[1] Darwin's early and principal American advocate, Asa Gray, wrote in his initial review of Darwin's *Origin* in 1860 that Darwin's vision drew on both Malthus and the seventeenth-century political philosopher Thomas Hobbes's *Leviathan*, a book that imagined human beings in a state of nature engaging in a "war of all against all," that rendered life "nasty, brutish, and short."[2] In a very real sense, Darwinism modeled the processes of the natural world on the doctrines of capitalist economics.

American Reception

Despite the widespread notion that Darwinian evolution had its largest immediate impact in the United States among orthodox Protestants who struggled to address its challenges to received religion, the initial reaction against Darwinism and evolutionary theory, in general, took place on the ground of science itself—although questions of its implications for religion were never far away. It was not until Darwin had won the allegiance of most scientists in the mid-1870s, that Protestant ministers and theologians began to criticize evolutionary thought for its challenges to Biblically-based Christianity. Initially, many of the leaders of the Protestant establishment at American universities and seminaries deferred to scientists, the majority of whom seemed intent on rejecting Darwinism for its affront to scientific truth. That is, the controversy over Darwinism in the years immediately following the publication of *Origin* was a scientific controversy, and the initial weight of opinion of scientists was opposed to it. The orthodox position of the fixity and distinction of species, based on the complexity of organisms and the inconceivability that such complexity could be produced through anything other than a deliberate act of design, was dominant.

The publication of *On the Origin of Species* in the United States was an event—here was a book, deeply learned and steeped in empirical observation, yet written to be accessible to an educated audience, that was arguing plausibly and eloquently for a position that defied the common sense of both the public and the scientific community. Even before the publication of an American edition, it was apparent that it was a bombshell. In Britain, the greatest publicist and advocate for the theory of evolution through natural selection was Thomas Huxley, who for his pointed presentation and unwillingness to back down in debate, earned the sobriquet "Darwin's Bulldog." The situation was different in the United States. There Asa Gray, Professor of Botany at Harvard, a friend, correspondent, and colleague of Darwin's, considered one of America's most important naturalists, but committed above all to a demeanor of reasoned scientific consideration, became the leading figure in the minority of scientists who initially were persuaded by Darwin. He wrote the first review of *On the Origin of Species* to appear in an American journal in March of 1860, before the publication of an American edition; while not uncritical of aspects of Darwin's argument, it was an endorsement of the main tenets of natural selection. In an analytical discussion, Gray evaluated the work in scientific terms—its empirical adequacy, its ability to "harmonize" (a word he, tellingly, used frequently) the vast diversity of observed facts into a meaningful whole, its explanatory power. For the next 15 years, Gray would write widely in favor of Darwinism, culminating in the publication of his essay collection, *Darwiniana* in 1876.

While Gray's position was initially not persuasive to the majority of American scientists and naturalists, his interpretation of Darwin strived to "harmonize" natural selection with a theistic argument for design. He saw evolutionary process as potential evidence of divine design, although he completely accepted a naturalistic approach that required no interference in the process of nature—evolution would run of its own accord. He also argued that the special status of human beings as possessing a divinely created soul was not incompatible with the process of natural selection, and that there were many developments—such as complex organs like the eye—that seemed hard to produce by the gradual modification identified by Darwin. Gray saw the choice between empirical and naturalistic scientific accounts, and religious faith, as a false choice, and unlike those who emphasized the challenge of science to religion, believed that the two were entirely compatible.

The majority of American naturalists were initially skeptical, not just of the Darwinian mechanism of natural selection, but of the notion that distinct species were not fixed, and that evolution and creation of new species occurred gradually over long scales of time. The most famous scientist in America, the Swiss-born ichthyologist Louis Agassiz, a colleague of Gray's at Harvard, was the leading scientific opponent of Darwinism. Although he rejected a Biblically-based account of creation, he believed that the order and design of the world depended upon the clear distinction and separate creation of species. Recognizing that the fossil record indicated that the organic world was not unchanging, Agassiz, in his early European career, had developed the theory that climate change, in the form of multiple Ice Ages, was responsible for the kinds of breaks in speciation found in the fossil record. By the time Agassiz came to the United States and Harvard in the 1840s, he was world famous, but had ceased to be a productive research scientist. Instead, he became a kind of public figure, giving popular lectures and representing what he regarded as the central truth and meaning of natural history to a non-academic audience. His vision was consonant with a long-standing tradition in understandings of the natural world that emphasized the diversity and complexity of design in nature as evidence of the mind and power of a creator.

Agassiz was indebted to the philosophical idealism of the German tradition, and very much sympathetic to America's own idealist school of antebellum Transcendentalists, who imagined the world as an expression of Mind, rather than simply a set of material facts. Gray was a Christian and a theist, but first and foremost, a scientific empiricist, who made his advocacy for Darwinism rest on observable evidence. Agassiz's use of empirical method and observation, on the other hand, was always in the service of the revelation of the glory of God's Mind—species were ideas, clear and distinct, before they were material things, and their material existence expressed their ideal nature. In classic idealist fashion, Agassiz dismissed empirically observed variation within species as merely transitory, and the classificatory categories as permanent and unchanging:

> while individuals are perishable, they transmit, generation after generation, all that is specific or generic, or, in one word *typical* in them, to the

exclusion of every *individual peculiarity* which passes away with them, and that, therefore, while individuals alone have a material existence, species, genera, families, orders, classes, and branches of the animal kingdom exist only as categories of thought in the Supreme Intelligence, but as such have as truly an independent existence and are as unvarying as thought itself after it has once been expressed.[3]

Darwinism was an attack not just on Biblical authority, but on the idealism undergirding Agassiz's science. Although the anti-Darwin position had great initial credibility, especially given Agassiz's prestige and authority, by the time of his death in 1873, there were very few naturalists who had not been won over to the evolutionary position, and Agassiz's stature was diminished.

It did not help that the initial Darwinian controversy coincided with the American Civil War and an increasing polarization around issues having to do with slavery and race. From the eighteenth century, there were two competing schools of thought about human racial difference—those who believed that members of all races had a common ancestry, known as monogenists, and those who believed in the separate creation of the different human races, known as polygenists. Agassiz was a polygenist. While he did not promote the proslavery political views of many polygenists, he did believe in a natural racial hierarchy. In his vision of an ordered natural universe, the black and white races were fixed and distinct, made by God in separate acts of creation, not members of the same species. To be clear, this was a position that ran counter to most Biblical understandings of human origins, which had emphasized the common descent of all human beings from an initial pair, Adam and Eve. The dominant school of polygenists imagined themselves as scientists, willing to buck the criticisms coming from Christians, committed to empirically derived positions regardless of appeals to Biblical authority. And, again, Agassiz, as a naturalist, was not committed to a Biblical account of creation, but certainly to a theistic one. In 1854, the physician Josiah Nott and the Egyptologist George Gliddon, building on the work of generations of ethnologists, published the most systematic and developed polygenetic account: *The Types of Mankind*. Polygenism was at its ideological height in the 1850s. Darwinism threatened not just the order of all of creation, but the very specific claims for natural racial hierarchy that polygenists were making. Of course, one did not have to be a polygenist to be a racist, or to commit to notions of white superiority, especially as an ideological justification for slavery. But not all racisms are created equal, and the polygenetic variety cast all non-whites out of the status of humanity, justifying a much more pernicious form of racism.

Among intellectuals in Boston and its environs, Darwin's implication for the racial justifications for slavery was recognized immediately—it dovetailed with abolitionist and antislavery politics. *On the Origin of Species* completely discredited polygenetic accounts of human origins, as well as Biblical justifications that had been used to define race differences. As we will see, new racial hierarchies would be built on the back of evolutionary theory, but after Darwin, scientific justifications for the idea that races were distinct species evaporated. The outcome of the Civil War involved a radical rethinking of racial hierarchy in the years of Reconstruction. There would be a long and concentrated backlash against the potential for racial equality that had been introduced in the 1860s and 70s, and in the last decades of the nineteenth century, newer forms of biological determinism and justification for racial hierarchy and separation within an evolutionary framework would gain prominence. The point here might be that the politics of Darwinism were up for grabs—there was nothing inherently progressive or conservative in Darwin's theories that might not be subject to reinterpretation to serve conservative or progressive ends.

Only when it became clear that Darwinian evolution was triumphing in scientific terms, did those committed to the priority of the Bible and religious belief begin to take it seriously as a threat to their own claims of authority. By the mid-1870s, theologians, ministers, and religious thinkers saw that they had to launch their own attack on evolutionary theory. The best known of these attacks was that of the Presbyterian theologian Charles Hodge, who entitled his 1874 critique, *What Is Darwinism?* Although very much concerned with analyzing the arguments pro and con, ultimately Hodge's concern was not to provide a critique of Darwinism in scientific terms but to follow out its logic to what he regarded as the ultimate moral and religious consequence of accepting Darwin's theory. His main argument emphasized the implications that he thought scientific theists like Gray, who wanted to have their cake and to eat it too, had tried to skirt. The critical element of Darwinism was not the doctrine of evolution per se, nor even that of natural selection, but the denial of teleology, purpose, design, and divine intention in the universe. No Christian, he argued, could accept the notion of a blind, random, process as the condition of nature. Even if Darwin himself had declared his own belief in God, according to Hodge, his theory led elsewhere. "[T]he denial of design in nature is virtually the denial of God."[4]

The Darwinian Sensibility

The debates around Darwin's arguments and claims were specifically addressed to a scientific theory and its implications for understanding of the natural world. But the way of thinking that emerged from the Darwinian frame was far more pervasive, informing ideas about literature and art, social theory, political ideology. General concepts, such as the idea of "adaptation," which stressed the process of people being fluid and labile creatures of the circumstances and environments they faced, rather than seeing human behavior solely in terms of inner motivations, for instance, would grow in the following decades to express the new sensibility. The idea that we are "products of our environment," so commonly expressed, owes its origins to this kind of generalized Darwinian outlook. Thinkers began to consider human beings as belonging to both the natural world and the social world and to ask how those two environments and orders were related to one another, how social development might be tied to evolutionary process. To think in anti-teleological ways, as the Pragmatist philosophers examined in the next chapter did, while not entirely attributable to Darwinism, certainly was aided by the reorientation toward nature and knowledge that Darwin helped to create.

In the realm of literature, the late nineteenth century saw the development of a new "naturalist" aesthetic. In works of fiction by authors such as Frank Norris, Jack London, Kate Chopin, Theodore Dreiser, Edith Wharton, and Stephen Crane, human beings were pictured as driven by natural conditions, environments, and their own animal desires, often resulting in self-destruction. Where literary "realists" such as William Dean Howells and Henry James sought a contrast to romanticism by emphasizing the conditions of modern urban life or the closely observed features of social circumstances, naturalists went a step further, basing their literary visions on a philosophical commitment to a kind of scientific "objectivity," a powerful fatalism in which persons' lives were controlled by impersonal forces of nature—blind, amoral, and instinctual. Where Darwinists had often imagined an evolutionary movement from lower to higher, naturalists often inverted the Darwinian sequence, emphasizing a reversion of "civilized" characters to the deep buried forces of nature, "red in tooth and claw." If some imagined Darwinian evolution as a simple matter of progress and improvement, literary naturalists tended to see the natural world in shades a great deal darker. In Norris's *McTeague (1899)*, for instance, the title character, driven by his insatiable greed and animal nature, ends up alone in Death Valley, handcuffed to the nemesis he has murdered. While literary naturalism often portrayed a powerful biological determinism, it did not have much of anything to say about the "origin of species" except to demonstrate that human beings were never far from their animal natures.

Darwinism had widespread influence on social thought of the era. Conventionally historians tend to divide this influence into a kind of conservative "Social Darwinism," and a progressive "Reform Darwinism," although in truth, social thinkers of every stripe drew on Darwinian images, tropes, and arguments. Although Darwin, as we have seen, cited the political economy of Thomas Malthus, those committed to a laissez-faire, anti-reform agenda, synthesized the tradition of political economy with new powerful invocations of the anti-design, self-regulating features of nature. In this version, progress in society, like evolution in nature, was a product of the relative success of individuals. The existing class structure was not the result of exploitation and oppression through the use of forms of property, but a natural outcome of the struggle for existence; those on top merited their position as winners in the competitive order; those at the bottom deserved their fate. Attempts at reform, from the point of view of laissez-faire Social Darwinism, were attempts to interfere with the natural process that produced progress and could only impede development. These kinds of arguments equated natural process with an industrial and emerging corporate economy that created class polarization, great sums of wealth for those at the top, immiseration for those at the bottom, and opposition to labor unions, social safety nets, and any regulation of industry.

The best known and most widely read of the so-called Social Darwinists was the British polymath and theorist, Herbert Spencer, who saw progress and laissez-faire as inevitably linked. Spencer and his acolytes were fond of invoking "survival of the fittest" and "the struggle for existence" as the creative force of evolutionary progress. Any attempt to interfere with or diminish the struggle for existence, from this point of view, was a brake on this creative force. But Spencer was not an orthodox Darwinist, either. He had little to say about natural selection and the conditions of variation, and his notions of success had more to do with passing on acquired characteristics than to reproduction of biological traits. Unlike Darwin, his vision was also deeply teleological—the highest realm of human evolution would be fulfilled and, like Marx, he imagined a future in which the state would disappear. In the decades immediately after the Civil War, Spencer was widely read in the United States, not just by academics, but by educated members of the elite. In fact, Spencer was more popular in the United States than in Britain. While Spencer has his American followers and imitators, such as John Fiske, probably the most widely known American figure identified with Social Darwinism was Yale Sociologist, William Graham Sumner.

Sumner was a caustic critic of all manners of reform, which he associated with misguided and unscientific "sentimentalism." An advocate for the limited state, and an especially harsh critic of taxation and redistribution of wealth, he pictured himself as an advocate for what he called "The Forgotten Man"—the small businessman who works hard and minds his own business, but who is constantly being put upon by sentimental socialists and reformers. In a series of works beginning in the 1870s and culminating in the classic sociological work, *Folkways* (1906), Sumner excoriated all movements to ameliorate suffering, to invoke humanitarian principles, and in general, as he titled his 1894 book, *The Absurd Effort to Make the World Over*. Sumner, who spent several years as an Episcopalian minister before becoming a full-time academic, never gave up the fierce anti-utopianism he directed at the fallen world in which he found himself. He embraced both the notion of the law-like natural forces of political economy and the laissez-faire ethic. In an 1881 essay, he wrote "The law of the survival of the fittest was not made by man and cannot be abrogated by man. We can only, by interfering with it, produce the survival of the unfittest." For Sumner, reform movements were simultaneously destructive of law and ineffective, since law would always out. Life was pain and struggle, "root hog or die," as he liked to say. The image of Social Darwinism as a kind of cruel justification of inequality and misery owes much to Sumner's writings.

> The sociologist is often asked if he wants to kill off certain classes of troublesome and burdensome persons. No such inference follows from any sound sociological doctrine, but it is allowed to infer, as to a great many persons and classes, that it would have been better for society, and would have involved no pain to them, if they had never been born.[5]

This strange synthesis of liberal ideas of unimpeded individual freedom and determinist ideas of necessity—of amoral process and moralizing work ethic—gave Sumner his particular voice. Social Darwinists sought to declare themselves advocates for a kind of objective observational science against the moralizing temper of social reformers, but couldn't resist their own moralizing of the status quo.

The social thinkers of this era who were opposed to laissez-faire and the endorsement of Gilded Age capitalism did not, as one might think, reject Darwinism; rather they embraced evolutionary thought and interpreted natural selection in an entirely different way. Lester Frank Ward played Asa Gray to Sumner's Agassiz. Often considered the founding figure of American sociology, Ward created what he called a "dynamic sociology," emphasizing evolution as a progressive force, but one that could be mobilized for human improvement. His entire sociology accepted the idea of evolution through natural selection, but instead of seeing human beings as passive actors in a natural process, he argued that the adaptations to nature that produced the human mind as a highly successful development created the conditions for human beings to consciously use their intelligence to direct history toward a higher moral condition. The use of mind pointed toward the preservation of the weak, the healing of disease, and the protection of human beings from a ruthless competitive order. All the greatest developments made by people were made through the cooperative use of mental powers. Ward was not alone. The British biologist Thomas Huxley argued in his Romanes Lecture, published in 1893 as *Evolution and Ethics*, that, while man was not in any sense "above nature," the world of morality and social improvement could not be derived in some direct way from the evolutionary process. Evolution was not a guide to ethics. Rather, human beings had evolved in such a way as to move beyond the competitive war of all against all that Social Darwinists imagined as the root of progress. Huxley contrasted the amoral "cosmic process" of evolutionary naturalism with the "ethical process" by which human beings carved out a set of principles opposed to untamed nature. The ethical world responded to nature in the same way that the gardener did—preventing weeds from taking over, preserving beauty and man-made order, nourishing the physically weak at the expense of the strong. "Interfering" in nature's design, in this view, was not unnatural, but the means by which the naturally acquired characteristics of human beings gave them adaptive success. Human progress was made through cooperation, through exerting collective control over nature, rather than through competition. Ward was acerbic in his critique of the false consciousness of Sumner and the Social Darwinists:

> When a well-clothed philosopher on a bitter winter's night sits in a warm room well lighted for his purposes and writes on paper with pen and ink in the arbitrary characters of a highly developed language the statement that civilization is the result of natural laws, and that man's duty is to let nature alone so that untrammeled it may work out a higher civilization, he simply ignores every circumstance of his existence and closes his eyes to every fact within the range of his faculties. If man had acted upon his theory there would have been no civilization, and our philosopher would have remained a troglodyte.[6]

The controversial economist and cultural critic, Thorstein Veblen, took the Darwinian argument for reform a step further than this, arguing that the so-called "successful" members of society, its elites, were not the fulfillment of evolutionary process, but an impediment to it. He inverted the Social Darwinian image of society. What he dubbed "the leisure class" he imagined to be a parasitic group, insulated by money and comfort from the struggle that produced progress. Veblen coined the term "conspicuous consumption," to point to the deliberate waste and lack of productivity of this class. And because social and economic elites had high status, their values further impeded innovation, improvement, and change because they inspired emulation on the part of those further down the social scale—to become successful in late nineteenth-century America was to become wasteful, to spend for the sake of demonstrating wealth rather than to be productive. Leisure class values were hegemonic, exerting their authority over the entire society in ways that were antithetical to progress—a progress that Veblen associated with engineers rather than capitalists. In Veblen's satirical take on American society, he turned a Darwinian vision into a radical critique of the class structure of an American plutocracy.

There were a variety of other responses to Darwinism by social and political thinkers—some of these, such as the feminist response to Darwinism, and especially the arguments about sexual selection that Darwin made in *The Descent of Man* (1871)—I will deal with in later chapters. Victorian anthropology, racial ideas, Pragmatic philosophy, movements for immigration reform and eugenics, birth control, and debates over Protestant modernism and fundamentalism: all were deeply informed by what I am calling the Darwinian sensibility. In the popular imagination, Darwinism was not always identified solely with natural selection, and there was enough ambiguity in Darwin's writings to admit of different interpretations. What all of those who thought in Darwinist terms in the late nineteenth century did share was the idea that nature was not fixed, that species evolve, that all living things share a common ancestry, that taxonomic classification was a frozen picture of a moment, rather than a set of universal and timeless categories. It was this destabilizing of nature, the sense that what had seemed permanently fixed about the world was not, that gave thinkers the possibility of challenging the given. But as much as Darwinian shedding of the fixed order of nature could be imagined as a basis for rethinking received wisdom, so, too, could it be imagined as the loss of certainty, and the opening to new and unfamiliar forms of control.

Notes

1 Charles Darwin, *On the Origin of Species: A Facsimile of the First Edition* (Cambridge, MA: Harvard University Press, 1964), p. 63.
2 Asa Gray, "Art. XV.—Review of Darwin's Theory on the Origin of Species by Means of Natural Selection," *American Journal of Science and Arts* 29 (March 1860), p. 70.
3 Louis Agassiz, "V. Book Notices. Prof. Agassiz on the Origin of Species," *American Journal of Science and Arts* 30 (July 1860), p. 151.
4 Charles Hodge, *What Is Darwinism?* (New York: Scribner, Armstrong, and Company, 1874), p. 174.
5 William Graham Sumner, "Sociology," *The Princeton Review* 57.6 (November 1881), pp. 311, 319.
6 Lester Frank Ward, "Mind as a Social Factor," *Mind* 9.36 (October 1884), p. 569.

2 Pragmatism and Antifoundational Thought

The late nineteenth century saw multiple attempts to come to terms with the modern philosophical inheritance developed in the seventeenth and eighteenth centuries. The powerful theories of knowledge, or epistemologies, that had defined early modern ideas about science and truth had served as challenges to ideas about revelation, divinely inspired truth, Aristotelian logic, and the authority of the Bible. The modern physical, chemical, astronomical, and biological sciences (grouped under the term "natural philosophy") had been enormously successful in providing both understanding and human command of the natural world. The metaphysical theories, or theories about the ultimate nature of reality, had created competing and irreconcilable visions, each of which claimed the authority of science. Ethical theories born of the early modern era sought to rethink human nature and motivation and to reconceive a natural, rather than merely a scriptural basis, for the good and the right. Political and social theories rethought the basis of political obligation, the sources of inequality, and ideas about liberty, often by appealing to natural law and more positive views of man's rational nature, rather than older forms of authority, including tradition and scripture. In all of these cases, early modern thinkers tended to show loyalty to one side of a bipolar divide. They were either rationalists or empiricists, idealists or materialists, deontologists or utilitarians, advocates for individual rights or for the collective good. In the late nineteenth century, in both Europe and North America, these schools came under sustained criticism, in part because they rested on absolute principles, on ideas of certitude and fixed order, and those principles were increasingly seen as limitations. Into the breach dividing rationalists and empiricists, idealists and materialists, stepped the philosophers of what the historian James Kloppenberg has deemed the *via media*—the middle way.

In the United States, this philosophy of the *via media* took its most prominent form in the philosophical school denoted by the term "Pragmatism." Pragmatism was an attempt to make knowledge, belief, and practice adequate to a world governed by science, and dynamism, a world in which all knowledge was provisional and partial, and the future was a realm of open possibility rather than of fixed design. One of the problems presented by the early modern inheritance was a central paradox in modern thought—the simultaneous elevation of objective detachment and subjective engagement. Pragmatists sought to heal that divide, to find a way to recognize the necessity of a world of values, emotions, and beliefs without foundations, and a world of expanding knowledge of the natural world that claimed to do without values and emotions. Like Darwinists, Pragmatists challenged the idea of a fixed hierarchical order, with its strict oppositions of mind and body; reason and emotion; fact and value. The inherited weight of early modern philosophy was what the philosopher William James called "the block universe," a system of fixed taxonomies and categories that were based on necessity.

The Pragmatic philosophers—Charles Sanders Pierce, William James, and John Dewey and their associates (such as Jane Addams, George Herbert Mead, Horace Kallen, Alain Locke, and many more) rejected what today we call "foundationalism," the notion that truth, knowledge, and morality rest on established bases that are certain and absolute. Foundationalism provided a bedrock framework for knowledge, in the same way that arguments for a fixed order in nature did. The idea that true knowledge would conform to how nature actually was, that the mind should be a kind of mirror of the world: this is the view that the Pragmatists challenged. The Pragmatists were antifoundationalists; controversially, for many of their contemporaries, that meant they were "relativists," or "subjectivists," that they destabilized the claims for objective truth and universal morality. The critics of Pragmatism were not entirely wrong, but their view of the philosophies developed by Peirce, James, and Dewey were often caricatures that concluded in images of nihilistic relativism that all of these thinkers were at some pains to avoid. In fact, their antifoundational critique was based on a belief in the greater power of the human mind to know the world, to liberate human beings from the constraints of hierarchy in favor of equality, and to situate knowledge and morality in the conditions of social existence, rather than in a world of logical necessity and free-floating abstractions. Pragmatic antifoundationalism pointed in two directions: toward the possibility of progress and overcoming the dead hand of the past, on the one hand, and toward a deeper appreciation of the role that habit, emotion, and history played in circumscribing knowledge, on the other.

Sometimes observers have tended to see Pragmatic philosophy as an instance of an anti-intellectual orientation in American culture, a kind of narrow practicalism, rejecting any interest in broad theoretical consideration. The Harvard psychologist cum philosopher William James, for instance, was known for invoking what he called, in an unfortunate metaphor, the "cash value" of ideas; there was a purpose in this metaphor, but for critics, it has been easy to say that Pragmatic philosophy was simply an expression of American capitalism on the philosophical plane. Many critics have sought to juxtapose philosophical movements in Europe to American philosophy, suggesting that the European, and especially German, forms of thought that provided the fierce critique of modernity in thinkers from Marx to Nietzsche to Heidegger to Foucault, created a much deeper and more far-reaching theoretically-inclined philosophy and that American Pragmatic philosophy has tended to float on the surface of things, never getting at the deep contradictions of modern life. I think this critique is wrong and based on a shallow reading of the Pragmatists, as I hope to demonstrate.

The Philosophical Inheritance

The forms of foundationalism in epistemology that the late nineteenth-century thinkers questioned had their roots in seventeenth-century philosophy, most dramatically in the writings of René Descartes and John Locke. The schools that descend from these two thinkers are generally referred to as Rationalism and Empiricism. The first finds foundation for knowledge in the power of the rational mind; the second in sense experience and observation. Descartes's famous experiment in doubt, in which he deliberately proposed to doubt all possible beliefs as a means of discovering what is indubitable, and using the indubitable as the "foundation" of all true belief affirmed that the evidence of the senses could be doubted, but that the existence of the doubting mind could not. Thinking was evidence of existence—sense data were not. From this experiment, Descartes argued that to know is to reject all received "truths"—whether those were Aristotelian or Christian—unless they could meet the standard of the rational mind—the standard of what he called "clear and distinct ideas." In addition, Descartes argued for what we refer to as mind/body dualism—he believed that the mind existed independent of the material world, having no extension in space, and therefore the knower could look upon the material world as an object of knowledge, entirely independent from the mind—Cartesianism created the theoretical basis for the ideal of objectivity. John Locke's *Essay Concerning Human Understanding* (1690) argued, in opposition to the Rationalist position, that the human mind, prior to sense experience, contained no ideas, and that all ideas are the product of the senses. The mind for Locke was a blank slate, a "tabula rasa," and all knowledge was acquired through reasoning from the foundations of sense experience. Like Descartes, in order to ensure the truth of knowledge, Locke made beliefs received second-hand subject to critical review, but the test knowledge had to pass through was empirical observation. What both Locke and Descartes sought to do was to remove error from the foundations of belief; belief could not be true unless it was grounded in certainty. Rationalism was always more committed to absolutes and certainty, since Empiricism was open to new experiences that would challenge older established beliefs. Empiricists, however, did cling to the certainty that no belief could be regarded as knowledge if it failed to be consonant with the empirical sources of knowledge. For Rationalists, mathematics was the model of knowledge, since its truths were imagined to be independent of, and prior to, experience. In general, one system privileged deductive logic, the other inductive logic; one tended to make ultimate reality ideal in nature and the other material. Descartes spearheaded a tradition that includes Continental European philosophers, including Spinoza, Leibnitz, Kant, and Hegel; Locke's Empiricism was dominant in Anglo-American philosophy, in a tradition that included Berkeley, Hume, and Mill. Two and a half centuries after the initial skirmishes that created the early modern forms of epistemological foundationalism, both had created a variety of offspring, but largely without challenging what had become dogmatic foundations.

In American philosophy of the mid-nineteenth century, there were three dominant philosophical orientations or schools of thought. The establishment philosophical outlook in the early Republic, taught at American universities, particularly Princeton, was Scottish Common Sense philosophy, a school that aimed to check some of the skeptical elements arising out of the empiricist tradition. Dugald Stewart, one of the prime figures in the school, saw his *Elements of the Philosophy of the Human Mind* (3 vols., 1792–1827) become a standard textbook in American colleges. As its name might suggest, Scottish Common Sense philosophy affirmed the God-given constitution of human beings as governed by a shared set of senses that went beyond the material senses of observation, and provided assurance that intuitive knowledge should not be subjected to skeptical doubt. This was particularly true in regard to ideas of morality and right and wrong. The second school was a group of philosophers, many of them centered around St. Louis, who synthesized a Hegelian philosophy of history, based on Absolute Idealism, with an educational agenda. In 1867, under the direction of William Torrey Harris, the St. Louis group founded *The Journal of Speculative Philosophy*, which occupied an important role in the development of American philosophy. The St. Louis Hegelians tended toward an orthodox commitment to Hegelian dialectical logic and idealism—they were generally not original thinkers. The third group, centered around Boston, were the Transcendentalists, who flourished in the 30 years prior to the Civil War. Like the Hegelians, and influenced by Kantian philosophy that came to them through British thinkers like Coleridge, the Transcendentalists—Ralph Waldo Emerson, Theodore Parker, Alcott Bronson, Margaret Fuller, Henry David Thoreau among others—were also philosophical idealists. They remain better known to the public today, largely one suspects because they were not narrowly a philosophical movement, but spoke in a much broader cultural register—as poets, essayists, lecturers, and reformers—and due to their radical challenges to orthodox Protestantism. This, then, was the philosophical context of the mid-nineteenth century: a strong body of Idealism and a lingering conservative legacy of ameliorative Scottish philosophy coming out of British empiricism. This synthesis of American philosophies would be disparaged by the Harvard philosopher George Santayana, in the early twentieth century, as an evasive "genteel tradition" for its failure to engage the concreteness and struggle of modern life.

Transcendentalism and Idealism belong to an era of geographical expansion, the breakdown of some existing hierarchies (and the reinforcement of others, such as racial hierarchies), and a dynamic economic order. The coming of a market economy—what some have called a market revolution—in the first half of the nineteenth century laid challenge to the idea of a self-sufficient agrarian economy organized around home production. For many, the integration into a national market economy through new forms of production, transportation, and communication could be experienced as the collapse of localism and the hierarchical order of the patriarchal family, and the birth of new kinds of freedom of both social and geographical mobility. Politically, the old politics of deference fell to a new putatively democratic revolution, as property requirements for the vote in all states fell away, and universal white male suffrage became the norm by the 1830s. In the wake of the Constitution's non-establishment clause, new sects and religions sprung up around the country, and religious choice—at least within the forms of Protestantism—was a reality for more and more people. To many, it appeared that the dynamic forces of history were breaking the grip of institutions inherited from the past. To be clear, other institutions, such as slavery, factory wage labor, and penal institutions were becoming more powerful during the same period. But in the Northeast and the West, if not the South, intellectual leaders pushed a cultural strain committed to anti-institutionalism, to the idea of the self-sufficient individual and the radical religious idea of a self completely free of sin. Hegelianism—a consciousness of history moving progressively through the opposition of ideas made manifest in the world—and Transcendentalism—an expression of radical individualism and the spiritual power to remake the world by discovering the divine in everyday life: both gave a kind of philosophical response to the newly transformed conditions of society.

After the Civil War, many of the processes that had been revolutionary in the first decades of the nineteenth century became the basis for a more highly regulated, consolidated social and economic order. The triumph of large-scale industry and distribution of goods, for instance, challenged the image of an open society of individual opportunity that had been central to the political ideologies of the antebellum era. The world of small producers was giving way to corporate consolidation, which reached an apex in the merger movement of the last decade of the nineteenth century. The complexities of modern social and economic life produced a sharpened clash between capital and labor, and the emergence of industrial unions such as the American Railway Union; a new middle class of salaried professionals and managers; increasing urban development and concentration; waves of new immigrants from Eastern and Southern Europe; the growth and transformation of higher education. Increasingly, large-scale and highly organized institutions—vertically and horizontally integrated corporations, labor unions, professional associations (such as the American Medical Association), city governments, and research universities—shaped the lives of Americans. In such a context, the antebellum untrammeled individualism of the past seemed less and less adequate as a way to negotiate the complexities of modern life. New conditions invited a mode of thinking more in sync with the institutional reality of late nineteenth-century life. While Pragmatic philosophy was not simply an ideological reflection of new social forms, it did aim to make sense of those forms in ways that existing empiricist and rationalist, materialist and idealist, and philosophies could not. The new world was imaginable in terms of ideas of procedure, of adaptation of means to ends, rather than individual minds freed from constraint.

The Epistemic Reconstruction of Charles Sanders Peirce

The epistemology of the new science was given its earliest expression in two articles that Charles Sanders Peirce published in *Popular Science Monthly* in 1877 and 1878: "The Fixation of Belief" and "How to Make Our Ideas Clear." These essays were the first two parts of a six-part series on the logic of science that introduced what was later to be called Pragmatism into the philosophical world. Peirce is often considered the most brilliant logician of the nineteenth century, and his philosophical and scientific writings have continued to inspire a coterie of devotees. In these initial essays, Pierce challenged many of the basic conventions and understandings about knowledge and belief, including providing a wholesale critique of the entire way of thinking that was central to the Cartesian tradition. In "The Fixation of Belief," he argued, first, that beliefs were habits that guided behavior, rather than abstractions belonging to a realm of pure ideation. So, he began by sinking belief into "practical" activity, routinizing it, seeing it as a feature of psychological composition, rather than seeing rational ideation as a transcending of the self and its habits in a realm of "pure reason." Rejecting Descartes' notion of a theoretical experiment in skepticism and doubt, Peirce argued that real doubt is a product of the necessary failure of habit to permanently "fix" belief and provide certitude. Doubt is, as in Descartes, the engine of inquiry, but it is not voluntarily chosen, or a product of rational deliberation in the abstract. Psychologically, Peirce saw human beings in a constant state of flux between habit and what he called "the irritation of doubt." Once doubt was resolved by fixing belief, no further inquiry would take place, but belief would once again be rendered habitual, until the next introduction of doubt. The question he aimed to ask is what the methods of fixing belief and ending doubt were, and what were the consequences of adopting any particular method. Instead of beginning his essay with a question of the conditions of epistemic truth, he created something like a sociological scheme of different ways of fixing belief—in the very method of his essay, he rejected foundational arguments in favor of consequential ones. That is, one of the distinguishing features of Pragmatic philosophy—its focus on the consequences of beliefs, rather than on their origins or foundations—was introduced in the form of Peirce's inquiry.

The notion of the fixity of truth—that to be true was to have an unchanging quality—was ironically subverted by Peirce's use of the term "fixation." Peirce argued that there were four methods of fixing belief: the method of tenacity, the method of authority, the *a priori* method, and the scientific method. The first was a method of simply refusing to entertain alternative beliefs, and vowing to adhere and remain loyal to one's existing beliefs, especially by isolating oneself from the presence of any alternative beliefs. The method of authority was exemplified by institutions such as church and state outlawing ideas and works that might contribute to doubt, thus preventing the presence of sources of irritation. The third method was to fix belief by appealing to systems of closed reasoning, in which all doubt could be reincorporated into positive knowledge by claiming reason to be independent of experience. This was the position of Rationalist and Idealist philosophy, of Descartes, Kant, Hegel, and Transcendentalism. The fourth, by far both the most difficult and the most successful according to Pierce, was the method of science, in which responding openly to empirical data would fix belief by changing it. Each of these methods, arranged in an implied historical sequence from lower to higher, has something to recommend it as a method of fixing belief—but for Peirce, only one of these, the method of science, has as its outcome the production of belief that is true. One of the distinguishing features of Peirce's argument was that the first three methods were destined to fail because belief is social, rather than individual, in its character. The presence of those who hold different beliefs in society meant that no one could successfully avoid encountering ideas that might generate doubt. Science, he imagined, would eventually produce consensus among those who were willing to adhere to its strictures.

All knowledge was the product of a "community of inquiry" rather than of autonomous and independent rational intellects. While Peirce believed in a reality independent of human beings that could be known, he shifted the ground of knowledge away from a mirroring of reality to an idea of shared belief and community, away from the isolated ego of Cartesian philosophy, to the socialized world of collective undertaking.

In the second essay, "How to Make Our Ideas Clear," Peirce challenges the Cartesian vision of "clear and distinct ideas," by taking the image of ideas as habits and aiming to demonstrate what it might mean for those ideas to be "clear." This essay introduced what William James later referred to as the principle of "the pragmatic method." Ideas are not made clear by being made purely rational, free from the messiness of concrete reality, as Descartes had proclaimed. Rather ideas were clear and distinct, rather than obscure and confused, only when they were evaluated in terms of the practical difference they made in volition: "what a thing means is simply what habits it involves….[T]here is no distinction of meaning so fine as to consist in anything but a possible difference of practice."[1] A belief was meaningless if it compelled no action. What Peirce had done was to insist that beliefs are the condition of action, and the actions produced by particular beliefs—the habits they compelled—are the entire meaning of beliefs. To cling to the dualism in which ideas and actions were entirely separate things was to create a fantasy in which the purification of ideas without any attachment to concrete reality made ideas clear, whereas for Peirce, ideas were clear and distinct from one another when they produced different habits of action. The old logic of abstraction embedded in "the doctrine of clearness and distinctness," said Peirce, "may be pretty enough, but it is high time to relegate to our cabinet of curiosities the antique *bijou*, and to wear about us something better adapted to modern uses."[2] The tone is patronizing, surely, but it points to Peirce's belief in the progressive nature of modernizing thought. Freeing logic from doctrines of self-contained necessity and sufficiency, and putting it into the action of consequence, was the game.

Pragmatic philosophy was doing a number of things in these essays, and laying the ground for the slightly different direction that thinkers like James and Dewey would take it. The antifoundationalism of Pragmatism pointed philosophy away from first causes, universals, fixed categories, and toward future outcomes, concrete particulars, and actions. Instead of thinking about ideas as principles, standing apart from the world and judging it, Pragmatism imagined ideas as habits, useful for getting around in the world, and to be judged in terms of their adequacy as tools. One might think of this as a kind of Darwinism of ideas; beliefs that were successful tools for navigating the world tended to be preserved. Beliefs had no essential truth apart from the environments to which they were adapted, and the methods used to fix them—as a consequence, instead of being frozen above time, they were constantly changing. Instead of an orderly universe defined by design, Platonic universal forms, and dialectical logic abstracted from particulars, Pragmatism imagined a logic enmeshed in a constantly changing competitive world and habitual action, disrupted by the constant failure of ideas to fix belief and the power of doubt to eliminate some beliefs at the expense of others. Now, for Peirce, this vision was tied to a telos, a belief in the final destiny of a truth defined by universal consensus, a state of total knowledge at the end of history. Peirce used terms like "destiny" and "fated" to characterize the goal toward which all inquiry was organized. His philosophical vision did so much to destabilize the claims of any universals, but by putting a fated consensus in the future, Peirce allowed for a developmental logic without foundations. Peirce, unlike James who would follow him, was committed to a metaphysical vision, whereas James imagined the possibility of what he called an "open universe" only being possible when all fixed metaphysics—notions of ultimate reality as knowable in some final sense—were scuttled.

William James: Pragmatism as Sensibility

Although Peirce was the more technically adroit and proficient thinker, James was the figure responsible for turning Pragmatism into a much broader and accessible sensibility. His popular lectures published as *Pragmatism: A New Name for Some Old Ways of Thinking* in 1907 laid out the case and implications for the new philosophy, but he had been edging toward its definition over the course of more than 30 years. James's comprehensive and radical *The Principles of Psychology* (1890) was a landmark work, at a moment when the idea of a science of the human mind and behavior was being formulated and established as an academic discipline. In it, James challenged the inherited faculty psychology that British empiricists (and Scottish Common Sense philosophers) had relied on—the notion that the mind was composed of distinct faculties such as reason, imagination, judgment, and will—by defining consciousness not as a fixed set of attributes, or collection of distinct ideas connected by logic, but as a fluid state of constant motion. The metaphor of "stream of consciousness" that James created has been a widely influential one, shaping techniques of literary modernism, for instance. James followed Peirce in thinking of the activities of the mind as "habits," ones adapted to the functions they performed—again, a kind of Darwinism in the field of ideas. And the famous theory of emotions—later referred to as the James-Lange theory—that he put forward undermined the notion that the interior feeling of emotion was prior to and separate from its physical expression; James claimed that, for instance, we don't cry because we are sad, but that the act of crying was the same thing as the act of being sad-the dualism of interior state and exterior expression needed to be rejected.

In his *The Varieties of Religious Experience*, given as the Gifford lectures in Edinburgh in 1901 and 1902, James redefined religion in terms of experience and consciousness, rather than as a body of theological doctrines or institutions. Although he adopted an empiricist method, importantly, he criticized materialist doctrine that "explained" religious visions as merely neurological or chemically based hallucination, rejecting what he regarded as a genetic fallacy. The physiological source of consciousness, he argued, has nothing to do with the truth or value of the belief, which was to be judged by its "fruits" rather than its origin. James was always interested in altered states of consciousness—experimenting with mind-altering substances like nitrous oxide, for instance—for their ability to break down the perceived limitations of the knowing mind. Religious experience was a way of expanding consciousness, for setting out a critique of the world, for pushing for something more against the limits of the material world. Arguing against Nietzsche's earlier critique of religion as a force opposed to life, James claimed that the intensity of religious experience produced something of greater value for human beings. Similarly, in a famous 1897 essay, "The Will to Believe," James argued that theism and scientific doctrine were completely compatible, that the attempt to limit belief to strictly observable phenomena was itself driven by a passionate desire of the will, that atheism was guided by a "fear of being duped." Arguing against the British philosopher William Clifford's "The Ethics of Belief," (1877), James carved out a space for theism on the grounds that evidence could not decide the case, and a belief in God could bring into existence a new addition to the universe, a new kind of moral orientation. James did not make an argument for the existence of God but for the epistemic legitimacy of belief in God in a world defined by the dominance of strictly empiricist accounts of knowledge. James's version of Pragmatism was always about expanding belief, creating a world of greater possibilities, welcoming both ideals and facts, religion and science, rather than subscribing to the fixed and given categories of systematic philosophy. Some of this was temperamental (although James would have it that all philosophy was a matter of temperament): James abhorred making definite decisions, and vacillated in his personal and professional life—a decision to do one thing always meant closing the door on another alternative.

In *Pragmatism*, James defended what he saw as a middle path between two philosophical temperaments—what he called the tough-minded and the tender-minded— with the image of Pragmatism as a genial colleague, open to all comers, a great "unstiffener" of rigid theories, an enemy of dogmatism in all its forms. Pragmatism was the liberalism of the open mind. Instead of starting with *a priori* commitments, Pragmatism, James argued, judged ideas on the basis of what they made happen, their adequacy in helping people live in the world, and navigate the conditions of existence. In other words, questions of value were never far from questions of truth; truth was to be defined as meeting needs, rather than simply reflecting an independent reality. James's theory of truth was probably the most controversial aspect of *Pragmatism*, for it challenged commonly held ideas about the meaning of the word "truth." He spent much of his work defending what initially appeared to be a counterintuitive notion of truth. For James, emotions, desires, and subjective needs were bound up in every statement of truth. The idea that fact and value, object and subject, thought and action, exist in opposition to one another was antithetical to the entire sensibility of Pragmatism. But the concept of truth, as broadly understood by James's contemporaries, was that a statement about the world was true when it copied or reproduced in the mind the actual independently existing reality. James denied that this was possible. "The truth of an idea is not a stagnant property inherent in it," he said. "Truth *happens* to an idea. It *becomes* true, is *made* true by events. Its verity *is* in fact an event, a process: the process namely of its verifying itself, its veri-*fication*." Because truth was defined by process, it was always open to change. The critics of Pragmatism claimed that James was arguing that the meaning of truth was entirely subjective, a matter of believing what one wanted to believe and calling it true. When he said the true "is only the expedient in the way of our thinking, just as 'the right' is only the expedient in the way of our behaving," many saw him claiming subjective utility as the only requirement to call something true, and that truth must therefore vary from person to person. Truth, says James, is something more than what people find it pleasant to believe.

> Pent in, as the pragmatist more than anyone else sees himself to be, between the whole body of funded truths squeezed from the past and the coercions of the world of sense about him, who so well as he feels the immense pressure of objective control under which our minds perform their operations? If anyone imagines that this law is lax, let him keep its commandment one day, says Emerson.

What the critics ultimately could not abide was James's belief that all truth was provisional, since this clashed with the notion that truth must be unchanging. "We must live today by what truth we can get today," he said, "and be ready tomorrow to call it falsehood."[3]

John Dewey and the Democratic Vision

Of the three major voices of Pragmatism, John Dewey, who was younger then both Peirce and James, had the most varied career, and took pragmatic ideas into a diverse array of genres. Dewey is today probably best remembered by the public as an educational theorist, the creator of a progressive educational orientation, but his voluminous writings touched on epistemology, religion, science, aesthetics, politics, social theory. Where Peirce emphasized community, and James the liberal self, Dewey took his version of Pragmatism—what he called "instrumentalism"—in the direction of a democratic vision. The early twentieth century was the age of "social democracy," the reinterpretation of democracy as more than a political doctrine of suffrage and representation, with a focus on the social meaning of equality. Dewey believed that the entire history of Western philosophy had been committed to a hierarchical vision of reality—a notion that there are higher and lower forms of reality, such as the difference between appearance (low) and essence (high), or between rationality (high) and passion (low). Pragmatic philosophy was a leveling form, an egalitarian philosophy because it rejected these hierarchies—rejected what Dewey came to characterize as the doctrine of aristocracy written in the language of philosophy.

Dewey's early career was one based on Hegelian philosophy. Although he scuttled the metaphysics and teleology of Hegelianism, as well as abandoning the Christian beliefs of his childhood, in some ways his thought maintained a Hegelian orientation or sensibility. This was particularly true in Dewey's commitment to overcoming dualisms and contradictions. He saw many of the inherited ways of thinking as committed to hierarchies in the form of dualisms or contrasting entities and forces: Labor vs. Capital, Man vs. Woman, Fact vs. Value, Intellect vs. Emotion, Thought vs. Action, Ideal vs. Material, Individual vs. Society, Art vs. Nature, Equality vs. Liberty. Dewey always sought to resolve these antinomies by demonstrating that they were really aspects of the same reality, viewed from different angles, rather than essential oppositions. In *Reconstruction in Philosophy* (1920), for instance, he articulated what he would later call a "new individualism," committed to the fullest realization of the self in a complex society. "Social arrangements, laws, institutions," said Dewey are "means and agencies of human welfare and progress. But they are not means for obtaining something for individuals, not even happiness. They are means of *creating* individuals"[4] This individual was not set in conflict with society, as Ralph Waldo Emerson had imagined in his landmark 1841 essay "Self Reliance." The old Enlightenment ideas had imagined a social contract between naturally autonomous individuals in a state of nature; Dewey insisted that vision belonged to an intellectual system that could not grapple with the nature of modern society. The potential for development and self-realization was the same thing as social realization, since educational, political, and cultural institutions were the conditions for the creation of selfhood. Dewey tossed out all the old Enlightenment-derived theoretical foundations of democracy and self-government based on natural rights, universalism, and rationalism, and replaced them with a future-oriented vision of democracy as a chosen way of life that could provide no inherent justification in nature. Individuals, like society, were made and not found. Having commitments to democratic self-fulfillment as a goal, Dewey believed that the task for Americans was to adapt their social means to ends of creating fuller and more-developed selves. Thinking about methods, means, and instruments was allowing a kind of proceduralism, informed by human desires, to provide a direction for the future. Dewey, like James, rejected the teleological vision of nature and history, the idea that there was something in the constitution of nature itself that propelled human beings in a necessarily progressive fashion. If "Progress" was not built into nature and God's design, the conclusion Dewey came to was that human beings were in control of their own destiny, that they could fulfill in both means and ends, the vision of a democratic way of life. Against the determinism and fatalism of some accounts of history, Dewey provided a vision of socialized freedom, of people acting together, collectively, in fulfillment of their social and individual potentials.

Conclusion

The Pragmatic sensibility would find large application in diverse areas of life and society, as we will see in subsequent chapters. Various thinkers took dispositions and tendencies in Pragmatic thought—its distrust of abstractions and fondness for concreteness, its anti-dualistic orientation, its embrace of a vision of science as a liberatory and progressive force, its challenge to orthodox and dogmatic thought—in a number of directions. Sometimes the power of modern thought is imagined as a great negative force, a kind of critical overthrow of the structures of meaning that ordered people's lives, what the social thinker Walter Lippmann famously referred to as the "acids of modernity." The powerful philosophical orientation of modern thought *has* been destructive in many of its orientation: the demythologizing tendencies of Marx, Freud, and Nietzsche have produced a critical sensibility, an interpretive strategy that seeks to pull down beliefs—faith in religion, reason, morality, the possibility of knowledge itself. To be clear, each of those thinkers believed that their critique was in the service of some larger human fulfillment, that the myths of the past had to be dispelled to produce a better future. While neo-Pragmatist philosophers of the late twentieth century, such as Richard Rorty, seem to be very much in line with the critique of received knowledge, the overwhelming disposition of the first generation of Pragmatists was not so much to expose the pernicious sources of received thought, as to provide a positive reconstruction of philosophy. They aimed to show, for instance, that people should trust science *because* its claims were not absolute, that religion (as in James) could provide a powerful value to human life, or (as in Dewey) could be deployed in secular form to reach for future goals, that understanding the volitional desiring, willing, and habitual content of knowledge would be a way to heal the alienation of the mind from the body. From their point of view, the universe of fixed types, absolute oppositions, epistemological foundations, designed and ordered reality, had to be evaluated in terms of its significance for human flourishing. They thought forms of belief and practice should be taken where one found them, rather than being referred to as expressions of abstract principles belonging to some transcendent realm. The recognition of the concreteness and specificity of human life was the source of a powerful commitment to finding frameworks of meaning for modern life that would recognize the capacity of people to make their own lives, but not under the conditions of their own making. If they imagined this project as a struggle for the existence of beliefs, tried out in the arena of practical outcomes, adaptation to the concrete conditions of modernity, they did so not as an expression of Social Darwinism, but as an attempt to find guidance through flexibility and method, to give to modern peoples the tools by which to make their lives together. This was the flipside to the acids of modernity, its creative orientation. To the extent that we, belonging to the Pragmatists' future, remain ambivalent about modernity—aware of the ways in which its potential for liberation is tied to its destruction of the bedrock of belief that had profoundly provided moral orientation in the past, for instance—we are, perhaps, still working within the practice that Pragmatism created, self-knowing creatures of habit.

Notes

1 Charles Sanders Peirce, "Illustrations of the Logic of Science. Second Paper—How to Make Our Ideas Clear," *Popular Science Monthly* 12 (January 1878), pp. 292–293.
2 Ibid., p. 288.
3 William James, *Pragmatism: A New Name for Some Old Ways of Thinking* (New York: Longmans, Green and Co., 1907), pp. 201, 222, 223, 233–234.
4 John Dewey, *Reconstruction in Philosophy* (New York: Henry Holt & Co., 1920), p. 194.

3 The Research University, The Idea of Culture, and The Social Sciences

[handwritten margin note: ※ influence of German univ./scholar.]

An educated public, thinking in the new naturalist modes of thought available in the late nineteenth century, was increasingly conscious of the conventional and arbitrary basis of categories previously presumed to be defined by essences and fixed nature. But if natural kinds, such as species, were not fixed, if reality was not designed or ordered, but in flux, the question of how to regard the traditional division of academic studies based on the inherited organization of knowledge was opened in a new way. The ancient idea of the distinct educational order of the *trivium* (grammar, logic, rhetoric) and *quadrivium* (arithmetic, geometry, music, astronomy) and their commitment to an educational purpose defined by knowledge received from the past had long been replaced by philology, moral philosophy, and classics as mainstays of the early American college. But this notion of an education rooted in inherited traditions was increasingly out of sync with the conditions of a new complex modern society. The period from the end of the Civil War to World War I saw a fundamental reorganization of knowledge: new academic disciplines created and old ones reformed; a shift in the orientation of knowledge, from a generalized common curriculum to specialized areas of study; a redefinition of the purposes of higher education; a systematic attempt to create new institutions and reform older ones; the creation of new means of communications, certification of expertise, and engagement with public life. This did not happen without a fight, one in which the advocates for an older classicism transformed it into a model to challenge the new research university and its protocols. But by the end of the era, an uneasy accommodation between the idea of the university as a vehicle for generating new knowledge (and wealth) through the process of research, and the idea of "liberal education" to provide the basis of public citizenship, had been reached.

The battles over higher education in the late nineteenth century were not just arguments over the most efficient way to organize knowledge—they were battles over ways of seeing the world. Should education be practical and "useful," on the one hand, or set against utilitarian goals by an advocacy for an idealized realm of "culture," on the other? Should higher education stand as a bulwark against the commercial order of corporate capitalism and its materialist values, or should it adapt itself to the nature of a modern economy and society? Should the emphasis be on transmitting learning and heritage from the past, or creating new knowledge in a future-oriented environment? Should all knowledge be modeled on empirical science, or was it possible to conceive of alternative models? Should education be a top-down affair, in which student choice was highly circumscribed, or should it be driven by students, defining their own paths of study? New models of authority, of complexity, of method, of ways in which to divide the world up into objects of study: all were at stake here. We might imagine the Culture Wars around higher education to be an artifact of the late twentieth century, when feminism, post-colonialism, and movements for ethnic and racial equality roiled the waters of a presumably long-established European-centered curriculum. Already, however, the question of what counts as knowledge, and w' at values it encodes, was rooted in the genesis of the post-Civil War R‧ earch University and its challenges to a classically-based curriculum, on ‧e one hand, and a generalized notion of "culture" on the other.

A number of important developments led to the transformation of the antebellum college and the birth of the modern research university. The leadership of a few critical individuals—Charles W. Eliot at Harvard, Andrew Dickson White at Cornell, and Daniel Coit Gilman at Johns Hopkins, among others—spearheaded the structural transformation. Eliot, appointed to the Presidency at Harvard in 1869, spent 40 years reshaping the oldest American college, founded by seventeenth-century Puritans, into one of the premier research institutions in America, and eventually, the world. White lacked the same sources of funding provided by the New England elite that allowed Harvard an alumni base rich in financial resources. But he harnessed his vision of a private research university, funded by the resources of businessman Ezra Cornell, to the contemporaneous movement by the Civil War-era congress to create land-grant Universities, focused on the agricultural and mechanical arts. White's vision of Cornell University, dedicated to both scientific aspirations and practical ones, balancing a liberal curriculum with one emphasizing practical sciences and technology, was one of the early models of what publicly-funded universities might look like. Gilman sought to create an entirely new research-oriented institution, with a focus on graduate education and the granting of the Ph.D.; Johns Hopkins was founded in 1876 and led the way in setting standards for educating scholars and generating research based on empirical methods. These three institutions suggested the various paths to the creation of a new system of universities in the decades after the Civil War. Institutions such as the University of California at Berkeley (founded 1868), Stanford

University (founded 1885), and the University of Chicago (founded 1890), among many others, became centers of higher research and education in the arts and sciences. The modern research university, both public and private, that we know today was essentially created in the decades prior to 1900, through a combination of philanthropy, business wealth, and government action.

The new disciplines created in the universities were part of a larger wave of professionalization that affected a wide array of occupations—law, medicine, government, engineering, as well as more narrowly scholarly ones. National professional associations, with explicitly articulated standards for education, self-regulation, credentialing, and ethics, multiplied. In the scholarly world, professionalization meant the establishment of disciplinary-based organizations, such as the American Historical Association (founded 1884), the Modern Language Association (founded 1883), and the American Physical Society (founded 1899); the creation of scholarly journals and publications; regular conferences and meetings; and oversight for training and credentialing of scholars. The American university system looked to the model of German scholarship and universities; many of the first generations of professional scholars who staffed the new departments had themselves been trained in Germany, and German scholarship represented the pinnacle of academic training and education in the mid-nineteenth century. The University of Berlin and Heidelberg University were widely recognized as the most important of the German universities. The preponderance of those who taught in American universities had done graduate work at one of the principal German universities. Johns Hopkins University began to award the Ph.D., or Doctor of Philosophy degree, as an indication of mastery of original research, in the 1870s; by 1900, the major Ivy League Institutions (Harvard, Princeton, Yale, Columbia, University of Pennsylvania) and several land-grant public universities, such as the University of Michigan, and the University of Wisconsin, were among the institutions granting Ph.Ds. Students continued to go to Germany, and it would be well into the twentieth century before American Ph.D.-granting institutions achieved global prominence. But the turn toward the research university, it should be clear, was an international movement with its clearest strengths in Europe, where state funding and long-established institutions were the conditions for the academic revolution. In the United States, by the early twentieth century, the Ph.D. degree—and the production of a dissertation based on original research—had become a requirement for employment as a faculty member at most universities.

The tension between an older generalist tradition of education, and the newer focus on highly specialized research was evidence of the ways in which the reformulation of knowledge in the late nineteenth century simultaneously opened new possibilities and constricted thought in very specific ways. William James, who helped shape the academic disciplines of Philosophy and Psychology, for instance, saw the focus on credentialing scholars as a way to substitute the emblem of scholarly achievement for the reality of it. In 1903 he declared that "the Ph.D. Octopus" had got hold of institutions of higher learning, and was threatening to strangle the creative potential of minds by producing conformists to a rigid model of education. American universities, said James, "ought to guard against the contributing to the increase of officialism and snobbery and insincerity as against a pestilence; they ought to keep truth and disinterested labor always in the foreground, treat degrees as secondary incidents," and "make it plain that what they live for is to help men's souls, and not to decorate their persons with diplomas."[1] The requirement of the Ph.D., at first instituted to provide an avenue for the promotion of original scholarship and creative work, had become a fetish, an end in itself. Given how unconventional James's own education was, a suspicion of an over-institutionalized approach to knowledge is not surprising. But the very development of a new approach to knowledge and learning, which was supported by James, seemed to produce its opposite, a greater respect for symbols, a worshiping of the external signs of success rather than internal virtue. James was not so far away from the Puritan suspicion of salvation through "works" (external means), rather than "grace" (the inner presence of the spirit). He seemed to desire the goal of the university—advancing scholarship—while suspicious of its means—the granting of the Doctoral degree.

The notion of producing and disseminating new knowledge as the central function of the university did not mean that the question of the public educative value of the university, or its moral purpose, was sidelined. One of the big questions raised by the rise of the research university was how its mission might be aligned with a broader concern about values, their inculcation, and their social consequences. So, on the one hand, the university was about creating and instituting new epistemic standards. On the other, those standards were not imagined as neutral or indifferent to questions of moral order, structures of meaning, and the kind of society that would be produced. Some historians have seen the decline of religious authority in higher education and the secularization of knowledge as a marginalization of morality in favor of building a professional ethos. Others have seen the early advocates of the research university as embracing "scientism": the belief that all knowledge was scientific and that science itself would solve the problems of modernity without recourse to values derived from religion, moral philosophy, political ideology, or other non-scientific sources. Still others have suggested that many of the founders and promoters of the post-Civil War university were "scientific democrats," committed to the notion best articulated by John Dewey, that scientific values were democratic ones, that education in science could supplant the religious and philosophical basis of morality offered by the antebellum college. The university, in this vision, would serve not only expertise-oriented technocracy but also broadly meritocratic and egalitarian values of widespread critical intelligence and reasoned deliberation. The students trained in the university would emerge on the other side as the leading edge in the creation of a scientific culture that opened the way for solving problems of governance and self-rule. As Gilman put it in his 1876 inaugural address at Johns Hopkins, a new institution with no allegiance to the antebellum vision of higher education:

> The object of the university is to develop character—to make men. It misses its aim if it produced learned pedants, or simple artisans, or cunning sophists, or pretentious practitioners. Its purport is not so much to impart knowledge to the pupils, as whet the appetite, exhibit methods, develop powers, strengthen judgment, and invigorate the intellectual and moral forces. It should prepare for the service of society a class of students who will be wise, thoughtful, progressive guides in whatever department of work or thought they may be engaged.[2]

The new orientation of the university, in this vision, was clearly not simply a commitment to scientific knowledge as an end in itself.

The Origins of the Social Sciences

Among the new disciplines created in the late nineteenth century were what today we recognize as the "social sciences": anthropology, economics, political science, sociology, and (sometimes) psychology. While the attempt to form some kind of scientific approach to "society," to apply the disciplinary methods and focus on empirical knowledge, has a pedigree that dates to Enlightenment social thought and moral philosophy, the notion of distinct disciplines in these areas, each with its own object of study and its theoretical and methodological concerns, was a novelty. And social science itself was not thought of as divisible in this way or each of these disciplines necessarily linked to one another, as the social sciences are today in most universities. Anthropology, or the science of man, for instance, was associated with biological science, psychology with philosophy, and political science with history. Other developing areas such as linguistics, crossed the boundaries between disciplines. The familiar distinction between the humanities and the social sciences that most institutions of higher education embrace today was certainly not understood clearly and distinctly in the past. And the idea that the human-made world is divisible into four quadrants or distinct phenomena, each with its own dedicated science—economy, polity, culture, and society—is more an artifact of mid-twentieth century social theory, as in Harvard sociologist Talcott Parson's famous general theory of action. Modern economics, for instance, draws its intellectual sources from what had been called political economy—but in the course of defining the new science, the attention turned to an image of "the economy" as a distinct object of study apart from politics, governed by its own laws.

There were alternative ways of conceptualizing the social sciences. The American Social Science Association, founded in 1865, provided the immediate form in which social science was institutionalized, but it was more deeply rooted in social reform and policy sensibility than what emerged in the following decades. Its own divisions—education, public health, social economy, and jurisprudence—were derived from older professions, focused on addressing social problems, and did not represent the distinct disciplines that would be formed by professional associations in the 1880s and 1890s. The idea that the Association was a vehicle advocating for solutions to social problems such as poverty, crime, and disease, even as it approached those problems with a modern "scientific" outlook, made it a difficult fit with the ethos of the emerging research university. That a scholarly science should aim for some distance from the immediacy of social problems, that its goal should be oriented toward the creation of new knowledge—with a faith that that creation would bring beneficial social results—rather than directly concerned with advocacy of reforms: this was more consistent with the imagined purposes of the late nineteenth-century university. The tension between public engagement and purpose, on the one hand, and academic autonomy, on the other, was built into the values that served to legitimate the new way of organizing knowledge. Some have characterized the movement away from the ASSA model as a turn toward the ideal of "objectivity" as a feature of social science. The history of academic social science has frequently been a contest between the advocates of an objective or "value-neutral" scientific ideal, and the advocates for an engaged social science premised on the idea that human beings are not natural objects and that social science is a form of self-knowledge.

When the new disciplines, professional societies, and academic departments were formed in the last two decades of the nineteenth century, the ideas that informed them had already achieved a kind of prominence in decades of discussion. One of the central contentions of eighteenth-century enlightened thought had been that applying the tools of empiricism and logic to the analysis of human social experience would lead to results akin to those reached in the realm of nature. And if the understanding of nature increased human power over it, and allowed people to control and subordinate the natural world to human ends, an understanding of human societies, their development, and their mechanisms would allow for the reconstruction of society on rational grounds. A science of society would, in this view, give people the power to shape their own futures. The question of whose values would dictate this future—would they be more egalitarian values of universal education, for instance, or would they use scientific and knowledge claims to value the authority of some at the expense of others—of course, was a matter of contention, and continues to inform public debate about the meaning of education to this day. But the idea that the forms of social order were not given in nature or by God, that human beings could remake the world into which they were born, that the authority of the inherited past was not a warrant for the existing moral order—these were central to enlightened social thought, and became the basis for creating sciences of society.

In a previous chapter, we have touched on some of the Enlightenment and post-Enlightenment forms the new scientific approach to society took. The most significant modern forms inherited by the American thinkers in the late nineteenth century were social contract theory; British political economy and moral philosophy; Marxism and other socialist theories of the first half of the nineteenth century; the sociology of the French philosopher Auguste Comte; stadial theories of social development arising out of the Scottish Enlightenment; and the evolutionary sociology of Herbert Spencer. In addition, a significant body of literature on "racial" differences and their specific social and characterological traits was part of the intellectual milieu in which the nascent social scientists of the post-Darwin era operated. It would not be wrong to say that the origins of American social science were imbued with various forms of white supremacist thought, for instance, including sometimes underarticulated ideas of ethnological hierarchy and European superiority. The influential evolutionary ways of thinking may have resisted the idea of a fixed and permanent hierarchy of peoples, for instance, but replaced it with the idea that societies could be seen in an evolutionary sequence, in which white Europeans were the most developed endpoint.

American thinkers were in constant conversation with European theorists, reformers, and social thinkers during this same era, so we should not imagine that American social science was an entirely distinct thing, rather than a variant on the forms of European social thinking that informed modern thought in its variety and totality. Nevertheless, the birth of American social science was indebted to strains of American ideology, as well as the corpus of European and international ideas circulating. The historian Dorothy Ross has argued that the specific frame of American social science was ahistorical in its orientation, concerned overwhelmingly with mechanisms and analysis of social processes without reference to the determinative power of the inherited past. This approach to social phenomena was deeply shaped by the ideological orientation of "American exceptionalism." The idea of American exceptionalism is a complex one, but its general meaning has been a belief that on the observable level, American social and political development was an exception to the rule that governed modern European development—so universal theories of history, such as Marxism, were not applicable to the United States. The ideology of exceptionalism linked a claim about the difference of American society from a rule governing other societies, with a claim of the moral distinctness and superiority of American society. The laws that operated in Europe were inapplicable to America. American society was free from the constraints of the past and its inherited feudal hierarchies, in this image, and so operated outside of patterns of historical development. Marx had famously written in 1852

> Men make their own history, but they do not make it just as they please; they do not make it under circumstances chosen by themselves, but under circumstances directly found, given, and transmitted from the past. The tradition of all the dead generations weighs like a nightmare on the brain of the living.[3]

This image of the past as the condition of the present, as a kind of burden that cannot be escaped, is antithetical to the ahistorical claims of exceptionalism. In what might be one of the principal historical sources of the exceptionalist doctrine, The American Revolutionary polemicist Thomas Paine had famously declared in his pamphlet *Common Sense*, "we have it in our power to begin the world over again."[4] Instead of a deeply historical social science that stressed the determinative power and constraint of the inherited past, the American social scientists responsible for founding and shaping the disciplines, oriented their analysis toward the observable present, creating a focus on replicable social processes, assuming the institutional reality of the present as a kind of natural given, rather than the conditions of history. History as an object of study and the basis for social scientific methodologies was central to many of the new sciences, as was an evolutionary framework. But history as the constraint of particularity, as a dominant force in society, was largely absent. When history *was* the context for understanding, say industrial order or institutional development, it was a transhistorical vision of a liberal society in which individual liberty and social harmony were ever-present in America that was the condition of any particular historical moment.

The key figures for understanding the first generation of academic social scientists include Richard Ely and John Bates Clark in economics; John Burgess and Frank Goodnow in political science; Albion Small, Franklin Giddings, and Charles Horton Cooley in Sociology; and Henry Lewis Morgan, John Wesley Powell, and Daniel Brinton in anthropology. Within each of the emerging disciplines, there were disagreements and intellectual conflicts, but the push toward disciplines and departmentalization encouraged the architects of these fields to stress what distinguished the discipline from its relatives, to argue in a more pronounced way for methodological and substantive differences between the study of, for instance, politics and economics, which had previously been linked, or sociology and anthropology—the former focusing on the character of modern society, the latter concerned more with "primitive" and non-Western peoples. The push for disciplinary distinctiveness was offset by the potential openness of the new disciplines, an openness that allowed for unusual combinations of thought by later standards. For instance, Thorstein Veblen was an economist, but his works read frequently as if they are sociological or anthropological, concerned with the structure of values and moral orientations as well as the distribution of goods. There is not space here to outline the different intellectual traditions within each of these new disciplines, but a brief look at the history of sociology suggests something of the way in which the philosophical thought of the previous century became the basis for the new disciplines.

The Science of Sociology

In many ways, sociology was a reaction against the perceived breakdown of inherited forms and practices, and from its inception in the mid-nineteenth century, it always included within it a kind of progressive or democratic attempt to overcome the fragmentation of nineteenth-century individualism, on the one hand, and a reactionary attempt to restore an older imagined feudal holism, on the other. As in the earlier Social Darwinist dispute between Lester Frank Ward and William Graham Sumner, sociology could mean a conscious attempt to collectively address the needs of a complex society, or it could mean an insistence on the natural and persistent nature of traditional authority against modern change. The idea of sociology as a distinct science was initially formulated by the French philosopher Auguste Comte in the 1830s, and as such was founded on a progressive image of a series of philosophies that moved from religious to secular authority—a science of society was a replacement for earlier forms of theological and metaphysical belief. Ward's approach to progressive sociology was influenced by Comte. Yet, by emphasizing that society was more than the sum of the individuals that composed it, sociology looked to the complex network of relationships in which individuals were bound, to suggest that modernity only appeared to be a source of fragmentation—in fact, modernity created a greater interdependence because of the specialized nature of practices and the division of labor. It is not surprising that the first American thinkers to embrace the term sociology were Southern pro-slavery theorists in the 1850s. By arguing that all societies were defined by mutual obligations up and down the social hierarchy and that societies were organic forms in which parts were subordinated to the whole, they could picture slavery as an antidote to the conflicts between labor and capital in industrial society. Those conflicts, the Virginian George Fitzhugh wrote in his *Sociology for the South* (1854), were premised on an idea that self-interest and individual liberty were ultimate goods, whereas sociology emphasized the ways in which a paternalistic slavery ended social conflict by subordinating the individual to the collective whole. The influential Herbert Spencer view of sociology, dominant in the United States in the 1870s and 80s, took the opposite tack, emphasizing the collective evolutionary development of individual liberty as a higher good, rather than an antisocial force. The insistence on sociology in Spencer and Sumner was on the law-like model of society and social development, rather than the mutual obligations of the collective. When Sumner in 1883 asked "What Social Classes Owe to One Another?" his answer was not the bonds of social unity and responsibility, but only the most minimal framework for the protection of property and individual liberty.

The sociological vision of the world that was developed during this era had a lasting consequence, not just on academic practice, but on the larger vocabulary and ways of thinking about society in the public sphere. Concepts such as "attitude," "role model," "assimilation," "social adjustment," "alienation," "cultural lag," and "reference group," for instance, although they appeared in sociological discourse much later in the twentieth century, would provide later Americans ways to talk about and explain the world they lived in. Here was a secular vocabulary that purported to explain human behavior as governed by laws and forces produced by the collective arrangements of the social order. In other words, the sociological view of the world was not narrowly an academic one; it had a role in shaping the larger public discourse outside of debates within the ivory tower. Central ideas that formed the stock of early sociological thought, such as Adam Smith's ideas about sympathy as a kind of social glue, or the French sociologist Gabriel Tarde's idea of imitation as the principle of social solidarity, or the German sociologist Ferdinand Tönnies idea of an opposition between Gemeinschaft and Gesellschaft (roughly "community" and "society"), or Max Weber's ideas about bureaucracy, secularization, and modern "disenchantment," although not always central to the specific forms of early academic sociology in the United States, would radiate out from their academic sources over the course of the following century.

Sumner and Ward were not entirely representative of the late nineteenth-century founders of American sociology, although they all drew on common sources: the political economy of Adam Smith, Darwinian evolutionary thought, and Common Sense philosophy, among others. One of the central figures in institutionalizing sociology was Albion Small, the founding head of the first department of sociology in the United States, at the University of Chicago in 1892, and also the founder and editor of *The American Journal of Sociology* in 1895. Small's own graduate work had been done in Germany in economic and political subjects, and he had completed a Ph.D. at Johns Hopkins in History in 1889. His sociological views synthesized these fields. Like his contemporary at Columbia University, Franklin Giddings, Small saw the origins of sociology not in Comte, but a half century earlier in the moral philosophy and political economy of the Scottish thinker Adam Smith. Smith's *The Theory of the Moral Sentiments* (1759) had sought to demonstrate that the source of morality lay in a kind of proto-sociological process, based on what Smith called "the sympathetic imagination": by identifying sympathetically with others as the basis for guiding one's behavior, the social world was internalized in the self. Sympathy was the "glue" that held the social order together and regulated individual behavior. In Giddings's sociology, this sympathetic mechanism would become the basis for what Giddings referred to as "consciousness of kind," by which he meant group identities—of ethnicity, race, social class, nation—that structured social interaction. Another early sociologist, Charles Horton Cooley, of the University of Michigan, developed a Smithian conception of the self as a product of sympathetic reflection in his concept of what he called "the looking glass self." This lineage of ideas, providing a kind of social psychological perspective, would be developed in a very influential way in the works of the Chicago Pragmatist, George Herbert Mead. Small also argued that Smith's *Wealth of Nations* (1776), which twentieth-century thinkers have consistently identified as a founding text of modern economics, was really the source of a sociological vision, one in which society was imagined as a self-regulating organism.

If we look only at the figures who founded the American Sociological Association in 1905—men like Small, Cooley, Giddings, Ward, and Sumner—we marginalize one of the most creative and significant founders of American sociology, the African-American historian, intellectual, critic, novelist, and activist, W.E.B. DuBois. The sociological program he shaped at Atlanta University, was part of a more activist reform-oriented sociology that also was developed at Historically Black Colleges like Tuskegee and Hampton. One of DuBois's earliest works was *The Philadelphia Negro* (1899), a pioneering empirical survey of urban life, and the first to attempt a systematic study of the social composition of a Black community. Because DuBois connected his sociological work to addressing social problems, his sociological vision was more "activist" than his white contemporaries. DuBois effectively redefined race as an object of study in this work. In the post-Civil War era, it was common to see educated white opinion consider "the negro problem" as an issue of morality, attributing crime, poverty, and other social ills to the intrinsic nature of

African-Americans, or as an attribute of racial "degeneration" in post-slavery conditions. DuBois challenged this view, demonstrating the ways in which racism and the constraints in employment, education, and other opportunities shaped Black lives. Poverty was, in this view, a social fact, but one which had definite structural causes in the environment of urban life. DuBois was pushing against a dominant racist ideology that attributed the characteristics of Black lives to biological, inherent, or received cultural attributes. Given that American sociology began half a century earlier as an attempt to justify slavery, it is striking that DuBois was able to transform it into an antiracist perspective, identifying race-based discrimination and oppression as the cause of what he still regarded as the "moral" condition of Black lives. Many years later, *The Philadelphia Negro* would take on the status of a classic, and come to be recognized as a landmark work in the history of sociology.

Victorian Anthropology

The study of so-called "primitive" peoples as a way to understand the earliest forms of human cultures and society also had Enlightenment roots. Eighteenth-century Scottish thinkers such as Adam Ferguson, Adam Smith, John Millar, and Henry Home (Lord Kames) had developed their ideas about the process of human progress by stressing a unilinear form of social development through a series of stages defined by modes of economic organization. They held that human societies moved through four stages, from most primitive or lowest, to most civilized and highest: hunter/gatherer, pastoral, agricultural, and commercial. These stages of history allowed for a universal model of what Dugald Stewart called "conjectural history." This approach to the evolution of human societies was not concerned with the particularity of different societies and their histories, but with creating a typology that could be applied to any society. This meant that the study of contemporary so-called "primitive" societies, such as American native peoples, was designed to serve as an image of an earlier, less-developed European society, and to measure the distance from that society on an evolutionary scale.

In the United States, the most significant of the stadial theories was that developed by ethnologist Lewis Henry Morgan. Morgan in his landmark *Ancient Society* (1877), argued that human societies progress through three stages: what he called Savagery, Barbarism, and Civilization. Each of these stages was defined by modes of production and property-holding, technology, language, kinship and family structure, governmental forms, and intellectual beliefs. Each was also divisible into three developmental substages (lower, middle, upper). The evolutionary discourse of Civilization stemmed from this conception. It's hard to conceive that the terminology that Morgan used here could be regarded as merely descriptive and neutral. Unlike terms such as "agricultural" or "commercial," terms like "savagery" and "barbarism" were loaded with moral attribution. On the one hand, this series of stages is anthropological, concerned with the way in which human institutions, organizations, behaviors, and beliefs have developed over time; on the other, it takes the form of a narrative of transition from animal to man, from nature to culture. How could the transition from Savagery to Civilization not be conceived in the image of progress, the story of Man overcoming his bestial nature through refinement and aspirations to a higher moral ideal? Victorian anthropology in the Morgan mode could reassert a hierarchy of peoples without the foundational notion of fixity or permanent status. The difference in human status was not so much a difference in biological identity as it was a difference in historical stage of development, although biological "race" and evolutionary stage would often be confused in the broader appropriation of Morgan's terminology, and Morgan was not above claiming that only "Aryan" peoples had reached the highest stages of Civilization. Morgan, along with his contemporary, the British social anthropologist E.B. Tylor, defined an evolutionary approach to the study of Man, but also a comprehensive one in which all facets of human practice were integrated. The idea of "culture," said Tyler famously, "is that complex whole which includes knowledge, belief, art, morals, law, custom, and any other capabilities and habits acquired by man as a member of society."[5] This idea that culture is a "whole way of life," became an important foundational concept for academic anthropology.

By defining the stages of human development first in relationship to the forms of technology and material production, and then seeing the ways in which those forms of production were related to the forms of the family and kinship, the use of language, political authority, and religion, Morgan adopted a materialist position on social development that shared a good deal with Marxist theory. In fact, Marx's partner Friedrich Engels drew heavily on Morgan's *Systems of Consanguinity and Affinity of the Human Family* (1871) for his important study of *The Origins of Private Property, the Family, and the State* (1884). Morgan had discovered that the kinship terms of the Iroquois (whom he had both studied in the field and advocated for) showed a matrilineal structure that he argued was held over from a period in which peoples held all wealth (primarily herds) in common. Only with the introduction of private property and inheritance was it necessary to restrict female sexuality in order to ensure that a man's property was passed to his biological descendants. Engels saw in this the basis for an argument about marriage and reproduction of wealth as the elements of class rule based on private property. This argument, in turn, was influential on later feminists who took it up as the basis of a critique of the family and the role of women. But Morgan's evolutionism, sharing a kind of progressive logic with Marxism, was far from Marxist theory; it had a unilinear form of gradual development and evolution, rather than a dialectical form emphasizing internal contradictions of a society and their generation of revolution. Instead of seeing conflict as the engine of social change, Morgan's vision saw societies as integrated wholes, occupying distinct places in a ladder of development.

Morgan's evolutionist model, perhaps even more than the Social Darwinism of some of his contemporaries, provided a model that could be used to legitimize imperialism. In the late nineteenth century, Europeans were expanding and developing colonies in Africa and Asia. The United States had its own expansionism and imperialism in the Pacific, and in the Philippines, acquired in the Spanish-American War at the end of the nineteenth century. *Ancient Society* was published at the moment of the so-called Indian Wars of the late nineteenth century, in which widespread arguments linking aboriginal peoples to "savagery" and arguing for their displacement and conversion to systems of private property holding and sedentary agriculture were afoot. Again, Morgan was himself an advocate for the Iroquois, but his theory of social evolution suggested that the more highly developed "civilization" could have a leadership role in civilizing primitive peoples, and leading the way for expressions of colonial moral uplift.

Culture and the University

While the new evolutionary anthropology was creating a concept of culture that referred to the whole way of life of a people, an alternative conception of culture was doing battle with the terms of a secularizing society and the kind of specialized knowledge that the research university was bringing into being. The shift over the nineteenth century was from the centrality of classicism—the notion that ancient Greek and Roman philosophy, art, and thought represented the defining pinnacle of education—to the idea of modern forms of thought rooted in the growth of science, and adequate to a complex and dynamic society as the character-forming elements of higher education. But there was a third player in the mix—a modern notion of culture that provided a moral and spiritual alternative to an exclusively classical curriculum, on the one hand, and an increasingly practical or pragmatically oriented course of study on the other. The idea of culture, in this instance, could provide a modern alternative to classicism, while still encompassing the lineage of Christian and Classical sources of aesthetic, literary, and moral values.

The post-World War II British Marxist Raymond Williams once said of culture that it is "one of the two or three most complicated words in the English language."[6] Its plural and conflicting meanings were a product of nineteenth-century responses to industrial and commercial changes, and in various ways, the thinkers who invoked it sought to create a source of integrative holistic meaning to counter perceived fragmentation, social breakdown, and secular challenges to religious authority. One of those ways was through the anthropological definition created by Tylor. Another was through a reinvention of art, literature, philosophy, and moral thought as a distinct realm of higher meaning and spiritual values. In 1867 and 1868, the British poet and critic Matthew Arnold published a series of essays which were then collected under the title *Culture and Anarchy*. In these essays, Arnold put forward a central argument—that contemporary society and politics could not rest on a kind of laissez-faire of individual taste and desire, but only on a commitment to some shared higher purpose. He defined culture as that higher purpose, famously identifying it with "the best that has been said and thought," and arguing for its emphasis on what he called "a pursuit of total perfection." Only those educated in the broadest way, who could draw on the resources of the best of human aesthetic and intellectual achievement, would have the power to face and give direction to the complex and divided future in a meaningful way. Arnold's was a critique of the anarchic elements of heightened individualism and the intellectual leveling implications of a modern move toward democracy. It was a critique of what he defined as the rule of the Philistines, those who cared only for material progress and were indifferent to aesthetic and spiritual values. The way to counter the narrowness of specialized functions in modern life, its materialistic orientation, its technical expertise, was to put forward a spiritualized realm of values. The Arnoldian notion of culture would have a lasting effect in sacralizing the realm of thought and the arts. Arnold noted the declining power of traditional religious faith in a supernatural world, a world in which the miraculous had been outlawed by modern science. Culture would serve as a kind of antidote to that decline, a surrogate religion.

In the United States, Arnold would have both his detractors and his advocates, but his image of culture as the basis for education exerted a strong pull for those who believed that science was inadequate as a moral guide for modern life. The suspicion that America was precisely the heart of the kind of materialistic vulgarity that Arnold abhorred, led many to see Arnold not just as a critic of modernity, but as a critic of America itself. But the Arnoldian notion of culture, which promised to elevate the moral nature, to equip human beings with the mental and moral resources to direct social change in progressive ways, did have a lasting influence in shaping the intellectual justifications for liberal education. That is, even as the research university became the cutting-edge model of higher education, the faith that higher education required a broad knowledge of the arts, literature, history, and philosophy—that provincialism and philistinism were both the enemies of character and social usefulness and purpose—informed the curricular base of American higher education. Arnold's ideas very much shaped the educational agenda of American liberal reformers and literary intellectuals of his era. Men like the poet James Russell Lowell, the radical Republican and religious universalist Thomas Wentworth Higginson, the scholar Charles Eliot Norton, and the magazine editors George William Curtis, Richard Watson Gilder, and E.L. Godkin, who are associated with "the genteel tradition" of Victorian literary culture, operated under similar understandings of the educative power of culture. Norton, for instance, was one of the originators of the idea of "Western Civilization" as a curricular subject, a codified integration of the broad sphere of culture and values based on Classical and Christian sources.

The question of higher education, how knowledge is to be organized, and to what ends, remains a battleground. The terms of that battle have not remained the same, although some of the broadest tensions that produced the modern research university have been rearticulated in newer forms. In a world that appeared to have no stable anchors, higher education provided a way to reorganize the given, to both preserve the past as a guide to the future, and to institutionalize a faith in a future that involved highly trained professionals, the navigation of public and private bureaucracies, and technical specialization. If religion was sidelined in the new model of education, it was possible to imagine the university as a kind of secular church, providing faith in spiritual and character development, in democracy and progressive specialization, in culture and instrumental knowledge.

Notes

1 William James, "The Ph.D. Octopus," in *Memories and Studies* (New York: Longmans and Greene, 1912), pp. 343–344.
2 Daniel Coit Gilman, "Inaugural Address," Johns Hopkins University, February 22, 1876, https://www.jhu.edu/about/history/gilman-address/.
3 Karl Marx, "The Eighteenth Brumaire of Louis Napoleon," (1852) in Robert C. Tucker, ed., *The Marx-Engels Reader*, 2nd edition (New York: Norton, 1978), p. 595.
4 Thomas Paine, *Common Sense* (1776) (New York: Penguin Books, 2005), p. 69.
5 Edward B. Tylor, *Primitive Culture: Researches into the Development of Mythology, Philosophy, Religion, Language, Art, and Custom* (London: John Murray, 1871), vol. I, p. 1.
6 Raymond Williams, *Keywords: A Vocabulary of Culture and Society* (New York: Oxford University Press, 1976), p. 76.

4 Progressivisms

The idea of progress has had many mutations and forms in its modern history. How the idea of progress was transformed into the ideology of Progressivism is a story of how a generalized belief in a unilinear view of history directed toward ever-increasing human improvement, became a covering term for a whole host of specific movements for social and political reform. The kind of persons who advocated this set of reforms and believed in the conscious power of human effort to solve social problems and create human betterment came to be called Progressives, and have given their name to a specific period in American history, designated the Progressive Era. While historians have challenged the unity and integrity of a 20-year period stemming from the election of 1896 to the U.S. entry into World War I in 1917, and have often indicated continuities of conception and reform concerns from the so-called "Gilded Age" of 1877 to 1896 that preceded it, the term Progressive has stuck as an indicator of a novel focus on social and political reform in the late nineteenth and early twentieth centuries. Progressivism, in this view, had its many particular manifestations: reformed notions of the classical liberal state and the laissez-faire view that accompanied it; movements to address the social dislocations created by industrial capitalism; new models of experiential education that rejected the rote learning of the past; conservation and management of natural resources; urban reform, directed at both the "machine politics" of the era and at public health and safety; movements for control of fertility to ensure a better future; advocacy for immigration policies, among many others.

As this list should indicate, such wide and disparate reform movements seem hard to unify under a common umbrella. The idea that there was one ideology and associated cultural movement called "Progressivism" is difficult to sustain. Was Progressivism a secular movement rooted in Protestant ethical and social values, or was it a movement committed to a new scientific ethos and opposed to the moral reforms and charity orientation of an earlier Protestant establishment? Was it backward-looking, attempting to restore a world perceived to be lost in the new industrial order, or was it forward-looking, attempting to overcome perceived deficiencies and beliefs inherited from the past? Did Progressives welcome corporate consolidation, or did they oppose it? Did Progressives embrace a pluralistic and cosmopolitan world of racial and ethnic difference, or were they advocates for Anglo-Saxon and white supremacy? Did they promote a new social democratic vision, or did they argue for meritocracy and the authority of experts? Was Progressivism conscious of the fundamental conflict of classes, or did it embrace an American exceptionalist idea of an individualist and class-free social order? It is easy enough to find actors who have been labeled Progressive on each side of these dualities. The great intellectual conflicts of the era—science and religion; tradition and progress; pluralism and homogeneity; equality and authority; radicalism and reformism—were contained in the battles *within* Progressivism as well as the battles *between* Progressives and defenders of the status quo. Progressivism was shot through with the contradictions of what one historian has called a "reluctant modernism."

Throughout Western Europe in the late nineteenth century, new concerns about what had come to be called "The Social Question," led to the rise of new political ideologies and social reform movements designed to address social dislocation. The idea of a generalized social question was at the center of a transatlantic body of thought. Like American scholars who trained in Germany, many educated Americans traveled to Europe to acquaint themselves with the various kinds of reforms and movements arising out of the problems associated with industrial capitalism and its accompanying social changes. A shared discourse in books, journals of opinion, and scholarly papers shaped a common concern with problems of poverty, crime, labor exploitation, family breakdown, increasing economic polarization, and public health. These were problems associated with industrialism, urbanism, and the disappearance of social stability in a fluid and dynamic society. The Social Question was ultimately an attempt to conceive of the complex problems of modernity as (1) diverse expressions of a single phenomenon or force; (2) an object of study, debate, and analysis; and (3) subject to conscious human control and solution. The question part of "The Social Question," as in its contemporary relatives "The Woman Question," "The Jewish Question," and "The Negro Question," was not an intellectual question in search of an answer, but a perceived problem in search of a solution.

Like the term Progressivism, of course, "The Social Question" could mean different things to different people. According to the University of Chicago Professor Ira Howerth

> This, then, is the social question of today: How are the economic institutions of society, in which so much power and privilege are concentrated,

and which are essential to the well-being of all, to be organized and conducted so that their benefits may be justly shared by all members of society, and thus the last refuge of the spirit of selfish domination be, like the Church and the State, in the hands of the people?[1]

The question here is fundamentally one of justice and the distribution of power and wealth. But, for others, the question might be more one of how to adjust workers to their new conditions so as to lessen misery but also avoid questioning the fundamental basis of the social order. Social reform, for both groups, might consist of something that an elite of critical thinkers and activists, using modern methods and institutions, did to and for those who were powerless to remake the world, or it might consist of a new ideal of cross-class cooperation, invoking the agency of the poor. The transatlantic world of the era was abuzz with political reforms to expand democracy, plans to use public funds to provide support and a financial safety net for workers and the poor, the development of progressive graduated taxation policies, educational solutions, the creation of social settlements such as Toynbee Hall in London and Hull House in Chicago, and other institutions designed to provide aid and cross-class social contact. Marx had famously declared that "the philosophers have hitherto only interpreted the world in various ways. The point, however, is to change it." Although Progressivism was not specifically Marxist in its orientation and analysis, it shared with Marxism and other left-leaning philosophies (as well as Pragmatism) the notion that philosophy could not stand aloof from the world, but must put intelligence at the service of solving the contradictions and evils of modern society.

In the 1870s and 80s, a host of prominent writers and thinkers sought to challenge the dominance of the laissez-faire view of limited government associated with nineteenth-century liberalism. Their concerns were that a view of an open society regulated only by the market forces of supply and demand was less a means of liberation, as Herbert Spencer and William Graham Sumner had it, and more an inadequate set of principles for dealing with the consolidation of modern life, the simultaneous growth of economic wealth, on the one hand, and poverty and immiseration on the other. Two of the best known solutions to "The Social Question" were put forward by Henry George in his *Progress and Poverty* (1878) and Edward Bellamy in his utopian novel, *Looking Backward* (1888). Working within the terms of classical political economy, and David Ricardo's "law of rent," George argued that the source of class polarization lay in increasing productivity pushing the cost of land use higher—the more wealth increased, the greater proportion went to landlords, rather than to labor. George's solution was a tax on rents that would push down the unearned returns of an unproductive parasitic class, and effectively redistribute income to labor. *Progress and Poverty* became an international bestseller, and George's followers in the "Single Tax" movement pushed for a non-socialist solution, consistent with the general embrace of capitalism, effected through tax policy. Edward Bellamy's utopian novel, *Looking Backward* (1888) imagined a world that had come into being by the year 2000, a world in which all problems of poverty, crime, and disease had been solved. Bellamy in effect argued that a new world of equality had come into being through an extension of the principle of corporate consolidation that was burying the old individualist proprietary capitalism of the early republic. Instead of a revolution that overturned existing property relations, Bellamy argued for continuity through bureaucratic rationality, technology, and increased efficiency. The competitive order that created social misery, for Bellamy, was replaced by a cooperative vision of large-scale institutions, the reduction of labor, and the expansion of leisure. Bellamy's novel inspired "Nationalist" Clubs, who sought to promote the principles outlined in *Looking Backward*. Although George and Bellamy's ideas received the most attention by reform-minded individuals during these decades, there were myriad other proposals and ideas put forward in the hothouse of social reformist thought.

The New Republic and the New Liberalism: Lippmann, Croly, and Weyl

As Bellamy's writing indicates, one of the major issues that occupied reform-minded thinkers was the role of the state and the political traditions associated with limited government. The old Enlightenment bodies of thought that provided the ground and foundation for American political theory—natural rights, limited government based on a structure of checks and balance, federalist division of powers between state and national governments—were viewed by many critics and reformers as outdated and out of line with unprecedented social conditions. Eighteenth-century thought had posited a universal set of principles in social and political thought—something called "human nature" was held to be a constant, rendering human motives and behavior calculable; human beings were rational and self-interested, but also sympathetic and benevolent; they were endowed by their creator with rights that could be not abrogated; political authority derived its power from the will and consent of the citizenry. Revolutionary era thinkers such as John Adams and James Madison had sought to affirm a practiced balance between what they regarded as an extensive liberty and the need to constrain power. The theoretical outlook of Enlightenment thought looked less to history and its particularity, and more to abstract principle and its universality. History and the authority of the past were constraints on the possibility of a rationally ordered polity and needed to be abandoned in favor of an appeal to timeless foundations. Increasingly, for many Progressives, the doctrines of federalist checks and balances, individual rights (for white men), and limited government, came to appear as belonging to a specific time and place and set of conditions, rather than having universal applicability. The theory of the state embedded in the U.S. Constitution, in this reading, was appropriate to an agrarian republic of small producers in a geographically diverse nation, but not to the new conditions of industrial and urban life.

The call for a new theory of the state and its practical application based on historical circumstances rather than universal principles was knit out of various encounters with labor and capital, corporations and consumers, law and justice. The fullest articulation of the new theory was in the writings of the so-called "new liberals" of the early twentieth century: Herbert Croly, Walter Lippmann, and Walter Weyl. Croly's *The Promise of American Life* (1909) laid out a full critique of inherited liberal theory as antithetical to democracy in an era of concentrated economic power. When the greatest threat to the widespread distribution of individual freedom had come from the power of the state, it had made sense to build into the theory of the state a constitution that constrained governmental power, through a federalist system of divided powers, and internal checks on interests. But, Croly argued, limiting the power of the state in an era of concentrated economic power in the form of corporations meant that liberalism produced less democratic freedoms. The inability of the classical liberal state to efficiently regulate distribution of resources to serve democratic ends meant that it was not neutral, standing above society and providing a framework of laws applied equally to all. The state, for Croly, always displays favor toward some and disfavor toward others. The new liberalism sought to judge the adequacy of the constitution and form of the state by its outcome—did it promote greater equality, and increase liberty for more people, or did it adhere to a putative neutrality that was in actuality a favoring of the wealthy and their ability to coerce workers, farmers, and consumers? "[R]egulation in the democratic interest," said Croly, "is as far as possible from meaning the annihilation of individual liberty," contrary to what the partisans of Gilded Age liberalism were arguing. The progressive state doesn't seek to challenge economic power so much as to use it for democratic ends. For Croly, "the interest of the whole community demands a considerable concentration of economic power and responsibility, but only for the ultimate purpose of its more efficient exercise and the better distribution of its fruits."[2] The old premise of individuality as a state of autonomous freedom of the person was a false premise, but pernicious because adhering to it prevented the use of social means to achieve social ends of greater democratic freedom and liberty. The new liberalism demanded a new social vision of democracy and an accompanying view of an activist state. "Today," said Walter Weyl, "no democracy in America is possible except a socialized democracy, which conceives of society as a whole and not as a more or less adventitious assemblage of myriads of individuals."[3]

Croly and Weyl were arguing for a new vision of an activist national government that provided the scale for the efficient regulation of economic institutions to serve the collective ends of socialized freedom. The old natural rights arguments were extinct. In their place was a vision of a society in which all were connected to, and dependent upon, all. The watchword of this new vision of the state was "efficiency," (something, the new liberals believed, private property and market exchange on its own did not provide). It did not seek to break up concentrations of economic power (sometimes referred to as "trust busting") in what Progressives regarded as a vain attempt to restore a romanticized Jacksonian America; rather, it saw the scale of the corporation as a matter of efficiency and sought to harness it to public and democratic ends. The regulatory or managerial state presented a counterbalance to the concentrated economic power of large corporations. It didn't seek to replace that power or to nationalize or socialize industry, as socialists desired, but to direct it toward the end of democratic freedom, now understood in social, rather than individualistic, terms. In 1914, Weyl, Croly, and Lippmann founded the weekly journal of opinion, *The New Republic*, which remained the most widely read and influential mouthpiece of the New Liberalism throughout much of the twentieth century. Progressives and later advocates for the expansive state of Franklin Roosevelt's New Deal in the 1930s, and the Great Society programs of the 1960s were steeped in the intellectual sensibility of *The New Republic*. With the coming of this new progressive vision of socialized democracy and the activist state, those who continued to adhere to the older liberal vision of limited government and the protection of private property, grounded in natural rights, came to be designated as "conservatives," despite the fact that the principles they sought to conserve were liberal ones.

The Ethos of Scientific Reform: Walter Lippmann, Jane Addams, Frederick Winslow Taylor

One of the features of the Progressive style associated with Croly and Weyl was its commitment to the idea that democratic governance was a scientific enterprise. For Progressives of this stripe, government possessed the means, through empirical analysis and identification of social and economic problems, to make conscious plans. The association of liberalism with "social engineering," as its critics would call it, dates from the Progressive vision of an active state as an instrument of democracy. The ethos of science undergirded the thinking of many reformers in these years. The moral reformers of the antebellum era, guided by evangelical Protestantism, had frequently seen social problems—alcohol abuse, prostitution, crime, poverty, slavery, and unemployment—as matters of vice, attributable to the sinful nature of actors. The solutions they proffered were framed in terms of sin and salvation, moral uplift, conversion, and the transformation of the individual. Organized reform by those committed to an ethic of benevolence and theological perfectionism had enormous impacts in shaping Victorian culture. While the association of social problems with moral dissipation did not disappear in turn-of-the-century America (and, indeed, continues in different forms to this day), one of the distinguishing features of those who sought solutions to "The Social Question," was the idea that reform should be conducted on scientific terms, which provided maximum flexibility, rather than on terms of religious faith and fixed policies.

No statement of the scientific ethos of Progressive reform was more influential than Walter Lippmann's *Drift and Mastery* (1914). Although in later years Lippmann, as one of America's most prominent journalist-intellectuals, would move in conservative directions, embracing notions of natural law and social hierarchy, for instance, the young Lippmann was committed to a vision of socialized freedom through the democratic possibilities of science. Lippmann redefined what had once appeared in the eighteenth century as an agent of progressive liberation—the appeal to laissez-faire and self-interest as a regulating mechanism against state-controlled economies—as a kind of purposeless "drift." Where earlier theorists of progress had imagined that necessary improvement was driven by the intrinsic nature of man, and that left alone man would inexorably progress through intellectual, moral, and social advancement, Lippmann saw human beings caught up in forces and changes they did not understand, and could not navigate. The old intellectual sources of guidance—religion and tradition—were dead habits, incapable of addressing the complex social realities. The old faith in private property, for instance, encountered a new corporate reality in which ownership, through stocks, was completely divorced from control, exercised by a salaried board of directors. Continuing to cling to beliefs about individual autonomy meant, ironically, that people had no control over their lives. To turn to science was to turn to "mastery," to refuse the folk beliefs people had relied on, and to bring a democratically-planned social reality into being. Lippmann found in a culture of science the cooperative mastery that would provide a meaningful communion for those who had had their old faiths destroyed by modernity. "Rightly understood," said Lippmann "science is the culture under which people can live forward in the midst of complexity, and treat life not as something given but as something to be shaped." Science "*is* self-government."[4] Lippmann viewed science, then, as both a method for solving social problems through applied intelligence, and as a bond uniting people in common purpose.

Clearly, Lippmann leaned heavily on the philosophical Pragmatism he had absorbed as an undergraduate at Harvard. His rejection of "habits" of belief in favor of reinvented purposive beliefs; his sense of science as a future-oriented discipline, flexible and open to human possibility, his refusal to separate the question of values from the question of knowledge; the faith that science meant a democratic breakdown of authoritarian and hierarchical structures of belief. While not all Progressives were Pragmatists, perhaps uncomfortable in letting loose the antidogmatic and anti-idealist temperament associated with that philosophical outlook, many did seek to incorporate a pragmatic, scientific effort into their reform sensibilities. Among these were figures such as Jane Addams, the Chicago reformer, who created and lived in America's most famous social settlement, Hull House, and remained active in numerous reforms. Chicago was a hothouse of pragmatic thought, associated with the University of Chicago, and various thinkers in philosophy, sociology, and psychology, including John Dewey and George Herbert Mead. Addams developed an approach to reform that sought to synthesize humanitarian values with a scientific attitude. She, and other women reformers of the era such as Florence Kelley of the National Consumers' League, crafted a community-oriented pragmatic outlook, heavily invested in solving social problems by living their commitments, rather than through seeking conversion or social control.

In *Twenty Years at Hull House* (1910), Addams used her own experience and ideas in creating the social settlement-- a house in which middle-class reformers sought residence in the urban slums, populated by new immigrants, workers, and the poor—to both reflect upon the accomplishments of the settlement movement in Chicago and to articulate the values that underwrote it. Reformers worked with residents to provide solutions to public health issues, issues of family breakdown across generations, housing and work conditions, to debate issues of public concern, and to recognize the cultural background of immigrants. In one of the fullest articulations of the motives of the reformers who came to live and work in the settlements, she emphasized the ways in which settlements synthesized the social needs of urban immigrants, the humanitarian sense and desire for usefulness of the reformers, and the experimental pragmatic nature of reform, providing a space to negotiate a new cross-class reality. The attributes that made the social settlement distinctive were "its flexibility, its power of quick adaptation, its readiness to change its methods as its environment may demand." wrote Addams.

> It must be open to conviction and must have a deep and abiding sense of tolerance. It must be hospitable and ready for experiment. It should

demand from its residents a scientific patience in the accumulation of facts and the steady holding of their sympathies as one of the best instruments for that accumulation.[5]

In language that sounded very much like William James's discussion of Pragmatism, she emphasized that science expressed a non-dogmatic approach to problems, a tolerance of different views, a willingness to engage in experiment, and to adapt to ever-changing conditions. The contrast was to a judgmental or moralistic style of reform, in which a fixed body of principles was applied, based on a sharp contrast between good and evil, and no attempt was made to bridge the social gap, to act with sympathy and tolerance.

A third vision of Progressive scientific efficiency, which could not be more antithetical to Addams's orientation, can be found in the work of the early business theorist, Frederick Winslow Taylor. Taylor was the creator of the principles of "scientific management," a theory of business management which purported to provide increased industrial productivity while simultaneously creating harmony between capital and labor. That is, Taylorism was more than a philosophy of business management—it affixed that philosophy to a utopian goal of ending social conflict, raising the standard of living of industrial workers, and increasing wealth for all. Taylor's system involved a subdivision of all labor tasks into specific measurable units, and time-motion studies designed to find "the one best way" to perform any task. The notion was to take control of labor away from the worker, his traditions, and the "rule of thumb," and to put it in the hands of managers, who would define the exact way each task was to be performed. In Taylor's mind, the worker would trade control of the labor process for increased wages based on greater productivity. The interests of managers and workers would be harmonized, and industrial production would move away from residual irrational and traditional practices to a highly efficient system. While Taylor shared the Progressive embrace of "efficiency," as in Croly, he pushed it toward ends antithetical to the image of democracy. Worker autonomy would be sacrificed, and workers would be turned into non-thinking task performers. Not surprisingly, the labor movement did not see Taylorism as an answer to the strife between capital and labor, identifying it as a movement to dehumanize workers and make them more tractable to the requirements of businesses. The rise of Taylorism in the late nineteenth century is an indication of the ways in which progressive faith in science and efficiency could be put in the service of causes that created greater fracture and conflict. If Lippmann wanted a turn toward conscious control of the democratic future, Taylor demonstrated that conscious control could be a means of further exploitation and affirmation of hierarchy. On the one hand, science was "democratic." On the other, it encouraged a cult of expertise, in which ordinary people would cede control to a new secular priesthood.

The Problem of Racial Progressivism

The main line of Progressive thought was concerned with the class inequalities produced by industrial capitalism—it was those inequalities that were at the heart of "The Social Question." This led those who saw white racial supremacy as the source of an on-going form of hierarchical oppression in the post-emancipation period following the Civil War in an anomalous position with regard to Progressivism. White Southern Progressives, in fact, contributed to the systematic construction of legalized segregation of the races and disfranchisement of Blacks. If Progressives in the Northern cities argued for education as a pathway to democratic participation, many Southern Progressives emphasized that voting restrictions based on lack of education and intellectual qualification—both of which were heavily associated with the African-American population—were legitimate means of progressive reform. There was a strong racialist orientation among some Progressives, North and South, as well. Rebecca Latimer Felton, a prominent Georgia feminist who pushed for a host of Progressive reforms, including equal rights for white women, was also a virulent white supremacist. She famously declared her support for lynching of Black men, who were subject to extra-judicial torture and killing on the pretext of having raped white women. "If it needs lynching to protect woman's dearest possession from the ravening human beasts," she proclaimed in 1898, "then I say lynch, a thousand times a week if necessary."[6] Madison Grant, conservationist and author of the influential and incendiary racist manifesto, *The Passing of the Great Race* (1915); Edward A. Ross, an influential Progressive sociologist at the University of Wisconsin and proponent of immigration restriction and eugenics, the progressive movement to consciously control fertility to breed a "better race" of people; Teddy Roosevelt, president and later standard bearer of the Progressive Party in the 1912 presidential election, who took up Ross's term "race suicide," to describe the failure of native-born white women to keep fertility apace with immigrants and non-whites: these, among many others, demonstrate the extent to which Progressivism could contain racialized ideas of progress that imagined non-Anglo Saxon peoples as impediments to social development and improvement. Not all Progressives were racialists, of course, but there was a strong strain of white supremacist and nativist thought amongst some Progressives.

It is not a coincidence that the nadir of race relations in the United States and the rise of Progressive thought were coterminous. The era from 1890 to 1920 saw a systematic effort to impose a new order in the post-confederate states: legalized segregation of the races, affirmed by the Supreme Court as meeting the 14th amendment requirement of equality before the law in *Plessy v. Ferguson* (1896); Black disfranchisement through the use of a variety of putatively race neutral requirements to register to vote; the use of racial terror to intimidate and punish African-Americans who fell afoul of the terms of racial subordination. What contemporaries understood as "The Race Problem," was frequently interpreted as a question of what white people should do with the presence of a large group of non-whites in their midst, premised on the idea that racial equality was not an option. And if the coming of industrial order had disrupted various local traditions and relations framing social life for white workers, in ways that could be imagined as a declension from a meaningful order, the emancipation of Blacks from the condition of slavery was hard to imagine as a loss for anyone but the white slave-holding elite and those who sought to romanticize a fixed hierarchical relation of whites and Blacks. After 1877 and the end of Reconstruction in the South, the attention of white reformers turned away from questions of racial justice, and toward questions of economic polarization and exploitation. The debate among Black thinkers was profoundly shaped by a vision of negative liberal freedom that white Progressives like Croly and Lippman were arguing was out of date and extinct.

The shadow of Frederick Douglass, the most prominent and highly regarded Black thinker of the nineteenth century, was long. Douglass's own universalist convictions were rooted in Enlightenment principles of equality, liberty, and education, on the one hand, and Romantic notions of individual growth, perfectionism, and self-making, on the other. The world of antebellum reform in which his ideas had been formed continued to shape his thinking, even as social and economic changes appeared to be cutting the legs out from under his vision. His death in 1895 opened a space in African-American discourse, revealing fissures in the orientation of Black thinkers—fundamental disagreements about both means and ends for achieving racial justice and equality in American society. While this period was a formative one for shaping modern African-American thought, the creators of this tradition of argument and theorizing had an ambivalent relationship to Progressivism as a movement. They both drew upon the strains of evolutionary thought, Pragmatism, and social science that informed so much progressive thought but found themselves appealing to moral universalism and Victorian ideas of culture as well.

1895 marked the beginning of national prominence for Booker T. Washington, a southerner born into slavery, who triangulated an ethical and materialistic vision that could offer something to Black agricultural and industrial laborers, white Southern segregationists, and white Northern philanthropists at the same time. In his famous "Atlanta Compromise" speech given at the Cotton States and Southern Exposition in Atlanta, he articulated a program of economic development and moral character training for Blacks, premised on the notion that full political and civil rights would follow upon economic success. Washington, in the midst of a wholesale movement to reaffirm white supremacy in the Southern states, ceded any Black claim to the vote, rejected any notion that Blacks should challenge the Jim Crow strictures of racial segregation, and emphasized the skills to be obtained through vocational and industrial education. In exchange, Black institutions such as Washington's own Tuskegee Institute in Alabama, would receive the financial support of white philanthropists, and both whites and Blacks would benefit from shared economic development. "In all things purely social," said Washington, "we can be as separate as the fingers, yet one as the hand in all things essential to mutual progress." Historians have debated the extent to which Washington's program represented a strategic and realistic accommodation to the conditions of Southern life during this period—to fight for civil rights was to anticipate violent suppression, and Washington offered an alternative that pointed in a progressive direction. From a philosophical perspective, Washington built upon a kind of economic determinist or materialist position that shared with the Marxist tradition the idea that politics and culture follow material change, rather than preceding them. He grafted onto that something that has come to seem in line with the Pragmatist revolution in the understanding of education. The vocational and industrial education that he advocated rejected the idea that education should concern itself with non-practical matters and that the classical or liberal tradition of the nineteenth-century college had anything to offer for those facing the conditions of modern life. If John Dewey asked students to know through doing, rather than pure reason, so did industrial education. Washington's program was, in some ways, an attempt to address the gulf between education and the conditions of modern society and economy. That said, critics of Washington have argued that the Tuskegee model of vocational education was training students for an economic order of small producers that was rapidly being displaced by the new conditions of corporate labor.

In the early twentieth century, a group of white and Black thinkers, mostly in the North, challenged Washington's vision and advocated for civil rights as an extension of the long legacy of the abolitionist movement. One of the major institutional expressions of this group came in the form of the National Association for the Advancement of Colored People (founded 1909). The polymath W.E.B. DuBois was a key figure in this organization, becoming the editor of its magazine, The *Crisis*. Earlier, he had developed a critique of Washington's program, published as Chapter 3, "Of Mr. Booker T. Washington and Others" in his landmark text *The Souls of Black Folk* (1903). His systematic analysis of the guiding assumptions and outcomes of the Atlanta Compromise inverted Washington's view of the relationship between politics and economics. Whereas Washington had seen economic success as the condition for political rights in some distant future, DuBois argued that in the absence of the right to vote, any economic gain could not be counted on—it was naïve to believe that laws governing property would be responsive to the claims of the disenfranchised. Who controls politics controls economy, and property rights did not exist independent of law. Further, giving up the claim for higher education was self-defeating, in part because higher education was necessary to train the teachers who would play an important role in Black colleges—vocational education was not a substitute for higher education, but dependent upon it. Accepting segregation also meant accepting a second-class status, and the cultural and psychological consequences of that, for DuBois were unacceptable. Douglass has argued in 1845 that slavery was a state of mind, as well as an external legal condition. DuBois thought that in order to be free and equal, one had to think of oneself as such. The epigram at the head of the chapter critiquing Washington was from Lord Byron's *Childe Harold*: "Hereditary bondsmen! Know ye not,/Who would be free must strike the first blow?" So, the fundamental disagreement between Washington and DuBois involved a disagreement about strategy and means, on the one hand, but also a conception of personhood and action, on the other.

The Souls of Black Folk is a complex text and is foundational for the history of Black thought. The question of whether it is a Progressive text, however, is not so simple to answer. DuBois had studied at Harvard with William James, and his outlook had been shaped by Pragmatism, as well as by the German philosophical tradition he encountered in his studies at the University of Berlin. But it had also been shaped by the genteel tradition and a kind of variant of Matthew Arnold's hierarchical conception of culture as "the best that has been said and thought." The book is modernist in its form—it consists of 13 chapters, each representing a different kind of writing, and as a consequence, a different kind of voice: autobiography, sociology, fiction, history, political critique, ethnomusicology. It is sentimental and Victorian at times, scientific and coolly analytical at others. Its themes of the doubleness and contradiction of Black life are expressed in its form as well as its substance. It walks a line between being a critical polemic on race relations, and a solution to the "Race Problem" by providing a bridge for its white audience to the inner life of Black Americans. The idea of a fractured and fragmented reality of contradiction that does not lend itself to dogma and simple solutions is combined with a kind of didactic moralism; it sits abreast an older system of transcendent fixed values and a modern commitment to the open possibilities of a fluid set of circumstances. Where DuBois seems most "Progressive" is in his confidence in the power of human consciousness to reshape the world, to scientifically address the problems of a dynamic modernity; where he seems least Progressive is in his welcoming of a kind of intellectual and cultural elitism that he would later associate with the doctrine of "the talented tenth." If Black emancipation and equality were to be achieved, it would be through the efforts of an intellectual avant-garde, and not through a kind of cross-class movement—the cutting edge of civil rights would be the educated Black and white elite coming to know one another. If that meant disfranchisement of the ignorant and uneducated, Black and white, DuBois argued, that was fine, as long as the line was not drawn on the arbitrary basis of race.

The Social Gospel

While the various Progressive ideologies of the late nineteenth and early twentieth centuries were often associated with scientific and fact-based secular approaches to reform, in contrast to the evangelically-based moral reforms of the antebellum period, American Protestantism also had a prominent role in shaping an ethically-based social movement rooted in Christianity. The term "Social Gospel" was used to describe a branch of liberal Protestantism concerned with addressing "The Social Question." What marked this religious movement off from other religious movements was its collapse of theology into the fabric of social relations. That is, instead of looking primarily to scriptural authority or abstract doctrine, those interpreting Christianity in social terms sought to see the presence of Christ in social relations. Their religion rejected doctrine in favor of experience, intellectual systems in favor of spiritual presence, and individualistic salvation in favor of social justice. It took ethical injunctions to love all men, to find the gospel message in the practice of everyday relations and social contacts, as the fullest expression of Christianity. Jane Addams, who found herself allied with the Social Gospel, described its practitioners as resenting "the assumption that Christianity is a set of ideas which belong to the religious consciousness," and advocating for the idea that Christianity "cannot be proclaimed and instituted apart from the social life of the community and that it must seek a simple and natural expression in the social organism itself."[7] Rejecting the Protestant insistence on the inner process of conversion as preceding works in the world, Social Gospelers collapsed the self into the social order. Protestant individualism, with its relationship with God unmediated by church hierarchy and external forms of action, was like economic and political individualism, inadequate to the conditions of modernity.

The most prominent advocates of the Social Gospel—men like Josiah Strong, Washington Gladden, and Walter Rauschenbusch—did not see religion as the dispensing of charity to the poor, but as active engagement in the lives and needs of others. Rauschenbusch argued that sin was not solely individual, a kind of expression of the corruption of the self, but that it was to be found in social institutions and practices, handed down from generation to generation. That means that salvation could not be an individual event, but that the Kingdom of God was only produced through the overcoming of the collective sins embedded in social forms. The old theology asked the individual to look within and involved a kind of withdrawal from the world. The new theology addressed itself to the reality of social evil and sought redress through the process of social service and reform. And like those who would argue that modern science was a form of democratic thought, Rauschenbusch argued that the social gospel, with the help of modern social science, transmuted hierarchical religion into a democratic form. "The social gospel registers the fact that for the first time in history the spirit of Christianity had had a chance to form a working partnership with real social and psychological science," he argued in 1917. "It seeks to put the democratic spirit, which the Church inherited from Jesus and the prophets, once more in control of the institutions and teachings of the Church."[8] Rauschenbusch struggled with his faith in an eternal and timeless Christianity and his faith in progressive development and a religion that changed to meet the new conditions of social life. The idea that the Social Gospel had to justify itself theologically, connecting it to the inherited Christian tradition, as well as in terms of social need, was the result.

Pragmatic Moralism and Reform Ideologies

A host of other ideas proliferated in the frameworks that Progressives developed to make sense of their world. How should children be raised and educated to prepare them for the dynamic order of which they were a part? Could new forms of leisure be effectively ordered to be regenerative, literally "recreation," rather than exist simply as the absence of labor? Could various levels of government recreate nature, in the form of parks, that would provide both aesthetic and health benefits to the public? How could public lands, such as forest and wilderness, be most efficiently managed for the public good? If politics was to be administrative and independent from forms of partisan corruption and graft, how could it remain responsive to democratic need? Again, Progressivism as a movement was intellectually diverse, internally contradictory in many respects, and lacking coherence. But as a sensibility, it sought to unite a sense of organized human control over the future with a moral vision that could not rest on older forms of foundationalism. The connections between Pragmatisms and Progressivisms, then, were not always direct, in terms of intellectual influence, but they tended to share a set of intellectual dispositions and attitudes. If the world was not "given," it could be remade. Social order and moral order were not two separate and distinct things. The appeal to timeless, abstract principle was inadequate to meet the historical conditions of a dynamic society. Progress was not automatic, but a matter of deliberate choice. Non-dogmatic tolerance and openness to alternatives, a world of debates rather than creeds, was the path forward. The limits of the various forms of Progressive thought—their inability to mobilize the ultimate commitments drawn from a metaphysical order that lay behind the application of social intelligence, for instance—were the same as their virtues. The "acids of modernity" that destroyed traditional beliefs Walter Lippmann would speak of in *A Preface for Morals* (1929), were the conditions of future possibilities, but also the limits on those possibilities.

Notes

1 Ira W. Howerth, "The Social Question of Today," *American Journal of Sociology* 1.3 (November 1895), p. 267.
2 Herbert Croly, *The Promise of American Life* (New York: MacMillan, 1909), p. 202.
3 Walter Weyl, *The New Democracy* (New York: Macmillan, 1918), p. 162.
4 Walter Lippmann, *Drift and Mastery: An Attempt to Diagnose the Current Unrest* (New York: Mitchell Kennerley, 1914), p. 275.
5 Jane Addams, *Twenty Years at Hull House* (New York: MacMillan, 1911), p. 126.
6 "Woman's Place on the Farm," *The Morning News* (Savannah, GA) (August 12, 1897), p. 3.
7 Addams, *Twenty Years at Hull House*, pp. 123–124.
8 Walter Rauschenbusch, *A Theology for the Social Gospel* (New York: MacMillan, 1917), p. 5.

5 Rethinking Woman and Man

The question of women's nature, rights, sex difference, and equality was one of the major arenas of debate and conceptualization that roiled the public sphere in the era between the Civil War and World War I. Drawing on a range of thought, from Darwinism to Freudian Psychoanalysis, Pragmatic philosophy, the new social sciences, and Protestant individualism, numerous thinkers reshaped the definitions of women, notions of family, sexuality, intellectual ability, civic participation, and the relationship between men and women. New definitions of women in nature and society also transformed the understanding of masculinity and men's identities. If modernist thought called into question the fixity and certainty of categories presumed to be God-given or found in nature, it found its largest challenge in the realm of sex difference, where the presumed universalism of the male/female divide was strongest. The idea that nature has ordained fundamental differences of body, social function, and character attributes, and that God had endowed men and women with distinct and complementary identities was one of the most potent organizing principles of thought. The idea that biological nature might provide the foundation for social forms was given additional strength by the pervasiveness of Darwinian thought. But science could also be deployed against long-standing biblically based arguments for women's subordination, and the egalitarian implications of some forms of liberal protestantism might also serve as a critical source for moving arguments away from a fixation on material bodily differences and toward the egalitarianism of souls. If, in the mid-nineteenth century, the identity of "Woman" was held by most thinkers to be singular and uniform, by 1920, an emergent pluralism founded on increasing recognition of divergence between urban and rural, immigrant and native-born, single and married, professional and working-class, white and non-white women, suggested that there were many ways of being female. The sharpness of the imagined difference between men and women was frayed by the imagined differences amongst women (and among men) themselves. This era provides us with the origins of a gender revolution that continues today.

The Idea of the Equality of Women

Although there were periodic moments in which individual writers sought to challenge the notion of the presumed inequality and difference of women from men in the previous centuries, it was not until the embrace of a radical rethinking of hierarchical conceptions of human difference that came with Enlightenment thought and the Age of Revolution in the late eighteenth century, that an attempt to formulate a vision of equality of the sexes in a more systematic way was born. In the English-language world, that movement is generally associated with Mary Wollstonecraft's *A Vindication of the Rights of Women* (1792). Writing in the idioms of Enlightenment thought, Wollstonecraft and others such as the American writer Judith Sargent Murray, sought to emphasize women's capacities as rational beings in contrast to those who sought to legitimate existing structures by emphasizing women's natural intellectual inferiority to men. These Enlightenment-era writings were radical in some ways, but it would be anachronistic to see them as laying out a vision of full political and social equality based on an understanding that women's and men's natures were identical. They argued strongly for women's education (which would be an important theme throughout much of nineteenth and twentieth-century women's rights writings), but they tended to justify education as a means of virtue and intellectual companionship in marriage—they argued not, as some later feminists would, against the family and domestic roles of women as forms of oppression, but for women's education as a means to make better families. In the American post-revolutionary moment, this meant a justification of women's education and public virtue in relationship to the role of motherhood—rational, educated women were necessary in order to raise sons to become citizens, not so that women could exercise their own citizenship rights. What is important here, however, is that the Enlightenment and republican-based arguments challenged one of the central legitimizing notions of women's subordination: that women were intellectually different and inferior to men. Women like Wollstonecraft and Murray claimed—in an argument that would be repeated by women's rights advocates such as Margaret Fuller and John Stuart Mill—that the picture of women's inferiority was circular, that women were denied education because of their presumed inferiority, and their lack of education was then offered as proof that they lacked rational capacity. The argument for women's education opened the door to seeing women's inequality in society as a function of social institutions and power, rather than the intrinsic capacities of women—the appeal to natural intellectual difference was found wanting as the basis for social inequality.

In the 1830s and 40s, at the height of the various reform movements associated with evangelical Christianity and Romantic thought—temperance and the abolition of slavery foremost among them—a new set of arguments synthesized the Enlightenment legacy of natural rights and faith in universal and rational principles with a greater focus on moral reconstruction and notions of spiritual development. Sarah Grimké, a Quaker abolitionist, responding to movements to prevent her sister Angelina from speaking against slavery to "mixed" audiences, containing both men and women, authored *Letters on the Equality of the Sexes* (1838). Challenging views that purported to demonstrate that the Bible affirmed women's subordination and difference from men, particularly due to Eve's culpability for violating God's command as described in Genesis, Grimké argued that women and men were spiritual and moral equals, that scripture had been corrupted by mistranslation, and used to draw an invidious distinction between men and women. As well as claiming Biblical authority for women's equality with men, Grimké pressed hard against any and all appeals to men and women's physical differences, arguing that to define the relative place of men and women by their bodies, physical strength, and reproductive functions, was to define human beings in animal rather than spiritual and moral terms. The two-prong attack of *Letters on the Equality of the Sexes* assumed the mantle of religious authority by denying materialist claims for inequality, on the one hand, and by reclaiming the Bible as a radical expression of spiritual equality of the sexes, on the other. Enlightenment thinkers had argued that women were equally rational with men; Grimké argued that more important than their rational natures, they were spiritually equal. That meant that not only did they have the same rights as men, but they also had the same duties. Women were required to agitate against the moral wrong of slavery, and anything that prevented them from doing so was unjust. Equality meant equality before God and equality in obligation to Him. The abolitionist movement, then, was the shaping ground for early women's rights advocates, including Lucretia Mott, Lucy Stone, and the Grimké sisters.

At the same time Grimké was putting forward an equal rights argument based on religion, the Transcendentalist Margaret Fuller emphasized an ideal of spiritual equality based on personal growth and potential. Unlike Ralph Waldo Emerson, whose "Self Reliance" (1841) marked out the radical individualism and anti-institutional commitments of Transcendental thought, Fuller argued that the Emersonian goal of individual self-perfection and expansion was not available to most women because they were excluded from it by the narrowness of social frames of womanhood. She sought Emersonian individualist ends by institutional means, arguing for education and the expansion of possibilities through transformation of the legal and social conditions of women. Importantly, Fuller maintained a position that men and women's natures and attributes were different and complementary. Her Transcendentalist metaphysics recognized the difference between the eternal universal Woman, in opposition to the universal Man, but in the practice of everyday life, this abstract reality became more fluid. "Male and female represent the two sides of the great radical dualism," wrote Fuller in *Woman in the Nineteenth Century* (1845). "But, in fact, they are perpetually passing into one another. Fluid hardens to solid, solid rushes to fluid. There is no wholly masculine man, no purely feminine woman."[1] Fuller's tract would be the most significant philosophical work on "The Woman Question" written by an American in the nineteenth century. It did three things that shaped the debate about women and equality in the later nineteenth century: establish the principle that sex difference was real in the abstract but not an impediment to equality—Fuller believed, for instance, that women were more "intuitive" than men; put forward her own exemplary and unusual education as an evidence of female capacity, in contrast to the arguments that women should not be educated because of their intellectual inferiority; argue that the goal of reform ought to be the fulfillment of the individual potential for growth and spiritual perfection. One of the powerful elements of what would later be called "liberal feminism" was the idea that women should aim to remove arbitrary barriers to individual achievement. In Fuller, of course, this idea was yoked to a Transcendentalist ethic, rather than to a meritocratic liberalism.

This was the philosophical situation when female (and some male) activists in the international antislavery effort, examining parallels between the conditions of enslaved peoples and women, developed the organizational movement for women's rights. In the mythology of feminist origins, this has come down to us as a key moment in which the first national Women's Rights convention was held at Seneca Falls, New York in 1848. The famous "Declaration of Sentiments," promulgated at Seneca Falls echoed the language of the American Declaration of Independence, specifically asserting that "all men and women are created equal," and laid out a program for women's rights. The historian Lisa Tetrault has convincingly argued that the attempt to define Seneca Falls as the origin of "The Woman Movement" in nineteenth-century America was the later work of Elizabeth Cady Stanton and Susan B. Anthony, who, engaged in sectarian battles within the movement, sought to create ownership for their own vision and control of the goals of women's rights. Throughout the second half of the nineteenth century, Stanton and Anthony were key figures in a wide range of proposed reforms: ending the legal subordination of married women, who through the law of coverture could not have economic autonomy and control of their own labor; arguing for equal pay for women; dress reform; liberalized divorce; women's rights to child custody; providing women with full citizenship rights, especially the right to vote; challenging segregation by sex in public venues; reforming religious doctrine and practice that used religious teachings as a way to reinforce women's subordination. Stanton was probably the leading intellectual figure in The Woman Movement, developing a radical and extensive critique of existing institutions and practices, and marking out a path for what she imagined was a universal claim of rights for all women.

In 1869, the British philosopher and political economist John Stuart Mill published an essay entitled "On the Subjection of Women." In it, he countered the principle philosophical claims supporting a hierarchical relationship between men and women and developed a wide-ranging and radical position on women's freedom and equality. Mill's essay won wide support from women's rights activists—Stanton in her own thinking built upon the universalist individualism of Mills's writing. The strain of thought developed by Stanton in the decades following the Civil War represents the foundation of what later generations would call "liberal feminism," although that was not a term used by Stanton or her generation of reformers, and her wide-ranging calls for reform (of the form of the family, of cultural beliefs and practices) would also be echoed in later more radical forms of feminist thought. But the dominant orientation of her thought was to extend liberal principles of individual rights and maximal personal freedom to women by overturning legal exclusions and social practices, opening doors of opportunity to women so they might take personal responsibility for their actions. Stanton's view represented an extension of Victorian liberalism, taking as its philosophical base the diminution of differences between men and women, the denial that women and men were fundamentally unalike. At the end of a half-century career as one of the leading political leaders and intellectual theorists of the movement for women's rights, Stanton expressed the radical individualism of her moral and social thought in a speech entitled "The Solitude of Self" (1892). Appealing to republican ideas of self-government and Protestant ideas of unmediated individual relationship to God, she put the case for women's education and enfranchisement on the existential condition of all persons—radically alone in the universe, and unable to rely on the support of others in the challenges faced in life and death. "The self," as a category, was unsexed—but also oblivious to the claims of race, ethnicity, class, and other differences between women. In contrast to those who argued for the idea that women needed neither education nor the vote because they were protected and cared for by husbands and fathers, Stanton argued that these relations of moral obligation were thin and ultimately unreliable, for existential reasons, rather than the failure of moral purpose of presumed protectors. The only way to ensure that women could meet the challenges before them was to provide them with the tools—education, economic autonomy, and political voice—to take care of themselves. The idea of women's "place" in a complex and interdependent order was dissolved in the emphasis on autonomy and individualism.

Like many of the radical challengers to existing practices and inherited institutions, one of Stanton's goals was to dethrone the authority of Christianity and the Bible as a source for claims of universal God-mandated positions. Scripture remained a powerful source of authority in late nineteenth-century America, although what the Bible said about contemporary issues was contested, as were the principles driving Biblical interpretation. In the debate over slavery and abolition, for instance, competing interpretations of scripture were arrayed on the sides of pro-slavery and anti-slavery positions. Advocates for women's rights faced a situation in which appeals to scriptural authority—and particularly to Genesis and the role of Eve in the Fall—were regularly deployed to support the existing order; to challenge women's subordination was to challenge God's mandate. One of Stanton's late-career projects was overseeing an analysis of the arguments based on scripture that were invoked to justify the inequality of women. Published in two volumes, *The Woman's Bible* (1895, 1898) sought to use techniques of critical analysis to suggest that the Bible was corrupted as a source by the substitution of men's desires and wishes for the vision of God. *The Woman's Bible* was not an atheistic denunciation of Christianity itself, but it was controversial, challenged many long-standing views of specific scriptural passages, and associated Stanton with other contemporary critics of religion. Many in the suffrage movement sought to distance themselves from the "irreligion" of this work; it was one thing to stand for equal rights and the vote, it was another to associate women's rights with a set of debates about religion, theology, and Biblical interpretation that were also a source of divisiveness in American culture. The critics of contemporary social arrangements could not help, in many instances, becoming critics of received religion, simply because religious arguments were so frequently enmeshed in support for the status quo and women's subordination.

In Stanton's own thought, as in that of many of her contemporaries, we can see a kind of paradox. Drawing on Enlightenment principles and the liberal individualism of Mill, women's rights advocates argued for equality on the basis that in matters of personhood and intellectual ability, men and women were the same, and therefore equally deserving of rights. But in making their case for inclusion of an entire category of persons, they had to recognize the distinctiveness and common elements that united women and separated them from men. The tension in women's rights thought between "sameness" and "difference" could take a number of forms, but it was impossible to evade. Many of the powerful advances that women's rights made in the late nineteenth and early twentieth centuries were premised on appeals to cultural ideals of women's difference from men. In the "separate spheres" ideology developed in antebellum America, women's natures were associated with domestic ideals of nurturance, moral purpose, and self-sacrifice, in contrast to the masculine competitive order of the marketplace and political life. Advocates for women's moral authority drew on this notion of female natural difference and moral superiority. Frances Willard, the head of The Women's Christian Temperance Union, the largest women's organization of the nineteenth century, for instance, pushed for women's suffrage on the basis of women's moral nature, arguing that women would prioritize the family and legislators would respond to the moral authority of women if they had the vote. Progressives like Florence Kelley strategically supported protective labor legislation for women, drawing on the notion that women's natures and needs were different than those of men. For the dominant white middle-class leaders of women's rights organizations, the flipside of recognizing sex difference was a presumed shared unity of all women, obscuring the internal differences between women.

Darwinian Feminism

To the extent that biological modes of thought in a post-Darwinian universe shaped notions of sex difference, attempts to argue that men and women were the same fell back on claims that the variation within the human species was not a binary difference between men and women. The idea of a singular fixed and permanent nature of human beings had been a casualty of the idea of natural selection. Twelve years after the bombshell that was *On the Origin of Species*, Darwin published *The Descent of Man* (1871), introducing sex difference as a basic opposition and complementing the idea of natural selection with that of sexual selection. The idea of sexual selection emphasized the ways in which physical differences between males and females were a product of the mechanisms of sexual attraction and fitness to reproduce that increased reproductive success. Differences between the sexes in terms of natural ornamentation, body shape, physical strength, and secondary sex characteristics (e.g. facial hair) were a result not of natural design, but of selective process. Sexual selection complicated the story of natural selection by emphasizing the ways in which the requirements of sexual reproduction aided in the survival of sex-specific traits that would have no survival value outside the struggle for sexual mates. The classic example might be the peacock's colorful plumes, which survived and evolved by attracting the peahen, rather than by contributing to survival against predators and other natural conditions. While Darwin's interest in *The Descent of Man* was demonstrating the ways in which human traits evolved naturally and had many forerunners in the animal world, in the discussion of sexual dimorphism he inverted the roles of male and female in the human species, as contrasted to the general pattern of nature. Sex-specific ornamental traits in the animal world, he argued, were frequently found in the male of the species; males competed with one another for the sexual interest of the female, and any attribute that aided in being successful in the mating process, would be reproduced. The male frequently had more colorful and dramatic features than the female. In the human world, the pressures of competition for mates were the opposite—the attributes of physical beauty, sexual attractiveness, and the presumed techniques for drawing the attention of mates were overwhelmingly associated with women, and women themselves were not motivated by physical attraction. In both cases, random variation produced outcomes that pointed toward sexual differentiation, and the notion that male and female within a species evolved not toward uniformity, but toward opposition.

The Descent of Man was widely read in the United States. It was far less controversial than *On the Origin of Species* had been, even though its emphasis on the animal-human continuum that had only been hinted at in *Origin*, was front and center. To some extent this is a measure of how widely the evolutionary ideas in the first text had passed into general educated opinion, winning over the majority of scientists, and shaping the understanding of fluid and progressive change. But it was also a measure of the extent to which Darwin could provide powerful new intellectual support for claims of female inferiority, or of naturally produced sex difference as the basis for social forms. The new science had many uses, but one of the most prominent of them was to give ideological heft to the conservative case against sex equality. Just as social Darwinists used evolutionary thought to justify an existing social hierarchy, so did advocates for women's domestic identities. Darwin argued that women's brains were less highly developed than men's for instance. Darwin's emphasis on sex difference dovetailed with a growing body of medical and scientific studies that sought to define the biological differences between men and women. Some of the same thinkers who believed that Darwinism provided support for claims of biological hierarchy among the races were also attempting to measure and provide empirical evidence for sex hierarchy. Edward Clarke, a physician and faculty member at Harvard University, in 1872 authored what became an infamous work, *Sex Education; or, a Fair Chance for Girls*. Clarke argued that women's physiology made them incapable of higher education on the level of men, and conversely that the fate of human reproduction would be negatively impacted by educating women, since the physiological energy women deployed in their education would result in infertility. At a time of the growth of women's educational institutions and a women's rights agenda, Clarke's book sparked a strong and immediate response. Many of the advocates for women's equality from the Enlightenment era forward, had seen education as the way to overcome the belief in women's incapability and intellectual inferiority; by using modern science to affirm that hierarchy, the defenders of the status quo shifted the question back to a question of pre-social essential nature, rather than one of social exclusion. A tradition of arguing for the "natural" basis of sex differentiation in humans on the basis of observations of the animal kingdom was one result. Those who accepted an evolutionary model of human social development saw women, like children and "savages," as occupying a less-developed evolutionary position than European men. Much of Victorian sexual science was dedicated to deriving women's social situation and condition from their presumed biological natures, rather than emphasizing the ways in which modernity made biological fixity *less* a determinant of social practices. The idea that women's menstrual periods, for instance, incapacitated them and rendered them unequal in the sphere of education was held by Clarke and a wide variety of sexual scientists. It was not until the psychologist Leta Hollingworth performed rigorous studies of menstruation and mental capacity in the 1910s that demonstrated that this was not the case, that this supposed scientific conclusion was put to rest.

This emphasis on the ways in which Darwinian and biological arguments—and scientific arguments in general--were deployed to reinforce existing hierarchies is only one side of the story, however. A number of thinkers who sought equality for women saw in Darwinian science a potential for liberation and a rethinking of women's condition free from the moral and metaphysical constraints of older ways of thinking. In particular, they embraced the appeal to science as a way to critique the dominant authority of religion and Biblical interpretation. For centuries, the claim that woman was a secondary creation--Eve made from Adam's rib—that God had mandated as subordinate to man had given an ultimate sanction to women's unequal condition. Further, the claim that Eve's temptation had brought sin and evil into the world, and therefore women were morally responsible for the corrupt nature of the world, was used to argue for the notion that women did not possess the attributes of self-government. The heavy weight of theological support for women's subordination seemed, to some, as challengeable by the increased status of science as an alternative authority. The consequence was a reading of Darwin and sexual selection that pushed back against the emerging sexual science of the later nineteenth century. A small number of what some historians have dubbed "Darwinian feminists," including Charlotte Perkins Gilman, Antoinette Brown Blackwell, and Eliza Burt Gamble, sought to use Darwinian ideas about sex differentiation to provide a critique of women's subordination. In doing so, however, they frequently found themselves reproducing a commitment to the idea of natural sex difference in mental and moral attributes that had provided the basis for thinking of social relations as an expression of natural capabilities.

Gamble, for instance, used Darwin's *The Descent of Man* to argue that, contra Darwin himself, women were the more highly evolved sex. Her *The*

Evolution of Woman (1894) sometimes reads like a satire of Victorian sexual science, but Gamble was deadly serious. She argued that Darwin himself systematically misread his evidence to promote the idea of masculine superiority, but that the "passivity" of women against the more combative and aggressive forms of masculinity was actually a sign of the more highly developed sympathy and moral sense of the female sex. Man wastes his energy, using it for non-productive ends; woman's energy is conserved for the parental nurturance and cooperative ethos that was the basis of the evolution of civilization. Gamble reproduced separate spheres ideology—women as agents of moral development in the domestic sphere, men as agents of competition and self-interests in the marketplace—but inverted it as a claim for the biological superiority of women as the agents of evolutionary advancement, and in particular the origins of society as a collaborative form. A generation earlier, Blackwell had argued for the equality of the sexes based on complementarity and division of function. Female and male were different, but neither was superior. Building upon the evolutionary writings of Darwin and Spencer, but criticizing their overemphasis on male development, Blackwell argued that the greater developmental complexity of species, the more male and female functions were balanced against one another, and the equilibrium of nature was achieved. Men's powers in bodily strength, locomotion, and sexual ardor were offset by women's powers in bearing offspring, creating domesticity, and parental love. Both male and female had intellectual powers, but women's were more immediate and intuitive—they were not lower on an evolutionary scale, but part of a balanced higher order. By appealing to science and the systematic study of nature, these thinkers sought two things: (1) to put arguments for women's rights on the ground of empirical fact and a system of knowledge open to argument, rather than religious authority; (2) To demonstrate in their own writing and thinking that they could stand on the same intellectual ground as male scientists.

Gilman went in a different direction than Gamble and Blackwell. Her *Women and Economics* (1898) used Darwinian arguments of sexual selection to demonstrate the ways in which women had been arbitrarily cut off from the struggle for existence that might have been selected for higher personal attributes. The competition that women engaged in was not a struggle for existence against nature, but a struggle against other women to obtain a mate. Women had become less evolved because of the abnormal adaptive force that made their livelihoods dependent upon their sexual attractiveness. The overemphasis of sex traits, said Gilman, flew in the face of modern commitments to specialization and organizational division of labor. Fortunately, sexual differentiation was balanced by the fact that females inherited attributes from males as well. "Is it any wonder that women are over-sexed?" asked Gilman. "But for the constant inheritance from the more human male, we should have been queen bees, indeed, long before this."² Gilman's vision built upon Darwinism, but was more sociological than those who would argue directly from the natural world to the social world. Instead of emphasizing the different but equal qualities of women, she argued that social institutions needed to be reformed so that women could more efficiently and effectively aid in the evolutionary process. Social interference with the natural process was to blame for women's condition. Her solution for women was to put them back into contact with the world of work—this would mean a radical rethinking of the structure of the family and the entire separate spheres ideology upon which it rested.

Feminists and Freud

The term "feminism" was not one used by the nineteenth-century thinkers and activists who saw themselves as arguing on "the Woman Question" or as part of the "the Woman Movement." As the historian Nancy Cott has argued, "feminism" came into being in the second decade of the twentieth century, just as women were moving into the final push that would achieve the long-sought goal of women's suffrage in 1919. The new idea of feminism took from the older movement some of its commitments—to a rejection of hierarchy on the basis of sex, to suffrage and legal reform, for instance—but based itself on a new modernist understanding of self and culture that the older women's rights thinkers did not systematically share. One of those new understandings was a refiguration of the role of sexuality—of women's sexual desire and pleasure as a goal independent of procreation. Nineteenth-century theorists and writers had not ignored sexual behavior and desire, but they had tended to see it, as the Darwinian feminists did, as figuring in the differences between men and women. The long-standing nineteenth-century view of bourgeois womanhood had stressed female sexual purity and "passionlessness," and had seen sexual desire and aggression as a specifically masculine trait. Woman's moral nature, as in Gamble and Blackwell, took the form of selfless parental love, while man's nature possessed something more of the animal sex instinct. There had been nineteenth-century radicals such as Victoria Woodhull who had advocated for "free love," by which she meant women's agency in deciding when and with whom to have sex, against the strictures of marriage and the male control of female sexuality. But the mainline of the Woman Movement, as much as it challenged women's subordination in law and custom, did not put forward the idea of women as sexual beings. For a theorist like Gilman, in fact, it was the attempt to organize women's identities around sex that was the problem, since it prevented women from fulfilling themselves through work and economic activity.

Feminism as a new political identity for women drew on a number of changes occurring in early twentieth-century society. Already in the 1890s, a cultural representation of "the New Woman," which emphasized an independent spirit, professional status, higher education, and physical activity, was the subject of a popular discourse. The growth of women in the professions, in literature and the arts, and in social service careers, as well as in the increasingly feminized occupations of secretarial and office work led cultural commentators to create the New Woman as a "type." Particularly in large urban areas such as New York and Chicago, middle-class women in the professions, graduates of women's colleges, or the new co-educational institutions such as the University of Chicago, provided a non-familial base from which to construct a new ideological outlook for women. Active in politics, social clubs, and urban life, some of these women came to participate in emergent bohemian enclaves, such as Greenwich Village in New York City. Political and cultural radicals like Emma Goldman, Mabel Dodge Luhan, and Crystal Eastman developed a kind of unconventional mode of life as a challenge to bourgeois manners and forms of behavior. In New York, the circle of women cultural radicals took on the name Heterodoxy as a symptom of its commitment to unconventional opinion. The feminism of the Heterodoxy circle was frank in its embrace of a new psychological mode of emancipation, and its view that female sexual desire had long been subject to denial, control, and antipathy. To be psychologically free was to liberate the self, and fundamental to the new conception of self was sexual pleasure. The Woman Movement had railed against the sexual double standard for women by arguing that standards of female chastity should be applied to men; the feminists argued that standards of male sexual freedom should be applied to women.

At the moment this new feminist mode of thought was coming into being, Sigmund Freud's psychoanalytic school of thought had already laid the groundwork for a radical rethinking of human nature and consciousness. In the decade after his only American visit, in 1909, Freud's work would be subject to a wide popularization and integration into new modernist understandings of selfhood. Freud's relationship to feminism was complex—and ambivalent. Many of the first generation of young women who identified as feminist embraced Freudian thought for its emphasis on women as sexual beings, and for what appeared to be an ethic of sexual emancipation opposed to bourgeois standards of self-control and repression. The idea that inherited ideas of sexual morality and their accompanying commitment to a spiritualized image of female sexual purity needed to be jettisoned, and that the path to freedom was both political *and* psychological, provided feminists with a framework within which to interpret Freudian thought. Freud's focus on the repression of desire as the condition of neurosis and pathology lined up with the ideas of the feminist anarchist Emma Goldman that the social oppression and psychological repression of women were two sides of the same coin. But Freud was far from being a sex egalitarian, and many of his doctrines and views reproduced notions of female inferiority. Although the Freudian idea of "penis envy" as a factor in female psychology was not fully developed until the 1920s, and would later become the basis for some feminist critiques of Freudian thought, earlier hints that Freud regarded women as lesser to and secondary to men were abundant. His famous case study of a Viennese young women, pseudonymized as "Dora," represents a systematic dismantling of women's sexuality and neuroses; his 1914 essay "On Narcissism," pictured women's inability to form love attachments of a non-narcissistic kind: whereas men transfer their own self-love to women, women, in Freud's view, frequently only seek to be desired and are incapable of an object-oriented love. Feminist and modernist thinkers read Freud in a variety of ways; in the second decade of the twentieth century, he could be heralded as a fresh analytical and scientific voice exploding the conventional received morality in ways that redefined freedom for women.

Freud's popularity dovetailed with the new psychological and sexual interests among bohemian modernists and feminists in the early twentieth century. Non-Freudian ideas emphasizing women's sexual desire and freedom were central to the writings of the sociologist Elsie Clews Parsons and the founder of the modern movement for family planning and birth control, Margaret Sanger. Parsons's 1906 discussion of the evolution of the form of the family provoked a strong backlash among conservative moralists for its recommendations for "trial marriage," and its suggestion that the alternative to the undemocratic nature of prostitution that commercialized the sex function by separating it from the family function, was "the toleration of freedom of sexual intercourse on the part of the unmarried of both sexes before marriage."[3] Sanger's crusade to make contraception available, severing sex from procreation, and putting the creation of offspring in the hands of women, was shaped by her reading of the British sexologist Havelock Ellis and his emphasis on sexual freedom; women could not be free if they could not control their own sexual behavior and its reproductive consequences. The tension in the thought of Progressive reformers like Parsons and Sanger was between the notion of a kind of rational approach to sexuality—making it subject to planning and experiment—and what appeared to be an expressive notion of sexual freedom and growth. Both Sanger and Parsons, for instance, were attracted by the Progressive vision of eugenics—the deliberate, conscious, and scientific control of reproduction in social terms--even as they stressed the opening of sexual choice for women.

African-American Challenges to The Woman Movement

The trajectory of African-American thought on sex difference, and especially claims for the rights of African-American women tended to move in an opposite historical direction from the dominant white middle-class women's movement, challenging the notion that "women" were an undifferentiated group that all shared the same interests and goals. For Black women, their personhood had been degraded by long association, through slavery and beyond, with animality, and with a lower place in a racialized hierarchy. The very definition of white women's sexual purity and civilizing mission was constructed against an alternative image of Black women as sexual beings, closer to nature and less civilized. So, when Darwinian feminists and sexual liberationists looked to reclaim the bodily, material, animal nature of women as a challenge to a "cult of true womanhood," they did so to invert the dominant values that constrained white women by idealizing them. That did not appear to be an option for Black women, who had been excluded from this idealized image of womanhood. In addition, although the Woman Movement was born in abolitionist circles (Frederick Douglas, for instance, was one of the signers of The Declaration of Sentiments at Seneca Falls), in the battles over suffrage, leaders such as Stanton deployed racist arguments as they saw the Radical Republicans during Reconstruction drive to amend the Constitution to provide suffrage rights for Black freedmen and not for women. The unfavorable comparison made by Stanton and others between educated and "refined" white women, and newly emancipated Black men, drove a wedge between Women's Rights activists, and the movement for Black freedom and equality. While the universalizing tendencies of Stanton's rhetoric would appear broad, in reality, they associated the desired rights of women of Stanton's class and race with all women, obscuring the fact that the concerns of Black and white women were different.

Educated Black women deployed what some have called "respectability politics" as a response to the situation that they faced. They often sought inclusion on the ground of their cultural refinement and their embrace of conventions of class-specific language, dress, and manners. Black leaders, like Mary Church Terrell, thought about their responsibilities through the lens of an ethic of social uplift. The educated Black elite, in this vision, were to push for various Progressive reforms, but also provide a model of genteel womanhood to advance the cause of "the race." Unlike white women's rights groups, Black clubwomen assumed a double responsibility—the future of "the race" rested on the success of Black men, as well as women, and instead of fighting the exclusions imposed by male domination, Black women often saw their goal aligned with achieving masculine power in the market, politics, and the family. Precisely because Black men faced the specter of "feminization" and denial of their authority on the terms expressed in white communities, Black women saw as part of their goal the elevation of Black men. Ida B. Wells-Barnett, for instance, was one of the most powerful voices in criticizing the Southern practice of race-based lynching of men. Like W.E.B. DuBois's doctrine of the talented tenth, this elite-based politics faced in a different direction from the Progressive era attempt to socialize democracy.

The tensions in Black women's thought at the end of the nineteenth century are most evident in Anna Julia Cooper's *A Voice from the South* (1892). Drawing on a discourse of "Civilization," Cooper puts her own agenda for women on the basis of European thought, and explicitly at odds with what she regarded as the lack of cultural resources of any kind in non-Western traditions. She invoked Matthew Arnold's ideal of culture, as well as the feudal and Christian traditions as the source of moral authority for women. Associating women with the ennobling influence of the home, she called for uplift and racial rebirth from a condition of degeneracy. "Now the fundamental agency under God in this regeneration, the re-training of the race, as well as the ground work and starting point of its progress upward," Cooper declares, "must be the *black woman*" (p. 28). Cooper deployed the notion of women's natural sympathy and morality as the basis for Her regenerative work. "[T]here is a feminine as well as a masculine side to truth," she said, echoing separate spheres ideology. There "are related not as inferior and superior not as better and worse, not as weaker and stronger, but as complements—complements in one necessary and symmetric whole."[4] For Black women to adequately play their missionary role of civilizing and uplift, they must have higher education. As white women were moving toward a claim of women's right to education for their own benefit, Cooper was reviving an older ideal of women's moral leadership, based on female nature and higher education. Instead of advancing a vision of women's moral right, then, she aimed to justify women's activism, education, and social responsibility by appealing for admission to the very genteel tradition of moral uplift that the scientific reformers and the New Woman had associated with the constraints of nineteenth-century images of women. The paradox of women's rights ideologies—aiming to dissolve the different statuses of men and women by appealing to the group identity of women—was amplified for Black women. Cooper was arguing that the white leaders of the Woman movement were ill-positioned to speak for the entirety of women, and regularly sacrificed Black women on the altar of racial purity. If any group could speak for all humanity and generalized notions of equality, it was Black women, excluded on the basis of both race and sex. Those who were most marked by the prevailing prejudices of the day were, according to Cooper, the most aware of the principle of universality as a meaningful goal.

Masculinity Remade

As women's economic and social conditions changed under the forces of industrial development, education, and middle-class professionalism, widespread criticism of prevailing arrangements in the spheres of work, family, and sexuality opened the door to new ways of conceiving of women's identities and potentials. But the change in women's status was also necessarily a change in ideas of what it meant to be a man. The masculine/feminine binary was available as a rich source of symbols for thinking about modernity itself, and provided a vocabulary for discussing progress and degeneration; autonomy and dependency; conflict and cooperation; freedom and responsibility. The reaction against changes in women's status and condition, and changing ideas about women's identity, provoked a periodic "crisis of masculinity," that has come to be an ongoing aspect of modern thought; masculinity is in an apparent permanent condition of crisis. In fact, the word "masculinity," as a term to describe the universal qualities associated with male identity, did not come into widespread usage in the United States until the end of the nineteenth century, driven by a desire to reinvigorate male identity. Notions of manliness that preceded it were tied closely to middle-class Victorian moralism and stressed values of personal responsibility, self-control, honesty, integrity, and familial duty. The newer notions of masculinity, in contrast, stressed attributes such as aggression, physical strength, bravery, and military virtue. The ideal of masculinity sought to revive attributes associated with primitive and non-white persons that white highly educated elites feared were being eclipsed by a feminized modernity. The great ambivalence about "Civilization" was that the values associated with it—refinement, social service, humanitarianism—were imagined as both higher on an evolutionary scale, *and* overwhelmingly associated with feminine values.

The 1890s saw a wide range of movements across the cultural sphere to address this fear of decadence and "softness": the popularity of college athletics, especially football; a new "muscular" Christianity; the Physical Culture movement, stressing exercise and fitness; the rise of men's clubs; organizations invested with a militarized sense of social services such as the Boy Scouts and the Y.M.C.A. The idea of a masculine ethos in crisis due to the comforts of modern life, and the insulation of men working in offices and bureaucracies from the struggle for existence, was a common theme. Teddy Roosevelt's famous 1899 speech to Chicago's male elite advocated for a restored virility that would synthesize primitive aggression and military virtue with the higher evolutionary goals of civilization, and justify an expanding American imperialism at the same time. Criticizing "the timid man, the lazy man, the man who distrusts his country, the over-civilized man who has lost the great fighting, masterful virtues," Roosevelt preached

> the doctrine of the strenuous life, the life of toil and effort, of labor and strife; ... that highest form of success which comes, not to the man who desires mere easy peace, but to the man who does not shrink from danger, from hardship, or from bitter toil...[5]

White men of the educated classes imagined themselves as beset by challenges to both sex and race hierarchies. The feminized world of comfort and leisure represented a female claim to be the civilizing force, upturning the authority of masculine leadership; the primitive world of "savage" violence represented a challenge to men who had lost the will to compete on the stage of instinct and aggression.

Biology and Culture

While Darwinian evolutionary thought in many ways opened up the question of sex difference during this era, by the time women's suffrage had been achieved through the Nineteenth Amendment to the Constitution, the ground had begun to shift away from claims that sex difference was exclusively a biological fact, and that social relations could be read as expressing an underlying biological reality. In part, this was due to the Darwinian idea that biological reality was not itself fixed. If history took the same evolutionary form as nature, awareness of the changing nature of the family, of political rights, and of moral development could underwrite a critique of the necessity of existing relations, as if they were immutable. It was not until the 1970s and the rise of so-called "Second Wave" feminism that feminists would come to sharply differentiate between cultural attributes, defined as "gender," and biological attributes, defined as "sex." In the late nineteenth and early twentieth centuries, those who sought to affirm or challenge existing relations did not have the vocabulary to speak of "gender" (which is why I have avoided using the language of gender here). But the more questions of sex differences were configured as differences of values, and not just physical attributes, the more the discourse shifted away from biology and toward culture and psychology. The intellectual upheavals of modernity were ones in which, increasingly, the human world was seen as human-made, and not derived from divine authority, or fixed categories of being. This meant that the fundamental organizing principle of sex difference that had been imagined as foundational was newly up for grabs, even as the persistence of social and political forms defined by sex difference remained a powerful conservative force.

Notes

1 Margaret Fuller, *Woman in the Nineteenth Century* (New York: Greeley & McElrath, 1845), p. 103.
2 Charlotte Perkins Stetson [Gilman], *Women and Economics: A Study of the Economic Relation Between Men and Women as a Factor in Social Evolution* (Boston, MA: Small Maynard and Co., 1898), p. 72.
3 Elsie Clews Parsons, *The Family: An Ethnographical and Historical Outline with Descriptive Notes* (New York: G. P. Putnam's Sons, 1906), p. 348.
4 A Black Woman of the South [Anna Julia Cooper], *A Voice from the South* (Xenia, OH: Aldine Printing House, 1892), pp. 28, 60.
5 Theodore Roosevelt, *The Strenuous Life: Essays and Addresses* (New York: Charles Scribner's Sons, 1906), pp. 9, 3.

Part II

The Contradictions of the Democratic Imagination

1920–1962

6 Cultural Relativisms and Modern Hierarchies

The twentieth century inherited from the nineteenth competing conceptions of culture: one tied to stadial anthropology and its evolutionary and materialist framework, as in the writings of Morgan and Tylor; the other tied to aesthetic and intellectual values and purpose, as in Matthew Arnold's conception. The first opened the door to pluralizing culture, by imagining that there were distinct groups, each maintaining their own particular way of life, even as it arrayed those cultures into a framework of progressive development from Savagery to Civilization. The second imagined a unified singular object even as it associated that object—art, literature, philosophy, thought itself—exclusively with a European tradition and body of work. Culture, for Arnold, was the pursuit of perfection, a higher plane of experience and development, defined by beauty and wisdom. But there was only one culture. There was no notion in Arnold that alternative traditions—say, China or Islam—had anything to do with Culture. Rather, Arnold's culture derived from the two fountainheads of European thought, the Hellenic and the Hebraic, Athens, and Jerusalem. While the anthropological and aesthetic concepts of culture seemed to be opposed or competing ones, they did have a number of things in common: they both assumed an integrated or holistic set of values and beliefs; they were both defined in opposition to the natural world or the biologically given; and, importantly, they both assumed a progressive vision of culture as development and improvement. Both were offered as responses to the perceived fragmentation and individualism of modernity, but neither offered a restorative vision of a presumed return to some earlier golden age. As much as the Arnoldian vision of culture appears to be a conservative one—dedicated to the preservation of an elite tradition—Arnold and his peers imagined it as a way to shape the future. Like Pragmatism and Progressivism, both conceptions of culture were future-oriented.

But as ideas about progress came under suspicion in the twentieth century, partly in response to the events of the first half of the twentieth century—two World Wars fought with industrial technologies, the rise of totalitarianism and industrialized genocide, the use of atomic weaponry—but partly in response to philosophical critiques that dismantled teleological views and challenged forms of absolutist morality and thought that underlay the vision of progress, a new understanding of culture would set itself in opposition to both evolutionary anthropology and the aesthetic perfection ideal associated with Arnold and his American followers. The advocates for this new vision of culture would use it to supplant the powerful biological and materialist frameworks that informed late nineteenth-century social thought, by emphasizing the symbolic and creative realm of human beliefs, and their power to constitute the artificial world in which people lived. In doing so, they aestheticized the collective lives of people and their shared beliefs. Darwinism didn't go away, but it no longer exercised the extensive grip on social thought it did in its heyday, and in the early twentieth century, it had to grapple with the complications arising out of the rediscovery of Mendelian genetics. If Darwinian thought had revealed a world unmoored from fixed foundations, it had also opened the door to biological determinism. The idea of culture also posited a comprehensive, sometimes deterministic, entity to explain human behavior, but freed that determinism from biology. The anthropologists, psychologists, cultural critics, historians, and political thinkers who championed the new, non-evolutionary view of culture, used it as a tool to fight against racialist ideas of biological difference and hierarchy, fixed sex difference, and sexual morality rooted in biology. The tension in this conception of culture was its scientific or "objective" claim to free social observation from the prejudicial values of Anglo-Saxon supremacy and higher "civilization," on the one hand, and its use to promote an alternative set of values—liberal and cosmopolitan visions of a democratic and tolerant way of life—on the other.

This turn toward a non-hierarchical conception of culture in the first decades of the twentieth century can be seen as part of what the philosopher Morton White many years ago called "the revolt against formalism" in American social thought. What White meant by this is a turn away from universalist, abstract, rationalist principles or rule-based logical thinking for understanding behavior—such as those favored by political economists—in favor of approaches that seek understandings based on historical and cultural contexts and an organic view of society and social behavior. This was the philosophical milieu of Pragmatism but also of the cultural and institutional economics of Veblen and the "new history" of James Harvey Robinson and Charles Beard. By rejecting formalist dualisms and fixed categories of thoughts, social thought ventured onto the ground of thinking about society in fluid and organic ways. Historicism—the doctrine that events and their meanings have to be understood in the particularity of their historical condition, not as representatives of a "type,"—was one expression of this anti-formalist outlook. The critique of the fixed developmental logic of evolutionary anthropology was another.

Franz Boas and the Rise of Cultural Relativism

The German émigré Franz Boas was the central figure in constructing a new anthropology that rejected the evolutionary frame of Victorian anthropology. At Columbia University, Boas established the first American Ph.D. in Anthropology, where he trained the modernist generation of anthropologists, who defined the field in the first half of the twentieth century. Boas's students during the almost 40 years he taught at Columbia, included Ruth Benedict, Margaret Mead, Edward Sapir, A. L. Kroeber, Robert Lowie, Zora Neale Hurston, Gene Weltfish, Melville Herskovits, and Ashley Montagu—a virtual who's who of American anthropologists, folklorists, and linguists. Many of Boas's students were women, which was still unusual in academia, despite the fact that higher education and the professions were opening up to women during this period. The particular modernist challenges to established forms of race and sex hierarchy associated with the Boas school, help to explain why the field—like psychoanalysis and other new sciences—would have particular appeal to women breaking the bounds of convention. Boas did not reject Darwinian evolutionary theory but argued that there was no empirical evidence for an evolutionary hierarchy of races or culture within humankind. Scientific inquiry should function without bending its knee to established prejudice. In *The Mind of Primitive Man* (1911), Boas systematically emphasized that the differences between different groups of people could be explained entirely on the basis of historical and environmental differences; that human beings of all groups possessed the same mental faculties; that there is much greater variation within races and ethnics groups than between them. Most importantly, without denying that there might be more "advanced" civilizations compared to "primitive" peoples, he argued that the empirical evidence for a single uniform evolutionary process from lower to higher was nonexistence. That meant that arraying peoples according to a presumed uniform standard of development was inadequate, not just for moral reasons, but for scientific ones. In order to understand any particular cultural attribute—say, for instance, ritual forms, attitudes toward death, or principles of self-control—it would be necessary to see it in terms of its particular historical development and its relationship to the other needs and practices of the society, rather than as an attribute that was higher or lower on a scale defined by the prejudices of modern Europeans. This was the doctrine of cultural relativism, and its central challenge to the evolutionary vision of social development shared by Social Darwinists, Reform Darwinists, and Victorian stadial theory alike.

Cultural relativism, although it has often been conflated with epistemological relativism and moral relativism, is not the same as them, nor does it necessarily imply them. Modernist thought produced a host of relativisms in a challenge to foundational and absolutist thought. But there is no evidence that Boas, for instance, thought that knowledge was subject to variable standards—he believed in a scientific ideal of freeing the study of Man from forms of subjective prejudice, and the rhetorical force of his arguments is aimed at displacing error rooted in prejudice with truth based on empirical observation. Pragmatists like William James might have suggested that truth was a variable thing, that all knowledge is relative to the conditions and habitual understandings that form its backdrop, but that was not Boas's stance. Nor was Boas saying that all moral values are just a matter of subjective attitudes and beliefs and that therefore we can make no judgments about the behavior of peoples, as if this was a warrant for human sacrifice, cannibalism, and sexual libertarianism. His point was that in order to understand people who were unlike educated modern Western Europeans, it was necessary to see cultural attributes in terms of their meaning and integration into the societies of which they were a part, rather than expressing a kind of step in a sequence toward a singular goal. Many of the critics of various relativisms have sought to equate them and then to characterize them in such a way that virtually no one would subscribe to the beliefs that relativists supposedly hold. The equation of relativism with moral indifference, for instance, is hard to square with the fact that those charged with the sin of relativism are often the least indifferent, and most committed to a broad and tolerant perspective opposed to narrow provincialism. What Boas was concerned with was the distorting effect of proclaiming a set of values held by one group of people into a standard to evaluate all of them. The fight Boas had was both against popular prejudice and ethnocentrism (a term, incidentally, coined by the arch-conservative William Graham Sumner!), on the one hand, and against the certitude of those who would hold their own standards as having an absolute and objective validity, on the other.

What Boas's approach did was to sever understanding of cultural difference from racial or biological difference. Boas was not opposed to the use of biological approaches to the study of Man, as put forward by physical anthropologists, but he was opposed to the *a priori* conflation of biology with cultural aptitude. One of Boas's most famous studies (1912) was his challenge to the racialist ideas of craniometry—the nineteenth-century science of fixed hereditary intelligence and evolutionary hierarchy based on the study of the volume and shape of human skulls. Arguing against the strict hereditarian ideas that associated skull size and shape with distinct racial groups, Boas sought to demonstrate that the American-born children of recent immigrants differed from their parents in the shape of their heads, indicating that environment played an important role in shaping physical features and that head shape, therefore, was not a reliable index of racial identity. Boas regularly argued that the observable differences in behavior and social practices between peoples were mistakenly assigned a biological basis, when the more obvious reason for these differences were matters of education and environment. On the one hand, he began the process of exploding the legacy of racial science and typology and arguing a more universalist understanding of general human capability, and its variation across the species. On the other, he pushed cultural differences between human beings in a way that made uniformity of "human nature" disappear in the concreteness of group differences. Boas was in a pitched intellectual battle with nativists and racialists who claimed immigration was "mongrelizing" the United States. His arguments emphasized the adaptive power of immigrants to their new conditions, as opposed to those who regarded immigrants as "unassimilable," but his engagement pointed to the ways in which cultural relativist ideas could both legitimate human difference and collapse it at the same time.

Anthropology as Cultural Criticism: Mead, Benedict, Hurston

Boas's most famous student, Margaret Mead, played an outsized role in the intellectual history of the mid-twentieth century. She was widely known to the public as well as to academic audiences, frequently engaging in public debate and contributing her voice to a variety of media. For many years in her later career in the 1960s and 70s, for instance, she published a monthly column in the women's magazine *Redbook*. One of the interesting elements of cultural anthropology as a ground for public discussion is that it deployed the idea that studying those peoples who seemed to be the furthest away from, or least similar to, modern Americans, would provide the best means of reflecting upon modern society. The evolutionists had studied "primitive" peoples because they believed them to be earlier less-developed versions of modern Europeans—they could be construed as the living embodiment of Europe at an earlier stage of the civilizing process. The cultural relativists took the opposite tack—assuming that all peoples were equal, studying peoples whose practices and beliefs were different from modern Americans was a way to denaturalize the views of moderns by demonstrating alternative ways of being. If Americans continued to rely on arguments that the relations between the sexes and the form of the family, for instance, were given in nature, the cultural relativists could demonstrate the wide variety of practices in family form. The evolutionists might argue that the matrilineal family belonged to an earlier stage of cultural development that had been superseded by the more evolutionarily advanced forms of patrilineal descent and patriarchal order. The cultural relativists countered this argument by demonstrating the contemporary existence of particular instances of matrilineal descent in relationship to the whole culture of which it was a part, rather than as a stage of development. Mead, among all the Boasians, was the figure who represented to the public this critical challenge to the received normative order.

Her first book, *Coming of Age in Samoa: A Psychological Study of Primitive Youth for Western Civilisation* (1928) created a firestorm, and remained one of the most widely read works of academic anthropology throughout the twentieth century. Mead's concerns and perspectives dovetailed with the growing interest in Freudian critiques of sexual repression in the 1920s; cultural anthropology was to align itself with sexual liberalism in a modernist critique of the inherited forms of the Victorian family and Victorian sexual mores. Just by focusing on adolescent girls and their sexual behavior, she was inverting older notions of sex difference, in which women had been objects, rather than agents, of sexual desire. Mead purported to find in Samoan culture a set of practices with regard to adolescence and sexuality that offered a critical perspective on modern America. Premarital sex in Samoa was common, casual, and not a source of shame, for girls; adolescence was a period of sexual promiscuity and marriage was delayed in order to enjoy it; the typical pattern of adolescent "stress and strain" in American society was nowhere to be found in Samoa, and there was no emotionally difficult psychological crisis involved in becoming an adult; generational conflict between youth and their parents was not common. The idea of adolescence as a discreet period of life marked by rebellion, risk-taking, and emotional conflict had only recently been created and given definition by the American psychologist G. Stanley Hall (1904). Mead's work sought to challenge the idea that adolescent development on Hall's or Freud's model was in some sense natural and culturally universal. *Coming of Age* is explicit in its framework of comparing modern America to Samoa as a scientific way to separate the natural from the cultural.

Mead's conclusion was that the peculiarity of adolescence in modern industrialized society is due to the significance of plural conflicting beliefs and modes of life in a complex society, and the overwhelming focus on individual choice that puts the responsibility for finding a path through complexity on the emerging adult. In Samoa, she said, the homogeneity and simplicity of life offer no challenging problems—the path of life is unchanging and clearly marked out for youth. Because Samoa is unlike America in these ways, of course, it cannot provide a model of behavior for Americans, but it can suggest that the form American ways of life take are not necessary or inevitable. In this way, the study of a "primitive" culture can relativize modern life, show it to be open to change. Mead's progressive liberalism, then, becomes both the starting and ending point of her study. What should Americans take from the study of Samoa? That our educational system needs to reject inherited ways of life that assume uniformity and homogeneity of belief and practice. "[T]he child of the future," said Mead, "must have an open mind.... The child must be taught how to think, and not what to think. And because old errors die slowly, they must be taught tolerance, just as today they are taught intolerance."[1] For generations of cultural conservatives, for whom Mead became a symbol of all that was wrong with modernity, it was not only Mead's modernist commitment to sexual freedom that bothered them—it was this progressive image of the critical mind committed to the rejection of parental authority, and a tolerance that appeared indifferent to primary commitments, that was at the heart of the complaint.

Ruth Benedict was one of Boas's first students and was an instructor at Barnard and Columbia, where she taught Mead and others, so she was a generation older than Mead. While Mead's *Coming of Age* appeared as a shot in the Culture Wars of the 1920s, especially with its centering questions of female sexual morality, Benedict's lasting impact was based on providing the most systematic popular discussion of the idea of culture itself. Her *Patterns of Culture* (1934) aimed to do something beyond what Boas and Mead had done—to provide an overview of the central tenets of cultural relativism and its challenge to a variety of other beliefs: biological racism, modern individualism, industrial capitalism itself. Besides asserting the primacy of culture as the basis of human difference and diversity, as well as the power of collective beliefs over individual consciences, Benedict made an argument that culture was not simply a collection of traits held by particular groups, but that it was an integrated pattern—cultures were more than the sum of their parts. If culture was "patterned," it meant that it possessed a kind of internal coherence, that all of its parts were bound together in service of a more general shared orientation. Benedict compared this coherence to the individual personality—culture was like a personality writ large—and to the stylistic identity of forms of art. The consistency of purpose of a culture gave it its identity, rather than just being an assemblage of forms of kinship, ritual practices, preparation of food, and forms of shelter, unrelated to one another. Her explication of her chosen three examples of cultures—the Zuni, the Dobu, and the Kwakiutl—reads like a kind of aesthetic interpretation, where each expresses in a multitude of ways, a coherent orientation toward the world. In fact, Benedict used the terms "Apollonian" and "Dionysian," used by Nietzsche in his famous analysis of Greek tragedy, to describe the integrated purpose of two of the cultures she analyzed. Benedict was a cultural holist, stressing the uniformity and homogeneity of culture as a set of standards regulating behavior of all of its members. The doctrine of cultural relativism, in this sense, was a challenge to images of individual autonomy and the rationality of human actors.

Despite the fact that Boas, Mead, Benedict, and the other cultural relativists had pulled down the evolutionary framework of Victorian anthropology, they did tend to reproduce the hierarchy of societies in their writing, particularly in the sharp distinction that Mead and others made between "primitive" societies and "civilization," a distinction preserved in the subtitle of Mead's opus. A later generation of critical anthropologists in the 1980s and 90s would argue that the origins of anthropology in European imperialism and colonialism have been carried throughout its entire history. The very idea of "culture," central to the discipline, had been a way of depoliticizing what was inherently a political relationship between Western industrial nations and the colonized peoples of Asia, Africa, and the Americas. By imagining some societies as simple and homogenous, having a kind of integrated unity that was denied to the complex industrial societies of the West, anthropology romanticized a fantasy of lost wholeness. Benedict was at some pains to deny the romantic primitivism of cultural relativism—anthropology, she said, does not "have necessary connection with a romantic return to the primitive. It is put forward in no spirit of poeticizing the simpler people,"[2] but her denial seems strained. Unlike Marxism, which imagined all societies as beset by internal contradictions arising out of the materially-based class structure, the anthropological idea of culture evaded politics. The liberal tolerance and cosmopolitanism that cultural relativism represented was complicit in driving a stake into the very particularism and difference that Northwest Coast native peoples, Trobriand Islanders, and Amazonian tribes represented to them. This was clear in the object-subject relations of anthropology; "primitive" peoples were always the object of study, Western social scientists always the possessor of knowledge. As much as the desire to democratize or remove hierarchies was a driving force in cultural anthropology, the critics of the late twentieth century would argue, anthropology failed to adequately reflect on its own assumptions and values as expressions of hierarchy.

Zora Neal Hurston, who was a central figure in the African-American cultural movement of the 1920s known as The Harlem Renaissance, took the Boasian prescription in a different direction than Mead, Benedict, and others who went on to forward academic anthropology. She was a student of Boas's, and although she never completed her Ph.D., took the anthropological and ethnographic outlook of the Boas school as the basis of a life-long concern with Southern Black folklore. Although Hurston is best known for her novel *Their Eyes Were Watching God*, her collection of folklore *Mules and Men* (1935) represented an application of Boasian cultural relativism in a new key. Hurston said that she had learned from Boas to see anthropologically, to see from the outside the world that she had grown up in as having a kind of value that needed to be preserved. We might regard Hurston as a kind of native ethnographer, inverting the pattern of participant-observer, in which an outsider comes to live with a group to study them, as Mead did with Samoans. Hurston studied at Howard University, and Barnard, and then came back to the Florida town in which she had grown up in order to collect folktales. Where Mead and Benedict used their analysis of "primitive" cultures to reflect upon and critique American society from the outside, Hurston used the distancing strategy she learned from anthropology as a way to elevate a distinct subculture of Black oral tradition as a source of historically-based identity and meaning. At Barnard, she had also studied with Melville Herskovits, who played an important role in defining the persistence of African cultural practices in the United States against those who argued that all African culture had been systematically expunged by the horrors of slavery. The antihierarchical perspective of Boasian anthropology would inform Hurston's practice.

For both Benedict and Hurston, the scientific conception of anthropology would be complicated by their reading of culture in aesthetic terms. The idea of a divergence between an anthropological or scientific conception of culture, and an Arnoldian idea that culture represented aesthetic and philosophical values, foundered on the commitment of Boasians to the worlds of art—in both Benedict and Hurston, the anthropological concept of culture was aestheticized. For Benedict, culture itself was the coherent work of art in which people lived; for Hurston folklore was an oral literary form that expressed the collective life of a people. Since culture was what was made by human beings, rather than what was given by nature, and it possessed a kind of expressive and stylistic unity, the idea that an anthropological idea of culture was not simultaneously an aesthetic one was hard to maintain. Surely, Matthew Arnold would not have included Black folk tales or Kwakiutl Potlatch ceremonies in his vision of the best that has been said and thought, and his idea of culture remained singular and unitary rather than plural. But the anthropological concept of culture, by removing human behavior from the determination of nature, turned human behavior into an artistic endeavor, with its own styles, themes, and values.

In the wake of *Coming of Age in Samoa* and *Patterns of Culture*, Benedict, Mead, Edward Sapir, and other anthropologists became part of an interdisciplinary movement interested in linking individual personality to culture. The Culture and Personality theorists also included psychologists and psychiatrists, many of them shaped by Freudian thought, such as Harry Stack Sullivan, Erik Erikson, and Abram Kardiner. Although there were a variety of approaches that fell under the Culture and Personality umbrella, the general concern of these thinkers was identifying the ways in which individual personality was shaped by culture and the ways in which, as Mead put it in describing Benedict's approach, culture was personality "writ large." These studies often focused on child rearing and the internalization of cultural values in the shaping of personality. The Culture and Personality thinkers were one of the first modern intellectual groups to open the door to thinking about human sexuality outside of binary heterosexuality as something other than pathological. Sexual norms varied from culture to culture, and some cultures provided recognized alternatives to American heterosexual norms. From the 1930s through the 1950s, this school of thought was influential, particularly in the attention it gave to what some of its members denominated as "national character." The idea of national character, in its heyday in the 1940s and 1950s, sought to construct character typology on the basis of national identity. Benedict's famous study of Japanese culture and character, *The Chrysanthemum and the Sword* (1946), commissioned by the U.S. Office of War Information, shaped American notions of Japanese character in the wake of World War II—and continued to shape discussion in Japan in the following decades. Mead turned the anthropologist's eye on American culture and character during World War II in *And Keep Your Powder Dry* (1942), and the transplanted British anthropologist Geoffrey Gorer analyzed both the American and Russian national characters in the Cold War era. The idea that all members of a nation were of the same character type, of course, put a scientific patina on ideas that tended to type people and collapse the diversity and range of personality within cultures and nations. One of the ironies of Culture and Personality theories is that, in delegitimizing the biological and racialist ideas of hereditary character, they ended up replicating some of the same stereotypical conceptions in cultural terms. Biological determinism was replaced by cultural determinism; both were committed to character typology. The result could easily provide a host of clichés suitable for cocktail party chitchat: Germans were rigid and anal retentive; Russians desired strong authority; Americans were "puritanical" in their sexual attitudes; Scandinavians were emotionally unexpressive and depressed.

The New History

At the founding of the American Historical Association in 1884, the guiding dictum to the study of history was that history is "past politics." Under the historian Herbert Baxter Adams at Johns Hopkins University, where scholars such as the future president Woodrow Wilson were trained, the study of history was developed as an empirical science with its principal focus on political life and events—the doings of nation states, the activities of statesmen and leaders. From the 1890s to World War I, a new generation of historians would reshape the understanding of the past in some of the same ways that Boas and his students had reshaped the idea of culture. The idea of historical relativism would come to stand side by side with cultural relativism. By introducing a relativistic and skeptical approach to the study of the past, the "new historians" sought to mobilize a concern for the contemporary implications of history. The idea that history would not aim for an Olympian objectivity, or neutrality, but would write about the past from the point of view and needs of the present was central to the new

Cultural Relativisms and Modern Hierarchies 111

approach. As one of the most influential of the new historians, Frederick Jackson Turner, put it in 1891 "Each age tries to form its own conception of the past. *Each age writes the history of the past anew with reference to the conditions uppermost in its own time.*"[3] Like the Boasians who called on anthropology to reconsider its own prejudices and assumptions, to adopt a more self-conscious position about its own limitations, the new historians sought to pull the rug out from what they regarded as the naïve empiricism of the reigning historical scholarship. Turner, James Harvey Robinson, Charles Beard, and Carl Becker would be the dominant voices in bringing economics, culture, environment, social and intellectual movements into historiography. By the mid-1930s, the idea that history was not something found, but something made by historians, that it contained inevitably a subjective element, and that this was not a cause for despair but a good thing, had reached the pinnacle of the historical profession.

Turner is most famous for an intervention he made in American historiography in a landmark essay delivered at the World's Columbian Exposition in Chicago in 1893: "The Significance of the Frontier in American History." Turner's Frontier Thesis would come to define the study of American history for the next 75 years. A historiographical revolution in the 1960s and 70s would overthrow the Turnerian vision of American history, but until then, its assumptions tended to define the image of the American past. The frontier thesis laid out an exceptionalist vision of an American history that turned its back on inherited European ideas and institutions. Turner argued for the power of an ever-receding frontier between "savagery and civilization" as the controlling element in the shaping of American history, American modes of thought and habit, and the forms of democratic life. Although presented as a claim drawn from empirical observation, the Frontier Thesis was mythological, encapsulating a picture of a distinct American identity, indebted to no tradition received from the past, forged in an encounter with the open land. Looking back at this text over the past 50 years, historians have found it to be ideological at its core, an expression based on the promotion of, and legitimation of, American nationalism and its territorial claims. Turner imagined the West as "empty land," erasing the indigenous peoples who lived there, or turning them into natural features of the wilderness; he associated democracy with the least democratic form of American government, appointed territorial governors; he overlooked or downplayed the role of the Federal Government, as opposed to ordinary "pioneers," in providing the material and intellectual basis for occupying the West; his theory had little to say about the central institution of slavery.

All of these criticisms are apt, but they tend to overlook what Turner was arguing *against*: a kind of blood-based hereditary nationalism. Herbert Baxter Adams and others had promoted the so-called "Teutonic

Seed" or "germ" theory of American democracy. In their view, the forms of American life were carried in the racial stock of Anglo-Saxon and Germanic settlers. In this context, Turner's argument for the shaping force of the environment was an anti-racialist and anti-essentialist position. The Darwinian sensibility was at work in Turner's theory—instead of fixed types and racial foundations, he argued for the mutability of persons and attributes in adapting to the environmental conditions of the frontier. All was process and change, rather than the stable continuity of the received past. The focus on a repeated liminal crossing as the force for breaking down distinctions and inherited categories is not entirely unrelated to the calls for cultural hybridity we hear in more recent iterations of postcolonial theory.

Charles Beard took on another mythic fixture of American political history—that the US Constitution was an expression of a purified or transcendent realm of political ideas, a moment when the participants in the Constitutional Convention put aside matters of petty politics to create a document of ideals. Beard's *An Economic Interpretation of the Constitution* (1913) insisted that the document should be seen in light of the specific property holdings and economic interests of the people who wrote it. The turn away from thinking of the Constitution as the outcome of a set of principles, held formally and abstractly, and thinking of it as the expression of interests, was, again, part of the turn toward concreteness, context, and specificity. Arguing against what he called "that noble dream" of historical objectivity, Beard later claimed that all historians had a point of view and an interest; that criticism of the economic interpretation as a violation of the principles of objectivity was itself a highly motivated stance, and not a disinterested one. The appeal to objectivity was, historically, an appeal to a conservative position, a rejection of the idea that history should be a companion, as in Marx, to revolution or democratic social change.

In his 1934 Presidential Address to the American Historical Association, "Written History as an Act of Faith," he argued that historians needed to reject not only the analogy of history to physics (laws of cause and effect) and biology (Darwinian organic development), but also to a too facile relativism that fails to understand the self-defeating nature of relativistic thought. Beard found it hard, however, to escape that relativistic orientation in his own writing and understanding. Recognizing that historians are guided by arbitrary decisions of periodization, subject matter, and matters of interest, the conclusion that Beard drew was that, although the forms that history takes—chaos, cyclical, unilinear progress—were not in the object that historians study, it was impossible to study history without some kind of faith in an order that was grounded in something other than the desire of the historian. Beard sought a kind of historical relativism without the negative connotations of relativism; history could not be science, it could only be a belief without foundation. Like Beard, Carl Becker had argued in his Presidential Address two years earlier, "Everyman His Own Historian," (1932) that history was a way of making sense of the present so as to guide behavior in the future—it had no epistemological ground in a realm of pure and disinterested knowledge. If cultural relativism was a way to use the diversity of "primitive" cultures to reflect upon the needs of the present in industrial America, Beard, and Becker were arguing that historical relativism had a similar purpose. History could be a form of cultural criticism. To know the distinctiveness of the past was to see the present in new terms. Even if the historian presumed that his obligation was to a fair and impartial view of past actors and events, his idea of what was fair and impartial was shaped by the needs of the present, from which he could not escape. But this was no reason to despair; it provided the legitimacy for studying history and gave it a vitality and purpose in contrast to the dull antiquarian view of knowing the details of the past for its own sake.

The Chicago School of Sociology

While the Boasian anthropologists turned to "primitive" cultures, and the New History turned to the American and European cultural, social, and economic past, the newly instituted Department of Sociology at the University of Chicago staked out its ground of reflection on modernity in the urban environment. The Chicago School of Sociology that developed after 1910, and flourished in the years between World War I and II, marked a distinctive American school of thought and dominated the field of sociology, as the Boasians dominated anthropology in those years. The central figure in Chicago sociology was Robert Park, and influential figures who were associated with the school, included W.I. Thomas and the Polish émigré Florian Znaniecki, authors of the landmark empirical study, *The Polish Peasant in Europe and America* (5 vols, 1918–1920); Ernest Burgess, co-author with Park of the "bible" of the Chicago school, *Introduction to the Science of Sociology* (1921); George Herbert Mead, Pragmatist and one of the principle theorists of the symbolic interactionist school of social psychology; and Louis Wirth, who defined "urbanism" as a cultural orientation and a way of life. Others in Chicago, such as the social reformer Jane Addams, and the Pragmatist philosopher John Dewey, were closely connected to Chicago sociology. Unlike the cultural holists, such as Benedict, that dominated anthropology, the Chicago sociologists were interested in looking at the urban environment in terms of its "social disorganization." Modernity, especially in its urban form, they believed, brought strangers into contact with one another in new ways, disrupting the cohesiveness of existing groups of people. The result was criminality, juvenile delinquency, gangs, prostitution, disease, and alcoholism. If cultural anthropologists were interested in the power and coherence of social norms, Chicago sociologists were more concerned with the breakdown of social coherence. Importantly, unlike the biological criminologists of the nineteenth century, who associated criminality and unsocial behavior with heredity, Chicago sociology defined such behaviors as results of social process. They shared with the Boasians the idea that social behavior was a result of environment and education, rather than biology.

Chicago sociology took from the Darwinian outlook not its biologism, but its concerns with the shaping power of environments—in this case the urban social environment. The approach was "ecological" in the sense of seeing social groups as forming a set of relations, and urban process as a kind of adaptation to the whole environment. Park had strong concerns with what he came to call "race relations"—before he came to Chicago he had worked at Tuskegee with Booker T. Washington—and with questions of immigrant assimilation. Chicago was a city marked by the strong presence of distinct racial and ethnic groups, so it provided an ideal space of observation to test Park's theories. Park's famous "race relations cycle" stipulated a series of stages by which foreign and outsider groups were incorporated into the dominant social order: competition, conflict, accommodation, and assimilation. Although later critics, especially in the wake of racial uprisings in the 1960s, would see the Chicago focus on process, adaptation, and accommodation as a kind of liberal evasion of the power structure of race and domination, the notion of "assimilation" as a sociological process has had a long staying power in American social thought. Chicago sociology proved to be attractive to racial and ethnic minorities. Black sociologists such as Charles Johnson, E. Franklin Frazier, Allison Davis, and the authors of *Black Metropolis: A Study of Negro Life in an American City* (1945), St. Clair Drake and Horace Cayton, were students or faculty members associated with the department. At a time when there were very few Chinese students doing graduate work at American universities, due in part to the Chinese Exclusion Act that had prevented Chinese immigration from 1882 forward, Chicago counted among its doctoral students Paul C.P. Sui, Wu Ching-Chao and Rose Hum Lee, the latter of whom became the first Asian American woman to head a sociology department in the United States.

Chicago sociology offered a space for the marginalized, for those who might look at the city from the point of view of an outsider. Park's famous essay "Human Migration and the Marginal Man," pointed to an alternative to the theories of evolutionary development based on race or internal development. Civilization, said Park, is produced by the contacts between peoples that have the effect of breaking up existing forms and habits of thought. If Turner imagined American development as a process of constantly crossing the boundary between civilization and wilderness, Park saw new forms of consciousness as produced by those who straddle the boundaries between peoples, belonging in neither one world nor the other. Drawing on the German sociologist Georg Simmel's image of "the stranger" as an urban figure, Park offered the marginal man as the type of the modern cosmopolite. The creative force of social development was

> a man living and sharing intimately in the cultural life and traditions of two distinct peoples; never quite willing to break, even if he were permitted to do so, with his past and his traditions, and not quite accepted, because of racial prejudice, in the new society in which he now sought to find a place. He was a man on the margin of two cultures and two societies, which never completely interpenetrated and fused.

This characteristic form of modernity—to be both on the outside and the inside—was Chicago sociology's alternative to the cultural relativism of Boas and his students, in which cultures were imagined as insular wholes. "It is in the mind of the marginal man-where the changes and fusions of culture are going on-that we can best study the processes of civilization and of progress."[4]

Anthropology Turns Its Eye on America: Middletown

The ideas associated with cultural anthropology began with an attempt to describe difference based on the gap between modern industrial society, and so-called "primitive" societies. Ethnography was presumed to be possible because those societies were simpler and more homogenous, and the observer could view them from the outside. But it was not long before someone imagined that Americans might understand themselves better if they regarded themselves as "other," imagining themselves as if they were from the outside looking in. The application of the tools of the anthropologist to the study of an American community resulted in Robert and Helen Merrell Lynd's *Middletown: A Study in Modern American Culture* (1929). The Lynd's study of the anonymized Muncie, Indiana, a medium-sized city in the American Midwest, sought to treat a modern American community as if were Mead's Samoa, Boas's Northwest Coast tribes, or Malinowski's Trobriand Islands. *Middletown*, like Mead's *Coming of Age in Samoa*, struck a chord with a larger non-academic public, who saw in social science an opportunity to examine American habits, practices, beliefs, and ways of life from an "objective" stance. The commitment to scientific distance, and the Lynd's own critique of modern America's "pecuniary culture," presented a tension in the work, but critique and epistemic distance—as in Samoa—seemed to be part of the same sensibility. To regard life in an American city as an anthropologist would a "primitive" culture created conceptual problems, since the predicate of so much anthropological ethnography was that primitive cultures were uniform, homogenous, integrated, tradition bound—the very things that modern society was not.

What *Middletown* did, in response, was to minimize the pluralistic and conflicted nature of modern society by erecting a representative or typical city as the site of "modern American culture." Despite various hedging on the issue, the Lynds wrote a book that was deliberately aimed at this typicality, and received as such by the wider reading public. The idea that the American Midwest, for instance, was more typical or representative of America; that a small to medium-sized city was more typical than a large city or a small town; that the relative absence of recent immigrants and Blacks would allow for a more straightforward understanding of modern life—this in a period of intense nativism and immigration restriction, and the prominence of the Klu Klux Klan in Indiana; the notion that it was more typical for a city to be "self-contained" than be in a relation of dependency and exchange on other nearby urban areas: these were the explicit factors driving the choice of Muncie as typical. When John Dollard published *Caste and Class in a Southern Town* (1937), for instance, he anonymized Indianola, Mississippi as "Southerntown," as if the South could not be typical of "America." And, unlike the tendency in the anthropological study of primitive cultures, the Lynds made a deliberate choice to make their study diachronic. If primitive societies were imagined as relatively unchanging and continuous, and therefore amenable to a picture taking at a single point in time, the whole idea of modernity was premised on rapid change and its consequences. What *Middletown* did was to study modern life in an American community under the pressure of change, using 1890 as a baseline for contrast. The idea of a portrait of a contemporary American way of life, then, was undercut by the idea that this was a life in motion, perhaps more suitably conceived as a motion picture than a photograph.

But the Lynds did use the kinds of anthropological categories that could be universalized. The book is divided into sections on "Getting a Living," "Making a Home," "Training the Young," "Using Leisure," "Engaging in Religious Practices," and "Engaging in Community Practices." In each of these sections, they sought to show the ways in which modern changes had transformed life: industrial standardization and mechanization of work; loosening of familial authority and sex roles; extension of formal education in public schools; commercialization of leisure activities outside the home; secularization; bureaucratization of community activity. The coming of the automobile and mass media (movies, radio, mass circulation magazines), the rise of a consumer-oriented leisure, and the standardization of taste all played a central role in the image of an emergent American way of life. It was hard not to read the Lynd's analysis as anything other than a tale of decline, in which commercial institutions were displacing community and family, religious faith and practice was superficial and moralistic, and the people of Middletown were caught in the process of changes they did not understand.

In this sense, the concerns of *Middletown* converged with a larger body of modernist cultural criticism afoot in the 1920s. This body of criticism includes fictional works such as Sinclair Lewis's satirical depiction of the middle-class boosterism of a Rotary Club civilization in Babbitt (1922) and Sherwood Anderson's depiction of the repressive forms of small-town Midwestern life in *Winesburg, Ohio* (1919); H.L. Mencken's scathing denunciations of the ignorance and moralism of the class of Americans he dubbed "the booboisie"; the cosmopolitan intellectuals who denounced former Democratic Party figurehead William Jennings Bryan's testimony at the 1925 Scopes Trial challenging the state of Tennessee's law against the teaching of Darwinian evolution in public schools. The stance that Middletown took spoke in scientific terms, but the critical view that was evident in Boasian anthropology helped to turn the Lynds' work into one of a growing spate of works that would be concerned with what a later generation of critics on both the right and the left called "mass culture." Once again, the attempt to think of the anthropological and aesthetic ideas of culture as different or opposed things foundered on the implied aesthetic distaste for the commercial forms of art and leisure that the Lynds found in their anthropological analysis of Muncie.

Making Meaning with Culture

What the Boasians, the New History, the Chicago School of Sociology, and the ethnographic study of American culture in *Middletown* shared was an attempt to move away from biological and evolutionary categories of analysis, and to see the behavior of peoples in ways that were simultaneously sympathetic to the objects of study, but distant from them. Chicago School sociologist W.I. Thomas, for instance, argued that if we are to understand social behavior, we have to be attuned to what he called "the definition of the situation," by the participants in it. Behavior was not independent from the subjective perspective of those participants and what they believed to be going on. Like the Pragmatist William James, who thought that ideas not only reflected the world but also created it, the dominant social thought of the first half of the twentieth century was committed to seeing the mind's creative power in the world. Social science needs to see, as the later cultural anthropologist Clifford Geertz put it, "from the native's point of view." But that, too, was insufficient. The process of modernity was a reflective process, a process of standing outside of one's belief and viewing them as if they belonged to someone else. This is why the metaphor of culture as a "mirror" was such a powerful and ubiquitous one. Anthropologists held up the mirror to Americans, allowing them to see themselves in new ways. Samoan girls becoming women could be a mirror to American adolescents, allowing them to see the peculiarity of their own conventions; the American and European past could be a mirror that might serve the needs of the present rather than stand apart from them; the racialized immigrant could be a marginal man, for Park, reflecting on the identity of the old and new worlds by belonging to both and neither; the Lynds could ask the members of the public to see themselves through the eyes of social science, to become aware of themselves as cultural beings in a period of rapid change, to imagine their typicality. Behind all of these ideas was a vision of collective self-making, of culture as an all-encompassing way of life, and as an aesthetic ideal.

Notes

1 Margaret Mead, *Coming of Age in Samoa: A Psychological Study of Primitive Youth for Western Civilisation* (New York: William Morrow & Co., 1928), p. 246.
2 Ruth Benedict, *Patterns of Culture* (Boston, MA: Houghton Mifflin, 1934), pp. 19–20.
3 Frederick Jackson Turner, "The Significance of History" (1891), in Everett E. Edwards, ed., *The Early Writings of Frederick Jackson Turner* (Madison: University of Wisconsin Press, 1938), p. 52. Italics in original.
4 Robert Park, "Human Migration and the Marginal Man," *American Journal of Sociology* 33.6 (May 1928), pp. 892–893.

7 Science as Culture
The Moral Order of Modernity

In Walter Lippmann's *Drift and Mastery* and the writings of some other Progressives, as well as in the intellectual justifications for the late nineteenth-century research university, we have encountered the idea that science and scientific knowledge were more than matters of epistemology. Rather, many thinkers imagined that they provided a mode of thought and belief that could provide moral purpose in the absence of the metaphysical claims of Christian religion or Enlightenment foundationalism. The idea of value-neutrality as a feature of science would come to be more widely articulated at various points in the twentieth century, but even the notion of value-neutrality is, ironically, a value statement—it proposes that impartial truth and disinterestedness is a higher moral good than subjective need and interest. In the course of the middle years of the twentieth century, a variety of advocates for, and critics of, scientific thought created a wide-ranging discourse about the meaning of science, its values, and its adequacy as a source of moral order. The question of science and values was not so much a question about the content of scientific knowledge, or its epistemological adequacy, as it was about whether science should have something more than epistemic authority, what a culture organized around science and scientific outlooks might look like, whether science could replace religion or merely complement it, whether science might need to defer to other sources of authority outside of it, whether scientific cultural and thought might be something less than an unalloyed good. As some intellectuals came to more systematically criticize modernity, they identified the centrality of a scientific ethos as responsible for the loss of moral order, as a source of fragmentation and amorality. Science as culture had its critics as well as its boosters.

The Lippmann–Terman–Dewey–Mencken Debate

One of the central questions raised by the appeal to scientific values and norms was whether a scientific way of life would create a more democratic culture or whether it would create a new priesthood of experts, whose authority would rest on understanding not available to the general public. In other words, was science democratic or elitist? Were its intellectual benefits widespread, or in the possession of a new aristocracy of knowledge? In a way, this question was an extension of the long-standing Enlightenment commitment to the idea that knowledge, freed from superstition, was the condition of self-government. Widespread literacy and an expanding attention to universal public education in the nineteenth century were components of the faith in the power of knowledge to create a more democratic and informed public. But the modern conditions of knowledge threw something of a wrench in this generalized ethic. As the research university expanded, it fragmented the possibility of comprehensive general understanding by emphasizing modern science as resting on specialization. The long years of study in a specific area of knowledge were increasingly the basis for making authoritative claims. The generally educated layperson, whose claim of self-government was based on breadth of knowledge and the development of critical intellect, appeared to be eclipsed by the expert, who could speak about one particular thing with a great deal of authority but lacked the comparable education in areas beyond the zone of expertise. The barriers of entry to the educated discourse of experts were high, and the more modern life rested on technical and specific knowledge—medicine, engineering, economic policy—the greater the distance between the will of the people and the knowledge necessary to navigate the complexities of modern life.

The very public discussion of the implications of scientific expertise for democracy in the 1920s has come to be referred to as the Dewey–Lippmann debate, although as historians have pointed out, John Dewey and Walter Lippmann were mostly on the same side of the debate, with some differences in tone and attitude, and opposed to those who believed that the mass of people were too irrational and unknowledgeable to be capable of self-government. Lippmann, who had enthusiastically endorsed a culture organized around science in *Drift and Mastery*, had not given up on science but appeared more skeptical of the capacity of ordinary people to understand the complexities of modern life in *Public Opinion* (1922) and its sequel, *The Phantom Public* (1925). Dewey's more enthusiastic vision of democratic life and its potentialities was expressed in *The Public and Its Problems* (1927). It should be noted, in contrast to those who have emphasized the opposition between the two thinkers, that Dewey wrote an enthusiastic review of *Public Opinion* in *The New Republic*, and concurred in its general conclusions. The focus on "public opinion" and its relationship to knowledge was at the center of this discussion, but it was not only expertise that was at issue in shaping public opinion. The rise of the field of public relations in the early twentieth century, and the development of mass journalism, as well as the understanding of persuasive techniques that informed modern advertising, pointed to a conception of people as manipulable rather than rational. In this context, both Lippmann and Dewey were affirming the idea of a democracy based on better instruments for the dissemination of knowledge, rather than Lippmann rejecting the possibility of democracy due to the inherent incapability of ordinary people to understand complex issues. But both Dewey and Lippmann were concerned about questions of how to turn expert knowledge into public support, or how it might be possible to avoid technocracy—the rule by a technocratic elite. If members of the public could not be experts in all things related to public concern, could they still govern themselves or would they have to defer to specialists? Dewey's answer, in part, was to suggest that democracy meant the conditions that allowed for the fullest specialization of individuals—for him, there was no conflict between scientific specialization and democratic flourishing since democracy could only be the condition in which each individual could realize his fullest gifts and capacities.

The reason Lippmann appears to present a more skeptical view about public intelligence than Dewey is that his analysis in *Public Opinion* is based on larger questions of epistemology, rather than intelligence or capability. That is, he was not arguing that members of the public lack intelligence or capability, which had been one of the strong arguments against democracy, both traditionally, and in the 1920s when he was writing. If democratic theory was based on a largely positive view of universal human capability, then anti-democratic thought often invoked an image of ordinary people as inherently irrational or lacking the intelligence to identify their own interests or the public good. This was not Lippmann's claim. Rather, he suggested that all people, outside of specific and narrow areas in which they might engage in scientific inquiry, were creatures of mental habit. In the Pragmatic tradition of Peirce and James, Lippmann suggested that our beliefs—what he called "the pictures in our heads"—were habits rather than purely rational ideation. Generalizations were simplifications, and new "facts" were constantly assimilated to what he called "stereotypes." Because all people could not be specialist experts in all matters relevant to public decision-making, people were in general guided by the generalized and simplified beliefs they held. The problem for government was not the irrationality and stupidity of the public, but the fact that all matters had grown increasingly complex, and the gap between the "pictures in people's heads" and the technical needs of policy were too vast. What was needed was a medium for translating expert understanding into public opinion. While Lippmann's own practice of a critical journalism addressed to the public might provide something of a model, the dominant forms of mass media journalism did not provide the means by which the public could know in a meaningful way. What Lippmann aimed for was the creation of a democratic public which could articulate the broad and general goals of the people, while expert specialists could translate those goals into specific policy solutions. But, given the tone of *Public Opinion*, it was possible to read Lippmann as arguing that modern problems of governance required expert scientific understanding and specialization, and the general public could never have sufficient education and understanding to make decisions about what was best for their own lives. Hence, the view of Lippmann as opposed to Dewey, who fully embraced the equivalence between democracy and science and was more optimistic about overcoming any temporary barriers to their union. Dewey saw the problem of the disappearing public in a modern society, but argued strongly that the remedy lay not in the authority of experts, but in "the improvement of the methods and conditions of debate, discussion, and persuasion"[1] The fault was not in the inherent limitations of the masses but in the failure to develop more fully the instruments of democratic life. Science and technical expertise were necessary to modern politics, but the decision-making was a matter of public decision-making, not technocratic control.

In contrast to the faith in the potential of a democratic public lay various attempts to limit the influence or voice of ordinary people in political life in the name of science, moves that were opposed by both Dewey and Lippmann. The clearest example appears in the explicit debate that Lippmann had with the Stanford University psychologist Lewis Terman in the early 1920s, after the publication of *Public Opinion*. Terman was one of the most prominent figures in the development of intelligence testing, creating the revised Stanford–Binet intelligence scale, the basis of IQ rankings. Terman was also a eugenicist who believed that intelligence was largely heritable. Intelligence testing was an area that seemed to have widespread application to business, education, and public life, and in the early twentieth century became a prominent aspect of the discipline of psychology. Lippmann responded to a specific set of findings that received a great deal of public attention. During World War I, the US Army had conducted intelligence testing on 1.7 million soldiers. One of the announced conclusions of those studies: the average mental age of white draftees was 13 years old. The implication was clear: the general intellectual capacity of the American public was on the level of children, and this public therefore lacked capability to make complex decisions or to understand the problems faced by a complex modern society. Racialists like the historian and polemicist Lothrop Stoddard seized on these findings to argue for a biologically-pure meritocracy, where intelligent whites of Western European descent would govern. Lippmann, in a series of articles in *The New Republic*, sought to dismantle the claims of academic psychologists like Terman. In other words, given a chance to embrace a set of findings that could support the idea of a public lacking intelligence sufficient to be capable of self-government in a complex modern society, Lippmann went in the other direction. He argued, not as an expert scientist, but as a public critic, against the authority of expert science and its hereditarian claims. Terman tried to discredit Lippmann's attack by appealing to the authority of the academic discipline, and Dewey ended up intervening in the debate on Lippmann's side. Both Dewey and Lippmann advocated a scientific way of life and thought *against* the claims of an actual existing science that purported to identify the merits of an intellectual elite.

The debate around elite vs. democratic rule was not just a debate about scientific expertise and the complexities of the administrative state, of course. Lippmann was at odds with those critics of democracy, like H.L. Mencken, who supported a quasi-aristocratic cultural elite but had a disdain for the narrowness of science as a ground of cultural authority. A vocal group of cultural conservatives—including Irving Babbitt and Ralph Adams Cram—in the 1920s expressed a deep antipathy to democracy, which they often associated with Romanticism and a rejection of tradition. Mencken was a conservative affecting a kind of critical cosmopolitanism that dovetailed with some of the sensibilities of the new liberals—a disdain for convention, for religious authority, and for middle-class moralism. But Mencken's satirical critique of democracy drew its sources from contrarians left and right: Friedrich Nietzsche, George Bernard Shaw, and Mark Twain among them. For Mencken, the vast majority of people were mindless and incapable of higher thought of any kind. In *Notes on Democracy* (1926), Mencken suspended his usual rejection of modern science—based on his own deep ignorance and misunderstanding of modern science as a kind of metaphysical "theology"—in order to embrace the results of intelligence testing, which confirmed his anti-democratic prejudices. Mencken, like his hero Nietzsche, saw democracy as an expression of envy of the superior man by the mob; its ethic of egalitarianism was nothing more than an attempt to destroy intellectual superiority and distinction through leveling. And Mencken's critical assessment of Lippmann's *Public Opinion* indicates that he and Lippmann were fundamentally on opposed sides of the debate about democracy, science, and the intellectual capabilities of members of the public. That is, Mencken was hostile to the entire project of democracy, which he saw as rising not from "the people," but from a misguided liberal elite, and which he associated with weak Christian moralism, sentimentalism, and an embrace of stupidity. Lippmann was with Dewey in affirming both science and democracy, expertise and public discourse; Mencken and Terman, on the other hand, and for different reasons, embraced an ethic of a superior elite against the follies of a democratic way of life.

Science and Disenchantment

That a world governed by science might create the conditions of undemocratic technocracy was only one of the concerns about science's cultural meaning. The commitment of modern modes of thought to a rationalized and secularized view of the world seemed to many commentators and analysts in the interwar years to destroy frames of meaning by which people might order their lives. The German sociologist Max Weber, who had died in 1920, and whose voluminous writings began to receive sustained attention in the United States in the mid-1920s, had centered his writings on the process of rationalization as the defining element of modernity. By rationalization, he meant that modern thought—and science as its exemplar—was committed to a systematic stripping of the world of mystery, tradition-bound purpose, and any metaphysical framework that could not be subordinated to the rational ordering of experience. Bureaucratization, secularization, and scientific thought worked hand in hand to "disenchant" the world. Science was the powerful intellectual emblem of a world without purpose other than the promotion of instrumental and logical ways of thinking. In his essay "Science as a Vocation" (1917) he wrote "The fate of our times is characterized by rationalization and intellectualization and, above all, by the 'disenchantment of the world.' Precisely the most ultimate and sublime values have retreated from public life…"[2] Science cannot answer the questions of how people ought to live, what purposes they should pursue, what makes a life meaningful. Unlike Dewey and his vision of science as a realm of values, for Weber science achieves its overwhelming intellectual power by refusing the world of animating values. Science is the emblem of meaninglessness. In Weber's most famous work *The Protestant Ethic and the Spirit of Capitalism* (1905, translated in 1930 by Talcott Parsons), He declared that the rationalized and secularized asceticism of modern capitalism, having lost its original religious framework, had become the "iron cage" of modernity, a compulsive orientation toward secular progress. "Specialists without spirit; sensualists without heart: this nullity imagines it has attained a level of civilization never before achieved."[3]

Weber's imagination of a disenchanted modernity drew on the writings of Friedrich Nietzsche, who had seen in the modern worship of science a "will to nothingness." Nietzsche, whose writings were increasingly influential in the first decades of the twentieth century, had criticized science not as the antithesis of religious Christianity, but as its extension. He had found in Christianity and its ethic an embrace of weakness, a hatred of power and the human will, an attitude he characterized as opposed to life. Science, with its secular orientation, would appear to have redirected the other-worldly telos of Christianity back to earth.

But modern science, Nietzsche argued in *On the Genealogy of Morals* (1887) expressed the ascetic ideals of Christianity—its mortification of the flesh, its distrust of the appetites—in a new and more relentless form. Science had progressively decentered human beings from the account of nature—Copernicus had dethroned the earth as the center of the universe, and Darwin had moved human beings into the natural world as an outcome of accident and natural process rather than special creation. More importantly, the scientific conception of truth, as Nietzsche imagined it, expressed a desire to embrace a neutral absence of will as the highest good. For Nietzsche, the self-evident idea that an objective truth, independent of human interest, need, and desire, was somehow good in itself needed to be questioned. The will to truth, as he saw it, was a will to nothingness, or the embrace of a kind of nihilism, which he identified as the diseased condition of modern life. In this sense, science denied both the metaphysical beliefs of religion and the naturalistic understanding of human beings as instinctual animals. The triumph of science was not the march of progress over error, but the loss of belief as a stable source of meaning.

For many literary and cultural intellectuals in the wake of World War I, this sense of loss could be figured as "disillusionment," a sense that a moral order that had once made sense, now appeared to be a fiction. Instead of the liberating sense of science as possibility, rising Phoenix-like out of the ashes of dead religious beliefs, that one finds in the optimistic writings of the Pragmatic philosophers, we have science the destroyer of illusions, and as a consequence, the destroyer of moral purpose. When Walter Lippmann, who had a genuinely favorable disposition toward scientific forms of thought, spoke of the "acids of modernity," this is in part what he meant. The scientific view of the world gave human beings enormous power over nature, but only at the cost of the illusion that the world was somehow made for, or centered on, man. Joseph Wood Krutch's critical analysis of the cultural condition of the post-war world, *The Modern Temper* (1929), saw the disconnection between an ever-more powerful scientific form of thought, and a chastened vision that attempted to see the world in human terms, as at the heart of the problem. "Time was when the scientist, the poet, and the philosopher walked hand in hand. In the universe which the one perceived the other found himself comfortably at home."[4] But that time, said Krutch, has passed. Scientific thought establishes a world in which the spiritual needs of human beings can no longer be met. The cost of the new epistemic order, with all its intellectual and practical power, was the loss of the moral and religious order that had seen the universe in ways that could not be squared with the new science. Science was, in this view, the inevitable destroyer of faith.

Toward History and Philosophy of Science

One of the ways in which intellectuals dealt with science was to adopt a position outside of it. That is, if science studied in empirical term the natural and social worlds, one thing was apparently not in its purview: science itself. If scientific modes of thought were replacing others, perhaps those others might have the opportunity to reflect on science from the outside. In the years between World War I and World War II, a battle was joined between historians, sociologists, and philosophers about how to characterize science as a human activity. What academics in the second half of the twentieth century would come to call "science studies" was knit out of the various approaches developed by other disciplines during this earlier period. The meta-scientific discourse asked questions such as whether there is a "scientific method," what the basis for scientific authority is, how did scientific practices and beliefs come into being, what are the institutional basis for scientific thought, do scientists share a common set of values and beliefs, how is science related to the societies in which it takes place. Understanding science as an epistemic and social activity was to reflect on modernity itself. One of the emergent tensions in some of these concerns was between philosophical and historical ways of understanding, and particularly between an increasing focus in history on contextualized understandings and an increasing focus in some forms of philosophy on the logical form of scientific arguments. The image of science in these two disciplinary approaches was so different that it often seems that they were creating their own preferred versions of what they thought science should look like.

On the philosophy side, the innovation of the interwar years was the prominence of a new school of philosophy, sometimes called Logical Positivism, sometimes Logical Empiricism. The characteristic concerns of this school would form the basis for a turn away from history and culture as arenas of philosophical concern, and the rise of what came to be called "analytic philosophy" in the post-World War II era. The coming of Logical Empiricism would presage the great divide in philosophy between Anglo-American analytic philosophy, and Continental philosophy; the latter was deeply entrenched in cultural and moral, as well as epistemic, issues. This, despite the fact that Logical Empiricism had European continental origins. The characteristic concerns of French and German philosophy from Hegel forward would be characterized by the Logical Empiricists as "meaningless." The coming dominance of a school that took a specific idea of what science is and should be as the model for all knowledge would also end up sidelining Pragmatism and other philosophical approaches that were open to a wider field of possibilities. Even in critiquing the fallacies of Logical Empiricism in the postwar world, as W.V.O. Quine famously did in his "Two Dogmas of Empiricism" (1951), analytic philosophy operated within its sensibilities and the grounds of the problems that the Logical Empiricists had deemed legitimate. The idea that philosophy should model itself on the rigors of what it imagined science to be eliminated the more far-reaching concerns that continued to inform philosophy within the broader culture.

The Logical Empiricists—Otto Neurath, Rudolf Carnap, Carl Hempel, Herbert Feigl, Hans Reichenbach, among them—were an intellectually diverse group, many of them having Central European origins in philosophical schools that flourished in Berlin and Vienna in the post-World War I era. With the rise of Nazism in the 1930s, a number of the most important figures joined the huge intellectual wave of émigré intellectuals that would reshape American intellectual life in the 1930s and 40s, coming to occupy positions at major American universities such as Yale, Princeton, UCLA, and the University of Chicago. While the range of Logical Empiricism was wide-reaching and expansive, in the sense that there were no specific doctrines that all of the figures identified with it necessarily held, it was also narrowing, based on the idea that if philosophy was to be scientific, it had to abandon many of its previous preoccupations. So, on the one hand, against the fragmentation and cultural particularity that was elsewhere being emphasized (e.g. the anthropological school of Boas), they focused on what they called "the unity of science," the idea that all science—liberated from meaningless metaphysical claims and imprecise ways of thinking—shared a universal epistemic and theoretical orientation. This meant, for instance, that a widening divergence between the methods of social scientists—based at least in part on *verstehen* or empathetic understanding—and natural scientists—based on objective measurement—could be overcome by finding the unifying elements that made them both scientific. The doctrine of unity was also part of what we might call a revival of Enlightenment thought in a modernist key—by claiming the uniform nature of human understanding, the Logical Empiricists aligned themselves with a progressive view of human social liberation and reform, especially in the Cold War era following World War II.

Many of them, with Carnap at the head, developed a doctrine of science based on what they called "verification." Verificationism emphasized that statements could only be scientific if they were capable of being verified through empirical observation. Statements that presented no means of testing that would prove them false or true were, for Carnap, "metaphysical," a term of disparagement. Carnap saw philosophy as a means of eliminating metaphysics from any claim of scientific authority. Statements that could not be verified he considered to be meaningless statements. A central challenge to the verificationist doctrine came from Karl Popper, who is often associated with Logical Empiricism, and shared many of its concerns, but saw himself as outside the school. Popper argued in *The Logic of Scientific Discovery* (1934) that the criterion for meaningful scientific statements could not be verification, but must be falsification. That is, science did not trade in certitude, and no statement of a scientific nature could be ultimately verified, since one would have to observe all future instances for it to be a verified universal claim. But in order for a statement to be scientific, there had to be clear means by which empirical observation could declare it false. The model of hypothesis testing that has become such a familiar part of the image of science involved this notion. Claims that could not be disproven were not science. Philosophy had once been "queen of the sciences," but in the twentieth century, claims about epistemology, method, and knowledge had been shuttled off to the various academic disciplines. Logical Empiricism represents, in some respects, a restorationist attempt to make philosophy important again by claiming authority over science, although it was not an authority most scientists might recognize.

The Logical Empiricist approach to science was to imagine it as a matter of form, method, and principle, rather than as a cultural practice or historically situated pattern of belief. The focus on language (the form of statements or propositions) and logic (the pattern of reasoning) was an attempt to abstract scientific practice and belief from the particular conditions of particular societies and traditions. The historical sociology of science pointed in precisely the opposite way. Instead of establishing criteria for scientific knowing, it asked what science was as a social practice and how it was to be distinguished from other social institutions. It started from the proposition that science was a collective project—it did not take place in the minds of individuals freed from time and place. In fact, it was a peculiarly modern practice, of recent derivation, and happening in Europe since the sixteenth or seventeenth century. That is, the idea that there was something called a "Scientific Revolution" in the seventeenth century was not, in this view, a consequence of the natural logic of the human mind, but something specific to the time and place in which it occurred. Of course this meant that modern science was something different from the classically-derived "natural philosophy" that came out of Aristotelian thought. The fact that science in the mid-twentieth century was becoming a highly organized collective project, often funded by government, that it had developed its own institutions and training, made its social elements more visible. Why did science flourish in some societies and not others? Were there intellectual traditions from which scientific thought drew, or particular occupations or forms of government that were more likely to produce scientific thought and activity? What the sociology of science seemed to say was that in contradistinction to the idea that science could be understood in theoretical terms, it was only through the empirical observation of scientists acting under particular conditions that we could come to understand what science is. Science is not logical form, but existing practices.

The figure most responsible for creating this perspective was Robert Merton, often seen as the founding father of the sociology of science. Beginning in the 1930s, with a doctoral dissertation that set out to illuminate the relationship between science and society in seventeenth-century England, Merton developed a large corpus of work dealing with questions of science as a set of institutional practices, but also as rooted in particular cultural dispositions. He would go on to become one of the most influential sociologists of the twentieth century, not just for his work on the sociology of science, but for his "theories of the middle range," his articulation of functionalist sociology, and his contributions to role theory—Merton, for instance, created the concept of the "role model" that came into widespread usage in the last decades of the twentieth century. Importantly, Merton sought to see science less in terms of its epistemic and logical claims, as the Logical Empiricists were doing, and more as something that resembled a culture in the anthropological sense. That is, instead of trying to establish a science that stood apart from society, free of its prejudices and values, Merton insisted that science was a value-laden practice, only possible under specific social conditions, that had its own ethos. The idea of a "scientific ethos" was first identified by Merton in 1937, and fully articulated in a 1942 paper that became the basis for a broad discussion about the values of science. In the Cold War world immediately following World War II, Merton's scientific ethos was regularly invoked as part of an effort to define the values of liberal democracy as consonant with the outlook of science. Liberalism, it was imagined, was tolerant, open-minded, and non-dogmatic; science was the emblem of an intellectual freedom unbound by the rigid strictures of the past.

Merton claimed that there were four norms that "are in varying degrees internalized by the scientist, thus fashioning his scientific conscience.": universalism, communism, disinterestedness, and organized skepticism. By the first he meant that science was in no way dependent upon a special status of persons, but was universally available to all—it was not the authority of a priesthood but could be accessed by anybody with the proper university training. By communism, he meant that scientists believed that the findings of science were not proprietary, but that science rested on a shared body of beliefs. Disinterestedness meant that scientists were committed to a set of professional standards and had high sanctions against fraud or misrepresentation. Fourth, scientists embraced a skeptical sensibility, a willingness to be open to new findings that would challenge existing belief. The image of science here is not altogether unlike that subscribed to by Logical Empiricists, but for Merton these were cultural norms, and not primarily epistemic principles. In effect, Merton's sociology of science "culturized" the Logical Empiricists' version.[5]

In the years following, it became common for sociologists and their fellow travelers to speak of something they dubbed "the scientific community." The idea that scientists formed a community, with a shared set of interests and practices was a way to bring together epistemic and sociological perspectives. The idea of "community," which has in our own day become a catchall for any group, no matter how separated in space and condition, whose members share an interest or identity, brought with it some of the notions associated with premodern life. A community—in contrast to the urban alienation of modern society with its fragmentation and marginal men—possessed a kind of homogeneity of interests and a bounded separation from the world. That one of modernity's most dynamic and progressive forces—science—should be refigured in communitarian terms, speaks to the contradictory nature of modern thought. But the idea of a scientific community was coming into being at a moment when the bureaucratic form of Big Science, based on massive government funding, was providing a sense of the future of research. The claim of a scientific community was also a claim for the autonomy of science, the notion that scientists alone shared the values that made science possible and that government entities should provide funding, but not direction. The image of science as corrupted by government was given its most lasting image in the Lysenko Affair, in which the Soviet Union endorsed the theories of the biologist Trofim Lysenko as state policy during the 1930s and 40s. Lysenko rejected Darwinian natural selection and Mendelian genetics and promoted a politically-guided policy of agricultural expansion based on what other scientists regarded as pseudo-science. Scientists in the Soviet Union who maintained their commitment to the intellectual autonomy of science and to genetics were heavily persecuted, imprisoned, and sometimes executed. Lysenkoism became a symbol of the ways in which political authority and ideology could corrupt science. The idea that scientists should decide through their own independent procedures and debates what constituted science, that the scientific world was an autonomous community that acted under its own directives, was a way for American science to simultaneously receive government funding and be intellectually autonomous.

By the 1950s, a widespread discourse about science, its methods and claims, its institutional existence, and its values had come to play a role in discussions of public life. This discourse included authors such as Robert Oppenheimer, former head of the Manhattan Project, responsible for the creation of the atomic bomb during World War II; The British polymath Jacob Bronowski, whose *Science and Human Values* (1956) arose out of lectures he gave at MIT in 1953; the Hungarian émigré Michael Polanyi, who fused religious, political, and scientific values in *Science, Faith, and Society* (1946); and Barnard Sociologist Bernard Barber, author of *Science and Social Order* (1952), among many other. The idea that the highly organized and specialized activity that was modern science had to be seen in light of its implications for the most widely held and generalized moral and political values was a stock element of modern thought at mid-century. As scientists were called on more and more to intervene in political issues—regulation of nuclear weapons, public health, agricultural policy—many people began to question the idea that science could be seen as an autonomous realm of pure knowledge.

The Two Cultures

In 1959 the British novelist and physical chemist C.P. Snow delivered lectures at Cambridge University that were then published as *The Two Cultures and the Scientific Revolution*. The "two cultures" thesis set off a firestorm in both Britain and the United States. Snow, staking out his authority on his claimed membership in both groups, argued that the divide between scientists and what he called "literary intellectuals" had grown so great that there was no longer the possibility of communication between the two groups. They had effectively become two distinct cultures, with fundamentally different understandings of the world they lived in. From his point of view, the traditional literary intellectuals were to blame—they had affected a deliberate ignorance of science as a point of pride and had rejected the central progressive values he associated with science. Part of the problem was the British system of education, which Snow contrasted with the American system—by focusing on tracked specialization, it had erased the possibility of a common bridging body of knowledge and heightened the divide. But it was, above all, the values and antagonisms of the literary intellectuals that lay at the heart of the problem. According to Snow, the literary intellectuals were all backward-looking, skeptical of change, Luddites who saw scientific developments as negative aids to an industrial capitalist society they abhorred. As several of Snow's critics noted, his choice to use George Orwell's dystopian novel *1984* (1948) as an example of the literary intellectual's refusal of the future seemed odd, since Orwell's attitude toward the future surely showed a concern for it, and it would be odd to see any scientists explicitly embrace the world he pictured. Many literary intellectuals had been steeped in left-wing politics and committed to a socialist future. Prominent figures such as the British Marxist Raymond Williams were very much concerned with the social and intellectual effects of scientific, technological, and industrial development; Snow's image of the literary intellectual, many of his critics claimed, didn't seem to match up with the actual existing intellectuals in Western societies. Snow couldn't quite make up his mind whether literary intellectuals were traditionalists or avant-gardists with a critical antipathy toward modernity. Scientists came off much more favorably in Snow's account; they were merely befuddled by the odd beliefs and attitudes of literary culture and had a much more optimistic, sensible attitude toward knowledge, progress, and the improvement of the world in which they lived.

Snow struck a chord, but not just because he identified a problem arising out of specialization and the decline of the nineteenth-century educated generalist, something that had been frequently observed by others, and not just because he framed the problem of intellectual division in Cold War terms, as he did. It was in large part his disparagement of the cultural authority of literary intellectuals, and his program for scientists and technologists to seize the mantle to remake the world in industrial terms that drew the ire of critics. It was also his choice to describe the difference as a matter of culture, to think of scientists as belonging to a culture, that gave a modern tone to his critique. In other words, he drew on an anthropological concept of culture to frame the role and place of science in modern life. In describing the culture of scientists, for instance, Snow pointed to "common attitudes, common standards and patterns of behavior, common approaches and assumptions." "C.P. Snow's scientists," said Steven Marcus, gesturing to Margaret Mead in his review of *The Two Cultures*, "might very well be Samoans."[6] In Lionel Trilling's lengthy critique of Snow, he saw the whole body of contrasts and evaluations between science and literature taking place in what he called "the cultural mode of thought."[7] The judgments that Snow made, the discriminations of his thinking, aimed to see the hidden pattern of thought, emotion, style, in the lives of "traditional" and scientific intellectuals; he used the concept of culture to make judgments that were ultimately aesthetic ones, matters of taste. So, Snow, a chemist by training, a novelist by avocation, stepped outside of both frames of reference to identify the characteristic attitudes and orientations of each by appealing to a third frame of reference: the anthropological concept of culture. It is clear that by "science" Snow understood natural science, but the very structure of the claim of a polar opposition between the two cultures makes social scientific perspectives disappear—they are the lens, rather than the object of vision.

What is striking is that such an extended discussion of Snow's argument took place in an intellectual world that had seized on the authority of science to remake traditional humanistic attitudes. Logical Empiricism represents the attempt to make philosophy scientific and more rigorous. Literary intellectuals in the period from the 1920s, when T.S. Eliot published his essay collection, *The Sacred Wood*, to the 1960s, developed an approach to literary criticism that rejected what they regarded as impressionistic criticism and a lack of rigor in the study of literature. The so-called "New Criticism" of John Crowe Ransom, Allan Tate, Cleanth Brooks, and others, sought to elevate the practice of literary analysis to something resembling a science. The adaptation of empiricism to the idea of "close reading" of literary texts was part of this effort. The New

Critics argued that the specifically literary text could be abstracted from its condition of creation—the author's intention, the social context, its ideological orientation—and treated as a discrete object, governed by its own structure and form. In some ways, this was like the contemporaneous movement in art criticism, with Clement Greenberg at its head, to emphasize formalism and formal analysis of visual arts. We might see this movement, at its height in the post-World War II era, as a kind of aesthetic "revolt against anti-formalism." The notion that the poem—and New Criticism privileged poetry over prose forms—worked in precise ways that could be identified with the tensions and contradictions contained in the language of the poem itself, allowed the New Critics to reject what they called "the intentional fallacy" and "the affective fallacy." The first referred to the idea that the meaning of a literary work should be identified with the intention of the author; the second that a work should be evaluated in terms of its emotional effect on readers. The New Critics removed both author and reader from the equation and treated the literary text as its own distinct object. It's hard to square Snow's vision of two cultures with a world in which literary critics and philosophers sought to borrow a vision of authority associated with empirical science and rigorous method.

Ambivalence

In the wake of the successful test of the Atomic Bomb in 1945, and before the world would come to know its destructive power, J. Robert Oppenheimer, director of the Manhattan Project, reminded himself of a line from the *Bhagavad Gita*: "Now I am become death, destroyer of worlds." While the general American response to the dropping of nuclear bombs on Hiroshima and Nagasaki was positive—it meant the end of a long war—in the years following, the anxiety about what science was capable of would only increase. The incredible power of nuclear physics to understand the world, to remake it, to provide the means to end the world, would require some kind of control over the destructive power—science could not be relied on as an ethical system. The idea that science was not inherently good or bad, that as a means of knowing it was epistemologically powerful, but amoral, might be seen as one of Oppenheimer's legacies, although in truth, it was Max Weber who gave this idea its most powerful earlier formulation. In 1954, Oppenheimer wrote

> if we are to take heart from any beneficent influence that science may have for the common understanding, we need to do so both with modesty and with a full awareness that these relationships are not inevitably and inexorably for man's good.[8]

Throughout the modern period, there was both celebration and suspicion about science's power and the way in which it might serve both the progressive and destructive ends of human desire. There is a long tradition of suspicion of what might be unleashed by the power of knowledge—Adam and Eve in the Garden of Eden, of course, but Faust and Frankenstein also. Modernist apprehension was based on the fact that science and its means of knowing had become central to the way of life in modern societies. Science might be able to contribute to moral order, to point to a way of life based on tolerance, open-mindedness, and lack of absolutist forms of power; but science, whatever it might be, did not operate as a force in itself. It was wielded by human beings in institutional contexts, pursuing goals that were not intrinsic to science.

Notes

1 John Dewey, *The Public and Its Problems: An Essay in Political Inquiry* (New York: Henry Holt & Co, 1927), p. 208.
2 Max Weber, "Science as a Vocation," in H.H. Gerth and C. Wright Mills, trans. and eds., *From Max Weber: Essays in Sociology* (New York: Oxford University Press, 1945), p. 155.
3 Max Weber, *The Protestant Ethic and the Spirit of Capitalism*, trans. Talcott Parsons (New York: Charles Scribner's Sons, 1930), p. 182.
4 Joseph Wood Krutch, *The Modern Temper: A Study and a Confession* (New York: Harcourt, Brace & Co., 1929), p. 12.
5 Robert K. Merton, "The Normative Structure of Science" (1942), in Norman W. Storer, ed., *The Sociology of Science: Theoretical and Empirical Investigations* (Chicago, IL: University of Chicago Press, 1973), pp. 267–278.
6 Steven Marcus, "Intellectuals, Scientists, and the Future," *Commentary* 30 (January 1, 1960), p. 165.
7 Lionel Trilling, "Science, Literature & Culture: A Comment on the Leavis-Snow Controversy," *Commentary* 33 (June 1, 1962), pp. 475–477.
8 J. Robert Oppenheimer, *Science and the Common Understanding* (New York: Simon and Schuster, 1954), p. 9.

8 From Protestant Hegemony to Religious Pluralism

The question of the role of religion as belief, as institutional framework, as lived experience, has been central to modernist thought. For some, the narrative of modernization has been one of secularization, the replacement of common religious frameworks for public life and moral order with instrumental, naturalistic, or rational frameworks. Declining religious faith and the rise of practices and ideologies disentangled from supernatural belief are, in this understanding, fundamental to the process of becoming modern. The secularization thesis, however, has had its share of critics. For some, pointing to continuing high levels of belief in God and the force and power of religious motivations in twentieth-century political movements, both Left and Right, the idea of a systematic shift from religious to secular forms of authority and belief seems overstated. For them, the persistence of religious belief as a moral, political, and social framework for large numbers of people is the story of an ever-contested ground of modern life, rather than a sweeping shift from religious to secular frames of understanding. The proponents of the secularization thesis, on the one hand, and those of the religious persistence thesis, on the other, often seem to be talking past one another. Secularization, says the one, does not mean the disappearance of religious belief, but a rearticulation of that belief as essentially private; people with deep religious convictions from multiple faith traditions can meet in the public square with a shared frame of reference, because public life is secular. Secularization, in this view, is not so much a decline in, but a relocation of, religious belief. It is a continuation of the long-term shift arising out of the Protestant Reformation of the sixteenth century—a turn from external public order to private individual faith. Even here, then, the argument is that secularism is itself a form of Protestant belief, rather than a neutral one. The advocates for religious persistence tend to see public battles and conflicts as arising out of religious convictions, and humanistic and/or atheistic frameworks as one position in a Culture War that is defined by the struggle for whose religious values will triumph, rather than by neutrality on the question of religious belief.

The struggle for the meaning of religious belief, for the very understanding of what religion is, took place in a world in which the fixed standards and orders received from the past in a world perceived to be unchanging were being called into question. What form should religious belief take if it was to meet the moment? Was religion to be a rock of stability in a mutable world, bringing it into conflict with new knowledge, new or different moral standards, different ways of life, and providing a means to constrain unleashed and destructive forces? Or was religion, in good Darwinian fashion, to maintain its cultural authority by adapting to the conditions of modern life, reworking its principles of interpretation to square with a changed intellectual world, re-evaluating what both the core and expendable elements of religious belief might be? We have come to see this as a battle between those committed to orthodoxy and those committed to modernism or liberalism. This gets the story only half right, for the proponents of orthodoxy were never defending an invariant religion, as much as they sought, in the grand tradition of restorationist movements, to do so. The historian of religion avers that religious belief and doctrine is always changing, that there is no singular content to orthodox belief, but that the idea of orthodoxy, and its flipside, heresy, have been powerful rallying cries for those who seek to imagine an unchanging and absolute vision of religious truth. That is, those who claim the mantle of religious orthodoxy are as much the result of modern thought as they are opponents of it. Conservative upholders of religious orthodoxy were often reacting and responding to changes, adapting what counted as orthodoxy to the unprecedented conditions of modern life. In fact, the very category of "religion" as a way to talk about belief systems and practices is modern; it requires a stance outside any particular system of belief to regard all of them as comparable.

The battles between religious conservatives and religious liberals were crosscut by the growing prominence of religious pluralism of a kind that had not existed before the late nineteenth century. While there were Catholics and Jews in early nineteenth-century America, they were small and discrete minorities. The public culture was dominated by a Protestant hegemony, and the extent of religious tolerance tended to be limited to Protestants of various sects and denominations. In the 1840s and 50s when large numbers of Catholic immigrants came to the United States from Ireland and Germany, some Americans responded with nativist movements which had a strong anti-Catholic component. The identification of Protestant Christianity with intellectual liberty and republican political order reinforced an idea that non-Protestant religions were antithetical to American values. From the 1880s through World War I, waves of new immigrants from Southern and Eastern Europe—Catholics from Italy and Poland, Eastern Orthodox Christians from Greece and the Slavic nations,

Jews from Russia and Eastern Europe—remade the Eastern seaboard and the Midwest, while Mexican Catholics were a prominent part of the population in the Southwest. The idea of a uniform homogenous Protestant America that had provided powerful cultural and public authority could no longer be assumed. Anti-immigrant sentiment could be both racialist and religious in orientation. So, if we assume that Protestant leaders had to respond to scientific change, such as Darwinism and geological science, industrial change and its creation of a class society amidst the breakdown of community autonomy and control, the new racial order of the post-Reconstruction South, and the rise of alternative sources of authority in the universities, they also had to grapple with a world in which multiple forms of religious belief and practice were becoming more prominent. In this context, freedom of religion and religious tolerance could appear to be a loss of authority for Protestants, rather than the conditions for strengthening religious authority.

The Coming of Protestant Modernism

One of the major developments of post-Enlightenment thought in nineteenth-century Germany was a new "scientific" or empirical approach to theology and Biblical criticism. The so-called "higher criticism" of the Bible sought to examine, using scholarly methods, the history of biblical texts and their versions. Historical criticism shifted attention away from the close reading or textual criticism, which was referred to, in contradistinction, as the "lower criticism." By situating the creation and variation of the books of the Bible in human history, and attempting to identify authors and the forms by which the Bible was composed and took its present form, the higher criticism, at least to its critics, threatened the integrity of scripture, and in particular, the idea that the Bible was the word of God, delivered directly and immediately through inspiration. To be clear, the intent of historical criticism was not to "debunk" the authority of the Bible. For the majority of scholars who took up some form of historical criticism, the idea was to establish a firmer more scientific basis for Christian belief, one that could be imagined to be compatible with modern forms of knowing. If one of the threats to religious authority in the later nineteenth century was the rise of secular intellectual authority in the form of the modern research university, the willingness of theological seminaries to sanction forms of scholarship that would compete with scientific authority on the terms of modern empiricist epistemology was really an attempt to coopt science to affirm religious authority.

In the era after the Civil War, American and English-speaking Protestant theologians took up German methods, as in so many other areas of study. The higher criticism entered the English-speaking world with a bang: the dispute over the publication in England of *Essays and Reviews* (1860), a collection of essays by theologically modernist Church of England clerics, far outweighed, in volume of written response, the controversy over the near-simultaneous appearance of Darwin's *On the Origin of Species*. The denial of Biblical miracles, the affirmation of the findings of German higher criticism, the embrace of progressive revelation, and other "rational" approaches to Christianity, suggested to some that attempts to square Christian belief with modern forms of secular authority could only destabilize the authority of the fixed truth to be found in the Bible. In the United States in the decades after the Civil War, several theological scholars took up the mantle of the higher criticism. The best known among them was the Presbyterian theologian Charles Augustus Briggs, who was tried for heresy and excommunicated for his publications, and particularly for the inaugural lecture he gave at the opening of Union Theological Seminary in 1889 in New York City. Briggs was always insistent that the identification of factual errors and multiple versions of texts did nothing to harm the authority of scripture, but in fact affirmed it. Turning a blind eye to such errors and variations, he argued, or pretending that they did not exist, was akin to admitting that their presence would undermine scriptural authority, while recognizing minor errors would not overturn his general idea that the Bible was "theophanic," organized so as to reveal God to man.

The sticking point between Briggs and his fellow Presbyterian critics—many of them associated with the conservative Princeton Seminary—was the idea of fixity of the Bible, and therefore the word of God. Although Briggs and his Princeton adversaries shared a commitment to empirical, factual study of the Bible, the latter developed the idea that the Bible was free of factual errors, and as the product of inspiration was therefore "inerrant." The higher criticism made the Bible appear to be the product of human beings, creating it under secular conditions, and therefore not a unified, absolute, and fixed source of authority delivered directly by God. The dispute focused on such technical matters as how the Bible was "inspired." Was it inerrant because every word was inspired, or did the form of inspiration permit minor errors and differences that did not change the general purpose and meaning of the text? Briggs, for instance, pitted the idea of "verbal inspiration" against the idea of "plenary inspiration." Verbal inspiration would argue that every word of the Bible was inspired in the precise form it was given. Plenary inspiration would argue that the overall purpose and meaning of the text was inspired, but that human beings might introduce errors and different ways of wording the text. The doctrine of verbal inspiration necessarily ran into contradictions with the empirical facts, while the idea of plenary inspiration that Briggs promoted allowed for the great variation to be found historically.

Conservative theologians like Archibald Hodge and Benjamin Warfield insisted that their doctrine of Biblical inerrancy was the orthodox position of Reformed theology, rather than simply a response to modernism. But they, too, tended to rely on the authority of empiricism and "fact," insisting that the Bible was a factual record. Modernist thought turned the Bible into an empirically observable set of documents, and the inductive method made the idea of verbal inspiration seem unreasonable and not consistent with the facts on the ground. Briggs and other modernist theologians sought to salvage God's authority by affirming the variety of God's revelation in empirical terms.

While the dispute over historical criticism of the Bible highlighted the challenge of reaffirming Christian belief in a culture which had kicked the legs out from underneath the idea of fixed, stable, and absolute truths, modernism and theological liberalism took many forms other than the higher criticism. Throughout the nineteenth century, movements and ideas that challenged some of the central tenets of Reformed theology, codified in the Church of England's Westminster Confession of 1646, moved much of American Protestant thought away from the dominant Calvinist orthodoxy inherited from the seventeenth century. A new emphasis on the power of human agency, rationality, empirical science, ideas about progress, as well as changing moral values and beliefs, sought to adapt Christian belief to the changing standards and ideas of the modern world as a way to strengthen faith. In New England, Unitarianism and its offshoot, Transcendentalism, claimed the authority of human reason and intuition against religious doctrines that increasingly appeared contradictory, such as the doctrine of the Trinity that made God simultaneously three persons (The Father, The Holy Spirit, and Christ) and one. The focus on the spiritual authority of the self, rather than on strict adherence to a faith codified as dogma, meant that conscience and intuition, for instance, trumped the written word. The dispute over slavery in the antebellum era led antislavery thinkers to the conclusion that there was no uniform and absolute moral authority in a scripture that often seemed to provide much more solid foundations for proslavery theorizing; many of them came to argue that moral ideals and standards were subject to historical progress, rather than fixed in the recognition of the legitimacy of slavery in the Bible.

For some, Christian notions of limited salvation seemed inconsistent with an increasing focus on spiritual egalitarianism and humanitarianism; the result was the movement toward "universalism," the notion that God will save and provide eternal life for *all* human beings, rather than only God's elect few. This universalist impulse could be expressed in a broader recognition that Christianity was only one of the avenues by which God might reveal Himself to man and that various World religions were equally legitimate means of realizing God's purposes. The Unitarian minister Thomas Wentworth Higginson, for instance, claimed in 1870 that all religions

> show the same aim, the same symbols, the same forms, the same weaknesses, the same aspirations. Looking at these points of unity, we might say there is but one religion under many forms, whose essential creed is the Fatherhood of God, and the Brotherhood of Man,—disguised by corruptions, symbolized by mythologies, ennobled by virtues, degraded by vices, but still the same.[1]

The attempt, of course, was to preserve some kind of fixed inclusive unity, that could meet the variety of conditions, but to do it at the expense of the fixity and truth of any particular religious doctrine. When the Chicago World's Fair of 1893 brought faith leaders from various religious traditions around the world to what was dubbed The World's Parliament of Religions, the agenda was to construct a forum for interfaith dialogue premised on the idea that all religions contained a common core of concerns. The ecumenical approach was concerned with demonstrating the commonalities of, and points of contact between, Buddhism, Islam, Hinduism, Judaism, and Christianity among other religions.

Christianity, throughout the late nineteenth and early twentieth centuries, also had to counter the philosophical critiques of religion that, unlike Protestant modernism, were actually concerned with debunking religious belief. Karl Marx famously declared that religion was "the opium of the people," and an illusion that kept the majority in a condition of oppression. The Marxist tradition argued that religion was an ideological expression of material conditions; man creates God, rather than God creating man. Marxism provided its own utopian goal, but a this-worldly one to supplant the other-worldly ends of Christianity. Friedrich Nietzsche's radical critique of Christianity as the expression of a "slave morality," and his proclamation that "God is dead," saw religion, and its self-destruction in nihilism and atheism, as the product of the human will. When Nietzsche's thought came to the United States in the early decades of the twentieth century, it was often those most concerned with the challenge to religious authority who took up his writings as the most penetrating critiques of religion. Sigmund Freud, in a series of books—*Totem and Taboo* (1913), *The Future of an Illusion* (1927), *Moses and Monotheism* (1939)—argued for the psychological origins of religion, and for those Americans who took up Freudian psychoanalysis as a critical tool, its atheistic sensibility was certainly part of its appeal. The difference between Protestant modernists and conservatives was that the former frequently believed they had to take the critiques coming from the likes of Marx, Nietzsche, and Freud seriously, while the latter tended to see the threat to religious belief as coming from the modernists and their attempts to adapt Christianity to new circumstances.

Perhaps more prominent than European theoretical critiques of religion was the growth of free thought, a movement that embraced uncertainty and skepticism as a response to dogmatic assurance and that aimed the tools of critical reason at the received Christian body of belief. In 1869, the British Darwinian T.H. Huxley coined the term "agnostic," as a new kind of belief that was neither the positive assertion of belief in God ("theism") nor the negative denial of God's existence ("atheism"), but the expression of the inadequacy of human beings to know ultimate and supernatural truths. In the United States, the agnostic position became most highly identified with the popular lecturer Robert G. Ingersoll, who was dubbed "The Great Agnostic." The arguments of agnostics like Ingersoll sought to demonstrate that none of the beliefs of Christianity, or alternatively other religions, could survive a critical evaluation of their foundations. In part, Ingersoll sought to impugn the power-based motives of the creators and promoters of religions, evaluate the consequences for liberty and thought of hewing to religious belief, and demonstrate that religious belief was not a product of the truth value of beliefs, but of accidents of birth, circumstance, and education. Ingersoll declared "The Foundation of Christianity has crumbled, has disappeared, and the entire fabric must fall." In its place, he claimed what he called "the religion of reason." But reason appeared to have only a negative consequence for religious belief, rather than providing a substantive body of belief. "[L]et us admit the limitations of our minds, and let us have the courage and candor to say: We do not know."[2] For Ingersoll, the great benefit of not knowing was that it allowed for maximal freedom of thought, unconstrained by fixed doctrine. The agnostic position of Ingersoll—always the belief of a small minority—expressed both the epistemic and ethical problem of fixed belief.

Similarly, while the vast majority of African Americans remained committed to the centrality of religiosity—a centrality articulated and emphasized by DuBois in the chapter "Of the Faith of the Fathers," in *The Souls of Black Folk*—some Black thinkers came to free thought and agnosticism/atheism, but often for different reasons than Ingersoll and his white colleagues. For many of these thinkers, the theodicy issue, or the problem of evil, was more significant than epistemological questions. Why had God permitted slavery to exist? What kind of God was it that sanctioned the cruelties of racial oppression and the violence done in its name? How could a society steeped in Christianity permit race-based lynchings? Frederick Douglass and others had emphasized the ways in which self-professed Christians were the most vicious slavers and that a particular interpretation of Christianity had given license and sanction to the system of race-based slavery. For Douglass this was cause not to abandon Christianity, but to affirm a "true" Christianity against the corruptions of American religion. For others in his wake, Christianity, and sometimes theism itself, could not be redeemed. A critical tradition of Black secularism and free thought would be a significant component of Black political thought through the twentieth century. Figures like David Cincore, R.S. King, Lord A. Nelson, and Hubert Harrison, in the late nineteenth and early twentieth centuries took the critique of Christianity to more definite agnostic and atheistic positions.

We might think of Protestant modernism as the middle way between the more radical critiques of religious belief, on the one hand, and the conservative attempts to construct a stable orthodoxy out of the received materials of the past. Modernists were willing to jettison ideas such as Biblical inerrancy; the literal truth of scripture as a historical record; doctrines that seemed cruel by Victorian moral standards, such as limited atonement and infant damnation; the idea of the authority of Christianity independent of scientific knowledge; and the idea that Christianity, or any particular variant of it, was the sole true religion. They did so, however, to affirm what they regarded as the core of religious belief—a faith in a world ordered by God, in which a larger moral purpose rested on a supernatural basis. For conservatives, the accommodations proposed by modernists turned faith into a relativistic practice and undermined the claims of transcendent and absolute truth. If religious doctrine was subordinate to historically changing standards of knowledge and morality, the idea that Christianity was the fount of truth and morality seemed imperiled.

From Theology to Religious Studies

Throughout the nineteenth century, proponents concerned with legitimating the intellectual validity of Christian belief and providing intellectual training for the ministry had created seminaries and institutions of higher learning to develop the scholarly field of theology. All of the features of emerging professions—degree granting and certification, professional standards, scholarly journals—were extended to theology as an academic discipline. But, with the rise of the research university, an alternative approach to thinking about religion challenged the theological approach. Theology assumed a position within a religious tradition, and was concerned with applying critical tools to developing doctrine; it assumed the validity and truth claims of the religious belief system within which it operated, and sought to analyze and stake out positions on a variety of issues—methods of biblical interpretation, mechanisms of salvation, the Christian view of history and the future, the nature of the human-divine relationship, etc. With the rise of secular institutions of learning, some scholars began to put forward a new, non-theological approach to the study of religion. The field we know today as religious studies was a product of a way of thinking about religion in social scientific, psychological, and humanistic terms that had Enlightenment-era roots, but became an academic subject in a comparative anthropological framework. That framework was less concerned with the truth of religious belief and more with its social and psychological function and purpose. The Scottish anthropologist James Frazer's *The Golden Bough* (1890) was one of the most prominent and influential works that sought a comparative framework for religious belief, including Christianity in its comparison with "primitive" forms of ritual and magical practice. The idea that Christianity was one form of some more general or universal category called "religion" that all societies possessed, situated the academic observer outside of Christian belief. While Frazer maintained an evolutionary framework of the kind that would be challenged by Franz Boas and his acolytes, he put Christian belief into a pre-scientific stage. From the point of view of anthropologists, Christian theologians could be regarded as propagators of mythologies, and not so far in advance of shamans and priests dispensing magical practices and truths.

Not all comparative study of religion was anthropological. The philosopher and psychologist William James created a framework for thinking about "religious experience" in a cross-cultural psychological way. Drawing on the long-standing commitments of American evangelical Christianity to the centrality of experience and spiritual conversion as the core of the relationship of man to the divine, James's Gifford lectures of 1901–1902, published as *The Varieties of Religious Experience* (1902), stripped religion of its formal institutional and theological elements. Religion, for James, as for Protestantism more broadly, was interior, experiential, a kind of orientation of the self toward the world. But James's analytical position lay outside religious experience, evaluating and describing its content, not for its truth or even its moral function, but for what it expressed about the values and needs of those who underwent its most extreme manifestations. James rejected the genetic fallacy that would make religious experience—visions, saintly ascetic purification, fixation on holiness or evil—simply a result of material and biological disorders, a matter of hallucinations and compulsions; the value of religious experience could not be reduced to epiphenomena of a materialist substratum. Rather, in good pragmatic fashion, James asked what religious experience added to the world, the value it brought to human life. Regardless of its truth or probability, James argued, religious experience was about the expansion of human consciousness and possibility, a desire that there be something more than a world governed by material reality and rational explanation. Religion was the vehicle that pushed past the limitations of normal consciousness. *The Varieties of Religious Experience* was generous in its salvaging of religion—as opposed to the critical dismantling often undertaken by agnostics and atheists—but it did so by making the content of doctrine and the role of ministry and the church essentially peripheral to the reality of religion. This general orientation toward religion was evident in James's earlier essay "The Will to Believe" (1896), in which he developed a philosophical defense of theistic belief as legitimate in a culture with epistemic commitments to empirical science. In fact, he argued that agnosticism was on no more solid ground than theism, since it was similarly driven by the desires of the passional self—the agnostic choice to suspend belief was, in practical terms, a denial of God, driven by a fear of being duped into believing something that might not be true.

The Reaction Against Modernism and the Modernist/Fundamentalist Controversy

The first decades of the twentieth century saw a reaction against the various forms of Protestant modernism, a reaction which blossomed in the 1920s into a very public dispute and controversy between modernists and conservatives. Between 1910 and 1915, the Testimony Publishing Company of Chicago, backed financially by Lyman Stewart, the founder of Union Oil, issued a series of 90 essays in 12 pamphlets collectively titled *The Fundamentals*. The authors of the individual essays represented a diverse group of ministers, theologians, and thinkers from a variety of Christian denominations, united by a concern with preserving a vision of Christian orthodoxy against what they regarded as the threat of modernism and theological liberalism. *The Fundamentals* sought both to articulate a set of doctrines deemed to be foundational and essential to the Christian faith, and to provide a concerted critique of modernist innovations, such as the higher criticism, adaptation to scientific naturalism, including evolutionary theory, and the modernist rejection of doctrines that could not be squared with historical, logical, and scientific understanding. Those who embraced the purposes and goals articulated in this series of essays came to be called "Fundamentalists," a term which has, over the course of the past century, taken on additional meanings and connotations. Fundamentalism was born as a rearguard action against Protestant modernism, so its definition of the essential and necessary components of Christian orthodoxy were those perceived to be under threat by adaptations to secular, scientific, and modern historical understandings. Fundamentalism sought, against an emerging pluralism, a uniform, fixed, and singular body of beliefs for evangelical Christianity. Doctrines of the virgin birth, the resurrection, the reality of miracles, the factual truth of the Bible, unmerited salvation, substitutionary atonement, the inspired nature of the Bible: these were all juxtaposed to what were regarded as the threats of higher criticism, and modern materialist science. The battle for the soul of mainline Protestant Christianity was engaged.

In 1922, the liberal Baptist minister Harry Emerson Fosdick delivered a sermon to First Presbyterian Church in New York City, entitled "Shall the Fundamentalists Win?" This direct attack on fundamentalist practices, if not beliefs, was published in the journal *Christian Work* and created a firestorm that redounded through the 1920s. Fosdick saw in fundamentalist attempts to regulate doctrine and control the church, as well as attempts to control state legislatures to mandate education consistent with the fundamentalist understanding of the Bible, a kind of intolerance. His argument was the classic liberal one—there is room in the church for people with modernist and fundamentalist views, as long as one does not seek to exclude the other. The threat of fundamentalism, in Fosdick's view, was in imposing a mandated dogma, it would drive from the church sincere Christians who believed that "We must be able to think our modern life clear through in Christian terms, and to do that we also must be able to think our Christian life clear through in modern terms." Fosdick was clear that fundamentalists and conservatives were two different groups: "All Fundamentalists are conservatives, but not all conservatives are Fundamentalists. The best conservatives can often give lessons to the liberals in true liberality of spirit, but the Fundamentalist program is essentially illiberal and intolerant."[3] The liberal image of Fundamentalism as an intolerant reactionary program aimed at imposing its own dogma as the one truth was central to Fosdick's critique. But Fosdick's liberal inclusion of opposing views was, in many ways, an expression of the very modernism that Fundamentalists saw as a threat: Fosdick was taking a side in the modernist/fundamentalist dispute, not simply offering a neutral position of inclusion of all perspectives—or, rather, the neutral inclusion of all positions *was* a liberal position. Fosdick's perspective conflated two things—the attempt to counter modernism by insisting on a set of core essential doctrines, on the one hand, and the attempt to shut down dissenting positions as heretical, on the other. Behind this was the notion, perhaps, that a commitment to fixity was antithetical to progress and open possibility. Fosdick and his intellectual compatriots' view of Christianity became ensconced in the magazine *The Christian Century*, which was to liberal Christianity what *The New Republic* was to Progressivism—an influential and long-lasting voice across the twentieth century.

Perhaps the greatest conservative response to Fosdick and modernism came from the Princeton School Presbyterian New Testament scholar, J. Gresham Machen. Machen was sympathetic to many of the elements of Fundamentalism but sought to distance himself from a thorough identification with the movement, partly as a matter of intellectual style. But he offered the most thorough critique of Protestant modernism to be found in the decades between World War I and II. In *Christianity and Liberalism* (1923) Machen argued that the crisis was not between two ways of being Christian, orthodox and liberal, but between two different and opposed belief systems: Christianity and liberalism. That liberalism uses the vocabulary of Christianity and disguises itself as a variant of Christianity, only makes it more difficult to see clearly that the modernist accommodations to science and social change created an entirely different philosophical outlook. That meant there could be no compromise between modernism and Christianity. "Modern materialism," said Machen,

> especially in the realm of psychology, is not content with occupying the lower quarters of the Christian city, but pushes its way into all the higher reaches of life; it is just as much opposed to the philosophical idealism of the liberal preacher as to the Biblical doctrines that the liberal preacher has abandoned in the interests of peace. Mere concessiveness [sic], therefore, will never succeed in avoiding the intellectual conflict. In the intellectual battle of the present day there can be no "peace without victory"; one side or the other must win.[4]

A house divided against itself, Machen seemed to say, cannot stand. All accommodation to modern science and belief was an introduction of the enemy inside the gate. Modernism might conceive of Christianity, à la the Social Gospel, as a way of living; for Machen, Christianity was rooted in doctrine, and the Christian life was impossible without the priority of doctrine. Machen's stance on Calvinist orthodoxy was, on the one hand, deeply antimodern and reactionary; on the other, his temper was libertarian, anti-statist, and modern in his concern with intellectual freedom. He always seemed to be saying that so-called liberalism was really illiberal and the source of intolerance. In the battle in the 1920s over the future direction of Princeton Theological Seminary, the bastion of Presbyterian conservatism, he lost to the liberals and at the end of the decade, departed to create an orthodox institution, Westminster Theological Seminary, in Pennsylvania.

The modernist/fundamentalist conflict received its greatest public presence in the media circus that surrounded the 1925 Scopes Trial in Tennessee. The state legislature had restricted the biology curriculum in Tennessee public schools to prevent the teaching of biological evolution, because it conflicted with Biblical accounts of origins. John Scopes, a teacher in the town of Dayton, deliberately contravened the law, and a trial ensued, but one designed to draw national media attention. Scopes was represented by the prominent attorney Clarence Darrow, and the prosecution enlisted William Jennings Bryan, former Democratic presidential candidate and secretary of state as a witness. While there were numerous issues at stake in the Scopes Trial—for Bryan, for instance, the democratic right of Tennesseans to control their schools, for Darrow, first amendment rights to free speech—, and there was little in the way of theological or biological debate, the trial was imagined as a battle between fundamentalist Christianity and its commitment to Biblical inerrancy, on the one hand, and modern scientific knowledge, on the other. This focus was crosscut by an emerging conflict, present throughout the 1920s, between urban cosmopolitanism and rural provincialism. Although Scopes lost the case, the result of the Scopes Trial was to give lasting weight to an image in the minds of educated secular thinkers that Fundamentalism was backward-looking, anti-intellectual, overly literalist in its interpretation of the Bible, and opposed to progress.

Religion in the Cold War World

The question of religion as thought and culture took a marked turn in the era following World War II. While the battle between theological liberals and conservatives continued—as it does to this day—religion was associated with political life in new and significant ways. In the Cold War context, this meant the identification of theism with nationalism. The international polarization after 1947 between capitalist liberal democracies and communist states—with the United States and the USSR at the head of the two opposed systems, engaged in a global struggle for political control of the non-aligned "third world" of developing states in Africa, Asia, and Latin America—actually meant a diminution of the polarization between religious liberalism and orthodoxy in the United States. Instead, a more ecumenical vision of religion was juxtaposed to the official state atheism of "Godless Communism." President-elect Dwight Eisenhower in 1952 famously declared "our form of government has no sense unless it is founded in a deeply felt religious faith, and I don't care what it is." Eisenhower invoked what was coming to be called "the Judeo-Christian tradition," a new idea that sought a common theological, ethical, and historical identity for Judaism and Christianity, against an older exclusive Protestant identification with individual liberty. The Cold War saw an embrace of a "tri-faith" America, neatly summarized in the sociologist Will Herberg's book, *Protestant-Catholic-Jew* (1955), as the descendants of Jews, and Catholics who had come from Europe or the Mexican territory seized in American expansion in the nineteenth and early twentieth centuries, were assimilated—not without conflict and resentment from some—into a new vision of American religion. This broad association of American society with theism was given form in such practices as adding "In God We Trust" to U.S. money or "one nation under God" to the Pledge of Allegiance. The Cold War era was a period of religious revivalism in evangelical terms, exemplified by the prominence of the Baptist Billy Graham's annual "crusades" beginning in 1947, and the close relationship Graham developed with American political figures. And while Protestant mistrust of Catholicism, and continuing antisemitism, remained as features of American Christianity, the push against forms of religious bigotry in the wake of Nazism fits the image of a broadly held, but largely doctrineless brand of thought that was dubbed "civil religion" by the sociologist Robert Bellah. In other words, the Cold War amplified the association of religion with political identity, making religious belief central, but did so by draining the specific content of religious belief from its significance. The theological conflicts that had animated modernists and fundamentalists were temporarily put aside by many in favor of a common assertion of faith.

But not all religious thinkers were indifferent to doctrine, as the rise of neo-Evangelicalism and neo-Orthodoxy in this period demonstrates. The 1940s and 50s were a formative period for modern evangelical Christianity. In addition to Graham's prominence, key figures such as Carl F.H. Henry and Harold Ockenga shaped a new, more activist, and engaged form of evangelical religion. Their institutional activities included the founding of the *National Association of Evangelicals* (1942) and the magazine, *Christianity Today* (1956-), to provide a conservative counter to the liberal *Christian Century*, as well as the founding of Fuller Theological Seminary. Henry's *The Uneasy Conscience of Fundamentalism* (1947) laid a roadmap for an assertion of evangelical Christianity in the public square. Criticizing fundamentalists for their attempts to counter the adaptation of Christianity to changing social issues by retreating to affirmation of doctrine alone, Henry called for evangelical Christians to engage the culture, but not by adapting to it as modernists proposed, but by seeking to change it to meet Christian doctrine. If the fundamentalist approach had been to build a wall against the forces of a scientific and secular order and to claim authority in the religious sphere of Christian churches, what Henry advocated was a direct departure, in which the causes of evangelical Christianity would be fought in the public square. If the Progressive Era Social Gospel had exemplified modernist rejection of doctrine in favor of social reform and action, Henry was arguing that evangelicals could not simply leave the claim of social reform and engagement to the modernists and liberals. Evangelicals had to hew to a conservative vision of doctrine, and not cede any ground to theological liberalism, but they also had to fight religious and secular liberals in public as part of the evangelical mission. Evangelical religion should not only be an expression of truth, but in order to succeed, it must make its truth relevant to the social problems of today. The problem, of course, would become evident: the more evangelicals acted like liberals, the more they were at risk of having their doctrine shaped to immediate social ends and needs, rather than maintained as a fixed and unwavering faith. The dilemma was: maintain the purity of the unchanging faith and become an increasingly irrelevant voice in a dynamic society, or apply the faith to social issues and find it increasingly swept up and determined by the culture. Evangelical Christians would follow the path Henry had demarcated throughout the second half of the twentieth century, but especially from the mid-1970s on.

Neo-orthodoxy represented an alternative turn away from some of the features of modernist religion, but different ones than fundamentalists and evangelicals had been concerned with. The American figure most clearly identified with neo-Orthodoxy was Reinhold Niebuhr, whose engagement with public issues also gave him a larger audience, including atheists who found his conceptions of personhood, tragedy, and complexity to fit the temper of Cold War-era thought. Neo-Orthodoxy disagreed with liberalism, not because of its commitment to higher criticism, nor its adaptation to modern scientific thought such as evolutionary theory. The question of Biblical inerrancy was not on the agenda of neo-orthodox thinkers. Rather, it found that liberal Christianity presented a simplified and rationalized vision of human agency and morality. For Niebuhr, modern thought had lost sight of the concept of sin as essential to human constitution, and until it recovered the Christian vision of sin, would provide platitudes incapable of managing the complexities of social, political, and personal action. Modern liberalism imagined that human nature was fundamentally good, and only corrupted by institutional arrangements. Once self-interest and agency in a democratic polity were realized, human beings could be free and self-determining. Niebuhr felt that this liberal anthropology was fundamentally naive, and therefore provided no basis for human beings to achieve goals of moral betterment. Without a strong sense of the universal corruption of humankind, that each of us has dark forces, selfish motives, inner violent desires, there could be no way to check or channel those dark impulses. Drawing on mid-twentieth-century existentialist thought and nineteenth-century precursors such as the Danish theologian Soren Kierkegaard, the neo-orthodox thinkers asked for a greater reflection on the misguided nature of utopian thinking. For Niebuhr, modern thought had lost the tragic sensibility, the idea that freedom and necessity were conjoined, that a fallen world meant a realistic encounter with the prevalence of evil. The simple moralism of idealistic and utopian thought denied the inherent contradictions of human nature. The result of the Niebuhrian sensibility was to center irony, tragedy, complexity, and paradox as central elements of Cold War thought. Neither modernism nor fundamentalism, liberalism nor evangelicalism, possessed sufficient critical and philosophical means for encountering what the poet W.H. Auden was calling "the age of anxiety."

One response to the pervasive uncertainty of the mid-twentieth century was the reinforcement of a version of religion as a kind of therapeutic psychological practice. Since the late nineteenth century, various thinkers had sought forms of spiritual practice, such as Mind Cure, with the notion that one of religion's principal goals was to provide directives for mental health in a troubled world. The conversion of religions into forms of self-help movements, a set of psychological aids that would parallel the growing popularity of Freudian psychoanalysis, was aided by the emergence of mass media—paperback publishing, radio, and television. In tri-faith America, therapeutic religion could take Jewish, Catholic, and Protestant form. The Rabbi Joshua Liebman had a bestseller with *Peace of Mind* (1946) by wedding a broad religious conception to a popular psychological outlook. "Prophetic religion now has an ally in what might be called revealed psychology," he wrote,

> a science that lays bare the secret diseases of man's troubled soul and provides a serviceable therapy for healing them. Fused together by terrible necessity, religion and psychology now bend forward, as one to succor stumbling humanity, to lift it up, anoint its wounds, and fill its cup to overflowing with the oil of peace.[5]

The Catholic radio Bishop Fulton J. Sheen responded with his own prescription: *Peace of Soul* (1949). And in 1952, the Protestant minister Norman Vincent Peale published his enormously successful *The Power of Positive Thinking*, which provided a set of practices and rules by which personal success could be achieved. These books came under theological criticism of course, and were not endorsed by the intellectual wings of the faith communities they purported to represent. But this version of religion as self-help was much more popular with the public than arguments over the inerrancy of scripture, Biblical criticism, adaptation to modern scientific understanding, or many of the doctrinal issues that were of concern to those who took theology seriously.

The triumph of a therapeutic vision of religion as self-help suggested that perhaps both the modernists, who sought to affirm a vision of religion compatible with modern knowledge and modern life, and the conservatives, who sought to maintain a fixed creed, had both misidentified their intellectual enemy. In a consumer society of abundance, the language of faith had become adapted to the language of psychological well-being, rather than to questions of epistemology.

Notes

1 Thomas Wentworth Higginson, *The Sympathy of Religions: An Address Delivered at Horticultural Hall, Boston, February 6, 1870* (Boston, MA: The Free Religious Association, 1876), p. 6.

2 Robert G. Ingersoll, "Why Am I an Agnostic? Part II," *The North American Review* 150.400 (March 1890), p. 338; "Why Am I an Agnostic? Part I," *The North American Review* 149.397 (December 1889), p. 749.
3 Harry Emerson Fosdick, "Shall the Fundamentalists Win?" *Christian Work* 102 (June 10, 1922), pp. 716–717.
4 J. Gresham Machen, *Christianity and Liberalism* (New York: MacMillan, 1923), p. 6.
5 Joshua Liebman, *Peace of Mind* (New York: Simon & Schuster, 1946), p. 15.

9 Pluralism and Cosmopolitanism

> If you know whether a man is a decided monist or a decided pluralist, you know perhaps more about the rest of his opinions than if you give him any other name ending in ist. To believe in the one or the many, that is the classification with the maximum number of consequences.
>
> William James[1]

We have seen already the challenges modernity presented to the idea that there was a singular American identity, defined by shared religion, ethnicity, or experience. These challenges became particularly pointed in the era around World War I. Boasian cultural relativism, Protestant modernism, and religious ecumenicalism, the growth of cities that put immigrant communities side by side, persistent questions about biological and racial differences, the power of an invigorated Federal government to integrate regional characteristics under a common umbrella: these and other forces and issues brought to the fore a central tension in modern thought between its homogenizing and unifying elements, and its production of variety and heterogeneity. In the second decade of the twentieth century, as the United States moved closer to entering the Great War on the side of Britain, large-scale fears of dual loyalty, especially among two of the largest ethnic groups, Irish and German-Americans, generated a discourse on "hyphenated Americans," and the notion that American identity should be associated with English social, cultural, and intellectual forms. While there were multiple positions articulated, the main line of the battle was drawn between advocates of a vision of America as a uniform "melting pot," and advocates of a vision of America as a culturally pluralistic nation. Although its origins lay in the early twentieth century, the terms of that debate would lay the groundwork for a century of battles over uniformity and cohesion, on the one hand, and multiplicity and diversity on the other. Just as battles over epistemology offered challenges to claims of uniform

DOI: 10.4324/9781003120803-12

and absolute knowledge, so battles over cultural identity offered challenges to claims of singular and fixed identity.

The Melting Pot vs. Cultural Pluralism

The term "melting pot," used to describe the United States as a uniform nation of assimilated immigrants, came from a play written by the British Jewish playwright Israel Zangwill, performed to great acclaim in the United States in 1909. There is some irony in the fact that Zangwill was not himself an American, but was responsible for creating this lasting image of American national identity and its assimilative power. Zangwill's protagonist, the Russian Jew David Quixano, proclaims "America is God's Crucible, the great Melting Pot where all the races of Europe are melting and reforming… Germans and Frenchmen, Irishmen and Englishmen, Jews and Russians – into the Crucible with you all! God is making the American."[2] The idea that "the American" was the product of the vast variety of peoples being melted into a single uniform type was consistent with other ideas of the era, such as Teddy Roosevelt's vision of a new American race, born out of the unity produced by some force (the frontier, American democracy, a break with the past) that melted away the particular distinctiveness of ethnic and national identity—language, folk tradition, religious beliefs, and practices. In fact, Roosevelt embraced Zangwill's play. It should be noted that the melting pot was <u>not</u> a metaphor that was used to refer to the melting away of racial differences between white and Black people, a division that white supremacy and the melting pot metaphor actually reinforced.

There was always a central ambiguity in the use of the melting pot as an image of American national identity. Were the different groups equal contributors to the new American race, each contributing its own elements to a collective identity? Or was there a single established American standard to which the new immigrants were to be "melted"? The idea of assimilation seemed to suggest the latter. The idea that an American identity had been formed in the preceding centuries and that much of it was derived from a dominant strain of Anglo-Saxonism—English law, language, and mores—could be deployed to suggest that immigrants had to lose the distinctiveness of their own ways and assimilate to that existing standard. The melting pot melted off the peculiarities of foreign elements, assimilating them to a norm represented by the Protestant Anglo-Saxon elite. The other variant of the melting pot emphasized the way in which elements specific to particular immigrant communities could be rendered as elements of the collective whole. Foodways might be a good example—today pizza, tacos, and bagels have become staples of the collective American diet, with only the gesture to an ethnic ownership or identity. What both variants of the melting pot accentuated was the desirability of creating a singular uniform identity and a rejection of the maintenance of distinct cultural practices and ethnic separatism. And melting pot ideology rejected, in large part, the insistence on biological differences between European peoples. Assimilation was possible because people were imagined as mutable, rather than possessing a fixed biological essence.

The critics of the melting pot on the nativist right, who were pushing for immigration restriction and eugenic policies of planned reproduction in these years, rejected the idea of assimilation. For figures such as Madison Grant, Edward Ross, Lothrop Stoddard, and Henry Pratt Fairchild, the melting pot was a "mistake" (as in the title of Fairchild's *The Melting Pot Mistake* [1926]). Grant's *The Passing of the Great Race* (1915), relying on the racial anthropology of William Z. Ripley's *The Races of Europe* (1899), which insisted on three distinct European racial groups with specific head shapes and corresponding character attributes—Teutonic, Alpine, and Mediterranean—saw the problem of immigration as not one of assimilation, but of "mongrelization." That is, many nativists and racialists believed that the melting pot ideology would create a mongrel, mixed-race people, inferior in kind to the Teutonic (or as Grant and others of his contemporaries preferred, the "Nordic") peoples who had populated the United States prior to large scale immigration from Southern and Eastern Europe. Interestingly, given the supposed Darwinian basis of Grant's understanding of racial types and hierarchies, he imagined racial mixing as always a reversion to "the lower type." The superiority of the Nordic type, apparently, did not extend to its power to elevate the inferior type. Immigration restrictionists, who finally succeeded in legally reducing European immigration through quotas in the wake of World War I, were arguing that an older Northern European racial identity was at the core of American identity. They rejected both pluralism and assimilationism in favor of reaffirming a "true" racially based singular American identity. Like the advocates for the melting pot, the racialists imaged an American identity that was singular, but unlike the assimilationists, they saw that identity in terms of racial purity, rather than synthetic mixture.

Against both the assimilationists and the racialists, a new set of ideas were created by young intellectuals such as Horace Kallen, Randolph Bourne, and Alain Locke. In a two-part article in the liberal journal of opinion *The Nation* in 1915, Kallen put forth the idea of what he called "cultural pluralism." His argument, as the title of his essay "Democracy vs. the Melting Pot" Indicated, was that the assimilationist ethic was fundamentally undemocratic. According to Kallen, a German Jewish immigrant himself, assimilation was coercive in that it asked members of immigrant communities to give up their identities as a condition of participation in American life. The democratic polity could only be said to be democratic if it recognized the significance of cultural identities, practices, and folkways for the lives of the people it represented. Because Kallen was a philosopher, trained at Harvard, and steeped in the pragmatic outlook associated with William James, his tendency was to see in the world diversity and multiplicity, rather than the ultimate unities of idealist philosophy. Behind modern Pragmatism on this issue was an eighteenth-century German philosophical outlook associated with Johann Herder, who had challenged both the emergent racial science and the Enlightenment abstracted universalism of his day, and had affirmed the variety and distinctiveness of peoples and their traditions. Applied to the world of social identities, Kallen's philosophical perspective aimed to straddle the traditionality of immigrant communities, and the progressive vision of social democracy. That is, cultural pluralism looked both backward and forward. Kallen argued that the preservation of cultural traditions, rather than the abandoning or overcoming of them, was necessary to achieve the fullest flowering of a democratic way of life. Yet, the preservation of tradition had frequently been seen by Progressives as a kind of narrow parochialism, a reliance on undemocratic and hierarchical practices. To be progressive was to reject the received authority of the past. What Kallen sought to do was to overcome the stiffening aspects of tradition by creating a world of multiple traditions, not antagonistic with one another, but harmonious. The metaphor he chose to describe cultural pluralism was telling—American democracy was to be a "symphony" in which all ethnic groups could contribute their own instruments and talents to the collective creation of aesthetic and political unity. The melting pot, presumably, was a monotone, a silencing of voices in favor of uniformity.

Randolph Bourne's response to the critics of "hyphenated Americans" and the insistence on assimilation went a step beyond Kallen's cultural pluralism. Bourne's 1916 essay "Transnational America" called not just for the preservation of distinct ethnic communities and identities, but for a transformation of those identities in conversation with one another. The idea that Bourne called for was a cosmopolitan one, "the first international nation," opposed as much to the provincialism of the "unmelted" ethnic as to the melting pot. "As long as we thought of Americanism in terms of the 'melting pot,'" said Bourne, "our American cultural tradition lay in the past. It was something to which the new Americans were to be moulded." Rather, he argued, "we must perpetuate the paradox that our American cultural tradition lies in the future." Calling for a cultural "dual citizenship" that allowed immigrants to both sustain and depart from any narrow provincialism—either that of Anglo-Saxonism or of self-preserving European communities—Bourne imagined a world of fluid and transformative identities, in which Americans of English descent had as much to learn from their immigrant peers, as immigrants did from them. Behind Bourne's critique of the effects of the melting pot was the expressed fear of deracination, of immigrants who had lost their old identities, only to be won over to a world of commercial culture, "the American culture of the cheap newspaper, the 'movies,' the popular song, the ubiquitous automobile." He juxtaposed his cosmopolitan ideal to what he disparagingly referred to as "cultural half-breeds," neither fully assimilated, but possessing only the rudiments of the national cultures from which they came.[3]

Alain Locke's adaptation and philosophical reworking of cultural pluralism came not from the generational break with Anglo-Saxonism represented by Bourne, nor by the vision from within an immigrant community represented by Kallen, but from his attempts to rework his experience as a Black man in philosophical terms. Like Kallen, he was a professional philosopher, trained at Harvard, and steeped in the philosophical Pragmatism and pluralism of the early twentieth century. He was also the first Black Rhodes Scholar to study at Oxford and a key figure in Black aesthetics. Although today Locke is primarily known for his promotion of, perhaps even creation of, the Black aesthetic movement of the 1920s dubbed "The Harlem Renaissance," in his 1925 collection, *The New Negro*, he also wrote widely in philosophy on value pluralism, cultural relativism, and aesthetics. His philosophical outlook was very much aligned with the anthropological work being done contemporaneously by Franz Boas and his students. But Locke came to cultural pluralism via knowledge of the ways in which a uniform Americanism was racially exclusionary. As Kallen said years later, in memorializing him,

> Locke's disposition had been first monistic or universalist. Pluralism and particularism imposed their reality upon him by the exigent harshnesses [sic] of experience. It is these which convinced him of the actuality of difference, which brought him to recognize that difference is no mere appearance, but the valid, vital force in human communication and in human creation.[4]

Whereas W.E.B. DuBois had difficulty completely abandoning a biological model of race which, despite its racist history, seemed to provide a basis for Black identity, Locke completely disentangled race from biological foundationalism and saw its formation in wholly cultural terms. Since values, cultural sensibilities, and aesthetic forms, in Locke's view, were created in the process of social contacts between groups, racial identity, both negative and positive, was not a persistent unchanging essence handed down generation to generation, but a shifting and fluid formation. Hence, he could write of "The New Negro," who, in his view, represented a break with the old. Whereas "the negro" in the post-Reconstruction era through World War I had been defined as a "problem," an identity imposed from without, in the urban and transnational modern world of the 1920s a new combination of peoples was rejecting the old politics of respectability, or art as an agent of social reform, in favor of a new, original, vibrant approach to reality. For Locke, the new negro was an emblem of a new race consciousness, rather than a transvaluation of the old. DuBois in 1897 had spoken of "the conservation of races," with the notion that it was the inherited biological and cultural "spirit" of the race that would be the basis for its future fulfillment. Twenty years later Locke rejected that formulation in the same way that Bourne had rejected racial Anglo-Saxonism. Racial formation in the crucible of the international Black capital that was Harlem was to be a counter to racism and its legacy, an embrace of positive difference as the condition of equality and democracy. Race, in Locke's view, was another word for "culture group," and was produced by the encounters of peoples with one another; his cultural pluralism integrated racial identity along the Black/white axis into the relations among diverse groups in ways that Bourne and Kallen, with their emphasis on immigrant communities, overlooked. Racial identity and immigrant ethnic identity, for Locke, were two sides of the same coin.

Black Nationalism and the Harlem Renaissance

Locke's attempt to develop race pride and cultural expression in a new key overlapped with, but was somewhat at odds with, a parallel attempt within Black circles to found racial autonomy on a more robust fixed essential identity. Black Nationalism, or the idea that all peoples of African descent had a common identity, set of interests, and cultural orientation, and should conceive of themselves as a distinct "national" group, aimed less at pluralism and more at racial separatism. There had been various articulations of this idea, stemming back to the writings of the abolitionist Martin Delaney in the 1850s, but it was given a new focus in the 1920s. The organizational expression of this, the Universal Negro Improvement Association (UNIA) was founded by the Jamaican intellectual and political activist Marcus Garvey and occupied a significant place in Harlem and other Black cultural capitals through the first half of the 1920s. Garveyism promoted an anticolonial internationalist perspective, arguing for a "Pan-African" national identity, Black economic autonomy in the form of investment and support for Black-owned businesses, and an assertive racial pride that would unify all peoples of African descent. Black Nationalism expressed a strong critique of the possibilities of racial equality in the United States and Europe, and, as a consequence, the movement for civil rights by organizations such as the NAACP. If Locke imagined race as the fluid product of social interaction, Black nationalists tended to see an inherent identity produced by birth and descent, and to imagine all Black peoples, on a global scale, facing the same conditions of colonialism and European domination. This led Black nationalists sometimes to make strategic alliances with white supremacist groups, who shared notions of racial essentialism and separatism. Even after the UNIA collapsed following Marcus Garvey's deportation from the United States in 1927, Black Nationalism remained a potent force. In the 1930s, Black intellectuals in the francophone world would put forward the idea of "negritude" as a shared cultural identity, a series of Pan-African racial congresses begun in the wake of World War I would continue into the 1940s, and many Black women in the United States and West Indies, such as Mittie Maude Lena Gordon, Ethel Waddell, Amy Ashwood Garvey, and Amy Jacques Garvey, would sustain and develop the Black nationalist perspective. While cultural pluralists had a more fluid notion of ethnic identity than Black nationalists, the latter were more cosmopolitan in their own way—they imagined their political movement and identities in international and transnational ways, whereas the cultural pluralists tended to frame their challenges to the Melting Pot ideology in terms of the American nation state.

The common ground for Black internationalists and Black cultural pluralists alike was the cultural center of Harlem in New York City. The increasing identification of Black artists and intellectuals with a distinct cultural attitude and a marked departure from Victorian moral uplift ideology created vibrant aesthetic movements in literature, painting, dance, music, and critical thought. Literary artists such as Langston Hughes, Claude McKay, Nella Larsen, Jean Toomer, and Zora Neale Hurston were at the center of this Harlem Renaissance, although it was something much broader than a literary movement. Something of the intellectual shift signified by the Harlem Renaissance can be seen in a 1926 essay by Hughes, entitled "The Negro Artist and the Racial Mountain." Hughes aimed his critique at the Black elite, who he saw as enthralled by respectability, understood in white terms, and ashamed of the lives, desires, passions, and cultural traditions of the people they claimed to represent. The desire for an imitative culture approved by white standards was the "racial mountain" that Black artists had to face. Against this, he proposed an art grounded in the life lived, an art that rejected evasion and gentility. "We young negro artists," he proclaimed,

> who create now intend to express our individual dark-skinned souls without fear or shame. If white people are pleased we are glad. If they are not, it doesn't matter. We know we are beautiful. And ugly too. The tom-tom cries and the tom-tom laughs… We build our temples for tomorrow, strong as we know how, and we stand on top of the mountain, free within ourselves.[5]

The model for aesthetic expression, as defined by Hughes, came from the Black working class and its lack of pretensions. The Harlem Renaissance was an expression of both the new modernist cosmopolitanism—drawing on the geographic mobility and transnationalism of the Harlem population—and, at the same time, the embrace of cultural particularism as the basis of identity.

And the fluidity of the aesthetic and its challenge to prevailing norms was emphasized by sexuality and identity among many of the central figures in the Harlem Renaissance. Although these figures did not refer to themselves as "queer" or "gay," later terminology that extended ideas about fluid sexuality and non-conforming identities, later scholars would come to see sexual heterodoxy enmeshed in the new forms of Black cultural expression. Alain Locke, Langston Hughes, Wallace Thurman, and Countee Cullen were circumspect in public, but all were queer Black men. Many of the women blues singers associated with Harlem night life—Ma Rainey, Bessie Smith, Gladys Bentley, Ethel Waters—were more overt in their presentation and performance of same-sex relationships, also frequently engaging in forms of gender cross-dressing. From the viewpoint of intellectual history, however, there is an interpretive conundrum. In most of the literary and critical work of the time, no explicit ideas or theories about queer sexuality were put forward—scholars have frequently had to infer queer identities from contextual sources such as private correspondence, rather than published work. That is, thinkers like Locke and Hughes *did* emphasize ideas about racial and aesthetic identity, but they *did not* develop any comparable intellectual framing of gender and sexuality. Since the concern of intellectual history is with ideas and thinking, we might make some inferences from the break with the past represented by the ideology of the New Negro and Black aesthetic expression, but we do not have evidence that any of these figures thought in terms of categories we might apply to their behavior and experience from the present. Locke was a theorist of cultural pluralism, but not gender pluralism or queer theory. Some of the Culture and Personality scholars of the 1930s and 40s, such as Ruth Benedict, would be more explicit in applying ideas about culture to issues of gender, sexuality, and identity.

Cosmopolitanism and Southern Distinctiveness

One of the features that the Harlem Renaissance shared with other cosmopolitan cultural movements of the 1920s was a self-conscious rejection of rural and small-town life, with its associated parochialism, in favor of an emphasis on the city as the site of modernity and aesthetic creation. The so-called revolt against the village, among literary intellectuals took a number of different forms, some of which we have touched upon—H.L. Mencken's sneering contempt for the anti-Darwinist Biblical worldview of Bryan in the Scopes Trial; Robert and Helen Lynd's critical perspective on the Midwestern middle class of Muncie, Indiana; the novelist Sinclair Lewis's satirical portrayals of "Main Street" and its "business civilization"; Sherwood Anderson's image of the grotesque crippling of character in *Winesburg, Ohio*. Many of the literary and artistic figures associated with the post-World War I era pictured themselves as "exiles" from a hostile America, an entire coterie making that exile realized in an expatriate existence in Europe, particularly in Paris. The so-called lost generation of Gertrude Stein, Ernest Hemingway, F. Scott Fitzgerald, e.e. cummings, John Dos Passos, Djuna Barnes, Henry Strater, and many others created the image of a modernist movement and style in which the cultural persona of a disaffected, disillusioned "type," often seemed to swamp the significance of innovative aesthetic and intellectual goals. The lost generation owed as much to the self-mythologizing created in the critic Malcolm Cowley's *Exile's Return* (1934) as it did to any developed body of thought. In the lost generation, we can see the origins of an image of the literary modernist inverting an American mythology that had set the established forms of European life as the opposite of an unencumbered self in the New World; American originality now rested with those who would flee the narrow constraints of a moralistic New World for the cultural sophistication and cosmopolitanism of the Old. But the lost generation, critical of Victorian literary realism and concerned, at least in part, with avant-garde experiments in the arts, had no analytic manifesto comparable to Locke's *New Negro*. The body of literary work produced by these artists was significant, but, with the exception of the critical writings of T.S. Eliot and Ezra Pound on poetry, there was little to mark the intellectual development of a theoretical body of ideas in which to think about modernist fiction and visual art.

When Randolph Bourne had put forth his vision of a cosmopolitan ethic of transnationalism—believing that America was the site of this new progressive ethic in contrast to the weary nationalisms of Europe—he used the American South as his foil; the white South, according to Bourne, was the most ethnically uniform region in the United States, and therefore the least vital. Bourne, of course, evaded the racial diversity of the South by writing Blacks out of his regional definition. But his image of the South as a culturally and socially distinct region echoed that of social scientists and Northern intellectuals who had been imagining the South as a "problem" for a generation in the wake of Reconstruction. The South's failure to industrialize on the model of a "New South," put forward by boosters such as Atlanta's Henry Grady; the images of poverty, disease, and violence as endemic to Southern life; the atavistic embrace of formalized racial segregation: all these constructed images helped to advance an agenda for modernization, for transforming the "backward" South into an American system of rationalized life and consumer capitalism. The idea of "southern distinctiveness," then, was coterminous with ideas of cultural distinctiveness and pluralism that were being developed elsewhere, but the image of the South inverted the modernity of cultural distinction, by affirming particularism as rooted in a past that could stand against the forces of modernism and homogenization.

The 1920s and 30s saw a literary "Southern Renaissance," that paralleled that of the Harlem Renaissance but defined "Southern" in such a way as to exclude Black authors. The white literary movement of Southerners—who frequently took as their central themes questions of Southern identity and history—included poets such as Allen Tate and Robert Penn Warren, and novelists Erskine Caldwell, Caroline Gordon, Thomas Wolfe, and, most prominently, William Faulkner. If the Harlem Renaissance writers defined a new, modern departure based on a cosmopolitan Black identity, white writers in the South often marked their modernist commitments by reevaluating their relationship to the Southern past. Against the "romance" of the Old South, the defense of the honor of the Confederate "Lost Cause" in the Civil War, and other staples of late nineteenth and early twentieth century ideological attempts to justify a South based on racial hierarchy and a vision of quasi-feudal nobility, the new Southern writers adopted a more critical and tragic sensibility. The South was distinctive precisely because of its internal contradictions, its burden of history, and its inability to assume the optimistic progressive vision so common in the rest of the United States. In an oft-quoted statement from his later novel *Requiem for a Nun* (1951), Faulkner wrote "The past is never dead. It's not even past."

This articulation of Southern distinctiveness was given its most sustained and critical voice in the manifesto of Southern "agrarianism," *I'll Take My Stand* (1930). The 12 authors who contributed to this volume—all of them poets, critics, and humanists—sought a philosophical affirmation of what they imagined to be a distinctive but threatened Southern way of life. Their agrarianism was a critique of modern American industrial society— its characteristic values, forms of work and leisure, its progressive instrumentalism, and its economic materialism. Not simply a literary manifesto, *I'll Take My Stand* proposed a contrast between the dominant culture of industrialism, and a Southern culture organized around an agriculturally-based society. And it relied, as so much thought of the time did, on an anthropological concept of culture. The humane values of the South, they argued, do not belong to "an abstract system, but a culture, the whole way in which we live, think, act, and feel. It is a kind of imaginatively balanced life lived out in a definite social tradition."[6] Art, literature, and religion were to be seen as linked intimately to social and economic practices. The agrarians proposed a culturally distinctive Southern conservatism, linked to a thorough-going rejection of industrial capitalism and the ideology of progress, creating a model for conservative thought that would challenge modern economic ideologies, whether capitalist or socialist. A life rooted in a relationship to the land, to non-commercial forms of leisure, to established traditions and practices: this was a vision that would later influence communitarian and environmental forms of thought, by presenting a contrast to the inevitability of the destructive values of industrial life. Of course, this vision elided or diminished significant aspects of Southern history and life—especially the centrality of institutions related to slavery, white supremacy, and racial segregation. "Slavery," said John Crowe Ransom, "was a feature monstrous enough in theory, but, more often than not, humane in practice; and it is impossible to believe that its abolition alone could have effected any great revolution in society."[7] The Agrarian manifesto, then, defended a racially hierarchical society, continuous with the past, committed to legal segregation—and it did so by putting race at the margins, rather than the center, of its social ethic and vision.

The idea of Southern distinctiveness was articulated in a more critical vein a decade later by the Southern journalist W.J. Cash in *The Mind of the South* (1941), an influential statement that has remained in print ever since. Like the Agrarians, Cash imagined a continuous South that bridged the Civil War era and claimed a distinctive intellectual and cultural outlook. Unlike the Agrarians, he in no way idealized either the Old South or the New. He found

> a fairly definite mental pattern, associated with a fairly definite social pattern—a complex of established relationships and habits of thought, sentiments, prejudices, standards and values, and associations of ideas, which, if it is not common strictly to every group of white people in the South, is still common in one appreciable measure or another, and in some part or another, to all but relatively negligible ones.[8]

Like the Personality and Culture theorists, the advocates of "national character," and the noted historian Perry Miller, who was simultaneously discovering in seventeenth-century Puritanism the "New England Mind," the commitment to finding a unified and singular identity amidst the diversity of individuals, structured the method and conclusions. But Cash's Southern mind was marked by violence, intolerance, individualism, and racial animus, more than by an ethic grounded in honor and communitarian values. Along with social scientists such as Howard Odum, John Dollard, and Hortense Powdermaker, who all wrote landmark works on Southern culture and society in the 1930s, Cash was more sensitive to the centrality of what, following Chicago School of Sociology terminology, was increasingly being called "race relations" in Southern society. The distinctiveness of Jim Crow institutions, laws, and mores—of lynching and racial terror--was being written into the idea of Southern distinctiveness in ways that the Agrarians would not have approved. The historian C. Vann Woodward would, beginning in the 1930s, emphasize economic class conflict and its relationship to race in Southern history, pushing against the emerging focus on the unification of shared values and outlooks represented by works, such as Cash's, that defined a Southern Mind, riven by mental contradictions, rather than a South riven by internal social conflicts. His *The Strange Career of Jim Crow* (1955) was an attempt to show that continuity between the Old and New Souths was a myth and that racial segregation did not belong to Southern "folkways" from time immemorial—*Strange Career* was an intervention against the arguments of Southern segregationists. But Woodward was responsible in his own way, as much as Cash, in giving intellectual weight to the idea of the distinctiveness of Southern society.

Regionalism, Populist Folk Culture, and New Deal Cultural Policy

Intellectuals in the 1920s tended to embrace cosmopolitan values, values associated with urban life, European expatriation, aesthetic innovation, and a critique of small-town and rural America; the 1930s represented a sea change in attitudes. Under the pressure of the Great Depression, high levels of unemployment, and what appeared to be the collapse of American capitalism, many thinkers turned to greater social and political radicalism. Marxist thought, Soviet-style Communism, and a pronounced concern with economic inequality and the lives of the oppressed exerted a strong pull on the sensibilities of intellectuals, and helped to shape a dominant cultural orientation on the Left. The rise of fascism and Nazism in Europe, and the sense among some that popular figures on the right, such as the antisemitic radio priest Father Charles Coughlin, represented an incipient American fascism, put issues of political ideology and action at the center of critical intellectual movements. Building on the cultural radicalism of earlier Greenwich Village bohemianism and radical social thought, articulated in small magazines like *The Masses* (1912–1917), publications such as *New Masses* (1926–1948) and *Partisan Review* (1934–2003) provided an outlet for Leftist and Marxist thought—although *Partisan Review* broke with the Communist Party in the mid-1930s and became the principal outlet for anti-Stalinist socialist and left-wing thought. Many of the writers for these publications and similar outlets were literary intellectuals and social critics—Mike Gold, Granville Hicks, and Max Eastman at *New Masses*, and

New York intellectuals such as Dwight Macdonald, Philip Rahv, William Phillips, and Clement Greenberg at *Partisan Review*. Gold and the circle around *New Masses* increasingly subscribed to the idea that art should serve revolutionary causes, and promoted the idea of proletarian literature as a vehicle for critiquing capitalism and creating working-class consciousness; the *Partisan Review* group was highly critical of the idea of literature as propaganda, had little use for explicitly political art, and embraced a commitment to modernist aesthetic originality in tandem with radical politics. Greenberg's famous *Partisan Review* essay "Avant Garde and Kitsch" (1939), for instance, expressed both the Marxist critique of capitalism and mass culture *and* the commitment to formalist experiment in the arts, synthesizing cultural cosmopolitanism and socialist politics. Marxists and Leftists of all stripes were part of the broader movement to embrace literature and the arts to advance politics by cultural means—a movement that Michael Denning has described as "The Cultural Front." Filmmakers, jazz and blues musicians, playwrights, novelists, and performers lent their weight to notions of collective action and the values of the labor movement against oppressive institutions and material exploitation.

If Sinclair Lewis's satire of middle-class business boosterism, *Babbit* (1922) represented the literary cosmopolitanism of the 1920s, novels such as John Steinbeck's *The Grapes of Wrath* (1939) and plays such as Clifford Odets's *Waiting for Lefty* (1935) expressed a Depression-era commitment to a kind of cultural folk populism, in which the struggles of workers, the poor, and the dispossessed were identified with the resiliency of American life. The Communist Party USA, which had been highly critical of the liberal reformism of Franklin Roosevelt's New Deal, after 1935 followed a "popular front" strategy of making common cause with New Dealers, who were advocates for an extensive welfare state, in opposition to the rising tide of fascism. Under Earl Browder, the CPUSA embraced a kind of patriotic Americanism, romanticizing the American working class as the heroic emblem of an anti-fascist struggle, and emphasizing American values of democracy and freedom. A lot of the folk populism on the left was the product of intellectuals who were not members of the CPUSA but were "fellow travelers," sharing some of the same concerns and interests with communists. The notion that farmers and workers were the "salt of the earth," and represented solid values of justice, fairness, and integrity, as opposed to the parasitic and decadent cultural and economic elite, represented a turn away from the cultural cosmopolitanism of the lost generation, and toward an affirmation of ordinary life. In the visual arts, this was represented in the regionalist paintings of Grant Wood, Thomas Hart Benton, and John Steuart Curry, who rejected the move toward modernist abstraction in favor of portraying the lives and struggles of ordinary people in the Midwest.

This turn toward "the people" was aided in large part by the cultural policies of the New Deal. Roosevelt's experiment in expanded government as a response to the crisis of the 1930s included a strong intellectual and cultural component that had not been present in previous iterations of federal policy. In New Deal agencies such as the Farm Security Administration (FSA) and the Works Progress Administration (WPA), intellectuals and artists were employed in new ways to advance a distinctively new vision of the American people in art and literature. The FSA, whose mission was to address rural poverty in the farm economy, created a photography project to document rural poverty, producing a body of photographs that expressed a new documentary aesthetic. Photographers who were to become some of twentieth-century America's most influential artists, such as Walker Evans, Dorothea Lange, Russell Lee, Arthur Rothstein, and Gordon Parks, documented the conditions of the Dustbowl, migrant laborers, poor sharecroppers, and depleted farmlands. Their images, which simultaneously depicted raw poverty and humanized the rural poor as heroic emblems of dignity and suffering, created a lasting challenge to the attempt of governments and bureaucrats to treat rural poverty as a matter of statistics and technological challenges, rather than as a human problem. The Works Progress Administration, from 1935 forward, housed employment projects for artists, writers, and performers. The Federal Writers' Project initiated a number of projects, most famously a series of state guides that defined the cultural, social, and economic identities of the individual states; and a collection of ex-slave oral histories, in which writers interviewed elderly African Americans who had been born into slavery. Under the WPA, artists created murals on public buildings, often depicting local history, and theater productions with similar themes of American regional identity, as well as social and political issues, were part of the Federal Theatre Project. While the justification for these projects was to provide employment for writers and artists during the Depression, the cultural consequences of the WPA programs affirmed a turn toward the folk populism and documentary aesthetic that was central to the thought of the era and created a lasting set of images associated with the New Deal. Localism and regionalism were very much in evidence in the WPA, but so, too, was the underlying notion that the Federal Government provided a unifying conception of the culture of the American people and that "Americanism" was part of the integrative cultural power of the New Deal that balanced that localism and particularism.

Internationalism

The onset of World War II in 1939, and the U.S. entry into the war following the Japanese bombing of Pearl Harbor in 1941, shifted the ground under the discourse of pluralistic particularism and American nationalism. The period after World War I had been marked by a retreat from international engagement, a simultaneous regime of new forms of immigration restriction founded on nativism, and a call for "100% Americanism" by groups such as the American Legion and a reinvigorated Ku Klux Klan. While the definition of Americanism continued to be contested ground, an assertive nationalism in the 1920s sought to define it in exclusionary racial, ethnic, and religious terms, not in cosmopolitan or universalist terms that invoked a set of ideals rather than fixed inherited characteristics. The movement toward greater international political isolationism, some of it predicated on a sense that the promises of U.S. entry into World War I had not been met, was offset by some of the movements toward cultural pluralism that flourished in the 1920s and 30s. But the rise of Nazism and the failures of the European order to create a lasting peace on the continent, as well as the stirrings of anticolonial movements in Asia and Africa, opened the door for some American thinkers to change the discussion from one of how or whether immigrants and racial minorities were to be integrated into a singular American national identity, to how the world could be remade by America or even as America. A new internationalism sought to minimize or reduce the differences between peoples on a global scale, and to stress a new role for the United States as a global leader in reshaping values and ways of life in a newly reorganized world.

At the forefront of the new internationalism was Henry Luce, the publisher of the news magazines *Time* and *Life*. In 1940, anticipating the U.S. entry into World War II, Luce published an editorial in *Life* entitled "The American Century." Pushing for remaking the world in the image of American political and economic practices and values, Luce also identified the role the United States was playing in creating a global culture that would unite all peoples under a shared identity. According to Luce,

> there is already an immense American internationalism. American jazz, Hollywood movies, American slang, American machines and patented products, are in fact the only things that every community in the world, from Zanzibar to Hamburg, recognizes in common. Blindly, unintentionally, accidentally and really in spite of ourselves, we are already a world power in all the trivial ways - in very human ways. But there is a great deal more than that. America is already the intellectual, scientific and artistic capital of the world. Americans —Midwestern Americans - are today the least provincial people in the world. They have traveled the most and they know more about the world than the people of any other country. America's worldwide experience in commerce is also far greater than most of us realize.[9]

The very thing that American cosmopolitans in the 1910s and 20s had disparaged about middle-class American culture—its commercialism, its materialism, its boosterism, its focus on practical invention—were, along with its scientific and artistic preeminence, for Luce, the sign of its internationalism. Parochialism and cosmopolitanism were collapsed into a single way of life. The world was to be unified as a kind of America writ large.

Wendell Willkie, the Republican nominee for President in 1940, pushed hard—against many in his own party--for the new internationalism, arguing that a narrow nationalism or isolationism was no longer a possibility under new conditions of the world. In 1943, Willkie published a best-selling volume, entitled *One World*, that documented his 46-day tour of the world in the midst of World War II. Given modern transportation and communication, said Willkie,

> There are no distant points in the world any longer… [T]he myriad millions of human beings of the Far East are as close to us as Los Angeles is to New York by the fastest trains. I cannot escape the conviction that in the future what concerns them must concern us, almost as much as the problems of the people of California concern the people of New York.[10]

Willkie was, like Luce, very much concerned with the exporting of American political and economic forms to a world in which the structures of Western imperialism were under challenge. The idea that people around the world, from vastly different societies, cultures, and religions, were more alike than dissimilar, that their interests could not be remote from one another, and therefore must be shared, formed the heart of One Worldism. In the post-World War II era, the photographer Edward Steichen organized an exhibit at the Museum of Modern Art in New York, entitled *The Family of Man* (1955) that brought this cultural universalism to a large audience. Curating documentary photographs from all over the world, this exhibit was intended to emphasize the common values, practices, needs, and concerns of all people, to focus on the similarity within the differences of skin color, religion, dress, and custom. That this ideology was for export—specifically in the Cold War context—was emphasized by the fact that what began as an exhibit for Americans became a traveling exhibit shown all over the world.

Conclusion

Sameness and difference—unitary and pluralistic identities—were central to discussions of what a modern society might look like. The attempts to emphasize the variety and heterogeneity of peoples, without making invidious distinctions between them, often foundered when met by those who insisted on singular norms, which often were exclusionary and did make invidious distinctions. But it would be a mistake to see these intellectual battles as ones between cultural conservatives and cultural modernists. The advocates for the melting pot and those for cultural pluralism were both modernists. The desire for homogeneity, under the cultural policies of the New Deal, was no less committed to a progressive vision than those who embraced the cultural politics of Black Nationalism and separatism. The nativists and eugenicists who argued against the "mongrelization" of the Nordic stock sought modern solutions; the Southern Agrarians might have insisted on a distinctive way of life against industrialism, but their conception of that way of life was bound up with the modern anthropological concept of culture. The forces of homogenization and cultural particularism went hand in hand in shaping the debates about American identity through the middle decades of the twentieth century.

Notes

1. William James, *Pragmatism: A New Name for Some Old Ways of Thinking* (New York: Longman Green and Co., 1907), p. 50.
2. Israel Zangwill, *The Melting-Pot, Drama in Four Acts* (New York: MacMillan Co., 1909), p. 33.
3. Randolph Bourne, "Trans-National America," *Atlantic Monthly* 118 (July 1916), pp. 90, 92.
4. Horace Meyer Kallen, "Alain Locke and Cultural Pluralism," *The Journal of Philosophy* 54.5 (February 28, 1957), p. 123.
5. Langston Hughes, "The Negro Artist and the Racial Mountain," *The Nation* 122.3181 (June 23, 1926), p. 694.
6. Twelve Southerners, *I'll Take My Stand: The South and the Agrarian Tradition* (New York: Harper & Brothers, 1930), p. xliv.
7. John Crowe Ransom, "Reconstructed but Unregenerate," in Ibid., p. 14.
8. W.J. Cash, *The Mind of the South* (New York: Alfred J. Knopf, 1941), p. viii.
9. Henry R. Luce, "The American Century," *Life* 10 (February 17, 1941), p. 65.
10. Wendell L. Wilkie, *One World* (New York: Simon & Schuster, 1943), p. 2.

10 Self and Social Order in the Cold War World

If the era of the Great Depression has sparked a renewed interest in Marxism and other forms of economic radicalism, the era following World War II has often been portrayed as a period of conservative intellectual retrenchment. In the context of a Cold War pitting the Soviet Union and Communism against Western European liberal democracy, the intellectual commitment to class politics and opposing forms of capitalist exploitation found less traction among intellectuals. Features of the image of the era's intellectual de-radicalization include a systematic attempt to stifle domestic dissent through a protracted "Red Scare," finding its most virulent expression in the politics of Wisconsin Senator Joseph McCarthy, and increasing revelations of the nature of Stalinist rule in the Soviet Union. Disillusionment about the "radical dreams" of the 1930s, combined with an increasing consumer-oriented abundance, an expanding middle class aided by the GI Bill for returning veterans and other government programs, and massive investment in higher education, created the conditions for the creation of a new intellectual sensibility.

While a number of critics of the New Deal and progressive thought formed a strong conservative intellectual movement during this era, the term "conservative" as a general descriptor for the thought of the era seems a misnomer. Rather, the post-World War world saw the ascendency of a New Deal-informed establishment liberalism, which would have been counted as among the most left-leaning movements to achieve intellectual hegemony in American history. Increasingly, however, these intellectuals concerned themselves with a kind of cultural criticism of modern abundance and American capitalism, rather than an economic criticism of class exploitation. The success of the labor movement and its gains, along with the very real movement toward reducing income inequality, allowed many on the left to imagine that a largely middle-class society had been achieved. In this context, the concerns of many intellectuals were with the psychological and cultural conditions of an expanding American middle class and its "way of life" rather than conditions of economic inequality;

they embraced a kind of liberalism that built on pragmatic, pluralist, psychoanalytic, and relativist roots in contrast to what they regarded as the unthinking acceptance of a totalizing vision of fixed and absolute truths. They gave this enemy the names "ideology," and "totalitarianism," and saw in uncritical habits of mind the underlying threat to liberal freedom. At the same time, out of the materials of a fluid, dynamic, and relativistic sensibility, they often aimed to create the image and idea of a stable, unified, and integrated social order.

At the heart of a great deal of Cold War-era thought was the characteristically modern problem of the relationship between self and society. This was the era in which a generalized psychoanalytical vocabulary reached its pinnacle of popularity, and terms like "neurosis," "anxiety," and "identity" were bandied about, as more and more Americans turned to Freud, not simply as a theorist or thinker, but as the architect of a therapeutic practice and process. The legacy of Nazism prompted a number of thinkers to see a kind of "soft totalitarianism" in the psychological impulse to conform to social conventions and shared collective norms of thought, rather than to embrace critical habits of mind. Many of those who the cultural critic Harold Rosenberg wittily described as "the herd of independent minds" saw in twentieth-century consumer society, awash in abundance and commercial forms of leisure, a new "mass culture" that blunted the critical impulse; the turn to religion as a solution to the anxiety of an age of nuclear weapons and political dystopias as a "new failure of nerve"; and the doctrinaire Anti-Communism of McCarthyism (as opposed to the "nuanced" Anti-Communism of liberal intellectuals) as a "witch hunt." The psychologizing of cultural and political issues—turning what had been considered as matters of "values" and "interests" into expressions of psychological desires and needs—was one common way in which social conflicts were reconceptualized as matters of the integrity of the self. Whereas Emerson in the 1830s and 40s had set "the individual" in absolute opposition to society, and Dewey in the early years of the twentieth century had argued that self and society were mutually interdependent, the critics of the Cold War years thought of the self, like Dewey, as a social product, but, like Emerson, one in danger of being over-socialized and subsumed by the forces of conformity.

A New Liberalism: The Vital Center

In the 1930s and through the World War II era, many liberals and progressives made common causes with Soviet-backed Communists. Anti-fascism, commitments to equality and ending exploitation, and a vision of progress creating a more just society seemed to unify liberals and leftists of all stripes. Even in 1948, when former Vice-President Henry Wallace ran for President as the Progressive Party nominee, and explicitly rejected the Truman administration's invoking of a worldwide battle between liberal democracy and Communism, he was backed by a strong contingent of leftists and left-leaning liberals. In 1947, at the beginning of the Cold War, a group of liberal political thinkers and activists formed Americans for Democratic Action, a group explicitly committed to furthering the goals of a post-New Deal expanded welfare state, but with a difference. ADA broke with pre-war liberalism by simultaneously setting itself against Communism. The liberal interventionists of ADA—including labor leader Walter Reuther, neo-orthodox theologian Reinhold Niebuhr, former first lady Eleanor Roosevelt, journalists Joseph and Stewart Alsop, and economist John Kenneth Galbraith—strongly supported NATO and the Marshall Plan for reconstructing postwar Europe in order to fend off Communist movements, and criticized what they regarded as the naïve idealism of Wallace and his followers. ADA redefined liberalism as a body of thought and as a political movement, and created a new liberalism, equal parts left-leaning domestic political agenda and internationalist strident anti-Communism. Cold War Liberalism set itself against Communism, but also against a reactionary conservatism, staking out a middle ground that historian and ADA member Arthur Schlesinger, Jr. would designate "The Vital Center."

In his 1949 manifesto for Cold War Liberalism, Schlesinger suggested that the battle for the hearts and minds of people in the new global order was also a battle between ways of thinking. In an "age of anxiety," when all the old certitudes had disintegrated under the pressures of industrialism and scientific challenges, Communism offered a therapeutic answer—by giving oneself up to the movement, the party, and its model of history, the self could find a place and a purpose that would relieve the sense of anomie, alienation, and dread characteristic of modern society and culture. Liberalism, in contrast, had a harder hill to climb. Yes, it could offer a vision of expansive freedom, of a world made better for more people, but at the cost of giving up fixed and absolute certainty, accepting that there was no utopia at the end of history, and embracing the relativistic and historicist sensibility of modern thought. How, said Schlesinger, was liberalism, with its partial solutions, its tragic outlook on life, its embrace of incremental progress, and its commitment to complexity rather than certitude, to become a "fighting faith," something that people would be willing to die for? "Communism fills empty lives," he proclaimed. The contrast was stark: "Free society alienates the lonely and uprooted masses; while totalitarianism, building on their frustrations and cravings, provides a structure of belief, men to worship and men to hate and rites which guarantee salvation." Democratic thought, according to Schlesinger, lacked the characteristics of a religion, but somehow had to compete with the power of totalitarianism to order life and give meaning. Democracy's "peaceful and rational virtues" included an abhorrence of fanaticism, a commitment to compromise, tolerance, and anti-dogmatism, a pragmatic and skeptical frame of mind, a willingness to be open to new ideas: all of which had the effect of emphasizing process, rather than substance. The transformed liberalism of the Cold War era had to imbue these characteristics with something of the force that totalitarianism offered. Schlesinger's answer was to promote a vision of the activist social welfare state that was linked to a vision of expansive equality and justice, one that would mobilize the participation and communion of citizens—what he called "the new radicalism."[1]

More often than not, Schlesinger and ADA's Cold War Liberalism has been noted more for its sharp and unrelenting anti-Communism and international interventionism, and less for the substantive view of a domestic radical agenda—full employment, universal medical insurance, expansive labor rights. Schlesinger's vital center was not the arena of compromise between Republicans and Democrats, liberals and conservatives. Schlesinger, like so many Cold War liberals, had no kind words for conservatism, which he regarded as an ineffectual commitment to "plutocracy" and business interests, lacking any intellectual and moral resources and appeal. American conservatism, in his view, was irresponsible, not up to the challenge of totalitarianism. His "center" was to be found where later generations would see a "radical left." On the one side, what he regarded as a moribund laissez-faire, business-friendly orientation; on the other, totalitarian Communism. Schlesinger explicitly rejected the model of the political spectrum that imagined that political ideas and affiliations ranged from Communism on the Left to Fascism on the Right, which would situate his left liberalism as sharing concerns with Communism. Rather, Communism and Fascism were more like one another, and what an earlier generation called social democracy or socialism under liberal government was wholly unlike either. The vital center was anti-Communist leftism, not moderate centrism. Its answer to the "age of anxiety" was to see the very forces producing anxiety and uncertainty as part of the answer. To be free was to recognize that problems will never be solved with any finality, that the ever-changing world would always generate new problems and new anxieties, and the best that people can do is to find and make purpose in a world unmoored from the certitudes of the past.

In retrospect, given the centrality of issues of Black civil rights to the 1950s and 60s, what appears evasive in the kind of Cold War Liberalism put forward by Schlesinger and his peers, is the marginalization of issues of racial equality in their discourse. In liberal and left intellectual circles among whites—in the pages of magazines such as *politics*, *Partisan Review*, *Commentary*, and *Dissent* in the late 1940s and 50s—the concerns of domestic left liberalism did <u>not</u> center on race and racial inequality, which were often absent from the problems of international affairs, social welfare, intellectual freedom, McCarthyism, middle-class conformity, and totalitarianism that white liberals were concerned with. This at a moment when central events in Civil Rights history—the Montgomery Bus Boycott, the Brown v. Board of Education Supreme Court decision, and the ensuing conflicts over school desegregation in Little Rock—were bringing new clarity to the Black freedom struggle, and even as the Soviet Union continued its appeal to non-white peoples in Africa, Asia, and Latin America by pointing to Jim Crow segregation as representative of the white supremacy of the West. Schlesinger's view was indicative. He gave much weight to "civil liberties"—free speech and freedom of association—but hardly any to "civil rights." "Most Americans," he said, "accept, at least in principle, the obligations spelled out in the Civil Rights report" of the Truman administration. And, even more startlingly in light of the Southern massive resistance to desegregation that was to come "the South on the whole accepts the objectives of the civil rights program as legitimate..."[2] For Schlesinger and many of his peers, the issue of racial discrimination, bigotry, and segregation had largely been solved, and it was merely a matter of gradualist implementation of equality in practice. After all, as the Swedish economist Gunnar Myrdal had argued in his massive work of social analysis of the race "problem," *An American Dilemma* (1944), American racism existed in contradiction to what was the dominant American Creed—an idealistic belief in equality, democracy, liberty, and individual freedom. In the following decades, many on the Left would come to argue that racism was central to "the American Creed," not an exception to it.

Cold War Liberalism also tended to be silent on the question of the relationship of the sexes and feminism, and if anything, affirmed a normative vision of the American family as indicative of what was increasingly called "the American Way of Life." In part, this was because the question of women's rights had taken a back seat to the cultural celebration of domesticity and home life as a response to men returning from war, although postwar domesticity was far from a retreat to nineteenth-century ideals of womanhood. This celebration was shortly to be challenged by new varieties of feminism in the 1960s and 70s. But the discourse of figures like Schlesinger did not avoid gendered language and images as part of their analysis of a reinvigorated liberal democracy. In order to battle Communism, liberalism, in its advocates' vision, needed to move away from its identification with a set of feminized values, and claim its status as a virile manly body of beliefs. *The Vital Center* was shot through with a rhetoric that associated the crisis of liberal freedom with the crisis of masculinity, echoing Teddy Roosevelt's invocation of "the strenuous life." Schlesinger's disparagement of the State Department as previously populated by "effete

174 *The Contradictions of the Democratic Imagination: 1920–1962*

and conventional men who adored countesses, pushed cookies and wore handkerchiefs in their sleeves," for instance, was also an endorsement of a new masculine and aggressive style of foreign policy.³ The new liberalism would have to be tough, assertive, willing to fight, rather than a bookish, home-bound, sentimental creed. Cold War liberals like Schlesinger participated in the "lavender scare" of the 1950s that associated homosexuality with subversion and weakness in the struggle against Communism.

Consensus History

The New History of the Progressive Era through the 1930s had emphasized not only a kind of historical relativism and recognition of historical revision as rooted in the changing needs of the present but had tended to see the past through the lens of social conflict and economic interest. Although American historiography did not speak with one voice, historians from Charles Beard and Vernon Parrington to C. Vann Woodward and Schlesinger himself in his earlier *The Age of Jackson* (1945), maintained a focus on class struggle that overlapped with the concerns of Marxism. Progressive historians were not theoretical Marxists in any sense, but they did see the struggle for power between economic and business elites, on the one hand, and the more egalitarian forces of workers and farmers, on the other, as central to American history. The idea that the Constitution expressed the economic interests of the social elites who wrote it; that the Civil War was a conflict between Northern industrial capitalists and a Southern backward-looking agricultural elite, and only incidentally about race-based slavery as the central institution of Southern society; that Reconstruction was more of a struggle between the Southern merchant-industrial elite and the planters than between contrasting Republican and Democratic visions of racial order: these were characteristic perspectives of Progressive historiography in the first half of the twentieth century. Having discovered "the economic interpretation of history," Beard and his cohort saw it everywhere.

Progressive history and its focus on social and economic conflict came under sustained criticism in the 1940s and 1950s, for a number of reasons. The term "Consensus History," first used by the historian John Higham as a critique of the failings of postwar historians, has come to be applied widely to a set of dispositions that were at odds with, and challenged, the prevailing Progressive History. While there was never a "consensus school" of U.S. historiography in the sense that its noted participants identified with one another as sharing a common intellectual framework, and it would be a misunderstanding to suggest, as some popular versions have it, that these historians offered a celebratory vision of the American past and present, the turn away from economic conflict as the driver of historical events and processes certainly did have something to do with the Cold War. But, as Schlesinger illustrated, one could leave lots of room for economic conflict in history while simultaneously developing a strong anti-Communist stance. The emerging forms of historical writing and understanding seem far from a vacuous affirmation of American exceptionalism and the role of the United States as an exemplar of liberal democratic values. With the partial exception of Daniel Boorstin, in full flight from the Communist identification of his youth, the most prominent of the so-called consensus historians—Louis Hartz, Richard Hofstadter, David Potter among them—offered up a critique of American thought, culture, and politics that was resonant with many of the same concerns as their contemporaries in sociology, political science, cultural criticism, and general social thought. While rejecting what they regarded as the limitations of Progressive History, they affirmed some of the important elements of that received tradition—the historical relativism, the critique of the idea of objectivity in history, the notion that written history is a form of public engagement, the idea that developments in fields outside of history could provide historians with a tool kit for achieving new perspectives on the past.

The two works, more than any others, that cemented the idea of a consensus history were Richard Hofstadter's *The American Political Tradition and the Men Who Made It* (1948) and Louis Hartz's *The Liberal Tradition in America* (1955). Notably, both were concerned with establishing a "tradition"—a continuous body of ideas, beliefs, and habits passed from the past to the present. The very frame of "tradition," linked with the singular definite article, implied that whatever differences one might find between political actors and their values at different moments in the American past, they all belonged to a coherent shared worldview. The point that both Hartz and Hofstadter were trying to make about that continuous common body of assumptions, is that they were excessively narrow and limiting, and had prevented American politics and society from offering a range of alternatives on both the left and the right. For Hartz, American politics, in the absence of a feudal tradition, was born "liberal," and possessed neither a genuinely conservative tradition committed to social organicism and a fixed hierarchy, nor a genuinely radical tradition that might aim to overthrow capitalist property relations in favor of a true egalitarianism. Hofstadter had written that American political actors and thinkers from the Founding Fathers through to the New Dealers of the 1930s and 40s "shared a belief in the rights of property, the philosophy of economic individualism, the value of competition: they have accepted the economic virtues of capitalist culture as necessary qualities of man."[4] What Hartz mean by "liberal," a term he qualified by attaching the adjective "Lockean," was largely what Hofstadter understood as "capitalist culture": a commitment to individualism, property rights, and the limited state. The British political philosopher John Locke was reinvented in the Cold War context as the founder of a distinct guiding set of principles, rooted in his famous *Second Treatise on Government* (1690), and then made the touchstone for all of American political thought and belief. Importantly, Hartz was not arguing that American political actors read Locke and then aimed to apply his principles in some deliberative fashion, as Marxists might read Marx. Rather, he was arguing that Lockean principles—man as a rational being in a state of nature, entering into a social contract to secure his liberty and property, and limiting the power of the state to that function— had become naturalized as the underlying operative assumptions of American life. What a later generation would call American "political culture" was founded on an unreflective and therefore unquestioned body of Lockean beliefs, so no one ever had to invoke Locke, but could simply invoke common sense. Not to put too fine a point on it, but for Hartz and Hofstadter, this was not a good thing.

Neither Hartz nor Hofstadter denied that there were conflicts between groups and classes in American history; what they tried to suggest was that the intellectual arena in which those conflicts took place severely narrowed the range of political solutions. In other words, they moved away from the idea that easily identified economic interests could tell the story of political life, and argued that there was no making sense of American history without understanding the world of beliefs in which action took place. Ideas structured and contained practice. Theirs was a brief for greater complexity against the simplistic reduction to economic interest. As much as consensus history was a response to the Cold War, it was also very much a response to the kinds of anthropological and psychological modes of thought that Boasian cultural relativism and the Personality and Culture theorists were developing. The historian Henry Steele Commager, for instance, in 1950 took as his object of study "the elusive thing I have called the American Mind," claiming "that there is a distinctively American way of thought, character, and conduct."[5] The economic interpretation tended to assume that human beings acted in rational and deliberately self-interested ways. The idea of culture, as it had come to be understood, suggested that the artificial world that people lived in—the world of tacit and structured shared bodies of belief—was determinative. It also suggested a kind of uniformity and homogeneity; culture might be another word for consensus. Except that the idea of consensus is itself misleading. It suggests, in good Lockean fashion, that historical actors entered into a body of belief as a deliberate act of consent. What was troubling for Hartz and Hofstadter, and others, was that the American political tradition was not a matter of consent, but of controlling ideas and assumptions—less an agreement and more a prison house. In other words, American liberal thought in the works of Hartz and Hofstadter was figured on the model of conformity and what contemporaries were calling, in disparaging tones, "ideology." Instead of American politics being anti-ideological, as so many were claiming, the implication was that Americans were ideological, but had absorbed the ideology so deeply that they were unaware of it.

One of the distinguishing features of Hofstadter's thought was his attempt to understand what he took to be "irrational" forces in history. This meant the use of psychological as well as cultural frames of analysis. If one of the major shifts in the understanding of human nature was the move from a nineteenth-century image of "economic man"—rational and self-interested, immersed in a world of labor and material things—to a twentieth-century understanding of "psychological man"—motivated by anxiety and psychic needs, immersed in a world of desires, susceptible to irrational appeal and manipulation—Hofstadter's historical writings are indicative of this shift. His *Age of Reform* (1954) famously invoked a world of "status anxiety" as the motive for late nineteenth-century displaced elites to enter the world of reform, and Agrarian populism as the product of delusional farmers living in a mythic unreality. His image of the American right as wrapped up in unreal conspiracy theories led him to characterize the McCarthyite right with the label "the paranoid style" in American politics. The tendency to explain the political inclinations of political enemies as a matter of psychological pathology runs through a great deal of liberal thought of the era. In the wake of totalitarianism and the images of mob psychology, the public concern with "brainwashing" as a technique of totalitarian states, and the question of how ordinary Germans had come to support Hitler, numerous thinkers were prepared to think about politics as an expression of psychological needs and tendencies. The image of "the authoritarian personality," as a particular type, with the strong need to create scapegoats and to use violence in service of political forms and ideologies that demanded conformity, ran through much of the literature of this era and overlapped with the tendencies of Hofstadter and other liberals to see political ideas on the right as rooted in psychopathology.

Totalitarianism, Ideology, and the End of Ideology

One of the central ideas that defined Post World War II thought, was the idea of totalitarianism. While the idea originated in the 1920s, it did not come into widespread use until the 1940s, and it was not until after the end of World War II that it came to dominate discussions of social and political order. Central to the notion of totalitarianism was that the old political divisions between Left and Right were inadequate to the understanding of a new kind of State that had come into being in the twentieth century and was embodied in both Soviet Communism and the Nazi's Third Reich.

In a way, this allowed the thinkers and policy elites of Western liberal democracies to apply their critique of Nazism in the 1930s and early 40s to a critique of the Soviet Union in the Cold War era. Sharply contrasted to traditional form of dictatorship, tyranny, and even the absolutism of earlier monarchs and rulers such as Louis XIV in France, the idea of totalitarianism moved the discussion away from a concern with the power of figures such as Stalin and Hitler, and toward a concern with more systematic and—as the name would suggest—totalizing forms of power. Authoritarian states, which centralized power in the ruler, had long existed; totalitarian states were imagined as uniquely modern, and their character as fundamentally different from any that had existed in prior ages.

While the image and concept of totalitarianism were ubiquitous in Cold War thought—in Schlesinger and ADA, in George Orwell's dystopian novel *1984*, in the writings of New York intellectuals such as Dwight Macdonald, Sidney Hook, and Daniel Bell, as well as in much more diffuse forms—the single most influential voice shaping the conception of totalitarianism was that of the German Jewish refugee Hannah Arendt. Arendt's *The Origins of Totalitarianism* (1951) not only aimed at a sweeping overview of the conditions of modern culture and thought that gave rise to Nazism and Communism but also provided a way of understanding and characterizing the logic and form of totalitarian states as a distinctively modern phenomenon. If modernity provided a new world of fluidity, unmoored from the fixed authorities of the past, it also, and as a consequence of that fluidity, provided the ground on which a new form of power could claim to bring the fragmented past into a cohesive and necessary unity. For Arendt, the forces of modernity meant that the resources ordinary people had in the past—their community and civic lives, their cultural and political traditions, their shared and stable belief systems—were destroyed. Industrialism, geographic mobility, urbanism, mass culture, secularism all powerfully reshaped ordinary experience. The modern individual was uprooted from the past, isolated, alienated, and morally ungrounded. This was fertile ground for a new state that was unobstructed by existing institutions and practices and sought to destroy any capacity for independent thought or action. The strategy of the new politics was a strategy of what Arendt called "total domination," one that worked power into any and every nook of experience and thought. Totalitarianism aimed to control not only public and political behavior but also sought to destroy all social bonds and the very nature of the self. Power was made "arbitrary," unrelated to any cause or resistance. "The aim of an arbitrary system," she said,

> is to destroy the civil rights of the whole population, who ultimately become just as outlawed in their own country as the stateless and

homeless. The destruction of a man's rights, the killing of the juridical person in him, is a prerequisite for dominating him entirely.[6]

The purpose of totalitarian states is not to rule over people but to "establish the superfluity of man," to crush everything that is human in people, so that state action is no longer controlled by the desires and needs and persona of human beings.

Central to totalitarianism in Arendt's conception, was "ideology," but she meant the term in a very specific sense. Not just generalized political belief, ideology referred to a mode of thinking, to what she called "the logic of an idea," as it was expressed in the various "isms" characteristic of modern political thought. Ideologies which provide explanations for every and any event, derived from an image or conception of history, are the perfect instrument for totalitarianism, not so much for their content (historical materialism for Communism, racial domination for Nazism), but for the way in which they present history as a matter of logical necessity. For Totalitarianism, ideology provides the brickwork logic of the historical next step—if the progressive destiny of history is to result in the triumph of the proletariat or the master race, whatever means necessary to produce those ends can be authorized. The totalizing logic of ideologies means that the various considerations that might have conditioned politics in the past—circumstances, concrete realities, traditions of political deliberation and decision making, morality itself—can be thrown aside to make reality align itself with political destiny and necessity. Because ideologies transform worldviews into "premises," they deny the possibility of contradiction—everything that does not align itself with the premise can be reinterpreted so as to remove the contradiction. The extermination of the enemies of the state, of whole classes and races of people, Arendt claimed, thereby becomes a necessary deduction from ideological premises.

Although Arendt herself is one of the postwar figures who is difficult to fit into an image of modern liberalism or to identify her in terms of conventional notions of progressive and conservative, the concept of ideology could be reconstructed by liberals to argue that American politics either had no ideology or that it had left ideology behind. The debate that ran from the mid-1950s and beyond took a sloganeering form: "the end of ideology." The sociologist Daniel Bell, the figure most associated with this idea, argued that the "isms" of Western political thought—and by these "isms" he meant Marxism and socialism, primarily, but also classical liberalism and organic conservatism—under the conditions of the modern West, were intellectually exhausted and no longer provided a meaningful logic for the future. His concept of ideology differed from Arendt's; like many intellectuals, his conception was shaped by Karl Mannheim's *Ideology and Utopia*, which had appeared in English translation in 1936.

"Ideology," he said, "is the conversion of ideas into social levers."[7] The power of ideology was that it provided a comprehensive cosmology with a plan of action for the future, functioning like a secular religion. But for reasons social, political, and philosophical, Bell argued, it was no longer possible to believe in the utopian goals of ideology. Politics in the West had become nonideological, governed by pragmatic choices, centrist compromise, piecemeal reform, in which stability and effectiveness were given central stage, and the heat and passion of ideology was moved off stage. If Schlesinger had argued that liberalism must become a "fighting faith" to challenge Communism, Bell argued that it was precisely the lack of fighting passion—their cool and moderate tone—that gave Western liberal democracies their character and their advantage. The Cold War was not one between two passion-filled competing belief systems, but between an ideological politics and a non-ideological one. Not surprisingly, the radical sociologist C. Wright Mills countered—"the end-of-ideology is, of course, itself an ideology," it is "a slogan of complacency circulating among the prematurely middle-aged, centered in the present, and in the rich Western societies."[8] In Mills's view, what he called NATO intellectuals had simply given up any hopes that the future might look better than the present, and had constructed an ideology that argued against the validity of organized political action. Mills's point was that there was no "outside" to ideology, that all people occupy a world of assumptions and structured beliefs that give meaning to their actions. Inaction was itself a form of action, pressed into practice by ideological need.

The Psychoanalytic Temper

The postwar era is one in which Freudian and neo-Freudian forms of psychoanalysis reached their height of intellectual appeal and dominance, both in academic and popular terms. Freud and Freudian thought, especially in the wake of Freud's late work, *Civilization and Its Discontents* (1930), became the basis for a widespread cultural criticism in works such as Lionel Trilling's "Freud and Literature" (1940) and Philip Rieff's *Freud: The Mind of the Moralist* (1959). Freud promised to reveal both the dark forces in human nature, and the ways in which they were disciplined, contained, and given expressive form in culture—how the self could be constructed out of the raw instinct of desire meeting the needs of social order. For figures like Trilling and Rieff, Freud became a kind of culture hero, a creator of a tragic sensibility that suited the world of Cold War concerns with the integrity of self in an unstable world. On the 100th anniversary of Freud's birth, the historian Benjamin Nelson imagined that the twentieth century could be remembered as "the *Freudian Century.*" Modernist intellectuals of every stripe looked to Freud, who offered wide latitude for interpretation in his voluminous corpus, becoming newly available in English beginning in 1953 in the 24 volume *The Complete Psychological Works of Sigmund Freud*, translated by James Strachey.

The neo-Freudians were central figures in American psychoanalytic thought in the mid-twentieth century, who departed from Freudianism by downplaying the biological and sexual elements and emphasizing the social and ego-developing elements in psychoanalytical theory. Unlike the orthodox Freudians, who were largely Austrian émigrés and devotees of Freud, the German émigré and American-born neo-Freudians attached themselves to the Culture and Personality movement. Erich Fromm, who was also associated with the Frankfurt School thinkers who sought a Western Marxist cultural criticism that drew on Freudian thought, was a principal figure in neo-Freudian thought. Other central thinkers included Karen Horney and Harry Stack Sullivan. Fromm's 1941 *Escape from Freedom* concerned itself with the ways in which modern forms of freedom that arise out of the historical rejection of established forms of authority give rise to a kind of insecurity of the self that can be resolved either by embracing an existential self-making or retreating to the security of new forms of authority—either authoritarian or conformist in nature. The desire to flee from freedom and its responsibilities under the conditions of modernity was exemplified for Fromm by the widespread appeal of Nazism to ordinary Germans. The notion that unfreedom had psychological roots tended to shift the discourse away from those who looked to the political sources of unfreedom. His vision of "the authoritarian personality," who desired both submission of the self and scapegoating of the other, became a central idea taken up by Frankfurt School émigré Theodor Adorno and his coauthors in their landmark *The Authoritarian Personality* (1950). Fromm's arguments were echoed in the many works that concerned themselves with "conformity" to group norms as a form of "soft" totalitarianism. Since the concept of totalitarianism emphasized not simply the control of behavior, the body, and material reality, but power over thought and the shape of the self, application of Fromm's argument to middle-class Americans suggested that a creeping fascist mentality that refused freedom was a threat in liberal America, even in the absence of the mechanisms of the totalitarian state. Horney's concern with what she called "the neurotic personality of our times," echoed the idea that the failure to successfully adapt to social conditions had created a breeding ground for psychological disease specific to the modern world.

Perhaps the most influential of the neo-Freudians, although he did not explicitly align himself with them and against Freudian orthodoxy, was Erik Erikson. His *Childhood and Society* (1950) brought to the center of cultural discussion a concept that has had a lasting influence on modern American discourse and thought: identity. "The study of identity," said

Erikson, "becomes as strategic in our time as the study of sexuality was in Freud's time."[9] Identity was a fluid concept, applicable as a centering device in many different discourses and framing of problems. It referred, on the one hand, to sense of self and self-formation, which Erikson rooted in a series of stages of individual development that each required the resolution of some characteristic conflict. Here he formulated the idea that adolescence was a period in which individuals go through what he called an "identity crisis," as they struggle for identity against "role confusion." But identity also referred to cultural identification, a notion of group belongingness that was the ground on which the stages of development would take place. He introduced a kind of historical relativism and social framework to the study of self-development. Erikson, in fact, attempted to create a psychoanalytical model for studying history. His *Young Man Luther* (1958) argued that Martin Luther's rebellion against the Catholic Church was part of a protracted "identity crisis," implying that the Protestant Reformation was itself an identity crisis writ large in which a Medieval Europe found its way to modern maturity. His approach dovetailed with increasing cultural concerns in the 1950s and 1960s about youth and their ability to transition from a protracted childhood to a mature adulthood. The moral panic over juvenile delinquency, the power of the "peer group" in teenage life, and serious works of cultural criticism such as Paul Goodman's *Growing Up Absurd* (1960) that found an absence of meaningful futures for teenage boys: all spoke to the notion that rebellion was a necessary stage, but one that could go off the rails into permanent alienation, on the one hand, or complacency and conformity on the other.

Sociology and Middle-Class Cultural Criticism

The postwar era saw a spate of sociological works that built on the concerns articulated by Fromm and others. Concerned not just with the "soft totalitarianism" of group conformity, but also with the consequences of material consumer abundance, and the highly organized collectivism of bureaucracies both private and public, these critics and analysts created an image of a middle-class society in which an older imagined individualism had been eclipsed by the forces of modern life. The expansive growth of home ownership, cars and appliances purchased on credit, government subsidies for education and home mortgages, and suburban development, in league with a new set of material gains by labor unions at the peak of their powers, tended to dissolve clear class lines, and aid contemporaries in imagining an amorphous "middle class" as a central American identity. Much of the popular criticism of the era represented a critique of suburban life. If urban cosmopolitan intellectuals in the 1920s had targeted rural and small-town middle America as characteristic of a narrow culture of Protestant moralism and business boosterism, in the 1950s they turned their eyes on the suburban bedroom communities, the tract housing developments, the cul de sacs, the flight from the cities and the enforced placeless homogeneity they imagined to be characteristic of the new middle-class society. The critique tended to combine a concern for the loss of independent thought to the forces of conformity with a distaste for the aesthetic form of suburban life—the "ticky tacky" standardized houses, the universal "picture window," the backyard barbeque. In popular works of social criticism by John Keats (*The Crack in the Picture Window*, 1956), A.C. Spectorsky (*The Exurbanites*, 1955), and Richard Gordon (*The Split-Level Trap*, 1961), suburban life was excoriated as a mind-numbing place of complacency and homogenous group isolation. What got little attention in these critiques was the racial dimension of white flight from the cities, and the enforced racial segregation of the suburbs. Ironically, these books were themselves the "middle brow" versions of a more developed and systematic analysis of middle-class life. Later revisionism, such as Herbert Gans's *Levittowners* (1967), which relied on a participant-observer model, would provide a strong empirical counter to the image of suburbia created in these works.

The "highbrow" version of middle-class cultural criticism included the business journalist William Whyte's *The Organization Man* (1956), and two sociological works, the liberal David Riesman's *The Lonely Crowd* (1950) and the radical C. Wright Mills's *White Collar* (1951). Although Riesman's work was an academic study, *The Lonely Crowd* became a surprise best-seller, its categories bandied about in educated middle-class circles. Riesman would land on the cover of *Time* magazine, and *The Lonely Crowd* would stay in print and go on to sell over a million copies. Whyte's *The Organization Man*, which focused specifically on the way in which corporate forms structured middle-class values and orientations, also received a great deal of public attention. Not only was the salaried middle class the object of these studies, it turned out that in good measure it was also the readership for them. The concern with organizational collectivism and the herd mentality was a kind of self-critique, a reflective demonstration that at least some portion of the educated middle class was self-aware, participating in a kind of jeremiad against its own perceived failings. All three works followed a classic form of historical declension—the transformation of an "old" middle class, defined by a different and apparently superior form of economic and social values, into a "new" middle class which had lost the older virtues and replaced them with a set of opposed, and apparently inferior, values. To be clear, of the three, *The Lonely Crowd* actually denied that it was charting a tale of decline and loss intended to call its readers back to a reaffirmation of those solid bourgeois values that had been lost, but the readers of *The Lonely Crowd*, for good reason, certainly interpreted it to be a lament for a disappearing moral order and form of character.

The central argument of *The Lonely Crowd* focused on the transition between two forms of what Riesman called "social character." Social character was the generalized shared group set of organized traits, the way in which societies inculcate in their individual members "modes of conformity." Every society, for Riesman, seeks to ensure the conformity of its members to the forms of social and economic organization characteristic of that society. *The Lonely Crowd* sought to delineate what was happening to social character in a shift from an age of production to an age of consumption. The nineteenth century in the West had been an age of industrial production and had produced a social character adapted to a dynamic and rapidly changing society in which material wealth and innovation were central. The form of social character of this age was what Riesman called the "inner-directed" character, and its elements were exactly what one might expect to see as classic bourgeois virtues: self-reliance, self-control, rational means to ends orientation, honesty, sobriety, order, and hard work. The inner-directed type contained all the necessary resources within—a fixed and stable moral code, a lack of concern with conforming to others' expectation, a sense of personal integrity and conscience. As modern societies shifted from producer-oriented values to consumer ones—with the rise of advertising, commercial leisure, large-scale bureaucracies, extended formal education—the form of social character was changing to what Riesman called the "other-directed" character, who navigated the world by being attuned to the perceptions of others and the need to fit in with the peer group or the work environment. The other-directed character was less driven by an internal motor, and more by a sensitivity to group dynamics. Riesman compared the inner-directed character to a "psychic gyroscope," set in motion by internalized values, and the other-directed character to "radar," constantly attuned to signals in the environment. The characteristic form of moral compulsion in one was guilt, in the other, anxiety. In chapters with titles such as "from the invisible hand to the glad hand," and "from craft skill to manipulative skill," Riesman described a transition and opposition between a society of individualism and fixed moral order, on the one hand, and a society of conformity to the group and an ever-shifting set of behavioral norms, on the other. The salaried professional and businessman in large-scale organizations; the over-socialized teenager in an ever-extended mandatory high school adolescence; the status concerns of consumers and their navigation of the world of commercial leisure; the anxious parents seeking the counsel of child-rearing experts: this world was imagined as one in which individual self-guided action was no longer possible or desirable.

The tone of Mills's *White Collar* was bleaker than *The Lonely Crowd*, in part because Mills was far more explicit in seeing the consequences for politics and freedom itself in the condition of what he called the new middle class. The old middle class of the nineteenth century was composed of farmers, small business people, shop owners; the new middle class was government bureaucrats, corporate office workers, professionals, clerks, and educators. The old middle class owned productive property; the new middle class was salaried employees in a condition of dependency. For Mills, the condition of work was also a condition that determined the possibility of democracy, of people making decisions over their own lives. The new conditions of work, for Mills, encouraged a sense of alienation and hopelessness, where workers had no ability to understand the larger forces and powers that controlled their lives. Mills was deeply indebted to the sociology of Max Weber, who had emphasized the modern forms of bureaucratization and disenchantment of the world, as well as to the emerging criticism of mass society that was becoming a central concern of twentieth-century social thinkers and critics. For Mills, as for Weber, rationality had come to be a feature of organizations and their processes, rather than being the character of individual minds; the more rationalized the world became, the less capable individuals were of exercising rational control of their own lives. For Mills, as opposed to Riesman, this was fundamentally a question of power. In another work, *The Power Elite* (1956), Mills would argue that an interlocking group of military, corporate, and government elites made all the decisions in American life, and that democracy was a mere appearance. The focus on the centrality of power in American life tended to distinguish Mills from many of his peers. For Mills, the political possibilities of the new middle class were defined by the problem of what he called "the cheerful robot." Office work was routinized and increasingly meaningless for the worker, but there was enormous pressure for workers to appear upbeat, engaged, and happy in the deadening mechanical repetition of such work. Under such conditions, was it possible for members of the new middle class to be critical and aware in such a way as to mobilize political convictions, or was apathy and indifference the essential character of middle-class politics? The portrait Mills's painted was of a kind of false consciousness, a class unaware of its own condition and therefore unable to take steps to remedy it.

This idea of a middle class living in a world of unreality was given a specific African-American orientation in the sociologist E. Franklin Frazier's *Black Bourgeoisie* (1957). Frazier was the most prominent Black sociologist of the mid-twentieth century, a long-time faculty member at Howard University, and, in 1948, the first Black president of the American Sociological Association. *Black Bourgeoisie*, first published in France as *Bourgeoisie Noire* (1955), was highly controversial both among sociologists and among the people it purported to describe. DuBois's legacy of the "talented tenth," had cast the educated black professional and business class as the leading force in the push for racial equality. Frazier offered, in contrast, a view of the Black middle class as a conservative force, pretentious, delusional, and obsessed with status and conspicuous consumption. Invoking psychoanalytic terms such as "inferiority complex" and "wish fulfillment," Frazier contrasted what he called "the world of reality"—the actual economic and social condition of the Black middle class—with "the world of make believe"—the fantasy of successful black businesses, celebrity, power, wealth, and status as depicted in Black periodicals such as *Ebony* and *Jet*. If *Black Bourgeoisie* offered a race-specific version of Mills's critique of the middle class, the criticism was more pointed, precisely because the desire of the Black middle class, in Frazier's view, was rooted in self-hatred and the wish to distance itself from the Black working class. Instead of realistically addressing the problem of racial discrimination and oppression, the Black middle class offered false images of achievement, an imitative vision of "society," an attachment to consumer values, a world of style without substance. Instead of the cutting edge of leadership in the movement for equality and racial justice, the Black middle class was a reactionary force, seeking white approval in imitative terms, and distancing itself from the Black masses.

The terms of middle-class cultural criticism also provided the foundation of Betty Friedan's famous *The Feminine Mystique* (1963). Often lauded as the book that launched second-wave feminism, Friedan's analysis gave a specifically gendered vision of middle-class insecurity, self-hatred, and false consciousness—and a specifically middle-class vision of gender. Friedan's suburban women were enmeshed in an unreal mythology, one in which the norms of middle-class domesticity were imagined by Friedan as sources of dehumanization and self-denial. Friedan went so far as to draw on studies of totalitarianism to declare the home a "comfortable concentration camp," in which housewives faced a progressive dehumanization. Interestingly, however, unlike Mills and others such as Paul Goodman, who identified the forms of meaningless modern bureaucratic work as the source of alienation and passivity, Friedan argued that work for women was the solution to the dehumanizing aspects of modern life. For her, work—in the form of middle-class careers—was the site of creativity, self-fulfillment, and personal growth, rather than the sphere of anxiety, routinization, and dependency as it was imagined by male critics of the era. Of course, her conflation of "women" as a group with middle-class college-educated women who had the option of professional careers, would come under much criticism as feminist forms of thought and critique multiplied in the decades following. Friedan herself had moved from being a journalist deeply concerned about labor and union issues in the 1940s to utilizing the postwar interest in Freudian psychology and Abraham Maslow's humanistic psychology, with its famous "hierarchy of needs," to define an agenda of human motivation for women. Maslow allowed her to move past the problem of material inequality, and to assume a culture of abundance in which the psychological and spiritual needs of self-development could become the basis of her political view. Although she was critical of both Freud and Marx (as well as functionalist sociology, and the work of Margaret Mead, among others), she drew on both, arguing, for instance, that keeping women in a condition of domesticity was driven by the needs of consumer capitalism to sell products. As much as Friedan constructed an argument against the prevailing practices, values, and modes of seeing she attributed to the postwar world, her own arguments were deeply indebted to the terms of the dominant postwar model of middle-class psychological and cultural criticism.

The concern with problems of individualism versus conformity that informed much of this thought found its *locus classicus* in the nineteenth-century French proto-sociologist Alexis de Tocqueville's *Democracy in America* (1835, 1840). Tocqueville, whose work had received little attention since the antebellum era in which the two volumes of *Democracy in America* were published, was rediscovered and reinvigorated in the Cold War context. Tocqueville was quoted by presidents and other political leaders, became a mainstay of the college curriculum, and was elevated to the status of central authority on American democracy. The Tocqueville revival of the postwar era was resonant with the turn to cultural and psychological modes of criticism. One of the most important aspects of Tocqueville's analysis of American democracy was his focus on the cultural and psychological consequences of democracy. He argued that, unlike European countries with established hierarchical institutions, democracy, by breaking the bonds of social dependency and obligation, created the conditions of mass conformity, which was only the flipside of the individualism endemic to democratic thought. Tocqueville was one of the first thinkers to construct a concept of individualism, which was to become a powerful idea in American thought. What he meant by it was a kind of anti-institutional belief in the autonomy of the person as a social actor, and he saw it as directly related to democratic egalitarianism. But without the hierarchies and institutions of aristocratic life, the lone individual was put in a precarious position—he needed to conform to public sentiment of the mass as a way to avoid alienation and disintegration of social order. The more individualistic the culture became, Tocqueville argued, the more narrow and constrained the range of thought was. Societies that were hierarchical and aristocratic valued diversity of opinion; democratic societies had to create order by psychological pressure to conform. Tocqueville's analysis was ironic, and in being so, served the interests of postwar thinkers who embraced notions of complexity and tragedy as indicative of liberalism. "In equality," said Tocqueville, "I see two tendencies: one which leads every man's thought into new paths and another which would force him willingly to cease thinking at all." Democracy provided "intellectual liberty," but "having broken the shackles formerly imposed upon it by class systems or men, the human spirit would be closely confined by the general will of the majority"[10] A book over a 100 years old, written in the era of Transcendentalism and the market revolution, became a kind of Cold War bible to describe the threat to freedom that resided within the very commitment to egalitarian freedom.

The Literary Imagination in the Cold War

In the academic world, one of the major turns in literary study was toward increasing formalism and rigor in the work of the New Critics. But this movement stood alongside—and at odds with—a broader kind of moral and cultural criticism that was tied to literature, and aimed more at the larger public as well as the academy. Writing about literature, for these critics, was a way to address the contradictions of modern culture. This group of thinkers included prominent figures such as critics Lionel Trilling, Leslie Fiedler, Harry Levin, Alfred Kazin, and Irving Howe; and critic/novelists such as Ralph Ellison, Norman Mailer, Mary McCarthy, and James Baldwin. The characteristic form of the essay—often published in magazines such as *Partisan Review* and *Commentary*—was their *metier*, and some of the best-known books of these writers were essentially essay collections: Trilling's *The Liberal Imagination* (1950), Baldwin's *Notes of a Native Son* (1955), and Ellison's *Shadow and Act* (1964). Unlike the New Critics, these intellectuals adopted a wide-ranging and comprehensive attitude, scanning not only literary texts but also broader forms of cultural discourse—Trilling, for instance, wrote on Jane Austen and Henry James, but also on Alfred Kinsey's sexology, Freudian psychoanalysis, the intellectual historiography of Vernon Parrington, and the social thought of anthropologists. These thinkers saw literature as a vehicle for something much broader, what Trilling called "the moral imagination': the ways in which societies configure beliefs, values, and modes of apprehending reality. In many respects, these intellectuals laid the groundwork—whether it was their intention or not— for the notion that literature was not a set of distinct aesthetic forms, with their own formal attributes, but an expression of ideologies and worldviews to be found in politics, social thought, and philosophy as well. They tended to walk a line that resisted the reduction of literature to politics, that sought to preserve the free imagination against dogmatism—while affirming that if one was to understand the society and culture and politics of the present, one had to see literary texts as the most developed expression of those things. These critics tended to align in many respects with the values of Cold War Liberalism—anti-dogmatic, committed to the literary imagination as a realm of possibility, concerned with the psychology of totalitarianism, embracing "complexity" against what they regarded as simplistic didactic moralism.

Trilling's opening essay in *The Liberal Imagination*, "Reality in America," and Baldwin's famous takedown of Harriet Beecher Stowe's *Uncle Tom's Cabin* in "Everybody's Protest Novel" are two of the best examples of this mode of writing. The first essay is an extended critique of what Trilling regarded as a simplistic equation made by liberals between "reality" and the material world, and their denial of the reality of the psychological and cultural world. In V.L. Parrington, Granville Hicks, Charles Beard, and the novelist Theodore Dreiser, Trilling finds "the chronic American belief that there exists an opposition between reality and mind and that one must enlist oneself in the party of reality."[11] The materialist conception of reality, said Trilling, is offered as the basis for political action, for fixing the inequities of the world, but in denying the reality and complexity of the human mind, it ironically offers no responsible solution—the observation of "reality" becomes a good and an end in itself. Trilling finds, on the other hand, that the intellectual resources of the novelist Henry James—denounced by critics as evasive, elitist, and failing to engage "the real"—provide a better and more profound political and moral vision. In his portrayal of psychological complexity and the reality of the world of ideas, James allows us to see that all political and social questions cannot be made simple, that the idea of an art that has its own deliberate intention to achieve political ends, sacrifices the aesthetic variety of the world to a utilitarian motive. Baldwin's attack on the protest novel is of a similar kind. While much of Baldwin's work as a Black writer is centrally concerned with the problem of race in American life—its psychological, social, and intellectual meanings—he rejects the tradition of writing about race and slavery that he sees extending from Stowe to the modern protest novel, as embodied in Richard Wright's *Native Son*, for its didactic moralism. The morality play of protest literature, he argues, has the effect of reproducing the dehumanization that it purports to portray by turning human beings into caricatures and creatures of their environment. "The failure of the protest novel," he writes, "lies in its rejection of life, the human being, the denial of his beauty, dread, power, in its insistence that it is his categorization alone which is real and which cannot be transcended."[12] Literature, for both Baldwin and Trilling, must aspire to face a more complex and tragic reality, must make us see the ironies and contradictions of human motivations, rather than be agitprop as the proletarian novelists and critics of the 1930s had declared.

The thought of these writers often dovetailed with the postwar American embrace of the philosophical existentialism of European writers such as Jean-Paul Sartre, Simone de Beauvoir, Martin Heidegger, Karl Jaspers, and Albert Camus, as well as the elevation of Nietzsche and Freud to the status of critical demigods. It is difficult to read Ralph Ellison's groundbreaking novel, *Invisible Man* (1952), for instance, without hearing the echo of Dostoevsky in a Black voice, the idea of radical alienation of selfhood, and the bleak canvas of a world in which the only meaning available was the one forged in the choices and actions of the self. Literary figures such as Richard Wright and Norman Mailer also took up existentialist ideas. Beginning in the 1940s, American writers and philosophers such as Hazel Barnes, Walter Kaufmann, and William Barrett, constructed a canon of European continental existentialism as a counter to the growing authority of Anglo-American analytical philosophy, on the one hand, and what many regarded as the troubling Marxist legacy, on the other. The central themes of existentialism—a denial of transcendental authority and structure in the universe, the problem of anxiety, dread, and terror as the condition of radical aloneness, human existence and being as itself not a given, but a problem, and the limits of rationality in such a world—sought to recover human existence as a moral problem, at the very moment academic philosophy was turning toward the solution of technical and logical problems. With no fixed or given meaningful order, existentialism created a vision of human self-making as an act of authenticity in an inauthentic and false world. Sartre's famous declaration in "Existentialism is a Humanism," (1946) that "existence precedes essence," sought to invert the philosophical essentialism that he saw as endemic to Western philosophy. The positing of the idea that human beings are radically free and responsible agents because they have only the being, the essence, that they create through their own actions offered a bracing alternative to forms of social and political radicalism, even as Sartre himself claimed a Marxist orientation in his own thought. Although Trilling and others remained wary of existentialist philosophy, they found themselves walking in similar tracks, raising the question of the moral vision in a world with no given moral order, looking into the "abyss" of a world without God or meaning. The existentialist equivalent of the common postwar idea of conformity was what Sartre called "bad faith," a kind of evasion of the conditions of existence through living a life grounded in social convention.

The Conservative Mind

While the dominant Cold War Liberalism set the terms for a great deal of the social and political thought of the era, it also had its critics, not just from the Left, but from the Right. But the liberal image of the American right tended to downplay the extent to which a body of thought highly critical of modern liberalism was given any traction in the public culture. For them, liberalism only had serious critics from within its own walls.

Hofstadter, in *The Age of Reform* described the "New Conservatism" of his era as an oxymoron: "It is in itself a capitulation to the American demand for constant change, and hence a betrayal of conservatism at the outset."[13] Trilling notoriously denied that there even existed a conservative body of ideas in American life: conservative impulses do not "express themselves in ideas but only in action or in irritable mental gestures which seek to resemble ideas."[14] Historians today, however, are very aware of a host of thinkers who sought to construct a body of developed thought as a counter to the establishment liberalism that rested on the extension of the New Deal welfare state and the internationalism of the World War II state. Postwar conservatism found its voice in the establishment of the journal of opinion, *National Review* in 1955 under the editorship of William F. Buckley. Buckley had made a splash as the author of a critique of the dominant ideological and atheistic orientation of the modern university in *God and Man at Yale* (1951), based on his own experience as an undergraduate. He would come to be identified as the central figure in the conservative intellectual world, bringing together a variety of voices and positions united by their opposition to New Deal-style liberalism. He also served as a kind of gatekeeper, defining the range of acceptable opinion. He distanced the conservative movement from the reactionary and conspiratorial John Birch Society, an organization that had accused President Dwight Eisenhower of being a communist; Ayn Rand, the founder of the philosophy of Objectivism, and a sharp critic of religious belief; and *The American Mercury*, fallen from its heyday under H.L Mencken to become a fount of explicit and virulent anti-semitism. Buckley aimed at a kind of respectability politics, an attempt to keep the more disreputable forces associated with opposition to liberalism—racism, nativism, conspiratorial thought, anti-semitism, authoritarianism, fascist fellow-traveling—relatively contained, but certainly not absent. Buckley himself, for instance, defended Jim Crow segregation in the South, and his brother-in-law and prominent conservative intellectual Brent Bozell was an admirer of Spain under the authoritarian reign of Franco.

Unlike Cold War Liberalism which, ironically, created greater consensus among its partisans even as it elevated the idea of critical thinking, conservatism did not possess a unified ideological outlook, even as it struggled to argue for a coherent worldview. In part, this is due to the history of conservatism, which has developed its worldview in reaction to progressivism and liberalism. The British philosopher Michael Oakeshott in 1956 declared that conservatism was something more like a sensibility than an ideology—a feeling for the established past, an antipathy to novelty and change. What such an understanding of conservatism suggested was that there were no central doctrines common to the history of conservative thought. Conservatives could be statist or anti-statist; individualist or social holist; rationalist or sentimentalist; capitalist or anti-capitalist; reactionary or reformist. What tended to unify conservatives, and provide the foundation for what came to be a central aspect of the ideological and intellectual history of the second half of the twentieth century, was what conservatism was against. The opposition to communism, socialism, and welfare-state liberalism, which many conservatives equated with one another, was the driving force behind a great deal of conservative thought. Postwar conservatives fell into three groups, who papered over their intellectual differences and contradictions by opposing a shared enemy. These three wings of the movement were anti-statist libertarians or what were sometimes called "classical liberals" committed to limited government and individual rights; traditionalists, who opposed the perceived breakdown of received authorities such as religion, the family, and morality; and anti-communists, some of whom were ex-communists, and who saw communism as a threat to freedom and the American way of life, and often advocated for a more powerful opposition to communists both foreign and domestic. For the latter group, this often meant support for McCarthyism on the domestic front, and advocating policies such as the military rollback of communism in Eastern Europe. The expanded state of the anti-communists clearly pushed against the libertarian commitments; the traditionalists were often critical of individualism and capitalism as disintegrative forces, as opposed to the libertarians; and the traditionalist fondness for an enforced moral order was at odds with anti-communist and libertarian commitments to free thought. Frank Meyer reduced the conflicts and tensions between these three components of the conservative movement by crafting a "fusionist" movement as an umbrella for postwar conservative thought. Libertarianism and traditionalism, in his view, did not need to be at odds, since one of the points of reducing State scope and action was to prevent the use of concentrated liberal power against traditional authorities.

While Buckley and Meyer were key figures in bringing disparate anti-liberal forces together in a kind of intellectual synthesis, the conservative intellectual movement included figures from the reactionary to the liberal: neo-agrarian Richard Weaver, the communitarian sociologist Robert Nisbet, the Austrian economist Friedrich von Hayek, the political theorist Russell Kirk, the poet and historian Peter Viereck, the ex-communists James Burnham and Whittaker Chambers, the economist Frank Knight, the anarcho-capitalist Murray Rothbard, among many others. One of the central hubs of conservative thought in the United States was the University of Chicago, where Austrian-influenced free-market economics came to dominate the economics department, and where some figures associated with the Committee on Social Thought emphasized a conservative counter to liberal social thought. Much of the opposition to statism, to the use of the economic theories of John Maynard Keynes, which emphasized the use of state policy and spending, and to the growth of the welfare state in Europe and the United States, took place under the auspices of an international organization, The Mont Pèlerin Society, founded in 1947 under the leadership of Hayek. Historians have seen this organization as key in shaping the philosophy of what came to be called "neoliberalism," with its faith in the power of markets. Hayek's influential *The Road to Serfdom*, which argued that any form of state planning and economic regulation was a gateway to expanded government power and the loss of liberty, had been published in the United States in 1944, and then in a condensed and simplified version for a mass audience in the magazine *Readers' Digest* in 1945. Hayek, and many of the free-market economists and political theorists who followed, such as the Chicago economist Milton Friedman, did not necessarily think of themselves as conservatives, even though they published in outlets such as *National Review* and had common cause with conservatives against the state. Hayek even explicitly distanced himself from Buckley and traditionalist conservatives, claiming the identity of classical liberalism in his 1957 address to the Mont Pèlerin Society, "Why I Am Not a Conservative."

Hayek was probably the most prominent voice of the free-market, anti-statist position in the years after World War II. Russell Kirk was his counterpart on the traditionalist wing. In 1953 Kirk published *The Conservative Mind*, an attempt to provide both a history of Anglo-American conservative thought and to define a body of conservative principles—two goals that were somewhat in tension with one another. Kirk found the little magazine, *Modern Age* in 1957. If *National Review* was the postwar conservative counter to *The New Republic*, more directly engaged with concrete politics and policy, *Modern Age* was a conservative answer to *Partisan Review*, a more frankly intellectual, philosophical, and cultural venue for traditionalist thought. *The Conservative Mind* located the intellectual source of conservative thought in the writings of the eighteenth-century British Whig, Edmund Burke, helping construct Burke as the patron saint of modern conservatism, just as liberals were constructing their own patron saint, John Locke. In particular, Burke's critique of the French Revolution, and his endorsement of a vision of society as an organism growing through gradual modification, against the abstract commitment to universalist principles embodied in revolution, made Burke a model and fount of conservative thought. Although Kirk was "reluctant to condense profound and intricate intellectual systems to a few pretentious phrases," he felt the need to define in a clear way the "principles" of conservatism: "the essence of social conservatism is preservation of the ancient moral traditions of humanity." The six tenets at the heart of conservative thought, according to Kirk, were faith in a God-ordered society; embrace of variety against uniformity; commitment to fixed hierarchy in society; belief that private property is a necessary condition of freedom; belief in the prescriptive authority of tradition and prejudice; and a gradualist incremental vision of Providentially-based progress.[15] Against liberal secularism, homogeneity, egalitarianism, unbounded selfishness, rationalism, and innovation, Kirk imagined a Conservative moral order. That the principles of conservative thought were potentially contradictory, that they were not always coherent with one another, was less important than that they articulated an opposition to liberalism, socialism, and communism.

Conclusion

One of the important aspects of the broad political and social thought that proliferated in the 15 years after World War II was the extent to which partisans got one another wrong. Liberals imagined a pathological conservatism, driven by paranoid thinking, or a conservatism with no intellectual content at all—they were critics of conformity, but had a hard time seeing the diversity of thought in their midst, a thriving world of conservative philosophy and argumentation. Conservatives such as Buckley, Meyer, Hayek, and Kirk, constructed their own vision of liberalism that denied the explicit commitment that Cold War liberals were making to drawing a sharp line between totalitarianism and social welfare liberalism. The idea that the New Deal state was an incipient totalitarian order waiting to happen flew in the face of liberal commitments to civil liberties—although both liberals and conservatives were willing to modify their commitments to freedom of speech and freedom of assembly when it came to Communism. Perhaps both parties shared a variety of outlooks, and the distinctions that were being drawn amounted to what Freud had called "the narcissism of small differences." But that would suggest that there was indeed a "liberal consensus" in the postwar era and that the idea of a liberal consensus was something more than an ideological construct.

Notes

1. Arthur Schlesinger, Jr., *The Vital Center: The Politics of Freedom* (Boston, MA: Houghton Mifflin, 1949), pp. 105, 244–245.
2. Ibid., p. 190.
3. Ibid., p. 166.
4. Richard Hofstadter, *The American Political Tradition and the Men Who Made It* (New York: Alfred A. viii Knopf, 1948), p. viii.
5. Henry Steele Commager, *The American Mind: An Interpretation of American Thought and Character Since the 1880s* (New Haven, CT: Yale University Press, 1950), p. vii.
6. Hannah Arendt, *The Origins of Totalitarianism* (New York: Harcourt, Brace and Co., 1951), p. 451.

7 Daniel Bell, *The End of Ideology: On the Exhaustion of Political Ideas in the Fifties* (Glencoe, IL: Free Press, 1960), p. 370.
8 C. Wright Mills, "Letter to the New Left," *New Left Review* 5 (September 1, 1960), p. 19.
9 Erik H. Erikson, *Childhood and Society* (New York: W.W. Norton and Co., 1950), p. 282.
10 Alexis de Tocqueville, *Democracy in America and Two Essays on America*, trans. Gerald E. Bevan (New York: Penguin, 2003), p. 502.
11 Lionel Trilling, *The Liberal Imagination: Essays on Literature and Society* (New York: Charles Scribner's Sons, 1950), p. 10.
12 James Baldwin, *Notes of a Native Son* (Boston, MA: Beacon Press, 1955), p. 23.
13 Richard Hofstadter, *The Age of Reform: From Bryan to F.D.R.* (New York: Vintage Books, 1955), pp. 14–15.
14 Trilling, *The Liberal Imagination*, p. ix.
15 Russell Kirk, *The Conservative Mind: From Burke to Eliot* (Chicago, IL: Henry Regnery Co., 1953), pp. 6–9.

Part III
Rethinking Modernisms
1963–2000

11 Cultural Revolutions and Ruptures

The 1960s represent a moment in intellectual history in which, to all appearances, the world split open, and history was imagined in terms of rupture and a radical break from the past. A set of challenges to the modernist modes of thought that had governed philosophy, social thought, aesthetic theory, and politics were ubiquitous in the intellectual life of the era. Some have described the new sensibility and ways of thinking of the era with the term "post-modernism" to stress this break with the high modernism of the mid-century that the cultural critic Harold Rosenberg had dubbed "the tradition of the new." By the early 1970s, social and economic thinkers had designated the new forms of order "post-industrial society." In the sphere of philosophical and literary theory, the forms of European structuralist theory associated with Ferdinand de Saussure in linguistics, and Claude Levi-Strauss in anthropology, came under criticism by a new group of "post-structuralist" thinkers such as Michel Foucault, Jacques Derrida, and Roland Barthes. French Post-structuralism would dovetail with increasing concern in American philosophy and literary theory with the nature of language as both a medium of representation and a kind of self-contained system of contradictions; commentators dubbed this "the linguistic turn." The influence of "theory" remade the academic disciplines in the humanities, and spilled out into the broader public sphere. In the art world, the modernist aesthetics of figures like Clement Greenberg gave way to new forms of experimentation that eroded the distinction between art and life and between high and low culture.

Lost in the eagerness either to celebrate or deride a host of new approaches to reality operating under the sign of "post," was the extent to which these new forms of thought were less novel than they appeared, and in fact, were in many ways extensions of the modernist thought that had preceded them. If modernism introduced radical uncertainty in epistemology, a relativistic or pluralistic account of belief, a commitment to novelty and originality based on rejection of tradition and received practice, the so-called post-modern moment simply turned the modernist ethos

DOI: 10.4324/9781003120803-15

on modernism itself. It elevated irony over sincerity, the surface of things over depths, the quotation of the received past over the idea of originality. What it did not do is replace a vision of the world as stable and fixed, with a new kind of subjectivity and relativism, as some popular commentators at the time and since have suggested; modernism had already been busy embracing new psychologies, cosmologies, and epistemologies for a hundred years, and any dream of a stable world based on transcendent reason and objectivity had long given way to modernist doubt.

This is not to say that belief in objectivity, neutrality, dispassionate reason, and evidence-based knowledge had no continuing cultural and intellectual existence. The spheres of academic understanding in the arts, humanities, and social sciences, and the political and cultural worlds of art, literature, and public life, had largely gone over to an embrace of modernist critique, uncertainty, originality, and fluidity. But in popular sectors such as news journalism and technology, some combination of ideas of empiricism, objective knowledge, balanced moderation, and fixed truth continued to have traction. The triumph of modernist and post-modernist thought was never complete, but even those who imagined alternative forms of secure and reliable epistemic and moral commitments found themselves operating in a universe of "narratives," "paradigms," and "world views," in which the limitations of older ways of thinking and knowing were constantly being overcome by new ones. If modernist ideas had, like the Pragmatist philosophers, replaced absolute and fixed truths and categories with habits and stabilizing continuities based on gradualism and adaptation to new circumstances, the forms of thought that came to the fore in the 1960s replaced continuity with discontinuity, evolution with revolution, stability with rupture. The consciousness of a break with the past was everywhere, even as it built upon the dominant modernism that had ruled for a hundred years.

Paradigms, Epistemes, and Their Cognates: Kuhn, Foucault, Skinner

One of the single most influential works of thought in the second half of the twentieth century was a work written by an academic physicist turned historian of science: Thomas Kuhn's *Structure of Scientific Revolutions* (1962). Building upon the substantial work in science studies, in the decades since the 1930s, that had emphasized the sociology of knowledge and the historical development of scientific thought, Kuhn created a way to think about science as a culturally specific activity; his work derailed the image of science built by Logical Empiricists, analytic philosophers, and celebrants of science as the crowning achievement of a way of knowing that transcended culture, history, and human subjectivity. This was no mere academic monograph, but a transformative text whose arguments, terminology, and interpretive framework spread widely across the academic world, shaping understandings not only of science but also of the grounds of epistemology and the form of history. Terms such as "normal science," "incommensurability," and, most prominently, "paradigm," and "paradigm shift," entered into widespread usage. Kuhn's *Structure* sparked widespread debate among philosophers and historians of science, but also among a broader public concerned with the nature and authority of natural science. In the years between its publication in the early 1960s and its 50th-anniversary edition in 2012, *Structure* sold over a million copies and remains one of the most frequently and widely cited works in the humanities and social sciences.

Kuhn argued a number of points that countered common assumptions and understandings of how science operates. The history of science, he said, provides an alternative to models of science built on logical and abstract forms and principles, such as those provided by Carnap and the Logical Empiricists, or Karl Popper and his image of science proceeding through hypothesis testing and falsification. Kuhn argued that the observation of scientific activity in history demonstrates that science does, and has done, none of the things that its philosophical explicators imagine that it does. Instead, historical observation can help us to construct a model of science and scientific revolutions that is based on what scientists actually do, and not on theoretical and idealized models of scientific method. That observation leads to a number of conclusions: (1) Science in its normal day-to-day activities does not seek to overturn error or criticize its own operating assumptions in any way—what he called "normal science," to distinguish it from "revolutionary science," is a matter of puzzle solving and filling in gaps. What this means is that it is a deeply traditional and conservative activity, bounded by largely untested assumptions that are received from the past and taken as unquestioned authority. Scientists in their normal activities are not stepping outside of convention into a space of logic or objectivity, but operating inside something that looks like a culture, in Ruth Benedict's terms: a patterned and coherent intellectual whole. The image of the scientist engaging in constant hypothesis testing to falsify or verify a proposition had nothing to do with how scientists conducted themselves. Normal science essentially found what it expected to find, articulating and specifying elements to make them fit the received form of belief. And the vast majority of scientific activity took place under the conditions of normal science. (2) Science in its specific forms is always operating within the boundaries or terms of what Kuhn called a "paradigm." Kuhn used this term in a variety of not-always consistent or coherent ways, but what he seemed to mean by it is a foundational "discovery" that defines the goals and elements of any scientific practice. Sometimes a paradigm, in Kuhn's usage, seems more like a "worldview," sometimes more like an "intellectual framework," and sometimes more like an "exemplar," but in all cases it both puts limits on the kinds of questions that could be asked and provided a set of problems to be solved. (3) When anomalies that can't be explained under the existing paradigm accumulate, scientists do not abandon the existing paradigm unless they have an alternative paradigm, and even then, many will continue to cling to the old paradigm. If a scientist abandons an existing paradigm and enters into an independent stance without a paradigm, according to Kuhn, he ceases to be practicing science. (4) The process of scientific paradigm change is not an accumulative process by which the new paradigm incorporates within it the old paradigm; instead, it is more like a gestalt switch in which one sees the world through the terms of one paradigm or the other. The two competing paradigms are what Kuhn called, in one of the more controversial arguments of *Structure*, "incommensurable." One must operate in one paradigm or another, and one paradigm cannot be reworked to be made compatible or assimilable to the other. (5) Kuhn's claim was that paradigms constitute worlds and that when scientists go through a revolution that replaces one paradigm by another, they can be said to be living in a different world: paradigms are not only "constitutive of science," but in a real sense "are constitutive of nature as well."[1] Kuhn fundamentally challenged a view that nature stays the same, while the things we say about it change. In Kuhn's world, there is no paradigm-independent "nature" that might provide a stable source of authority to evaluate different theories or conclusions. (6) The reason that scientists opt for a new paradigm is not that it provides a better explanation for all phenomena under its purview. Scientists do not make decisions on purely rational and epistemic grounds but are motivated by aesthetic, contextual, and practical interests. (7) Scientists themselves are unaware of what they are up to, because they are socialized into the profession by textbooks which construct a false history of scientific progress.

The implications of Kuhn's argument were ground-breaking. Science does not proceed in a unilinear additive fashion, in which truth replaces error, and therefore, it is not based on the continuous gradual accumulation of knowledge. Instead, scientific revolutions are disjunctive and discontinuous—one way of thinking is replaced by another. More importantly, the new paradigm does not get the scientist closer to truth in any absolute sense, but replaces one way of seeing with another; since there is no observed nature outside of paradigms, there can be no way to evaluate the ultimate truth value of one paradigm compared to another. The model of science as the exemplar of progress, as an overcoming of superstition, prejudice, and inherited assumptions, moving ever closer to truth, said Kuhn, needs to be abandoned. This is not to say that Kuhn thought science was just like every other activity engaged in by human beings—in fact, he thought most of the fields of study in the humanities and social sciences were not really scientific, because they lacked the consensus of paradigms. The goal of Kuhn's book was not to dethrone scientific claims to authority or to argue that scientific knowledge was ultimately subjective, and therefore should not be regarded with greater authority than religion, folk wisdom, or moral philosophy, although many of his readers took it that way. Rather, it was to suggest that the distinctive characteristics of science were unintelligible if not understood as a practice of human beings in communities with shared beliefs—beliefs that made sense by telling scientists what to look at and how to look at it. In this way, Kuhn was the heir of the Pragmatic philosophy of Charles Sanders Pierce and William James, but with a difference. The idea that belief was "habit" sounds like the basis for Kuhn's idea of normal science; rooting knowledge in scientific communities sound like Peirce's vision of the social nature of science. But where James saw human beings making the least adjustment possible to make their new ideas fit with their existing stock of beliefs, and imagined a gradual continuous process of adaptation, Kuhn imagined revolutions as moments of all-or-nothing, in which one world view was displaced by another. The new beliefs had the effect of entirely displacing the old ones, rather than gradually adapting them to new understandings. The James view might hold for normal science, but James provided no way to talk about scientific revolutions in which an entire structure of belief went down in flames as the condition for a new intellectual order. Kuhn essentially overthrew the model of scientific change as evolution on the Darwinian model and argued that evolution of knowledge was a vision that contemporary scientists imposed upon their own past. He took the modernist critique of historical teleology a step beyond the modernists, in effect arguing that they were not sufficiently anti-teleological in their outlook. They imagined they had dismissed the idea that history had a goal or an end, but their faith in a progressive and gradual science coming ever closer to some kind of "truth" still clung to a model of movement from ignorance to enlightenment, and thereby imagined that earlier scientists were simply laying the seedbed for discoveries to come, rather than operating in a world entirely alien and foreign to the present. Present belief itself was ripe for wholesale replacement.

Kuhn's image of scientific revolutions as discontinuous was echoed in a more radical form by the French philosopher Michel Foucault, whose 1966 book *Les mots and les choses* was translated as *The Order of Things* in 1970. Foucault, in translation, would go on to be a major intellectual influence on late twentieth-century American thought, especially in the 1980s and 90s, through other works he wrote on the history of the penitentiary, the history of madness, and the history of sexuality. At the center of, especially, the later Foucault, was a conception of knowledge and power as produced in what he called "discourse." In *The Order of*

Things, which was subtitled "An Archaeology of the Human Sciences," Foucault argued for the cultural specificity of ways of knowing at various historical epochs, and their discontinuous relationship to one another. As the archaeology metaphor suggests, Foucault saw the epistemic forms of particular eras as striated rather than continuous—the history of thought was to be understood in terms of distinct layers, rather than as an evolutionary process. Foucault called the characteristic ways of organizing experience and constituting the objects of knowledge of an era an "episteme." Unlike Kuhn, who imagined particular scientific fields of study as governed by paradigms, Foucault was interested in something both more general and pervasive, on the one hand, and less articulated and conscious on the other—the episteme was the mode of order that reached across widely different areas of study, but provided their common epistemological underpinning. Foucault's argument focused on the disjunction between what he called the Classical and Modern epistemes in Europe, the first running from the mid-seventeenth century to the late eighteenth century, the second from the early nineteenth century to the present. Each episteme tied together, in Foucault's analysis, the study of language, of biology, and of wealth. The discourses around each of these areas were not independent from one another. Rather, the forms of culturally defined ordering and knowing, of thinking in categories and relations and abstractions, were shared across disparate areas of study. The episteme was something more like what we might imagine to be a culturally defined epistemic unconscious; it was the ground on which some objects became visible, and others absent. It was the condition for the possibility of thinking and knowing within a culture. And, for Foucault, it was the counter to a history of ideas built on continuity and evolutionary development. The shift from the Classical Episteme to the Modern Episteme was a rupture or break, not a development, growth, or evolution.

Foucault's arguments were more radical, but also, for many American thinkers, more easily dismissed than Kuhn's, because they were offered in a theoretical language derived from sources such as Nietzsche and the French structuralism stemming from the earlier linguistic thought of Ferdinand de Saussure. In the mid-1960s, this was a body of thought that, for philosophers and historians of science, had not achieved intellectual traction in American life; by the end of the 1970s, Foucault, the literary theorist Jacques Derrida, and other important figures in French post-World War II thought would come to exert an important influence in sectors of American thought that sought to weld cultural criticism, linguistic analysis, and what was coming to be called "theory," into a new sensibility. Central to the structural linguistics of Saussure was the doctrine of the arbitrariness of the sign; this doctrine, in a modified and expanded form, suggested a radical discontinuity between the world of language, and the world of objects and events to which language presumably referred. Saussure had argued, first, that there was only a conventional relationship between words and what they signified and that all language was based not on essential meanings, but on oppositions. If meaning was defined by oppositions (white/black, up/down, nature/culture, etc.) rather than by reference to distinct concepts with their own essences, then language could be said to make or constitute the world, rather than reflect it. The things in the world did not, as empiricists might suggest, determine our images and ideas; rather our language ordered the world by attributing and creating meaning and opposition. Nature made no distinction, for instance, between a tree and a bush—that was a conventional distinction in language that ordered the world as people experienced it. When structuralism was applied not just to words and sentences, but to more elaborated forms of discussion, which Foucault and others had designated as "discourse," the conclusion seemed to be that human beings lived in a linguistic world of their own creation, which constituted its objects. If the world had no independent order, then it was malleable, subject to human imaginative ordering. The flip side of this, for Foucault and others, was that language constrained possibilities, that it demanded one think in only the ways it allowed—it was a site of power, a prison house from which no escape was possible.

Parallel to the continental European tradition of critical thought about language, was an Anglo-American philosophical turn toward language, in the works of Ludwig Wittgenstein, J.L. Austin, Gilbert Ryle, and Paul Grice, among others. The "ordinary language" philosophers concerned themselves with problems of meaning and intention—unlike the Saussurean structuralists and post-structuralist, they tended to see language as a matter of use in speech acts, rather than a system of structured oppositions. Austin, for instance, made a famous distinction between speech acts as "locutionary" and "illocutionary," which corresponded roughly to a distinction between the meaning of a speech act, and its action—language was understood as a vehicle that not only permitted people to say things but to do things. Questions of meaning were therefore wrapped up in the intentions of actors bounded by circumstances and contexts. The ordinary language philosophers in Britain had an enormous influence in shaping the so-called Cambridge School of Political Thought that included J.G.A. Pocock, Peter Laslett, John Dunn, and, most importantly, Quentin Skinner. In 1969, Skinner published a paper entitled "Meaning and Understanding in the History of Ideas," which utilized linguistic philosophy to lay out a methodological and theoretical approach to the history of political thought. That essay is now one of the most widely cited works in the field and has been subject to much critical attention. Skinner's essay represented a wholesale attack on a number of approaches to studying the history of thought that created what he regarded as false continuities between vastly different thinkers, and abstracted thought from the conditions of its argumentation in order to write a history of ideas free from any attention to the contexts in which political thinkers made their "utterances." The political philosopher John Locke, for instance, should not be identified with a body of thought called "liberalism," as so many had, because Locke had no such concept and would not have seen his writing as making a contribution to a lineage that later thinkers would construct. The Cambridge School approach came to be dubbed "contextualism," and rejected ways to think about history that involved notions of evolutionary development and continuity. The idea that one thinker "anticipated" a doctrine that was not yet fully developed, according to Skinner, implied an intention that historical actors could never have. The point of studying the history of thought was to discover the alterity of past ideas and the worlds in which they were developed. There could be no history of concepts or ideas, but only of the use of ideas in arguments in specific times and places. The idea that we might be able to identify a long-standing tradition of thought or philosophy, he claimed, obscured the reality of thinking in the past. Instead, we should see the canonical texts of philosophers and thinkers as utterances in a foreign tongue, which we can only reconstruct by seeing them in relationship to authorial intention and entirely dependent on localized meanings. Ordinary language philosophy could help historians to break up a false coherence and telos that Skinner found in ways of talking about ideas, and point understanding not so much toward political, social, or economic conditions, but toward the linguistic conventions, under which arguments were made. Instead of containing ideas, said Skinner, we should be thinking of texts as forms of action, and aim to reconstruct what they were doing, rather than just what they were saying.

What Kuhn, Foucault, and Skinner, among others, had in common was not just a rejection of ideas about progress in understanding the history of science, philosophy, and thought, but a more radical application of ideas about cultural relativism to the image of history. They broke up the assumed relationship between the past and the present, casting the past as a foreign country that was built on a different scaffolding than the present, providing a mirror in which to see the non-rational, culturally specific forms of thinking in our own time. On the one hand, this image of history offered a liberation from the past—no longer was the era before the nineteenth century a determinative burden, weighing on the present and providing a set of inherited constraints. On the other, the paradigms, epistemes, and contexts of the present were equally restrictive, not subject to rational criticism, a kind of linguistic frame or epistemic unconscious that offered a more severe form of continuity, enforced consensus, and containment within their own bounds. No scientist could step outside the paradigm, the episteme determined the possibility of thought, the ideological needs of the present were bound up in our ways of speaking, and could not be separated from them.

The New Left, and the Old

The 1960s was a decade, like the 1930s, identified with radical social and political movements and new forms of critical thought. The material conditions of the two eras, however, were unlike one another in fundamental ways. Of course, continuities of a growing consumer culture, mass media, and welfare statism linked the two decades. But the sharp distinction between an era of mass unemployment, Depression, and widespread belief in capitalist dysfunction, on the one hand, and an expanding economy of material abundance, knowledge-based work, and a vision of managed growth of a middle-class way of life, on the other, seemed to point in opposite direction. What came to be defined as the "Old Left," of Marxism, class-based politics, labor unionism, and the push for material equality through socialism, was challenged by a "New Left" seeking to go beyond Marxism, committed to a politics concerned with culture, psyche, and values as well as material inequality, a new emphasis on youth and American racism, and a critique of the global politics of the Cold War. The wholesale discrediting of Soviet-style communism, and its Marxist underpinnings, in the era of the Cold War and McCarthyism, helped contribute to a redefinition of what political radicalism might look like. Daniel Bell and other social thinkers in the 1950s had declared an "end of ideology," and the expectation that a liberal politics of moderation, gradualism, and compromise would replace the Marxist faith of the Old Left. The New Left was in many ways less a response to the inadequacies of the Old Left, and more to the perceived inadequacies and limits of an establishment liberalism wedded to the foreign policy goals of the Cold War, a slow roll on issues of racial inequality and justice, and a rejection of idealistic or utopian visions. The Old Left sectarian debates between Stalinists and Trotskyists, communists and socialists, and then between those who cooperated with the government investigations into domestic communism and those who refused to cooperate, seemed to the thinkers of the New Left to be largely irrelevant to current concerns. The morality play of the House Unamerican Activities Committee (HUAC) and McCarthyism in the 1950s appeared to belong to a different era for the thinkers of the New Left. If the historians and theorists had imagined history as a series of breaks with the past, the New Left provided a kind of practical enactment of a worldview defined by a break with the Old: new conditions, New Left.

In 1960, the radical sociologist C. Wright Mills published an article in the newly established British journal *New Left Review*, entitled "Letter to the New Left," which was then reprinted in 1961 in *Studies on the Left*, a Madison, Wisconsin based journal that became the center of New Left criticism and theory in the following decade. In it, he laid out a vision of the character of a New Left against what he regarded as the moribund conditions of post-World War II politics of complacency and fatigue. "To be 'Left,'" he said, "means to connect up cultural with political criticism, and both with demands and programmes." Insisting on a utopian vision of possibility, Mills argued for a radical critique of institutions and existing social forms and political ideas. One of those ideas, on the Left, was belief in the working class as the agent of historical change, despite the abundant evidence that the industrial working class had settled into an accommodation with consumer capitalism and was no longer a radical force. Deriding what he called the "labor metaphysic" of the Old Left as "a legacy from Victorian Marxism that is now quite unrealistic," Mills pushed for a new agent of emancipation: the young intelligentsia. The growth of universities had created the conditions for an educated body of students, who, providing a radical rethinking of the conditions of possibility, were primed to act as the agents of change and emancipation. Looking at the activism of white and Black students in the Civil Rights Movement, as one example, Mills shifted the identity of the Left from a working-class movement to a student-led movement.[2]

Two of the most prominent organizations identified with Left politics of the era were Students for a Democratic Society (SDS) and the Student Non-Violent Coordinating Committee (SNCC), both founded in 1960. Although SDS grew out of the student wing of an Old Left organization, the League of Industrial Democracy, it quickly established its own identity in the early 1960s by refusing the sectarian stances and fixations of the Old Left and came to national prominence and visibility for its opposition to the beginnings of the Vietnam War in 1965. SNCC was a Civil Rights organization, which grew out of the student sit-ins at segregated lunch counters in the South, and, embracing the non-violent philosophy of Martin Luther King, Jr., sought direct action through protests, sit-ins, voter registration drives, and other challenges to Jim Crow. Both groups mobilized "youth" as a category of action, suggesting that the calls for maturity and anti-utopianism in politics were the voices of an elderly impulse to resignation and acceptance of the status quo.

In 1962, SDS prepared a manifesto that expressed a particular way of thinking that has captured something of the way in which New Left thinkers built upon the concerns of the middle-class cultural criticism of the post-World War II era, and attempted to synthesize leftist structural criticism of society with the focus on individual self-fulfillment characteristic of the consumer culture of abundance and its therapeutic orientation. Tom Hayden, a student at the University of Michigan, was the principal architect of SDS's "Port Huron Statement." The ghost of "lonely crowd" conformity, apathy, and middle-class quiescence hung over the manifesto, as did the anxiety and existentialist psychology of potential hopelessness in a world armed with nuclear weaponry. Hayden stressed the need for a new idealism to counter the world-weary resignation of his elders; by putting "values" at the center of the statement, Hayden invoked, without any explicit reference, what Jane Addams had called the "subjectivity necessity" of politics, how it represented an outlet for a middle-class generation "bred in at least modest comfort," counseled by their elders to accept a world without utopian aspirations. The Port Huron Statement was both a political and cultural critique. It found life in the world of consumer capitalist abundance to be a source of both oppression (economic, racial, and global), on the one hand, and of soul-deadening inauthenticity and alienation, on the other. It took language from existentialist philosophy and the human potential movement and made the aspiration for individual self-fulfillment a central feature of its political purpose.

> Men have unrealized potential for self-cultivation, self-direction, self-understanding, and creativity. It is this potential that we regard as crucial and to which we appeal, not to the human potentiality for violence, unreason, and submission to authority. The goal of man and society should be human independence: a concern not with image of popularity but with finding a meaning in life that is personally authentic: a quality of mind not compulsively driven by a sense of powerlessness, nor one which unthinkingly adopts status values, nor one which represses all threats to its habits, but one which has full, spontaneous access to present and past experiences, one which easily unites the fragmented parts of personal history, one which openly faces problems which are troubling and unresolved: one with an intuitive awareness of possibilities, an active sense of curiosity, an ability and willingness to learn.[3]

This idea of personal "authenticity" was linked to a social and political vision of what the statement called "participatory democracy." The idea that electoral politics was a sufficient form of democracy was part of the problem of a dissociated public. In order for politics to be meaningful, in SDS's vision, it required a collective effort in which people working together could take control over their own communities and practices; in a mass industrialized society, the answer to enforced apathy and helplessness was democratic action as a form of community building. While the Port Huron Statement is full of specific criticisms of racial injustice, poverty and economic inequality, the interlocking power of corporations, military, and foreign policy elites, it contains no theory of history and society, no fixed intellectual system, to counter the once-powerful presence of Marxism on the Left. In fact, it seems to suggest that thinking in "systems" and fixed ideologies was part of the problem. Its vision was moral, open, idealistic; its tone critical but optimistic. The sense throughout is that the New Left cannot draw on any of the established, now exhausted, resources of political thought, but must reorient politics to a new set of unprecedented conditions.

As the student Left grew more radicalized through the 1960s, it became factionalized and its early idealism and non-dogmatic orientation gave way to more specific political and theoretical influences: Maoism, the Frankfurt School Marxism of Herbert Marcuse, a Third-World critique driven by post-colonial movements, including the writings of Franz Fanon, an embrace of violence as a revolutionary means of action. SNCC, which had shared much of the idealistic vision of racial justice found in the Civil Rights Movement rhetoric of the late 1950s and early 1960s, moved away from reform, non-violent protest, and integrationist politics to an embrace of what SNCC leader Stokely Carmichael (later Kwame Ture) dubbed "Black Power." The tensions between what younger leaders, activists, and thinkers thought of as an ineffective Civil Rights Establishment represented by figures such as Martin Luther King, Jr., and Bayard Rustin, and the demands for a more radical form of revolutionary cultural politics, tended to bring the divided nature of Black thought to the fore, although the actual political positions of various actors were more complex than a simple binary between "establishment" and "radical" would suggest. Young Black intellectuals seized on a more militant racial politics, drawing on the long-standing Black Nationalism of the Nation of Islam and Malcolm X, the insistence on the autonomy of the Black Left from well-meaning white activists, an embrace of armed self-defense by groups such as the Black Panthers, and the rise of a Black Arts Movement premised on the notion of a distinct cultural aesthetic. If the Harlem Renaissance of the 1920s had foregrounded culture and the arts as a space for the assertion of a new identity, the Black Power movement made culture and identity specifically political, and aimed at revolutionary change.

The decade was a revolutionary one in developing a sustained and diverse body of criticism and thought on the Black Left. Harold Cruse's *Crisis of the Negro Intellectual* (1967) was one of the landmark works of the decade, providing a sustained, if highly idiosyncratic, critique of the failure of liberal integrationist politics, Garvey-style Pan-Africanism, Marxism, and the rise of Black Power militancy. Cruse's polemic was marked by an equal-opportunity rejection of symbolic protest and what he regarded as so-called "revolutionary politics"; a takedown of central traditions in Black thought of integrationist vs. separatism, non-violence vs. violence, and faith in the major organizing forces of Garveyism and Marxism. Cruse was a contrarian, and it was often difficult to know what he was for, in concrete terms, other than Black self-determination cast in an alternative voice to the essentialism of Black Nationalism and Pan-Africanism. His message was that Black cultural politics had been disconnected from the actual strategic needs of community building, economic self-help, and the actual conditions of Black life in the United States. Black thought was often, in Cruse's view, intellectual posturing, symbolic statement, an affirmation of culture as a kind of substitute or expression of politics. Cruse was a Black nationalist in his own way, but one that refused the slogans of Black Power and Back to Africa, and the essentialist notion of race homogeneity. *Crisis* spoke to a moment of radical rethinking but did so in such a way as to emphasize what Cruse imagined as the historic failures of Black thought and politics from the Harlem Renaissance to the mid-1960s. Many Black students and thinkers might not have agreed with Cruse on the specifics, but the idea of a crisis in thought that demanded a departure from the received tradition made *Crisis* obligatory reading for Black intellectuals and activists.

The Meaning of Art

The year 1964 signaled a moment in the history of aesthetic thought that appeared to represent a turn away from the high modernism of avant-garde art and art criticism of the Cold War era and toward something new. If critics like Clement Greenberg, Harold Rosenberg, and Meyer Schapiro had created influential ways to understand art in terms of form and style, they were also all committed to the construction or affirmation of an aesthetic canon based on high modernist principles. Greenberg, in "Avant-Garde and Kitsch" (1939), for instance, had drawn a sharp line between art and mass culture, and associated the latter with capitalist industrial production and propaganda, in contrast to the aesthetic value of high art. For modernists of the post-World War II era, when New York City displaced Paris as the international center of art, avant-garde art embodied values of complexity and experimentation that refused commercialism, that sought to liberate art from the sterile conventions and conformity of mass culture, that favored an art of originality and innovation. Two essays were published in 1964 that pushed hard against the presumed orientation of an aesthetic establishment: the young New York intellectual Susan Sontag's "Against Interpretation," and the philosopher Arthur Danto's "The Artworld." What Sontag was to refer to as a "new sensibility," seemed everywhere afoot, and the old understandings of how to think about art, and its relationship to critical thought and social conditions, were under challenge. The break in aesthetic standards was more apparent than real, and the movements in art and criticism were in many ways extensions of what theorists of the avant-garde since the early twentieth-century Dadaists had already laid down. But consciousness of a departure at this moment in the first half of the 1960s became the basis of a much-discussed idea of "postmodernism" in art in the decades to come.

New artistic movements in the late 1950s and early 1960s pushed beyond the Abstract Expressionism, or "Action Painting" as Rosenberg had it, of Jackson Pollack, Willem de Kooning, and others: Minimalism, Happenings, and, most prominently, Pop Art. Each of these challenged tenets of mid-century modernism. Minimalists pushed against the notion that abstraction was "expressive," and toward a concern with a more clinical idea of pure form absent romantic notions of art; the idea that art necessarily involved fixed objects with enduring qualities such as paintings and sculptures was challenged by the focus on performance and events in Allan Kaprow's much-discussed "Happenings"; Pop Art, in the hands of artists such as Andy Warhol and Roy Lichtenstein, used the elements of mass commercial culture in new ways, breaking down the presumed hierarchy of art and kitsch. Warhol's Brillo Boxes, Campbell's Soup Cans, and reproduced images of Marilyn Monroe asked the viewer to look at the ubiquitous design environment of consumer culture in new ways. The idea that Hollywood films, fashion, comic books, and advertisements could be figured as art if recontextualized by artists challenged a vision of art conceived as an autonomous realm of culture, and the idea that aesthetic value and mass culture commodification were fundamentally at odds. Jazz music in the 1940s and 1950s had created its own Be Bop avant-garde and intellectual audience, undermining the ideas of modernists such as Theodore Adorno, who had difficulty conceiving of popular music as anything but commercial repetitive forms with no aesthetic aspirations. The simultaneous emergence of pop musicians and performers, such as Bob Dylan, who asked that their work be regarded with some level of seriousness, meant that the modernist hierarchy of highbrow and lowbrow, art and entertainment, was being unmade both from above and below. Hollywood cinema was challenged by the importation of European films, with their own claims to art: Bergman, Rossellini, Antonioni, and others. The French New Wave filmmakers such as Jean-Luc Godard and François Truffaut took the conventions of Hollywood cinema and both celebrated them and turned them inside out through formal innovations. By the end of the 1960s, the old Hollywood Studio system had lost its prominence to a new generation of American "auteurs." What was high and what was low? Where was the line between commercial and aesthetic forms? What could art continue to mean in a mass-mediated culture?

Sontag's "Against Interpretation" appeared in this milieu of reevaluation of art. Her essential argument was that the hermeneutic desire to find meaning in art was driven by an attempt to contain and limit the power of aesthetic experience, and should be rejected; interpretation was "the revenge of the intellect upon art." What she meant by interpretation was an intellectual exercise of replacing the art object with its presumably hidden meaning, and her principal exemplars of this practice were the Marxists and Freudians who peeled away the sensuous surface of the artwork in order to find property relations or libidinal desires lurking underneath. Although her argument could be read as an anti-intellectual embrace of what she called "the erotics of art," against "the hermeneutics of art," it was also a highly intellectualized position, ranging widely in its references, making a historicist argument that interpretation has become a deadening practice only under the conditions of an over-saturated modernity. Although she focused on visual art, her target was not the dominant formalist criticism of Clement Greenberg—she and Greenberg in fact shared a concern with form. She seemed more concerned with a general discourse that could be found in Cold War modernist literary critics such as Lionel Trilling and Leslie Fiedler, although she never mentioned literary criticism as a practice. What she was targeting was an intellectual sensibility, rather than a specific critic.[4]

Her essay represented a shift away from high modernist criticism in a number of ways. Firstly, she emphasized the power of aesthetic experience, linking the senses and their engagement as the thing being threatened by the project of intellectual "containment." "Interpretation" was her version of what "the end of ideology" was for the New Left, but in aesthetic terms—it opposed itself to passionate engagement. A cool and distanced intellectual understanding could be no replacement for the intensity of experience she sought to recover, even as the enthusiasm she evinced was delivered in a cool and distanced tone. Against interpretation did not mean "against criticism," but rather, a redefinition of the role of the critic. The critic should aim at description and analysis of the work of art as an aid to aesthetic experience; criticism should help the audience to "see," and feel, rather than to understand. Secondly, she directed critical attention to what we might call the surface, rather than the depth, of art objects. Not merely formalist in her orientation, she drew a sharp distinction that set meaning against sensuous apprehension, depth against surface. When later critics would talk about a postmodern sensibility, this idea that the surface of a work of art doesn't refer to a fixed content underneath, but points out to other forms and shared languages, seemed to be one of its elements—which is why postmodern thinking emphasized parody, irony, play, pastiche, and the continual deferral of meaning. Thirdly, she elevated film as a form worthy of criticism in formal terms, at a time when, for the critical establishment, movies were still largely associated with Hollywood and mass culture—although the films she had in mind were mostly European art films or American avant-garde cinema. Although Sontag was in no way a populist or a promoter of popular culture, her ideas had the effect of remaking the very image of what constituted art, and, hence, what deserved critical attention. The movement in aesthetics was a continued challenge to any essentialist notion of art, any attempt to delimit "art" as a distinct field of objects with a fixed ontological standing.

The question of what art actually was, in a culture that seemed intent on erasing boundaries between art and life, was at the center of Arthur Danto's essay. His answer was largely that the definition of what constituted art varied, depending upon theoretical understandings that were embedded in what he called "the artworld." Ancient notions of mimesis, ideas of beauty, romantic notions of self-expression, or modern German philosophy of aesthetics as disinterested pleasure: these were reconceived as the theories of particular intellectual worlds or distinct cultures. That term—"artworld"—would come into wide play in the last decades of the twentieth century as art became harder to define in formal or essentialist terms. Instead of attempting to create a universal definition of art, Danto particularized and relativized the understanding of what constituted art to the specific cultural practices of artists, critics, museums and galleries, and theorists. Art is what the artworld understands art to be, and any object or practice can be reconceptualized as art. But what makes objects that were once not considered to be art into art is not a progressive change in taste, but a change in the *theory* of art. The artworld operates on the basis of theoretical dependency, much as Kuhn's scientists operate in a paradigm that defines what objects can be seen and how they can be seen. "It is the role of artistic theories," Danto said, "these days as always, to make the artworld, and art, possible."[5] While Danto did not quite say that artworlds were "incommensurable" with one another, he did make them discontinuous. What is art in one world is not in another. Inverting the presumed relationship between aesthetic theory and art, he made the latter dependent upon the former, rather than vice versa. We don't develop theories of art to explain a pre-existing body of objects, but our theories make the objects art. Without theories of art, we cannot have an artworld. Danto's was a response to the specifics of the moment—he used Warhol's Brillo boxes, Lichtenstein's blown-up comic strip panels, the work of Robert Rauschenberg, Jasper Johns, and Claes Oldenburg, as examples of works that could not be comprehended within older artworlds and their theories. Since artists themselves, much like Kuhn's scientists, did not know what they were up to, the philosopher of aesthetics had an essential role to play in defining and bringing into being works of art and the artworlds in which they existed. But if the artworld was alien to the naïve member of the public, and only insiders who were socialized into its standards and ways of seeing were able to operate in its terms, it also represented an insular turn, the building of a wall between the public and aesthetic values. On the one hand, relativizing the definition of art made it seem possible to say "it's art if I say it's art." On the other, artists, patrons, critics, and exhibitors seemed bound within the systemic power of an impersonal world to constitute, through its theories, what counted as art.

Simultaneous with Sontag's and Danto's reconceptualizations—one in the voice of the public intellectual, the other in that of academic philosophy—another revolution in aesthetics was brewing that sought to bring art, culture, and politics together: the Black Arts Movement. As Black political thought turned toward Black Power and a more radical Black Nationalism, the Black Arts Movement sprung up as the aesthetic wing of the attempt to redefine Black identity and agency. Beginning in 1964 with the opening of the Black Arts Repertory Theater and School in Harlem in 1964, Black Arts was shaped by noted figures such as the poet/playwright LeRoi Jones (later Amiri Baraka) and Maulana Karenga, the creator of the African-American holiday, Kwanza. Black Arts was not simply an assertion of Black identity but involved a critique of dominant aesthetic standards and criteria as rooted in racial hierarchy. Black Arts tended to focus more on literature, especially poetry, and theater than on the visual arts, but saw all of the arts as expressive of a cultural identity that was unavoidably political. Rejecting notions of the autonomy of art, proponents of Black Arts shared in the critique of high mid-century modernism for its elitism and assumptions about what constituted a canon of works defined by putatively apolitical criteria. The arts establishment was a white establishment, one that systematically denigrated the creative work of Blacks. Black Arts looked back to the Harlem Renaissance but offered a much more radical and separatist vision of Black aesthetics than earlier movements. Larry Neal, who was one of the most prominent advocates for, and theorists of, the movement, called for a "Black aesthetic," rooted in cultural tradition and in the Black community, but breaking with a history of Black artists who had sought recognition on white terms. The Black aesthetic was to be explicitly political, refusing the notion that culture and politics were separate spheres. "The motive behind the Black aesthetic," said Neal, "is the destruction of the white thing, the destruction of white ideas, and white ways of looking at the world." For Neal, "much of the oppression confronting the Third World and Black America is directly traceable to the Euro-American cultural sensibility."[6] The movement, then, was aimed at creating a new sensibility, in which aesthetics, ethics, and politics would be unified. But the Black aesthetic advocated by proponents of the movement, had its own contradictions—not merely a critique of white cultural ideas and standards, much of the movement contained its own hierarchies, evinced in the misogynistic, homophobic, and antisemitic rhetoric it sometimes deployed in the service of its challenge to racial hierarchies. Nevertheless, some of the most prominent figures to arise out of the Black Arts Movement—the poets Audre Lorde and Nikki Giovanni, for instance—were women, and the main force of its aesthetic was one rooted in racial pride and critique of dominant white cultural standards.

Post-Industrial Society

By the late 1960s and early 1970s, a consciousness of a break with the past had become ubiquitous. The fullest systematic invocation of a change in the very nature and organization of society, akin to the discovery in the 1830s and 40s of a new social order defined by industrial capitalism, was the idea of "post-industrial society." The term is associated most strongly with Daniel Bell, and we might even see it as an extension of his earlier "end of ideology" thesis, which seemed to point to a break with the past and a set of conditions that rendered the old class politics of Marxism no longer viable or attractive. What Bell meant by post-industrial society was a shift from a material goods-producing economy to a service and knowledge-based economy, one in which workers manipulated symbols rather than made things. The emphasis in a post-industrial society is on the use of knowledge to produce technical solutions and processes and to provide for social planning. The expansion of universities, the increase in the number of workers employed in the management of transportation, communication, and technology at the expense of manufacturing, the creation of a scientific and technological elite, and a growth of consumer material abundance: all seemed to be elements of a new kind of society. Unlike Marxism, which had predicted that only an end to capitalist property relations would create the conditions for a new social order, Bell and many of his followers saw a fundamental transformation occurring within capitalist societies, rather than in replacement of them. Western Marxists looked at the same phenomena and increasingly used the terms "late capitalism," or "advanced capitalism," with the implied teleology of a coming revolution, to characterize them. The idea of post-industrialism didn't seem to suggest that industrial production had disappeared, any more than industrial society had made agricultural production disappear but that the dominant organization of the society was determined by knowledge and information technologies, rather than by material forces. But post-industrialism, as a catch-all, was notoriously vague, and many of Bell's critics were skeptical about whether it made sense to close the book on an industrial age while the factories were still pumping out goods. The historian and cultural critic Christopher Lasch, in his review of Bell's *The Coming of Post-Industrial Society* (1973), said "the case for the transition to post-industrial society cannot easily be refuted, because it was never stated with any precision to begin with."[7]

Bell followed his analysis of post-industrial society with *The Cultural Contradictions of Capitalism* (1976), in which the idea of an older model of industrial capitalism and its emphasis on bourgeois virtues of self-control, work, and deferred gratification was the mirror in which to look at a capitalism that had produced, contra Marx, not a revolutionary proletariat, but a hedonistic culture of self-gratification. Bell famously declared in the introduction to the paperback edition that he considered himself "a socialist in economics, a liberal in politics, and a conservative in culture."[8] The enormous success of capitalism in creating material abundance, in his view, meant that the values necessary to sustain capital accumulation and efficiency were being countered by a need to reject those values in favor of the promotion of consumption. Harkening back to the *Lonely Crowd* vision of a mass society unmoored from bourgeois discipline and "inner direction," Bell identified the problematic transformation not in terms of an anxious other-directed self, but of a wild uncontained libidinal self. The counter-culture of the 1960s and 1970s, with its slogan of "sex, drugs, and rock and roll," for Bell, had abandoned a work ethic and embraced an ethic of pleasure and selves liberated from convention. This was another version of a society that had lost its mooring in a fixed and stable material reality. Bell's post-industrial society was a world in which knowledge and symbols had taken the place of goods and things.

Conclusion

The consciousness of a break with the past, or the idea that history was discontinuous, had many iterations and forms in the 1960s. But modern thought since its inception had always produced notions of sharp distinctions between past and present, even if offered as "ideal types" rather than as empirically observable societies. Sociology had insisted on polarities such as tradition vs. modernity, community vs. society, status vs. contract. Anthropology had insisted on gradualism and evolution but then had constructed ideal types of savagery, barbarism, and civilization in its progressive account. What the new forms of thought did to extend and counter these earlier modernist ideas was to deny the bridge that evolutionary thought had provided, and the progressive narrative that went with it. One paradigm had no more absolute truth value than another; the meaning of art made sense only within the art world that created it; the New Left set aside the intellectual and theoretical disputes bequeathed by earlier generations of radicals, and put youth in the seat formerly occupied by labor, the entire history of Black political thought was called into question. The idea of a break with the past could become a source of liberation, an ability to criticize the existing order from the outside, on radically different ground. But the idea of rupture could also mean a loss of the connection to the past and to the cultural, intellectual, and political resources it brought with it.

Notes

1 Thomas Kuhn, *The Structure of Scientific Revolutions* (Chicago, IL: University of Chicago Press, 1962), p. 110.
2 C. Wright Mills, "Letter to the New Left," *New Left Review* 5 (September 1, 1960), pp. 21–22.
3 Students for a Democratic Society, *Port Huron Statement* (New York: Students for a Democratic Society, 1962), p. 5.
4 Susan Sontag, *Against Interpretation and Other Essays* (New York: Farrar, Strauss, and Giroux, 1966), pp. 17, 23.
5 Arthur Danto, "The Artworld," *The Journal of Philosophy* 61.19 (October 15, 1964), p. 581.
6 Larry Neal, "The Black Arts Movement," *The Drama Review: TDR* 12.4 (Summer 1968), p. 30.
7 Christopher Lasch, "Take Me to Your Leader," *New York Review of Books* (October 18, 1973), https://www.nybooks.com/articles/1973/10/18/take-me-to-your-leader/.
8 Daniel Bell, *The Cultural Contradictions of Capitalism* (New York: Basic Books, 1978), p. xi.

12 The Social Construction of Everything

How does change happen?

The influence of the turn to language, the theoretical concern with the power of ideas and discourse to shape reality, and the social upheavals of the 1960s and 1970s—especially in feminist and Black thought—produced a new way of thinking that built upon the historicist and relativist strains of modernism that derived from nineteenth- and early twentieth-century revolutions in thought. Marx, Nietzsche, Freud, Darwin, Dilthey, James, and Boas: all had called into question the fixed nature of reality, forms of absolutism, and the claims of established sources of authority. They did so in the service of liberating consciousness and/or the picture of the world from its artificially imposed limits, in creating the conditions for what they regarded as a new, fluid, open future of greater freedom and possibility. But by creating powerful and systematic theories that purported to get at the root of social order, morality, religion, and the forms of nature, they not only criticized received limitations but also ironically aided in modernist attempts to control reality, to create more centralized and totalizing ways of regarding life.

In the last third of the twentieth century, one of the principal ways in which these contradictory impulses—to critique existing knowledge and modes of thought, and to systematize new forms—was expressed was in the language of what came to be called "social constructionism." By the end of the century, the anti-essentialist ethos underlying social construction arguments had become one of the most prominent features of intellectual life across a wide body of disciplines and patterns of thought. It could be deployed piecemeal in arguments that a particular phenomenon or category of phenomenon was socially constructed, or it could be deployed in a more totalizing way, suggesting that all categories were artifacts of social life, and that discourse produced its objects rather than reflecting or mirroring them—that there was no element of "nature" that did not already have culture all over it. And the concept of culture that went along with social constructionist arguments was one that expressed forms of social dominance and power, rather than simply generalized belief. Although

DOI: 10.4324/9781003120803-16

much of this discourse focused on ideas about the social construction of race and gender over and against the claims of biological essentialism, the idea of social construction was not limited to these putatively "natural" categories. Social construction became a ubiquitous term of analysis and critique. Even when the language of "social construction" was not present, the sensibility it represented often was; it was one of the pervasive modes of thought of the age—demystifying, skeptical, critical, but also confident, enlightened, and totalizing.

The vocabulary of social thought in the last third of the twentieth century would have seemed alien and untranslatable to thinkers at the beginning of the twentieth century, even as the ideas behind that vocabulary owed an enormous intellectual debt to that earlier period. It included a set of keywords that oriented thought in specific ways: social construction, yes, but also essentialism, gender, critique, identity, multiculturalism, sexism, racism, homophobia, late capitalism, whiteness, postmodernism, hybridity, neoliberalism, discourse, social imaginary, orientalism, post-colonialism, code shifting, linguistic turn, cultural representation, the public sphere. This new vocabulary sat side by side with the received vocabulary of the late nineteenth through the mid-twentieth centuries: capitalism, ideology, culture, class, progress, community, bourgeoisie, proletariat, liberal, radical, conservative, social structure. But much of the distinctive vocabulary of earlier eras had evaporated; nobody spoke any longer of "the social problem," "the woman question," and like formulations. Civilization, melting pot (as a real thing rather than an ideology), anomie, alienation, the negro, cultural lag, national character: all had an antiquated sound inconsistent with the newer images of society.

The language of "social construction" arose out of the sociology of knowledge, and its mid-century forms in the writings of Karl Mannheim and Robert Merton. Its *locus classicus* was the sociologists Peter Berger and Thomas Luckmann's *The Social Construction of Reality* (1966). Although the various advocates for later social construction arguments did not hew to the theoretical positions advanced by Berger and Luckmann, the term "social construction" proved too hard to resist. The growth and expansion of the term moved outside of academic sociology, and became a central term across the humanities and social sciences, particularly in new disciplines such as "cultural studies," which took over some of the domains that sociology had previously claimed, but concerned itself with humanistic phenomena such as popular culture, film, music, visual art, and literature. The form of social constructionism that proliferated especially in the 1980s and 1990s took root as a key idea on the intellectual Left, as a way to denaturalize claims of the given nature of social and biological arrangements. There is some irony in the fact that Peter Berger, then, was one of the most visible neoconservative intellectuals of those decades, a fierce critic of the idea of secularization, and a prominent advocate for the centrality of religion to modern society. One of Berger's dissertation students, James Davison Hunter, would go on to define the terms of a contemporary "Culture War" in religious terms in the early 1990s. That a work which was intended to stress the common creation of a shared stable world of everyday reality became the basis for a language of radical criticism of the existing order suggests that the dual nature of sociology—a source of social holism and organicism, on the one hand, a source of demythologizing the givenness of social reality on the other—was baked into social constructionist thought.

Berger and Luckmann were primarily interested in grafting the focus of the sociology of knowledge and its object, "the symbolic universe," onto the classical sociological tradition that had achieved its greatest theoretical articulation in the mid-twentieth century. Instead of being concerned with the way in which particular systems of knowledge were expressions of power, as the Marxist conception of ideology would suggest, they were concerned with the creation of an intersubjective world that provided the basis for a shared reality. Terms such as "socialization" "institutionalization," and "legitimation," were central to their vision. The point of social construction, in their view, was to address the central theoretical question of sociology—what makes society hold together? Their treatise was addressed to what they regarded as the inadequacies of general theories of society that downplayed the symbolic world of ideas and knowledge in which people collectively operated. They regarded the existence of social constructions not as something to be critiqued and overthrown, but as the way in which human beings participated in a coherent and cohesive world in which objects of knowledge were shared with others. They imagined a social world that was at odds in fundamental ways with a natural or biologically given world, but in a positive or creative sense. "Man is biologically predestined to construct and inhabit a world with others," they said.

> This world becomes for him the dominant and definitive reality. Its limits are set by nature, but once constructed, this world acts back upon nature. In the dialectic between nature and the socially constructed world the human organism is itself transformed. In the same dialectic, man produces reality and thereby produces himself.[1]

Social Construction as Radical Critique

In the 1970s, 1980s, and 1990s, this idea of social construction would be taken up by critics who saw it as a way to denaturalize, or call into question, the givenness, stability, and existence of the status quo. To identify the process of social construction was to unveil the agency behind the constitution of a common-sense, taken for granted, reality. The term "social construction," as the philosopher Ian Hacking pointed out, contains an ambiguity—it points to both a process, and to a product. The process is the means by which the things in which people believe come into being, as when we say "human nature" is socially constructed. The product, labeled a "social construction," was a fixed thing: a category, a phenomenon, a thing in the world. "What a lot of things are said to be socially constructed!" exclaimed Hacking in 1999, before listing, based on titles in a library catalogue, a set of ideas and objects, including gender, nature, illness, authorship, danger, quarks, deafness, knowledge, vital statistics, as well as more very particular things: serial homicide, the women refugee, the child viewer of television.[2] The point of much social constructionist thought was to "unfix" these products or things, by revealing them to be the artificial creations of the process of social belief, "reified," and treated as having an independent reality. In another sense, social constructionist arguments represented an attack on the philosophical and scientific belief in a natural ontology or reality that existed independent of human interest and mind. For those who clung to a philosophical or scientific realism, a commitment to the independent reality of the objects of our knowledge, the difference between their view and that of the social constructionists might be summed up in the distinction between "discovery" and "invention." Realists believed that knowledge is discovered or found; social constructionists, that knowledge is invented or made by social processes.

Two of the central features of the critical social constructionist view were what I will call anti-naturalism and anti-essentialism. The first denies that nature provides fixed constraints, limitations, or guidelines for social life and its norms, and that it is only in the artificial, created world that such constraints come into being; because nature gives no such constraints, the categories and objects we live with are open to the possibility of change—human beings created them, and they can change them. For instance, if nature defined the biological differences between the sexes in terms of emotional, intellectual, and moral characteristics, such differences would be fixed, but if such differences were socially constructed they could be imagined as open to reconstruction; what human beings have made, they can unmake. Note here the strong contrast with the legacy of eighteenth-century Enlightenment thought, that made its appeal to nature as the basis for a critique of society. By appealing to natural law, natural equality, and a universal human nature, those early modern thinkers—Locke, Rousseau, Jefferson, and Adam Smith among them—sought to align social reality with the natural world against the introduction of artificial distinctions; social constructionists went in precisely the opposite direction, arguing that the appeal to nature was itself a social and ideological appeal, and needed to be rejected.

Anti-essentialism was closely paired with this antinaturalism. A long tradition of Western philosophy, going back to Plato and Aristotle, had prioritized distinguishing between the essence, core, or necessary features of a person or object, and its accidental, contingent, or superficial attributes, and giving moral preference to the essential over the accidental. Although much modern thought, as we have seen, refused the idea of essence—as, for instance, in Darwinian rejection of the notion that species are defined by their essences—social construction arguments took anti-essentialism to its furthest extent. The criticism of categories of things and people was premised on the notion that those categories had no essence that could function as an unmoving anchor or a source of fixed identity. Modern anti-essentialism tended to replace the idea of essence with that of relation, on the one hand, or variation on the other. Structuralist and post-structuralist thought saw the meaning of terms defined by their relationship to other terms—often in the form of oppositions. Social construction arguments leaned on the idea that entities were defined in relationship to the social contexts in which they were produced, rather than to some underlying essential or natural reality. So, there were no essential qualities of, say, motherhood, because motherhood was a social relationship based on gender and generational relationships. They also tended to reject essentialism as reductionistic, an attempt to simplify the variety of phenomena into fixed types.

There was a certain irony to the antinaturalism and antiessentialism of social constructionist thought. The implication of the idea that a trait, category, or person was not natural or essential, but socially constructed, was that if that entity could be demonstrated to be natural or essential, it would somehow confirm its moral and ontological rightness. In other words, social construction arguments tended to accept the idea that nature had some kind of moral authority, if it could be validated. They simply refused the metaphysical claim that such a nature or essence existed. But there hasn't been and needn't be any necessary connection between nature and social rules. As much as appeals to nature have been common as the basis for prescribing social norms and identities, so have arguments against such prescriptions. Nobody (except maybe Nietzsche!) would argue that because human beings are naturally blood thirsty and aggressive that nature prescribed murder as part of a moral order. The ideas of culture and civilization had tended to suggest that, in fact, human nature was a problem to be overcome, and that civilization should not be premised on nature, but opposed to it. But in the social constructionist worldview, moral order was not defined in opposition to nature so much as being defined by the absence of nature. Taken to its logical conclusion, there was no space outside language, culture, and society in which an independent and pre-social nature could be held to exist.

Another feature of the social constructionist sensibility, both in the thinking of its advocates and its critics, was the tendency to regard the claim of social construction as a kind of argument about whether objects of knowledge were real or not. That is, by demonstrating that some category was socially constructed, the implication was that it was somehow not real, that the only kinds of realities that could qualify as such were ones that weren't socially constructed. But what Berger and Luckmann, for instance, were saying is not that because reality is socially constructed it's not really real at all, but that the reality was of a different kind than had previously been supposed. To put this another way: showing that race, for instance, was socially constructed by the development of biological ideas of inheritance that linked presumed physical characteristics to characterological traits, implementing rules defining heritable identities, and then using those to pursue policies of racial segregation and hierarchy, only means that race is not a biological reality. Race is a reality because its social and ideological consequences are real, just not biologically or naturally or essentially real. But the demystifying tendencies of social construction arguments could, and often did, lead to a conflation of claim of social construction with the claim of unreality.

Anti-Psychiatry and the Problem of Mental Illness

One of the principal sources of the social constructionist sensibility lay in a movement that converged in the early 1960s around a critique of psychiatry, its practices, and concepts of mental illness. The anti-psychiatry movement drew on several strains of thought, exemplified by its most prominent promoters: Thomas Szasz, R.D. Laing, and Michel Foucault, and the early works associated with each of them. The American Szasz's *The Myth of Mental Illness* (1961), the Scottish Laing's *The Divided Self* (1960), and the French Foucault's *Madness and Civilization* (1961) converged on a moment when critics had taken to labeling modern society as sick, diseased, its values distorted by repressive notions of normality. The Beat poet Allan Ginsberg's famous poem *Howl* (1955) had invoked a series of images of spiritualized outcasts—homosexuals, drug addicts, psychiatric patients, the down and out—as a counter to the diseased values of a mainstream America that worshipped money, commerce, technology. Laing, in his existentialist analysis of schizophrenia as an authentic way of being in an insane society, dovetailed with the emergent counterculture of the 1960s. "In the context of our present pervasive madness that we call normality, sanity, freedom," said Laing, "all our frames of reference are ambiguous and equivocal."[3] Who is mad: those who embrace the strategic use of nuclear weaponry, or those who believe a bomb lives inside themselves? Szasz, drawing on right-wing critics of communism such as the philosopher Karl Popper, argued in a libertarian mode that what he later called "The Therapeutic State," in the absence of a waning theological worldview, had looked to psychiatric medicine as a means of social control and to punish dissent. By the end of the 1960s, he was equating the concept of mental illness in modern society with the concept of witchcraft in early modern Europe. Foucault provided something more of a deep history, based on a Nietzschean vision, of the redefinition of behavior as madness in ways that provided for new forms of clinical power and control.

There were serious differences in emphasis between these thinkers and their ideas, but they all spoke to a moment in which suspicion of powerful modern institutions and their role in defining deviance and social norms was coming to the fore. One of the main issues raised by the critics of psychiatry was the status of mental illness as a diagnostic category and the ways in which it was used to maintain power, marginalize, and control persons whose behavior did not align with dominant norms. For Szasz, he began with a kind of demythologizing outlook at the beginning of the 1960s, arguing that illness, as a medical condition, was physiological and that mental illness was simply not disease; he maintained a faith in medical science but saw its extension to mental conditions as non-scientific. By the end of the decade, he was arguing that mental illness was socially "manufactured," and then deployed to institutionalize and manage people by defining them as deviant.

The anti-psychiatry movement converged with rising gay liberation and radical feminist movements in the late 1960s and 70s in their critique of the use of psychological terms to define homosexuality and specific gender-based sicknesses. As we have seen, feminists through the twentieth century had an ambivalent relationship to Freudian psychoanalytic theory; in the 1970s, feminist thinkers often took on the broader history of psychological science and psychiatry as well, critically targeting concepts such as "hysteria," that had defined women in the nineteenth century as overly emotional, neurotic and/or pathological. Sexual scientists, including those in the Freudian tradition, from the late nineteenth century forward had consistently defined homosexuality as a disorder, and the homosexual as a maladjusted person suffering from a mental pathology. Feminist and gay rights advocates identified psychology and psychiatry as handmaidens to the dominant classes and norms in society, rather than as value-neutral scientific forms of knowledge. Szasz and others had pointed to the nineteenth-century disease of "drapetomania," which had defined enslaved people who sought to escape slavery as suffering from a mental illness. One result of the activism against psychology and psychiatry as instruments of social control was the successful campaign to have homosexuality removed from the American Psychiatric Association's *Diagnostic and Statistical Manual of Mental Disorders (DSM)*, which was accomplished in

1973. There is some irony in the fact that this reversal was accompanied by a pathologizing of anti-homosexual attitudes as a form of mental illness, metaphorically if not clinically; in the 1970s, "homophobia" became the term to describe anti-gay belief and behavior.

Foucault's *History of Sexuality*, vol. I (1976, English trans. 1978) moved the question away from whether a particular form of sexuality was a sickness toward a much broader constructivist framework. Among all of Foucault's writings, this slim volume was probably the most widely read in the United States, and became one of the main foundational texts for the intellectual field that has come to be known as Queer Theory. In it, Foucault argued that not only was homosexuality a constructed category, but the very idea of sexuality, in general, was a product of modern scientific discourses, which have been instrumental in constituting people's identities. Arguing against the twentieth-century idea that the nineteenth century had been a period in which a natural sexuality was repressed, and that the sexual revolutions of the twentieth century were aimed at liberating a preexisting sexuality from its repression, Foucault claimed that sexuality was a wholly modern construct. In the distant past, for instance, there had been same-sex acts, but until modern sexual science, there had been no type of person called "the homosexual," (or, for that matter, "the heterosexual"). The idea of sexuality turned sex from a behavior to an underlying essence of identity. The modern conception of personhood, defining the health, well-being, and integrity of people by invoking what was presumed to be a pre-social disposition, was really, in Foucault's reading, a consequence of the power of scientific discourses to label, create, and order people. Sexual liberation turned out to be its opposite, not a form of freedom, but a form of totalizing power that constituted the objects it purported to free. The attribution of essential identities to people, and people's need to operate within the terms of modern discourses that constructed those essential identities, made the very idea of sexuality a means of regulating modern life. It's hard to overstate the significance of Foucault's argument for the triumph of social constructionist thought in the ensuing decades.

Theoretical Foundations

While many things were said to be socially constructed—most prominently race, gender, and sexuality—the theoretical source of social constructions arguments lay in a more abstract shift that built upon the modernist ideas and sensibility developed in the previous century. One principal source was what has been called "the linguistic turn"; a more developed consciousness of language as a medium, with its own structure, that does not simply reflect or mirror an independent reality. Instead of looking through language at a world independent of it, much of late twentieth-century thought saw the world being constituted by language. When the French Deconstructionist Jacques Derrida declared, in a much-quoted (and controversially translated) statement, "there is nothing outside the text," ("il n'y a pas de hors-texte"), he perhaps meant this—all meanings are textual and never eventuate in a place where meaning runs up against some solid untextual reality. In some ways, the turn toward language was a continuation or extension of the turn toward an anthropological conception of culture earlier in the century; if culture, rather than nature, created the worlds in which people lived, then there could be no direct, unfiltered, contact with empirical objects in the world. Culture determined what could be seen and what could not. Structuralist and post-structuralist theories of language saw a radical discontinuity between language and a non-linguistic reality. The terms "structure" and "Deconstruction" that arose out of this tradition of thinking about language lent themselves to the social constructionist imagination, even if most social constructionists were not engaged in anything that looked remotely like the deconstructive practice of literary scholars like Derrida.

A second source of social constructionist thought lay in the late twentieth-century revival of Pragmatic philosophy, or at least the version of it associated with Richard Rorty. Trained as an analytic philosopher, Rorty moved in the 1970s toward a thorough critique of the central questions of that dominant school of thought, and in doing so became a kind of public intellectual, with a large intellectual audience outside of philosophy. His *Philosophy and the Mirror of Nature* (1979) argued that the central Western philosophical tradition, and its updating in the form of analytic philosophy, had created a set of problems based on a vision of knowledge conforming to the objective world. For Rorty these problems, under conditions of modernity, no longer made sense as philosophical problems—they were creatures of a particular vocabulary and way of seeing, but not universal in any sense. Rejecting the idea that the purpose of philosophy is to hold a mirror to nature, Rorty pointed toward a social vision of philosophy as a creative, but ultimately ethnocentric, way of being. Science could no longer be imagined as separate from or above culture—he leaned on the ideas of Kuhn and other thinkers to reject correspondence theories of truth in favor of something that looked more like an aesthetic or creative purpose for philosophy, although a deeply socialized one. Rorty's reinvention of philosophical Pragmatism, as much as it identified John Dewey as one of its principal sources, had the effect of departing from the classical Pragmatists' commitment to a culture organized around the innovations of scientific thinking. The attack on the claims of science to stand outside of culture, which were not specific to Rorty alone, contributed to the arguments that science was socially constructed.

A third source of social construction thought came out of Marxist and Freudian roots, and was encapsulated in the phrase "the social imaginary." A number of figures, drawing on earlier ideas articulated by French thinkers Jean-Paul Sartre and Jacques Lacan, began to use this term in the 1970s and 80s to refer to the social reality that was imagined, as opposed to the material relations of social structure. The social imaginary was ideological and symbolic; it was the comprehensive vision of social totality, and therefore was a kind of social reality itself, since it shaped the actions of people who conceived of their society in particular ways. In 1983, the political scientist Benedict Anderson published a book entitled *Imagined Communities: Reflections on the Origin and Spread of Nationalism*. At a moment when the nation state as a fundamental reality was being called into question by the forces of globalization and the elevation of trade as a challenge to the notion of self-contained political entities, Anderson's opus struck a nerve. Nations, he argued, are not ancient and rooted in traditions, culture, or ethnic inheritance, but are modern and imagined. The nation is a kind of social construct, an imaginary reality by which people identify themselves with a larger group. Unlike the face-to-face community, with its bounded form, nations were communities only in the social imaginary. Coincident with Anderson's influential conception of the nation, the British historian Eric Hobsbawm was arguing that traditions, contrary to the idea that they were handed down from time immemorial, were invented in modern nations as means of creating identities that could be imagined as having a stable root in ancient times. These ideas—the nation as imagined community, and the invention of tradition—contributed to the critical tendency to see what had previously been taken as a given, a kind of inherited historical reality, as an ideological product, a construction. Neither Anderson's nor Hobsbawm's ideas were shaped by the kind of linguistic thought of structural and post-structuralist theory, but they dovetailed with the critical tendency to see discourse as producing, rather than reflecting, its objects. Nations and traditions were made, not given.

From Racial Essentialism to the Social Construction of Race

White Liberals and progressives had sometimes treated race as a secondary issue, but at various points in the twentieth century had also embraced a critique of racism, segregation, and racial discrimination, especially in the 1960s and beyond. The term "racism" did not have an ancient lineage either. In the first half of the twentieth century, racism could sometimes refer to discriminatory prejudice, attitude, and behavior, but it was often used to describe movements, such as Nazism or immigration restriction, that had an explicit purpose of advancing the racial identity of a group. "Racism" was something more like nationalism or ethnic pride.

The difference between "racism" and "racialism" was less clear than later uses of the terms would indicate. Mid-century white liberals did adhere to a view that racism was a problem, often viewed as rooted in psychological prejudice (as in the psychologist Gordon Allport's *The Nature of Prejudice* (1954)), and they often supported a vision of racial equality. But they also tended to believe that racism was an attitude or belief about a previously existing natural or biological reality. They believed that there were naturally occurring differences between groups of people defined by a fixed inheritance. The difference between mid-century ideas about race, and those that came to prominence in the 1980s and 1990s, was that the former criticized and sought to eliminate racism, while the latter criticized the idea of race itself. Those who came to argue that race was a social construct denied that there was a biological substratum upon which racism rested. For some of those critics, the very concept of race needed to be abolished, because race was created for no other purpose than to draw a hierarchical relationship between peoples.

Advances in genetics and population studies allowed critics to argue that race was not a meaningful concept in biological terms. Geneticists had found that the genetic variation within so-called racial groups was far greater than that found between racial groups. The old idea that racial groups were defined by a uniformity of inherited "stock" had no scientific basis in modern genetics. Broad physiological features such as skin color and hair, which had been used to group peoples into distinct racial types, were surely heritable, but the concept of race tied those features to some more essential identity. The fact that there were "white" people with darker skin than some "Black" people, for instance, suggested that racial identity was not a mere matter of such physiological difference. As critics noted, the ways in which racial identities were defined were social, including rules of descent. The prevailing practice in many parts of the United States, from the era of slavery forward, had been to define race according to proportion of descent. If more than one great-grandparent or grandparent was Black, the individual would be considered legally Black. Being born into slavery was itself a marker of racial identity. During the Jim Crow era of racial segregation in the South, states adopted the so-called "one drop" rule: if one identifiable ancestor was Black, the person was designated Black. If the mother was Black, even if the father was white, the child was Black. The widespread practice of rape of enslaved peoples by whites meant that a large proportion of the Black population had some European ancestry. The idea that biological races were pure distillations of a uniform type ran counter to the empirically observable facts on the ground, and the ways in which the law, rather than biology, was used to define race. Race, for historians such as Barbara Jeanne Fields, and philosophers such as Kwame Anthony Appiah, was ideological or cultural all the way down. "Race," said Fields "is a purely ideological notion. Once ideology is stripped away, nothing remains except an abstraction."[4]

One of the consequences of thinking of race as a social construction was to create a new consciousness of "whiteness," and a burgeoning field of whiteness studies in the academy, spilling out into the broader public sphere by the end of the century. David Roediger's *Wages of Whiteness* (1991), Theodore Allen's *The Invention of the White Race* (1994), and Noel Ignatiev's *How the Irish Became White* (1995) were among this wave of studies. If race was a social construction rather than a biological fact, these critics and historians claimed, it was time to turn the spotlight on the unmarked status of white identity against which Blackness had been defined. The purpose was not to glorify or celebrate white identity, but to demythologize and denaturalize it. The white race had never existed through the vast history of human societies—it was wholly a modern invention, resting on a hierarchical conception of peoples, and, for these thinkers, one that needed to be unmade. Ignatiev, for instance, edited *Race Traitor: The Journal of New Abolitionism*, with its slogan "Treason to whiteness is loyalty to humanity." The title linked the crusade against whiteness to the nineteenth-century crusade against slavery. By destabilizing Blackness as a biological fact, the new critics of whiteness pointed to the artificiality of a white identity that had often been defined in such a way as to exclude groups who were now included as white: Jews, the Irish, Italians among them.

A related set of arguments on the social construction of gender were prominent in these decades as well. I will deal in more detail with those arguments in Chapter 14.

The New Essentialism

The turn to arguments that emphasized the contingent, arbitrary, and non-natural definitions of social categories such as race and gender did not go uncontested. The more frankly biological determinist arguments that rejected entirely the cultural and linguistic approaches of social constructionism are addressed in the following chapter. But there were also thinkers during this same period, especially in the 1970s and 80s, who invoked essentialist ideas as the basis for a critique of racism and sexism. Two of the most prominent thinkers in this vein, although very different from one another, were Molefi Kete Asante and Carol Gilligan. Throughout modern history, the assertion of ideas of essentialism has never been unequivocal in its political implications. Sometimes essentialist arguments have been used to assert claims of social hierarchy rooted in a presumed presocial nature; other times, as with Black nationalists and Pan-Africanists, essentialism might be a tool to challenge existing hierarchies.

Asante was the most prominent spokesman for the late twentieth-century academic field of Afrocentricity, which had its institutional base at Temple University in Philadelphia. Drawing on traditions of Black Nationalism and Pan-African thought, as well as Black Power and the Back to Africa movement of the 1960s and 1970s, Afrocentricity argued for a common shared African identity in contrast to the categories imposed by Europeans. The notion that there is a core African culture, and that it is shared by people of African descent in vastly different parts of the world, that the systems of education imposed by Europeans have sought to erase African modes of thinking and being, and that an Afrocentric approach is necessary to overcome the racist denigration of African peoples and restore their identities as agents rather than objects of European power: these ideas lay at the heart of the Afrocentric ideology. In the late 1980s and early 1990s, an academic dispute spilled into the public sphere and intersected with the developing ideologies of Afrocentricity; Martin Bernal's book *Black Athena* (1987) argued that ancient Greek culture, long regarded as the fount of European civilization, was rooted in Egyptian and African civilization, and borrowed heavily from those sources. Many scholars denounced Bernal's book for its historical inaccuracies, and the dispute brought the field of Afrocentrism into a more prominent place in public discourse. Critics derided the field as promoting false history and mythology in the service of a contemporary cultural identity that was not rooted in African societies and cultures at all.

Carol Gilligan's challenge was to an emerging feminist anti-essentialism. Gilligan was a psychologist who's *In a Different Voice* (1982) argued that, based on empirical studies, women use a different form of moral reasoning than men do, and that the models of stages of moral development put forward by psychologists had assumed the male position. Men, according to Gilligan, tend to abstract rational and logical modes of thinking about right and wrong; women, on the other hand, privilege what she came to call the "ethics of care," a concern with the well-being of people, especially defined by a sense of relationship. Gilligan's position, it should be clear, was a feminist position that sought to expand the range of moral thinking by listening to women's reasoning. Although Gilligan claimed that "the contrast between male and female voices are presented here to highlight a distinction between two modes of thought … rather than to represent a generalization about either sex," it was hard not to read her as arguing that men and women were fundamentally different from one another, in ways that tended to replicate the image of women as less rational and universalistic in their thinking.[5] At a time when many feminists were claiming that arguments for men and women's difference inevitably fell back into the hierarchical stereotypes inherited from the past, Gilligan seemed to be pushing in the opposite direction. A decade later, the long shadow of

Gilligan's willingness to confirm essentialist stereotypes was evident when John Gray published his enormously successful bestseller, *Men Are from Mars, Women Are from Venus* (1992). The naturalizing of the differences between men and women now found itself in an oft-repeated cliché.

Conclusion

Social Construction arguments were often attached to progressive political views because they detached the given world from the idea of necessity. If X is socially constructed, went the reasoning, it is open to change. If X is socially constructed, then we can see the agency that lies behind it and the ideological work it is doing. And, yet, social construction arguments have not been necessarily committed to a politics of change and reconstruction, and appeals to nature have continued to have their power to upset existing hierarchies. Appealing to "natural law" as the basis for radical movements for equality is one example. The claims of more recent gay rights activists that sexual orientation is a natural disposition as a way to counter those who would regard it as a choice, and therefore not a given fact, is another. Similar arguments would come to inform queer theory and the transgender movement—freedom now could mean a freedom to be who you already were, your essence, against the artificiality of social conventions and categories.

Notes

1 Peter L. Berger and Thomas Luckmann, *The Social Construction of Reality: A Treatise in the Sociology of Knowledge* (Garden City, NY: Doubleday, 1966), p. 183.
2 Ian Hacking, *The Social Construction of What?* (Cambridge, MA: Harvard University Press, 1999), pp. 1–2.
3 Ronald David Laing, *The Divided Self: An Existential Study in Sanity and Madness*, new edition (New York: Penguin, 1965), pp. 11–12.
4 Barbara J. Fields, "Ideology and Race in American History," in J. Morgan Kousser and James M. McPherson, eds., *Region, Race, and Reconstruction: Essays in Honor of C. Vann Woodward* (New York: Oxford University Press, 1982), p. 151.
5 Carol Gilligan, *In a Different Voice: Psychological Theory and Women's Development* (Cambridge, MA: Harvard University Press, 1982), p. 2.

13 The Return of Nature

Just as cultural theory pushed toward a radical denaturalization of categories, increasing emphasis on human genetics, culminating in the mapping of the human genome at century's end, provided a countervailing vision of reality—a reassertion of the biological as determinative. In the wake of the synthesis of Darwinian evolutionary theory and Mendelian genetics in the first half of the twentieth century, and the mid-century discovery of DNA and its structure, the idea that not just human physiology, but human psychology and social behavior, were coded in the deep structure of biological inheritance became a powerful means to revitalize, in new and sophisticated ways, the application of biological science to culture and human institutions. Many of the received ideas about race had been discredited, thanks in large measure to genetics and the conclusion by scientists that race was a biologically meaningless concept. The Social Darwinism of the late nineteenth and early twentieth centuries, and the Nazi use of hereditarian claims in the 1930s and 1940s had exposed the fundamentally ideological uses of biological claims as applied to social behavior. Eugenics, the ideas of managed and controlled fertility for purposes of social progress, for instance, had become permanently associated with racist and antiliberal modes of thought, whereas in the first part of the twentieth century, it was often part of a larger progressive agenda of human improvement. The Civil Rights Movement of the post-World War II decades had effectively challenged the use of racial categories as a principle for the hierarchical organization of society, and provided a model for a variety of later challenges to the use of biological identities in discriminatory ways: arguments for gay rights, and rights of the disabled, including deaf and blind people, rested on notions of human equality independent of biology. In the social sciences and humanistic disciplines, intensely aware of the ways in which biology had been invoked to justify hierarchy, any kind of appeal to biological determinism was now suspect. The social constructionist arguments and their kin had won the day. But in the broader realms of culture, in certain areas of philosophy, anthropology, and psychology, evolutionary thought and biological determinism were redeployed in very successful and prominent ways.

The proponents of this new biologism faced a war on two fronts: against the progressive and liberal culturalist arguments, on the one hand, and against newly reinvigorated assertions of religion, particularly Christian evangelical religion, on the other. The liberal secularists distrusted biologism because of its legacy of ideological use; the religious critics of biological arguments distrusted Darwinian evolutionary arguments for their challenge to Christian belief and created a countervailing theory of biological "Creationism" in response. The "Culture Wars" of the late twentieth century didn't always neatly line up with secularists and religious thinkers on opposing sides. That said, the thinkers associated with sociobiology and evolutionary psychology, the two principal forms of a reinvigorated biologism and scientism, often found themselves in the same corner with a newly militant atheist movement, critical of religious belief for its anti-scientific orientation. But the critics of sociobiology and evolutionary psychology from the secular side were often arguing that the problem with these new supposed scientific doctrines was that they were inadequately scientific, and tended to reproduce pervasive assumptions about society that were held for non-scientific reasons. The tendency to think about culture in biological terms often appeared to lead to a reduction of culture to biology, as opposed to a synthesis seeking a middle ground in the so-called "nurture-nature debate."

Background: The Genetic Vision

What physics had been to the first half of the twentieth century—from Einsteinian relativity to the culmination in the creation of nuclear weaponry—biology was to the second half: the scientific field that appeared to be reshaping the understanding of the principles of the cosmos. This is, of course, stating the contrast far too strongly, but the sense that biology was where the action and the cultural traction was, shaped public culture in the wake of the discovery of the structure of DNA and the technical mechanisms of heredity. What Darwin had articulated in relation to organic variation and evolution, and that the field of Mendelian genetics had identified in terms of the heritability of discrete traits, expressed and unexpressed, was given a specific physical structure and form in the discovery of the double helix form of DNA (deoxyribonucleic acid) by James Watson and Francis Crick in 1953. The metaphors that were used to describe DNA (and later, the use of DNA itself as a metaphor), were determinative of the way in which it became an idea both scientific and technical, on the one hand, and generalized and popular, on the other. From the beginning, the form of DNA and its productive process was referred to in linguistic terms. DNA was imagined as *a language, a code*; it was *read* and *transcribed* by RNA, and *translated* in the production of proteins. The four chemical bases of the "code" were given letters: A (adenine), C (cytosine), T (thymine), G (guanine), the so-called *alphabet* of DNA. Those letters were sequenced in ways that resembled words. The idea that DNA was a kind of master code of life meant that the genome, or complete DNA set of a species, could be imagined as a kind of instructional manual, a set of directives for the production of life. While scholars in the humanities and social sciences were taken by the "linguistic turn," the idea that languages constituted artificial realities, biologists were imagining that the actual chemical events happening on the molecular level within cells could be described as a kind of language, providing instructions for the natural construction of species. As much as this was a science without divine or metaphysical intention, it still remained difficult to speak as if there was no systematic intention or purpose in the production of the natural world.

The discovery of the structure of DNA and its mechanism of reproduction and translation gave a kind of specificity to the idea of the heritability of traits and encouraged a notion that DNA was a comprehensive and totalizing directive. By the last decade of the twentieth century, scientists had begun the complex process of mapping the human genome, identifying the entirety of the species-specific DNA code, a task that was completed in 2003. Increasingly, it was possible to imagine DNA in two ways—as the complete foundation and natural chemical base of all life and its specific forms—the determinative essence of all species—on the one hand, and as a distinct characteristic that allowed for the specific differences between individual members of a species. The development of the use of human DNA for purposes of identification—in medical, criminal justice, and other contexts—with the notion that each person had a unique DNA profile, encouraged views that the entirety of differences between persons could be explained by differences in DNA, that DNA was not only the template for physiological difference, but characterological difference as well. DNA, it was imagined, could tell us who we were. Beginning in the 1970s, scientific and popular ways of thinking, borrowed a metaphor from engineering to describe a kind of fixed determination of both species-specific and individual behavioral characteristics; they were said to be "hardwired." The idea of hardwiring represented a return to biological essentialism, determinism, and the idea of permanent and fixed characteristics. Hardwired functions for machines, particularly computers, are those that are built in as fixed, permanent, and necessary—they are part of the basic way in which a machine functions, independent of specific situational directives and applications. The idea of hardwiring in brain science was equated with innateness, with nature, with instinct, with determinism, and of course, with being "in the DNA."

In the last decades of the century, DNA itself became a metaphor for any trait, behavior, or characteristic that could be identified with being received from the past, and having some essential or unchanging quality. It was common, as it still is, for people to speak of occupations, interests, or abilities as being "in our DNA." The idea of transmission of family characteristics, such as a love of music, an interest in banking and finance, a willingness to take big risks, or a generosity of spirit, as being "in the DNA" walked a line between being figurative and literal, since many people came to believe that a great number of characterological traits were biologically heritable. When organizations and businesses invoked the metaphor ("customer service is in our DNA," for instance), everyone understood that this was not literal—but the use of the metaphor rested on a conviction that DNA provided a model of a kind of fixed, essential inheritance and identity. Just as the Darwinian image of nature as a competitive struggle for existence could be grafted onto a vision of a capitalist social order in the late nineteenth century, so a vision of DNA as a natural instruction manual or permanent identity code could be grafted onto a fluid, unfixed society, increasingly concerned with symbolic manipulation and information, as a way to gesture to a kind of stability that was not evident elsewhere. The desire to see cultural traits as expressions of some underlying biologically transmitted essence perhaps became more important for people questing for some certainty in a society that increasingly provided none, as well as providing justification for conservative reinstatement of social hierarchies.

It was in the domain of culture and character that ideas about biological inheritance became objects of contestation. The idea that particular human traits could be identified with specific gene sequences was non-controversial, as long as the discussion had to do with the inheritance of physiological traits, such as hair and skin color, height and size, genetic propensity for specific physical diseases, and the like. But when it came to characterological attributes—bravery, inventiveness, altruism, intelligence, for instance—and cultural forms and institutions—family structure, political party identification, forms of leadership and institutional organization, the claims of biological heredity rested upon much weaker grounds. Ultimately, trying to keep the spheres of non-controversial physiological inheritance distinct from controversial psychological and characterological inheritance could not be entirely successful. On one side were those social constructionists who gave as little as possible to the realm of nature; on the other side were those biological determinists who sought a complete explanation for all human behavior in DNA, and tended to see social and cultural forms as expressions of an underlying hardwired code.

Sociobiology and the "Darwin Wars"

In 1975, Edward O. Wilson published a book, entitled *sociobiology: The New Synthesis*. Wilson was a specialist in the social behavior of insects, but his book was something more of a manifesto for the broad application of the principles of evolutionary biology to the collective behavior of organisms, including human beings. He defined the object of study as "the biological basis of all social behavior." Although human behavior was the subject of only a small number of pages of a very lengthy book, for critics the specter of Social Darwinism and various attempts to use biological arguments to affirm existing social hierarchies was evident in the approach. Clearly, Wilson thought he needed to defend the specific social implications of his arguments, since he published a more extensive development of sociobiological ideas applied to human beings three years later in *On Human Nature* (1978). Those who applied Darwinian ideas to society in the late nineteenth century were social thinkers of various stripes, but they generally were not biologists. Wilson and the field of sociobiology mobilized the claim of scientific expertise as the basis for a challenge to the disciplines of the social sciences, and sociology in particular. In fact, Wilson explicitly invoked C. P. Snow's "two cultures" thesis in his argument for what he would later call "consilience," the notion that all knowledge is unified and that the humanities and social sciences must ultimately rest on a biological, chemical, and physical basis. Wilson's sociobiology was doing at least two things: making an argument for a kind of biological, and specifically genetic, determination of human social behavior; and making a proprietary claim about knowledge itself. Rejecting the weight of twentieth-century ideas of cultural determinism and pluralism in the understanding of human beings, Wilson argued that existing sociology was purely descriptive and concerned with surfaces and taxonomies, but that a true science of society would discover the deep genetic basis of social behavior. "It may not be too much to say that sociology and the other social sciences, as well as the humanities," said Wilson, "are the last branches of biology waiting to be included in the Modern Synthesis. Whether the social sciences can be truly biologicized (*sic*) in this fashion remains to be seen."[1]

Wilson's book generated a firestorm. Its most prominent critics were not social scientists, but biologists themselves, aware of the various uses to which biological arguments had been put in justifying social inequalities. While critics such as Stephen Jay Gould and Richard Lewontin, high profile figures in evolutionary biology at Harvard (as was Wilson), were clearly concerned about the political and social consequences of Wilson's sociobiology, they made their critiques of Wilson on scientific grounds—Wilson's arguments, they claimed, were reductionist, unsupported by evidence, and tended to a kind of circularity; they were grounded in ideology rather than in science. In the decade prior to the publication of sociobiology, a series of popular books arguing for the evolutionary basis of human behavior had come out: Desmond Morris's *The Naked Ape* (1966), Robert Ardrey's *The Social Contract: A Personal Inquiry into the Evolutionary Sources of Order and Disorder* (1970); Robin Fox and Lionel Tiger's *The Imperial Animal* (1971); and Steven Goldberg's *The Inevitability of Patriarchy* (1973) among them. In a period of social upheaval and challenges to an existing racial and gender order, these books often sought a reaffirmation of male and female roles and a justification of social domination as rooted in evolutionary behavior, appealing to the behavior of primates as a model of human social forms. In *Not in Our Genes* (1984), Lewontin and his co-authors made their case clear: "sociobiology is a reductionist, biological determinist explanation of human existence... The general appeal of sociobiology is in its legitimation of the status quo."[2] Linking sociobiology to Social Darwinism, they suggested that the invocation of evolutionary process was a way of saying that the present was the optimal outcome of natural process, and since it was biologically determined, could not be changed.

On the 25th anniversary of *sociobiology* in 2000, Wilson responded to his critics by characterizing them as Marxists who believed in the *tabula rasa* –the idea that human beings were a blank slate, and could be infinitely molded to a desired outcome. In other words, when met by criticism on scientific grounds, he attacked not the logic of the criticisms, but their presumed ideological motives. On both sides of a debate that burned hot in the 1970s and 80s, the argument over the relative weight of genetic factors in social behavior turned into a debate over who was being truly scientific, and who was guided by ideology. "As the century closes," said Wilson, "this dispute has been settled. Genetically based variation in individual personality and intelligence has been conclusively demonstrated."[3] In a kind of scientific triumphalism, Wilson equated the end of the Cold War with the end of criticism of sociobiology and genetic determinism. Even in his claims for a science free of ideology, Wilson could not resist a political vision based on a frankly conservative vision of nature. That the criticism of sociobiology was not put to bed but remains a part of modern thought, suggests that Wilson's view of science and consilience was a product of a large dose of wishful thinking.

Almost exactly contemporary with Wilson's *sociobiology* was Richard Dawkins' *The Selfish Gene* (1976). While Dawkins was concerned with developing an argument that the unit of survival in the Darwinian process was not the species, but the gene, and that genes were "selfish" in pursuing their own survival and replication, even at the expense of the species, his foregrounding of the evolutionary process was unlike that of Wilson and others who were committed to the idea that the basis for human behavior was fundamentally genetic. Dawkins specifically set human beings apart from other animals. He argued that human existence was biological, of course, but also that it was governed by culture and its transmission, rather than arguing that culture was itself an expression of biology. The lasting influence of Dawkins's book was its creation of the concept of the "meme," as a unit of cultural transmission, a kind of analogue on the cultural level of the gene on the biological level. He spoke of a "meme pool," and of cultural entities such as the idea of God, or a piece of music, or a form of clothing, as being units that were replicators, with a suggestion that the process of cultural replication could be understood as evolutionary, a competition for survival among memes. The idea of cultural progress, long questioned by skeptical modernists, was resurrected in Dawkins's account, particularly because he imagined science itself as composed of memes, the better and more adaptive scientific accounts outlasting their competitors. The tension in Dawkins's account lay between his willingness to offer a culturalist version of human behavior, and his desire to model that cultural process on that of biological evolution. The idea of "meme" was confused and unclear from the beginning. That its lasting appeal would be to providing a name for the circulation of visual jokes on the internet showed how the meaning of cultural units could be transformed in their appropriation.

Evolutionary Psychology

In the decades following Wilson's *sociobiology*, the specific application of evolutionary biology to human behavior came to be identified as evolutionary psychology. Evolutionary psychology tended to be less concerned with the mechanisms of social ordering such as the division of labor, caste hierarchies, and social structure, and more concerned with the understanding of personality traits and human behavior such as aggression, love and sexual attraction, anger, sympathy, and jealousy. Not a field of biology, but of scholars trained in psychology and anthropology, it was less centered on finding the specific DNA code for such attributes and more concerned with demonstrating the evolutionary adaptation and success values of particular behaviors. The foundational texts for evolutionary psychology, as much as it was shaped by Wilson's sociobiological agenda, lay in Darwin's twin texts, *The Descent of Man* (1871) and *The Expression of Emotions in Man and Animals* (1872). The key texts responsible for defining evolutionary psychology included John Tooby and Leda Cosmides, *The Adapted Mind* (1992), on the scholarly level, and Robert Wright, *The Moral Animal* (1994) on the popular level. A small group of scholars, including Tooby, Cosmides, Steven Pinker, David Buss, Martin Daly, Margo Wilson, and David Symons defined the newly emerging field from the late 1970s forward, creating new academic journals and centers, such as Tooby and Cosmides's Center for evolutionary psychology at the University of California at Santa Barbara.

Pinker defined the operating assumptions of evolutionary psychology in the following way in his best-selling *How the Mind Works* (1997):

> The mind is a system of organs of computation, designed by natural selection to solve the kinds of problems our ancestors faced in their foraging way of life, in particular, understanding and outmaneuvering objects, animals, plants, and other people…. The mind is organized into modules or mental organs, each with a specialized design that makes it an expert in one arena of interaction with the world. The modules' basic logic is specified by our genetic program. Their operation was shaped by natural selection to solve the problems of the hunting and gathering life led by our ancestors in most of our evolutionary history. The various problems for our ancestors were subtasks of one big problem for their genes, maximizing the number of copies that made it into the next generation.[4]

The arguments of evolutionary psychologists received enormous press coverage and generated controversy. Like Wilson, the prime figures in the field were highly critical of what they referred to as "the standard social science model," for assuming a vision of cultural determinism and a blank-slate vision of a highly mutable human nature. Social scientists and humanists returned the favor by criticizing evolutionary psychology for its biological determinism and the lack of attention to specific cultural forms. The method of evolutionary psychology, in contrast, was to assume a uniform human nature on the analogy of a universal human anatomy; the vision of "mental organs" as selected in the Pleistocene Era (roughly 1.8 million years ago to 10,000 years ago) when human beings were hunter-gatherers led to its characteristic form of argumentation. Looking at contemporary human behaviors, evolutionary psychologists sought to "reverse-engineer" them to show how they must have evolved in relationship to the presumed environment that ancient humans faced. The field, then, united an empirical approach to present behavior with a highly speculative approach to the past. Often beginning with identifying behaviors as cultural universals, evolutionary psychologists then presumed the universality was evidence of biological uniformity.

Evolutionary psychologists tended to reject the arguments that they were advocates for a new form of the kind of Social Darwinism that flourished a century earlier. Because they were in search of a universal human nature, they were not concerned with creating models of evolutionary stages of peoples, or emphasizing racial differences and hierarchies, although sex difference was often at the heart of studies. The most prominent conclusions associated with evolutionary psychology included David Buss's claims that men were hard-wired to prefer young nubile women, and women were attracted to high-status men, since this arrangement was most advantageous for reproductive success and survival; Martin Daly and Margo Wilson's claims that parents differentially bestowed love and affection on children that they confidently regarded as having strong probability of being genetic offspring; and John Tooby and Leda Cosmides's claims that human beings possessed a genetically adapted mechanism of "cheater detection." Each of these traits was held to result from its reproductive advantage under conditions of the distant past of the human race. Because evolutionary psychology put the weight of psychological formation on the Pleistocene, they often seemed to be suggesting that human attributes forged to be adaptive in one world, were out of step with the contemporary organization of human societies. As a consequence, their conclusions seemed to waver between arguing for the natural order of human social relations, and suggesting that humans had stopped evolving and now had a fixed set of attributes that were a mismatch for modernity.

This idea of a mismatch between human biology and the conditions of modern life was given additional weight in popular culture by the rise of what was called the paleolithic or caveman diet, one version of many fad diets characteristic of the twentieth century. The gastroenterologist Walter Voegtlin in 1975 published *The Stone Age Diet*, arguing that the modern diet of grains, fruits, and vegetables and processed foods was entirely out of sync with the human digestive system, which had been selected for in a world in which the principal source of human nutrition was animal protein. Human beings were genetically determined carnivores, and the physiological ailments of modern life could be tied to a deviation, in the past 10,000 years, from the presumed standard diet of man. The solution: eliminate all carbohydrates from the diet, and return to the presumed foodways that had ruled humanity for the vast majority of its history. Variations of the paleolithic diet, and the genetic arguments for it, would appear through the 1980s and 90s. Evolutionary psychologists did not generally argue for the return to the practices of the Pleistocene, but they shared with the promoters of the caveman diet the idea that modern life was governed by principles often contrary to the genetic elements that had been selected for in man's early life.

Race Essentialism and *The Bell Curve* debate

In 1994, the conservative political scientist Charles Murray and the Harvard psychologist Richard Herrnstein published *The Bell Curve*. Not simply an academic tome, *The Bell Curve* was designed to provoke, and provoke it did. The book argued that intelligence, as measured by IQ, was the best predictor of social and economic success in the contemporary United States, and revived in public discourse older debates about the use and value of IQ testing. Murray had previously caused a stir with a book that argued that the social policies of the Great Society programs of the 1960s had resulted in institutionalizing greater inequality and poverty. *Losing Ground* (1984) was a Reagan-era manifesto that called for the rollback of the welfare state and its manufactured dependency. *The Bell Curve* built on that argument by rejecting the notion that socioeconomic inequalities reproduced themselves through access to education, social supports and services, and class privilege, and saw those inequalities as explainable by relative differences in intelligence. In the most controversial chapter in the book—the one on which the vast majority of criticism came to fall—they argued that intelligence differed by race, to a small extent between Asians and whites, the former higher than the latter, but to a much larger extent between whites and Blacks. The reason for the relative lack of success of Blacks in American society, they held, was not structural racism, access to education, or other environmental factors, but this intelligence differential. While they hedged on just how much of that difference was genetic, since they sought to systematically downplay environmental factors, their main intent was to argue that at least some substantial proportion of differences in intelligence between the races was genetic. Failure to accept this as a conclusion of science, they said, was part of a continuing "elite wisdom on this issue, for years almost hysterically in denial about that possibility," and driven by ideology rather than fact.[5]

The result was predictable. *The Bell Curve* received enormous attention in the national press, especially in journals of opinion such as *The New Republic* and *National Review*. Racial liberals denounced the book as racist, arguing that it revived a body of racist and eugenic thought that had been sustained throughout the twentieth century, especially its later twentieth-century variants focusing on IQ and race in the writings of figures such as Arthur Jensen and Nobel Prize-winning Physicist William Shockley. Murray and Herrnstein relied on some of this work, much of it funded by the white supremacist Pioneer Fund. For many, the racial and eugenic arguments that had been used by Nazis and white supremacists invalidated the fundamental approach associated with the idea of IQ and a differential general intelligence based on heredity. The evolutionary biologist Steven Jay Gould, who, as we have seen, was also one of the most vociferous critics of Wilson's sociobiology, was quick to dismantle the claims of genetically based intelligence differentials related to race. Conservative defenders of Murray and Herrnstein argued for the scientific and qualified approach they appeared to take, in contrast to the shrill and knee-jerk reaction of their critics. As with the Darwin debates, each side accused the other of ideological intent. It's hard to deny that Murray, with a history of criticism of social welfare policies before he took up the issue of IQ, was simply pursuing a line of temperate reasoned academic research, rather than being motivated by ideology. The idea of IQ was, for some, like the idea of race itself, a social construction, a creation with built-in ideological content. For others, race was a biological reality, and IQ measured some natural ability that was an inherent possession of people. The middle ground between the biological essentialist and realist position, and the culture and social constructionist position, was hard to find.

The Politics of the "Gay Gene"

Almost contemporaneous with the *Bell Curve* debates was the appearance of a study by a team led by the geneticist Dean Hamer, purporting to have discovered a common set of DNA markers on the X chromosome of a group of gay men. The publication of a paper in the journal *Science* in the summer of 1993 sparked an immediate media reaction. The discovery of the so-called "gay gene," was taken up in the midst of a political controversy during the Clinton administration over allowing gay people to serve in the military. Hamer had turned to the study of the genetics of sexuality—and away from his previous cancer research—after having read Darwin's *Descent of Man*, with its focus on sex-specific divergence, and Lewentin et al.'s *Not in Our Genes*, the arguments of which he rejected as politically motivated rather than scientific. The response to Hamer's study was divided but in ways fundamentally different from those that met the claims about the genetic heritability of intelligence related to race put forward by Herrnstein and Murray. Although there was a strong component of social constructionism, following Foucault, among many gay activists, the notion that homosexuality was coded in DNA led many others to argue that because sexuality and what had been called "sexual preference," was not a matter of choice, it could no longer be debated as a matter of morality. The idea of genetic inheritance flew in the face of a long tradition of sexology from Freud, Alfred Kinsey, and others, who had seen sexual behavior as in large part a social product, even if they often characterized it as a kind of disease or disorder. Religiously based animus against homosexuality had assumed that homosexuality was a sin, and could be "corrected" through therapy designed to reorient the sinner's sexual desire into marital heterosexuality. In this context, the idea that homosexuality with a natural genetically inherited trait flew in the face of those who argued that it was "unnatural." The idea of homosexuality as a fixed biological attribute was, for those who took it up, a way to challenge the presumed moral fixity of a heterosexual standard.

This idea that homosexuality was not a matter of choice, but of biological determination, then, seemed to offer a different outcome than many of the other uses of biological and genetic arguments to naturalize hierarchy and existing norms. Many conservative and religiously based thinkers rejected Hamer's conclusions out of hand. But the idea of a "gay gene" also had its detractors among gay activists and thinkers, in part because the image of genetics was moving more and more in the direction of the scientific ability to modify, edit, and control gene reproduction. In 1996, the first mammal, Dolly the sheep, was cloned in Scotland. The idea of human control over genetic reproduction, of the ability of humans in the future to choose not only the sex of their offspring but also to edit genes to eliminate undesirable traits, raised the specter of eugenics in a new key. The idea that, having located a specific sequence of DNA that controlled sexuality, the dominant social groups would seek to modify it to ensure universal heterosexuality, was very much part of the discussion and response to Hamer's findings. And, at the same moment that the idea of a gay gene was being put into circulation, the legacy of gay liberation's pluralistic challenge to conventional forms of family and sexual behavior was being transformed into a rejection of the binary model of homosexual/heterosexual in favor of a new "queer" ethic that suggested that sexuality should be imagined as a spectrum or a many-headed animal, rather than a fixed orientation—as we will see in the following chapter.

By the end of the century, however, the initial optimism of those who thought they could identify a gay gene had dissipated. A series of studies had failed to confirm Hamer's initial findings, and the existence of a direct genetic link was roundly criticized by many. The idea of a "gay gene," as much as it proved inviting as a way to describe heritable sexuality, was always a kind of conscious simplification. Human sexuality, for many scientists, still had significant biological causes, including but not limited to genetic ones, but a singular gene, and one operating independent of the shaping power of social environments seemed highly unlikely. But the parallels to the issue of the heritability of intelligence remain striking. Both, for instance, relied on the study of identical twins to try to separate biological factors from social environment. A decade later, Hamer would follow his search for "the gay gene" with a book entitled *The God Gene: How Faith Is Hardwired into Our Genes* (2004).

Transhumanism

By the late twentieth century, especially with the development and use of personal computers and widespread technologies that were transforming every facet of life—labor, business, communications, and art among them—the notion put forward by Daniel Bell and others of a post-industrial society was newly christened "the information society." The idea of DNA as coded information dovetailed with a focus on new fields in the post-World War II world: cybernetics, computer science, and Artificial Intelligence (AI). The idea of feedback loops and neural networks as features common to the organic and mechanical worlds eroded the boundary between human and machine, equating biological and social "systems." The field of cybernetics, the study of self-regulating causal processes—both biological and artificial—was developed by Norbert Wiener and others in the post-World War II era, a time in which techno-utopianism was very much the object of skepticism and ambivalence due to the association of modern technologies with both nuclear weaponry and military destruction. "We have contributed to the initiation of a new science," said Wiener in 1948, "with great possibilities for good and for evil. We can only hand it over into the world that exists about us, and this is the world of Belsen and Hiroshima."[6] The optimistic dream of some that it was possible to create artificial forms of thinking and reasoning that would mimic—and even bypass—the human forms of cognition was born at the Dartmouth Summer Research Project on Artificial Intelligence in 1956. The fate of AI would wax and wane over the next half-century. Cybenetics, AI, and other fields, including linguistics and molecular biology, all contributed to the development of the field of computer science, which began to be institutionalized as an academic discipline in the early 1960s.

Modern thought has been deeply ambivalent about the moral and social value of new technologies. For every vision of a utopian world remade by technologies that have universalized freedom and eliminated exploitative labor, disease, and poverty, there has been a counter vision of a technological world of greater exploitation, social alienation, and more efficient means of controlling people, including their minds. In the wake of the horrific events of the mid-twentieth century, the dystopian warnings seemed more frequent and salient. In the last decades of the twentieth century, however, technological utopianism had been given a kind of rebirth, fueled by the growth of new industries that came to be described simply as "tech," and associated with innovation and an imagined new kind of capitalism in places such as California's Silicon Valley. The promise of machines that would remake the world, of a libertarian world in which "information wants to be free," of a revolt against the control of information by existing hierarchical institutions, easily merged with the legacy of the 1960s counter culture in the thought of figures such as Stewart Brand, the founder of The Whole Earth catalogue. The decades of the 1980s and 1990s, in which the internet was being born and nurtured, were a period in which it was very much possible to imagine new technologies as the source of not just a revolution in business, but a social and cultural revolution.

One of the forms that late twentieth-century techno-utopianism took was what came to be called transhumanism. The belief that human beings were merging with machines, that it might be possible to use new technologies to "enhance" human beings, to move beyond being human, although in its most radical form always the province of a small group of advocates and believers, began to receive much popular attention. No longer was AI simply the realm of chess-playing machines, or solving mathematical problems; some people came to believe that all human cognition could, and would, be replicated by machines that could do it faster and better. The traditional human being would become obsolete. This vision could take many forms, with many political resonances. A left-wing feminist version of overcoming the divide between human and machine, for instance, was articulated by Donna Haraway in *A Cyborg Manifesto* (1985), in which she urged a rejection of the kind of fixed boundaries (man/woman, nature/culture, self/other, animal/machine) that would limit utopian possibilities for feminism. Overcoming dichotomies, as anti-dualists such as John Dewey had earlier proposed, was a means of opening up political possibility, of flattening hierarchies. If Darwinism had destroyed the boundary dividing human from animal, in the new world of the late twentieth century, the divide between human and machine had to go.

More typical of the transhumanist vision was the work of those futurist thinkers coming out of the AI field, best represented by the writings of Ray Kurzweil. For Kurzweil, human carbon-based life intelligence, complex as it is, is completely assimilable to machine-based intelligence, and since consciousness and thought can be reduced to neural networks, it is possible for machines to be conscious, intelligent beings. There is no fundamental difference in the thought process of advanced computers and human beings. Kurzweil embraced a kind of historical technological inevitability. "The accelerating pace of change is inexorable. The emergence of machine intelligence that exceeds human intelligence in all its diversity is inevitable."[7] He imagined this as a continuation of the evolutionary process. Since machine-based intelligence will be so advanced (in a mere 100 years in the future), traditional humans will cease to have purpose. All new technologies will be created by the new transhuman beings. For Kurzweil, this is a good thing. Transhumanist futurists often seemed to have little familiarity with traditions of ethics and philosophical and social thought, nor of the weight of empirical finding that would be necessary to sustain their vision. Neither *The Bell Curve* authors nor the AI futurists, could come up with a commonly accepted definition of the central concept of intelligence (Kurzweil relied on the Turing Test—if a computer can answer in such a way as to convince a person that it is a conscious being, then it is conscious). Instead, they imagined that the reality of intelligence was reducible to a single quantitative standard measuring an objective outcome.

Conclusion

The idea that all manners of social behaviors and traits were best understood through the framework of biological heritability, and that DNA could be the master metaphor for understanding human society and its forms, was a powerful form of thinking in the late twentieth century. It carried with it a shadow of the Social Darwinist impulse of the late nineteenth century, but often stripped of some of the evolutionary hierarchies that characterized that earlier body of thought. What was most innovative about this later thought was the way in which it wedded and twined the vision of information technology as code with the vision of DNA as code, linking the biological with the mechanical.

Notes

1. Edward O. Wilson, *sociobiology: The New Synthesis*, 25th Anniversary Edition (Cambridge, MA: Harvard University Press, 2000), p. 22.
2. Steven Rose, Richard C. Lewontin, and Leon J. Kamin, *Not in Our Genes: Biology, Ideology, and Human Nature* (New York: Pantheon, 1984), p. 236.
3. Wilson, *sociobiology*, p. 8.
4. Steven Pinker, *How the Mind Works* (New York: W.W. Norton, 1997), p. 21.
5. Richard J. Herrnstein and Charles Murray, *The Bell Curve: Intelligence and Class Structure in American Life* (New York: Free Press, 1994), p. 315.
6. Norbert Wiener, *Cybernetics: or Control and Communication in the Animal and the Machine* (Cambridge: MIT Press, 1948), p. 28.
7. Ray Kurzweil, *The Age of Spiritual Machines: When Computers Exceed Human Intelligence* (New York: Penguin, 1999), p. 253.

14 Gender and Sexuality

It is common to refer to the various isms that have come to characterize modern thought in the singular: racism, liberalism, conservatism, Marxism, post-modernism, feminism. This usage obscures the fact that any of these isms rarely possess a unified consensus body of belief and that each presents variations in emphasis, and often internal contradictions, that make them far from singular and uniform. The term "feminism" is one of the most contested of these—over the past decades, beginning in the 1960s, there have been liberal feminists and socialist feminists, sameness feminists and difference feminists, maternalist feminists and gender-queer feminists, intersectional feminists and essentialist feminists; eco-feminists, separatist feminists, Third World feminists, libertarian feminists, lesbian feminists, Black feminists, middle-class feminists, Christian feminists. In other words, a great deal of intellectual diversity is hidden behind a term that appears to speak in a unified way. The history of feminism, then, is really a history of an essentially contested term, a battle over the meaning of gender, sex, equality, and the forms of social, political, and economic life. From one point of view, the plurality of feminism has been one of its greatest strengths, an indication of a powerful, rich body of thought; from another it has been a weakness, turning feminisms away from a common problem or enemy and toward fragmentation and in-fighting, and providing anti-feminists with rhetorical power to argue against feminism by generalizing a particular position as expressing "feminism in general."

We might regard the proliferation of feminisms in the last third of the twentieth century—and the reaction against them—as a sign of the significance of contestation over one of the fundamental ideas and organizing principles found in all societies. For the challenges to long-standing ideas of the family, the gendered division of labor, sexuality, the relationship between nature and culture, embodiment, the meaning of equality, and the operating principles of capitalism itself, the intellectual history of feminisms is one of the principal places to look. Feminist thought and its derivatives—concerns with the politics of gender and sexuality in gay liberation, queer theory, and the men's rights movement—provided the ground on which the forces of social constructionism and linguistics often did battle with both religiously derived traditionalism and biological essentialism. Gender might be imagined as the quintessentially modern idea, because it points to a moment in which deeply embedded ideas of fixed biological difference as the basis for social distinction came under repeated and profound question. If the fundamental difference between men and women was not fixed in nature, but, like race, was a product of highly variable social and cultural forces, what aspects of human life could be imagined as retaining any fixed definition? For those who sought to resist the reframing of gender by various feminisms—evangelical Christians, biological essentialists, and advocates for what was increasingly referred to as "the traditional family," among them—the moral order of an imagined world was at stake. So-called liberal feminists often found themselves comfortable with some challenges to the received moral order, but unwilling to follow their more radical compatriots in challenging even more fundamental aspects of the given world. And some radical feminists were to unexpectedly find themselves in the twenty-first century as defenders of a fixed notion of womanhood against the claims of a transgenderism that grew out of their own radical rethinking of the relationship between men and women.

Feminism in Waves and the Thought of Betty Friedan

Historians and the broader public have generally spoken of the history of feminism through use of the wave metaphor: first-wave feminists were held to triumph in the realization of women's suffrage through the 19th amendment to the Constitution in 1920. Historians imagined that the movement for women's equality, which had been funneled into the movement for voting rights, then receded in the mid-century, only to be followed by a "second wave" of feminism in the 1960s and beyond. Some have speculated about a third, and even fourth, wave, implying that feminism differs generationally, that its history is a lapping at the shore, an ebb, and flow amidst an ever-rising tide. This way of thinking, however, has been called into question by those who have found continuity and expansion of women's political activism over the course of the entire century, and who regard the wave metaphor as tied to cyclical accounts of activism followed by reaction. The advantage of the idea of a "second wave" feminism is that it allows us to see something of both continuity and rupture in a new mode of intellectual thought about gender and sexuality. The language that feminists adopted sustained older ideas from the movement for women's equality in the nineteenth and early twentieth centuries—the language of rights, of equality, of individual autonomy, for instance—but also incorporated Marxist, neo-Freudian, post-structuralist, post-colonial, and existentialist elements, among many others. Talk of "patriarchy," of sexism, of sexual power and rape, of "sexual politics," of "compulsory heterosexuality," and "the traffic in women," of "consciousness raising," of "women's liberation" and a "women's culture," of making the personal political, of "the male gaze," of "woman-identified women," of breaking "the glass ceiling," and therapeutic self-fulfillment, demonstrates the range of new vocabularies and ideas among a variety of different feminisms over the course of the last decades of the twentieth century. As with so much thought in the late twentieth century, it was appealing to imagine a break with the past, and a new vision of women's freedom and equality, but we should always remember that the constant change in modern thought has also been undergirded by continuity over the past century and a half.

It is conventional to date the origins of second-wave feminism from the publication of Betty Friedan's *The Feminine Mystique* (1963); as with the famous meeting of women's rights advocates at Seneca Falls, NY in 1848, so much commentary about the history of feminism has grown up and become encrusted around the canonical status of Friedan's text, that some historians have felt the need to critique what we might call the mystique of *The Feminine Mystique*. The idea that this text landed as a kind of spark that ignited a new consciousness in women, that it gave a name and a common assurance to women that they were not alone in their unarticulated discontent and psychological unease, has become a kind of cliché in the understanding of the history of feminism. Not that the cliché was entirely without truth. What Friedan's book did do was to set the terms of a particular kind of feminist thought rooted in the educated upper middle class, a feminism that took a culture of abundance and the material comforts of a middle-class suburban life for granted. When that variety of feminist thought encountered the transformations and fragmentations of the later 1960s and early 1970s, including student radicalism, the Black Power movement, and the so-called sexual revolution of the counter culture, it provided some of the elements—the focus on consciousness and psychic identity, of a culture that had to be unlearned, for instance—that would be transformed into a critique of middle-class feminism. As revolutionary in some respects as Friedan's book was, it also borrowed heavily from the mainstream of middle-class cultural criticism and psychological self-help of the era.

Friedan's principal argument was that a cultural ideal of womanhood that emphasized female fulfillment in the capacity of wife and mother had worked, in the post-World War II era, to push women into the role of "occupation housewife," but that women felt a widespread discontent—which she referred to as "the problem that has no name"—in this role. For Freidan, the solution to what she saw as the dehumanization of women was equal opportunity in the world of work. The professional career was, for Friedan, the space in which women could realize their potential. Liberal or middle-class feminism argued that the idea of a fixed division of labor—men in the workforce, women in the home—was inimical to the health and well-being of both men and women. The program was reformist rather than revolutionary—it accepted the norms of a capitalist society and a form of liberal democracy built on individual rights. Friedan argued that women's domestic duties actually required very little labor and time—boredom and alienation was what plagued American women, not the burden of unpaid labor. Her vision was one that required a change of consciousness and a legal push to prevent discrimination against women in the workforce, but not a change in the responsibilities of men. She drew on Freud, Marx, Abraham Maslow, and his hierarchy of needs, among many other sources, to fashion an argument about a kind of false consciousness operating against the higher needs of women for fulfillment through work. The class-based assumptions Friedan generalized when she spoke of "women" would come under sustained criticism by various other feminists in the ensuing years.

What was absent in the vision of *The Feminine Mystique*? Besides class differences, Friedan avoided the issue of sexuality as a source of freedom. She largely accepted a Freudian view that pathologized male homosexuality as a product of frustrated women domineering over their sons. But the idea that heterosexual monogamy, on the one hand, or sexual violence, on the other, were issues central to women's oppression, as later feminists would argue, was not on her radar. In her view, unhappy housewives acted out the lack of meaning in their lives by extramarital affairs; equality in the workplace would produce happier and more fulfilling marriages. As President of the National Organization of Women (NOW) in the late 1960s, she explicitly sought to separate the women's movement from lesbian activism, warning of a "lavender menace" that would associate NOW with a challenge to the heterosexual family. Later feminists would aim their criticism of patriarchy (a term that never appeared in *The Feminine Mystique*) at the institutions of heterosexual marriage and the family as an engine for reproducing inequality. She also had nothing to say about race and how Black women's lives and needs might differ from those of whites. In the late 1940s and early 1950s, Friedan had been active in labor circles, and as an advocate for more radical unionism; by the time she wrote *The Feminine Mystique*, and under the pressure of the anti-Communism of the 1950s, she was imagining social problems as cultural mystification, rather than as class exploitation. Critical of the weight of social scientific and psychological ideas about women's nature and social identities identified with Freud, Margaret Mead, and the functionalist sociology of Talcott Parsons among others, Friedan appeared to be offering a radical alternative to a dominant ideology. Her feminist critics over the next decades, however, would suggest that she was *too* wedded to a dominant ideology, and insufficiently critical of the structure of power in American society.

Radical Feminism

The challenge to NOW's leadership and the perceived limitation of its liberal feminism came from a variety of places: women who had been active in the Civil Rights Movement and the student left, increasingly conscious of the ways in which these movements reproduced male domination; lesbian activists, increasingly visible in urban centers like New York, especially in the wake of the Stonewall Riots that sparked the Gay Liberation Movement; Black women immersed in the struggles for Black Power and the rethinking of Black and Third-World radicalisms, among others. The late 1960s and early 1970s saw a proliferation of thought, writings and political manifestos that defined the central issues of a radical feminism: Shulamith Firestone's *The Dialectic of Sex*; Ti-Grace Atkinson's The Feminists' pamphlet "Radical Feminism,"; Kate Millet's *Sexual Politics*; Carole Hanisch's essay "The Personal is Political"; Susan Brownmiller's *Against Our Will: Men, Women, and Rape*; Anne Koedt's *The Myth of the Vaginal Orgasm*; Germaine Greer's *The Female Eunuch*; Jill Johnston's *Lesbian Nation: The Feminist Solution*; Andrea Dworkin's *Woman Hating*; Gayle Rubin's "The Traffic in Women"; and Robin Morgan's collection of radical feminist writings, *Sisterhood is Powerful*. Groups such as The Redstockings, The Feminists, and New York Radical Women were the spaces in which women met to develop a radical rethinking of women as an oppressed class, and to propose an agenda of what was dubbed Women's Liberation.

Although the term "radical" has often been equated with extremism, its meaning, and the way in which those identifying themselves as radical feminists used it, speaks to its etymology: radical means of the root, or going to the root. Radical feminists argued that in order for women to be free and equal, they had to change not just behavior, attitudes, and legal structures, but had to uproot the foundations of the social order and its central organizing principles. At the root of women's unfreedom, in this view, lay a systemic commitment to a social and political order undergirded by sex difference. They challenged sexism, the belief in a hierarchical relationship between men and women, and patriarchy, a system of rule by men and its pervasive expression in all of the institutions, beliefs, and practices of the social order. As long as women were identified with the requirement of biological reproduction, they would be systematically oppressed as a class. "The feminist dilemma," said Ti-Grace Atkinson,

> is that it is as women—or 'females'—that women are persecuted, just as it was as slaves—or "blacks"—that slaves were persecuted in America:

Gender and Sexuality 253

in order to improve their condition, those individuals who are identified as women must eradicate their own definition. Women must, in a sense, commit suicide, and the journey from womanhood to a society of individuals is hazardous.[1]

The entire identity of "woman," from this point of view, is the expression of a system of power, and must be undone. Friedan challenged a "myth" of feminine identity; radical feminists challenged the very basis of the category which defined them.

Shulamith Firestone's *Dialectic of Sex* (1970) developed the most systematic theoretical position of early radical feminism. Drawing on elements of the Marxist and Freudian traditions, as well as the existentialist Simone de Beauvoir's *The Second Sex* (1949), she constructed a systematic theory of history and what she regarded as the conditions that made feminist revolution possible. Firestone argued that Marx and Engels's historical materialism had not gone far enough because it had refused the primacy of a biological division of labor that represented the earliest form of oppression. The exploitation of women was based on their biological role in reproduction—procreation, the means of *reproduction* in society, was prior to the economic means of *production*, and therefore more foundational; the sex difference was historically prior to the development of social classes—and private property—that was at the heart of Marx and Engels's theory of history. Calling for what she called a "cybersocialist" feminist revolution, she located oppression in the form of the family, and called for its elimination.

> ... [J]ust as the end goal of social revolution was not only the elimination of the economic class *privilege* but of the economic class distinction itself, so the end goal of feminist revolution must be, unlike that of the first feminist movement, not just the elimination of male *privilege* but of the sex distinction itself: genital differences between human beings would no longer matter culturally.[2]

Embracing the development of technologies that both eliminated labor and created the condition for artificial reproduction, she sought a liberation of not only women but also children, from both the oppression of family and the repression of sexuality. She started her critique with a biological essentialism and foundationalism but ended by saying that the conditions of biology had been transcended through historical process and that revolutionary freedom meant the elimination of the functional categories of male and female derived from biology. Only when women were no longer mothers (and men no longer fathers) would all people be free.

Many feminists were unwilling to go as far as Atkinson and Firestone; to build a movement on the identity of women, on what radical feminists often referred to as "sisterhood," for the purpose of ending that identity seemed to some others to itself be an internalization of misogyny—women who no longer wanted to be women. The problem frequently faced by feminists was the dominance of antifeminist arguments that began with biology, as Firestone did, but then removed it from history to argue for biological identity as a necessary constant in defining women's social roles and psychological constitution. The notion that "biology is destiny" had been a source for various essentialist accounts—women, said advocates for the norms of the family, were destined to be mothers and caregivers; as a consequence, they were characterized as more loving and emotional, less aggressive and rational, than men. Nature created complementarity between men and women, both anatomically, but also psychologically and socially. The social roles of women were held to stem from their biological natures.

Against these arguments, many feminists deployed a critical distinction between sex and gender. In a 1975 article, the feminist anthropologist Gayle Rubin defined what she called "a sex/gender system" as "the set of arrangements by which a society transforms biological sexuality into products of human activity, and in which these transformed sexual needs are satisfied." Rejecting both the terms "patriarchy" and "mode of reproduction" used to describe the political forms by which women were oppressed, Rubin argued that sex/gender systems could be hierarchical or not, but that every society necessarily had to create institutions and meanings out of the raw material of biological difference. There was nothing in the biological and natural that determined the inevitability of any form of the sex/gender system, any more than the various kinship terms in societies were given in nature. Drawing on the structuralist anthropology of Claude Levi-Strauss, and Freudian psychoanalysis, she developed an argument centered on kinship categories and the development of sexual identities. The sexual division of labor, she claimed, was not given in nature, but was a taboo: "a taboo against the sameness of men and women, a taboo dividing the sexes into two mutually exclusive categories, a taboo which exacerbates the biological differences between the sexes and thereby *creates* gender."[3] This idea, that gender was a cultural creation, a way of organizing and giving meaning to an underlying biological sex, allowed women to separate a biological, presumably fixed, identity from an unfixed cultural identity, an identity ripe for remaking through political action. Sex was nature; gender was culture. Biology was not determinative of the forms of gender. Rather, biology only became meaningful and social under the conditions of the creation of cultural values, norms, and institutions. Although Rubin's position was more nuanced, the appeal to an absolute divide between sex and gender, nature and culture, was an attractive analytical lens for feminists seeking to identify what could be changed, and what was fixed. Gender became one of the keywords or dominant ideas of the last third of the twentieth century. Designed to distinguish between nature and culture, the irony was that, in the larger cultural appropriation of the idea, gender and sex difference served for many Americans as synonyms.

The Feminist Critique of Radical Feminism

There was never a radical feminist consensus on all matters; radical feminism was more a sensibility, a critical rethinking of social foundations through the category of woman as an oppressed class, than a set of agreed-upon doctrines. Internal debate, such as that between lesbians ("The Woman-Identified Woman" (1970) was an early manifesto by the group Radicalesbians) and those who thought sexism could be uprooted in a way that preserved some form of heterosexuality without privileging it, characterized the movement from early on. What that meant was that the creation of a space in which a radical rethinking of sex roles, male dominance, and cultural ideas of normative family and sexual order became possible, was the condition for a splintering of the movement. While the issues, as with factionalism within any political movement, were complex and cannot be fully addressed here, three of the main issues of criticism and conceptual conflict were over (1) issues of the universality of the category of woman as a social class; (2) questions of sexuality; (3) the very nature of a binary distinction between men and women. Because the gender revolution was taking place at a time of other social upheavals—including the Black Power movement, the incipient Gay Liberation movement, and a counter culture challenging the norms of middle-class society with regard to work, sex, living arrangements, and consciousness itself—the characteristic conflicts of feminism both contributed to and drew on shifts taking place in the larger culture.

Prominent early radical feminists had conceptualized "woman" as a political class, characterized by a common ascribed identity, an identity it was held, that was historically and conceptually prior to differences between women on the basis of class, race, ethnicity, and sexuality. Thinkers such as Firestone and Atkinson, and groups such as Redstockings were arguing that the problems that women faced were as women, rather than as differently situated individuals who happened to be women. The idea, for instance, that barriers to professional advancement were a feminist problem, a result of the root definition of "woman," implied that all women suffered from such barriers. The idea that the family was a mechanism for reproducing male domination, or that the "sex/gender system" ascribed common identities to all women across the class structure, seemed to many to collapse the differences between the different kinds of families women had, and to do so in such a way as to privilege the concerns of educated white middle-class women as the universal concerns of "womanhood." The liberal feminism of Friedan, the radicals had argued, asked for no structural changes in the foundation of society, in part because it was a feminism that had a class and economic stake in the existing order; it was reformist rather than revolutionary. But the most prominent voices of early radical feminism, and their intellectual heirs, came to be accused of an agenda that tacitly and unknowingly assumed similar priorities to that of liberal feminism.

The most vocal critique came from women of color and Black feminists. Women of color had been active in the movement from the earliest stages of Women's Liberation and radical feminism. By the mid-1970s, many of them had come to the conclusion that the movement's domination by white women meant a reproduction of racism, and a failure to acknowledge the specific and different conditions of Black, Hispanic, American Indian, and Asian women, many of whom identified a dual loyalty, oppressed by both sexism and racism, in their own political allegiances. The idea that the category of woman in feminist theory contained within it an unexamined racism became part of the critique. Drawing on the radical feminist techniques of consciousness raising, and invoking the feminist tenet that the personal is the political, women of color challenged white feminists' simultaneous claim to include all women, and their marginalization and erasure of the cultures and experience of non-white and non-middle-class women. *The Combahee River Collective Statement* (1977) was the earliest developed statement of a new Black feminism. The collective was a group of Black socialist lesbian feminists in the Boston area that had formed in 1974. Rejecting the idea that it was possible to separate systemic sexism from other forms of oppression, it affirmed that the collective was "actively committed to struggling against racial, sexual, heterosexual, and class oppression, and see our particular task the development of integrated analysis and practice based upon the fact that the major systems of oppression are interlocking." The idea that women were a single unified class and that oppression on the basis of sex was prior to, and more foundational, than other kinds of oppression, could not account for the experiences of Black women. The statement coined the term "identity politics"—a term that would be taken up and transformed by various critics both right and left in the coming decades—and argued that "the most profound and potentially most radical politics come directly out of our own identity, as opposed to working to end somebody else's oppression."[4] The Combahee statement laid the groundwork for the critical race theorist Kimberlé Crenshaw to develop, in the late 1980s, the analytical framework of what came to be known as "intersectionality"—the idea that multiple forms of oppression intersect and that racism, sexism, classism, and homophobia are systems bound up with one another.

A more expansive statement of feminist women of color was *This Bridge Called My Back* (1981). Edited by Gloria Anzaldúa and Cherríe Moraga, this book brought together women of color, many of them lesbians as well, who articulated a deep distrust and disappointment in white feminists, as well as an attempt to define a new and more inclusive vision of sisterhood. The Black lesbian feminist Audre Lorde wrote, in an open letter to the white lesbian feminist Mary Daly, that as radical as her critiques were, they too easily embraced a racism of their own. "The oppression of women knows no ethnic or racial boundaries, true," Lorde said, "but that does not mean it is identical within those boundaries.... [B]eyond sisterhood, is still racism." And, in another essay, Lorde was more acerbic:

> If white American feminist theory need not deal with the differences among us, and the resulting difference in aspects of our oppressions, then what do you do with the fact that the women who clean your houses and tend your children while you attend conferences on feminist theory are, for the most part, poor and third world women? What is the theory behind racist feminism?[5]

The arguments made by feminists of color were developed and extended to a broader public in the writings of bell hooks (née Gloria Jean Watkins), whose many books became the source for a radical Black feminist criticism accessible to students and non-academic audiences. Although her first book, *Ain't I A Woman* (1981) drew the ire of Black feminists such as Barbara Smith (one of the authors of *The Combahee River Collective Statement*) and Cheryl Clarke for matters both large and small (no footnotes; homophobic lesbian-hating; fundamental misunderstandings of Black history; no experience with Black feminist organizations), hooks would go on to be a voice that could bridge the academic world of feminist theory and the concerns of those whose lives in Black communities fell outside of a developing feminist network. In particular, *Feminist Theory: from Margin to Center* (1984), represented an explicit reinvention of radical feminism. A thorough-going critique of the dominant forms of feminist thought as based on assumptions of white privilege and a universalization of women as an oppressed class, her point was not to dismiss feminism as saddled with hierarchical baggage, but to redeem it as a broader political program that aimed to dismantle all forms of domination. She rejected reformist and liberal individualist forms of feminism, but she also sought what she imagined to be a more inclusive project, one that included men, that argued for the significance of families as sources of strength and that rejected what she saw as the implicit privilege and political retreat of woman-centered communitarian alternatives developed by separatists. Hooks became the most widely-known Black feminist theorist in the final decades of the twentieth century.

Another critical body of thought incorporated post-structuralist thought and the focus on language in an effort to undo some of the binary or oppositional categories central to both mainstream culture and much feminist thought. In particular, the binary distinctions between man and woman which lay at the heart of radical feminist criticism, and the distinction between biology and culture, or sex and gender, that provided what was, at least provisionally, a set of firm analytical frames. Out of this critique came a new body of thought in the late 1980s and early 1990s: Queer Theory. Michel Foucáult's *History of Sexuality vol. I* was highly influential in developing a critical body of thought that sought to "queer," or disruptively trouble and call into question, fixed categories around issues of gender and sexuality. Feminists, such as the poet Adrienne Rich, had earlier laid down a critique of what was increasingly referred to as "heteronormativity," or the idea that central institutions, values, and ways of seeing reinforced the normality of a fixed heterosexual identity. Rich had referred to this in a 1980 essay as "Compulsory Heterosexuality." The move from thinking in terms of categories of sex (man/woman) to thinking in terms of categories of sexuality grew out of the linkage that feminists and lesbian activists had made between a social order organized around male power and the channeling of sexual behavior into the form of heterosexual marriage and the family. To be free was not simply to transform the social roles of women, but to open up the possibility of a radical polymorphous sexuality. The appropriation of the idea of "queer" from being a negative slur and epithet to representing a challenge to control and power was part of a new ethos. But Queer Theory, in the writings of thinkers such as Eve Kosofsky Sedgwick and Judith Butler, made the idea of fixed sexual identities, either heterosexual or homosexual, an effect of language and power, further undermining the idea that there could be a natural fixed category of lesbian or heterosexual identity.

Butler's *Gender Trouble* (1990) took aim at the sex/gender distinction developed by feminists over the previous decade. Butler argued that by affixing gender identity to a presumed prior biological reality, feminism had actually re-essentialized it—"gender" was presumed to be socially constructed, but constructed on a prior fixed biological reality. Instead of destabilizing the claims of a fixed identity based on sex, Butler found that gender, in the hands of feminist theory, tracked sex—only biological women could be gendered female, and only biological men could be gendered male. What appeared to be a distinction was, in fact, no distinction at all, and gender collapsed back into sex. Like the Marxist commitment to tying ideologies to their presumed material base, the feminist use of the sex/gender distinction didn't free gender from sex determination but made gender identity an expression of an underlying biological reality. If feminism was serious about challenging the forms of domination around the presumed differences between men and women, Butler appeared to be arguing, it needed to free gendered identity from *any* biological foundation. Instead of thinking of gender as an identity, or its outward form (clothing, body, manner) as expressing an underlying identity, gender should be conceived as a kind of performance. Drawing on the practice of drag performance, which she argued parodied the idea of gender as an expression of an inner self, Butler aimed to destabilize what the idea of gender sought to make stable—a clear and absolute distinction between Man and Woman. "If gender attributes, however, are not expressive but performative," she said, "then these attributes effectively constitute the identity they are said to express or reveal."[6] The Combahee River Collective Statement had put forward identity as the basis for politics, against a universal idea of "woman"; Butler's post-structuralist theory argued that the construction of "identity" limits politics by trapping people in the very categories they seek to overcome. A politics in which gender performance is unmoored from any biological sex, she argued opens new possibilities that feminist theory had foreclosed. There was no escaping the categories of thought, but they could be subverted and destabilized performatively.

As influential as Butler's *Gender Trouble* was in creating an idea of queerness, of gender performativity, of a non-binary world of sexuality and gender, its effectiveness for a more activist feminism appeared less significant. In part, this was due to the opaque and difficult language in which her ideas were put forward, her reference to an extensive and complex body of philosophical thought, her engagement with what for many appeared to be abstruse trends in French literary theory. For academic feminists and queer scholars interested in critical theory and cultural critique, Butler's text became a touchstone and dovetailed with the larger social constructionist sensibility of the era. For feminists concerned with law and the state, with social practices and institutions, there were other priorities. The push to provide protections from sexual harassment and rape, to focus on women's access to health care and family planning on the basis of bodily autonomy, to create pay equity and equal employment standards for women, took precedence over troubling gender ideology on the philosophical level.

Pornography, Violence Against Women, and Sex-Positive Feminism

In the late 1970s and 80s, the increasing fragmentation of feminist thought over matters of race, ethnicity, sexual identity, and class, on the one hand, and essentialism and social constructionist thought on the other, encountered a more explicit and polarizing issue: sex itself. Out of the early radical feminist critique of sex as a tool of patriarchal power, many feminists developed a conception that linked objectification of women, a counter-cultural "free love" ethic of sexual libertinism, pornographic representation, and sexual violence, as part of a common project to dehumanize and control women. The early radical feminist Robin Morgan famously declared in 1974, "pornography is the theory, rape is the practice." As pornographic films, magazines, and literature became more widely and commercially available in the 1970s in the wake of the Supreme Court's overturning of state restrictions on free speech grounds, many feminists organized against pornography, picketing bookstores, and movie theaters that provided sexually explicit material. The movement against pornography culminated in city ordinances in Minneapolis and Indianapolis defining pornography as a civil rights violation in 1983 and 1984; the authors and promoters of those ordinances were Andrea Dworkin and Catharine MacKinnon, who also provided the theoretical understanding of sex, power, and pornography that underwrote the new proposed laws. One of the central claims that MacKinnon made in her legal writings was that women were harmed by a regime that treated their bodily autonomy as a matter of speech. MacKinnon's approach dovetailed with the Anglo-American linguistic philosophy of J. L. Austin and others, who had argued for the idea that language was both semantic and performative—it involved both "saying" and "doing." Challenging the First Amendment rationales of protected speech for pornography, she argued that pornography is speech only incidentally—its significance lies not as a vehicle to promote thought or ideas, which would be legally protected if such were the case, but as a form of action. Pornography *is* violence against women. "At stake in constructing pornography as 'speech' is gaining constitutional protection for what pornography *does*: subordinating women through sex."[7]

By the late 1970s, a backlash against anti-pornography feminists was developing among other feminists, and a major rift opened up between the two groups, making explicit what had been an initial contradiction in early radical feminist thought between a desire for sex liberated from its patriarchal distortion, on the one hand, and opposition to male sexuality as rooted in patriarchal power, on the other. Those opposed to the critics of pornography, such as the writer and critic Ellen Willis, dubbed "prosex" (and later "sex-positive") feminists, argued that sexual pleasure for women was an important feminist goal. Willis and others were not uncritical of pornography as a form of commodification of sex but found anti-pornography feminism to fall into the trap of reproducing Victorian ideas of women as "above sex," of moralizing about sex in ways that fed into a good girl/bad girl image of sexuality characteristic of a male-dominated society. Willis, in a series of essays written in the late 1970s and early 1980s, referred to the antipornography feminists of Women Against Pornography (WAP) as "conservative feminists," even as their lineage came out of early radicalism. The willingness of antipornography feminists to join forces with a resurgent religious conservativism that opposed pornography on the grounds that sexuality should be funneled into the heterosexual male-led family seemed to confirm Willis's criticism. The question of sexual ethics and behavior—not just on questions of pornography, but on ideas of normative sexual behavior, the understanding of sexual "consent," and the relationship between sexual fantasy and social action—drove a wedge between feminists, with long-standing consequences for the future of feminist thought.

The Response to-Feminism

The feminist redefinition of women in terms of a binary distinction from men was underscored in the concept of gender, but the concept of gender was relational; it defined women in relation to men, and vice versa, rather than in terms of some essential elements of women's nature. The transformations of the understanding of women, then, necessarily entailed transformations in the understanding of men. The response to feminist criticism and thought by those concerned with its implications for men was also a response to changing social conditions. A shift toward greater labor force participation by women was driven in part by feminist ideas, but also by economic compulsion in a service economy. By the 1980s and 90s, the "breadwinner" model of manhood characteristic of the mid-century, had become economically unsustainable. For middle-class married couples with children, the two-income household was increasingly the norm, as it often had been for many working-class families. The decline of industrial manufacturing jobs, and the concomitant weakening of labor unions that had provided the basis for middle-class incomes by which men were able to support a family, also helped push women into the workforce. The professions were more open to women, but so were expanding areas of clerical work in the so-called "pink collar" sector, and the Civil Rights Act of 1964 had made job discrimination on the basis of sex illegal. Men appeared to be under pressure from two directions: a feminist critique of their privilege, and an increasing economic precarity in a post-industrial economy.

The response to these changes took a number of forms. Among those prominent in an increasingly politically-engaged religious right—groups such as Jerry Falwell's Moral Majority, James Dobson's Focus on the Family, and the men's group Promise Keepers—the push was to restore what was an imagined Biblically-based vision of the family with ideals of male leadership and gender complementarity, a program supported by many evangelical women and central to the successful battle waged against the

Equal Rights Amendment (ERA) to the Constitution. Alongside it was a secular men's movement divided, in ways not initially apparent, between those sympathetic to feminist criticism, who sought a redefinition of manhood and masculinity that would end male domination, and those hostile to the claims of feminism. The latter emphasis would eventually produce a men's rights movement, convinced that men were the victims of double standards and that law, family law in particular, was systematically organized to benefit women. Works such as Herbert Goldberg's *The Hazards of Being Male: Surviving the Myth of Male Privilege* (1976) and Warren Farrell's *The Myth of Male Power: Why Men are Disposable* (1993) helped to define the tone of this side of the men's movement. Also, in the late 1980s and early 1990s, a series of prominent books such as the poet Robert Bly's *Iron John* (1990), and the essayist Sam Keen's *Fire in the Belly: On Being a Man* (1992) sought to redefine manhood for a new era, often invoking mythopoetic and archetypical ideas as a means to link a presumably primitive and essential masculine nature to the requirements of a new kind of society. The men's movement, like feminism, was divided between those who advocated for an essentialist identity—linking anatomy to psychology and sociology as given in biology—and those who sought to reform and remake, rather than erase masculine identity entirely. What might being a man look like in a society organized around feminist goals of gender equality?

The body of thought most sympathetic to, and derivative of, feminist theory took the form of academic Men's Studies, on the model of Women's Studies programs. The general perspective of Men's Studies, sometimes also referred to as Masculinity Studies, was social constructionist and critical; it often aimed a critique at forms of masculinity that were organized around dominance, aggression, violence, and misogyny. This set of characteristics were said to define a masculine ethos, sometimes referred to as "toxic masculinity" in the mythopoetic men's movement of the 1990s, a term that has since achieved much more general usage. Other scholars referred to "hegemonic masculinity" as the form in which male-identified characteristics had enforced social power and domination. The sociologist Michael Kimmel was one of the leading figures in this field, authoring and editing a slew of books on masculinity beginning in the early 1990s. Insisting that the feminist project to make gender visible meant that the unmarked category of "man" had defined a kind of unquestioned norm, Kimmel argued the anti-essentialist line: "Manhood is neither static nor timeless. Manhood is not the manifestation of an inner essence; it's socially constructed. Manhood does not bubble up to our consciousness from our biological constitution; it is created in our culture."[8] Men's Studies was, in a sense, parasitic on feminist thought, both an expression of feminism and a reaction against it. Kimmel even titled one of the chapters of his *Manhood in America*, "The Masculine Mystique," in a nod to Betty Friedan. Many of the studies of manhood sought both a critique of dominant forms of masculinity and a proposed form of manhood that could be made egalitarian and feminist. The idea seemed to be that manhood was redeemable, if stripped of its toxic content. Feminists struggled against the gendered order, looking to change it from below; the advocates for a new man might have to free themselves from their own self-punishing ideals of masculinity, but their very magnanimity in denying aggression and dominance often seemed patronizing and void of the structural element of power that many feminists pointed to. Thinkers like Kimmel made manhood into a cultural and psychological problem, rather than a structure of domination. The feminist response to Men's Studies was divided. Some admired it for its willingness to criticize masculinity (if not patriarchy); others found it a way of re-centering the discussion around men, rather than the gender relation itself.

Conclusion

By the end of the twentieth century, the discussion of gender, sex difference, sexuality, and questions of equality, power, and family structure had become a pervasive discourse, even if it meant that there was little agreement among the participants in the discussion. Some saw a backlash against feminism in the 1980s and a stalling of the movement; others saw the success of some feminisms in the fact that women who refused the label feminist, by and large subscribed to some version of gender equality. By uprooting the question of moral order from the fixed foundations of sex difference, feminist thought opened up the possibilities of its own fragmentation. If "woman" was an ascribed category, it could become fluid and open to redefinition. But the very understanding of the arbitrariness of the category, its fictive quality, led to the conclusion that it necessarily concealed difference; feminist thought brought every other difference (race, class, ethnicity, sexuality, colonial, ideology) into the frame of its analysis, making tenuous the idea that the centering object of feminist thought could provide some common identity and solidarity. Some feminists took up the notion of "strategic essentialism," the idea that embracing essential characteristics might prove useful for political purposes, but it was hard to see how this concept could avoid failing back into the very thing that the proliferation of feminist theories had exploded: the idea of a unified political class rooted in biology as foundational to the social order. Feminist thought bequeathed to the twenty-first century a set of issues that continue to provide the material for rethinking a social order wedded to sex difference.

Notes

1 Ti-Grace Atkinson, "Radical Feminism," in Shulamith Firestone, ed., *Notes from the Second Year: Women's Liberation* (New York: Radical Feminism, 1970), p. 33.
2 Shulamith Firestone, *The Dialectic of Sex: The Case for Feminist Revolution*, Bantam revised ed. (New York: Bantam Books, 1971), p. 11.
3 Gayle Rubin, "The Traffic in Women: Notes on the 'Political Economy' of Sex," in Rayna R. Reiter, ed., *Toward an Anthropology of Women* (New York: Monthly Review Press, 1975), pp. 159, 178.
4 *The Combahee River Collective Statement: Black Feminist Organizing in the Seventies and Eighties* (1977) (New York: Kitchen Table: Women of Color Press, 1986), pp. 9, 12.
5 Audre Lorde, "An Open Letter to Mary Daly," in Cherríe Moraga and Gloria Anzaldúa, eds., *This Bridge Called My Back: Writings by Radical Women of Color* (Watertown, MA: Persephone Press, 1981), p. 97; Lorde, "The Master's Tools Will Never Dismantle the Master's House," in Ibid., p. 100.
6 Judith Butler, *Gender Trouble: Feminism and the Subversion of Identity* (New York: Routledge, 1990), p. 192.
7 Catharine A. MacKinnon, *Only Words* (Cambridge, MA: Harvard University Press, 1993), p. 29.
8 Michael Kimmel, *Manhood in America: A Cultural History* (New York: Free Press, 1996), p. 5.

15 Culture Wars

Throughout the modern era, there have been a series of skirmishes in the public sphere that we might characterize as "cultural battles"—conflicts over fundamental values, beliefs, and cosmologies. Comstock laws regulating information about sex, alcohol prohibition, the modernist/fundamentalist controversy of the 1920s, The Scopes Trial, the comic-book scares of the 1950s, counter-culture rebellion of the 1960s, academic freedom controversies: all speak to cultural conflicts that went beyond issues of economic freedom or political rights to clashes over issues such as the meaning of personal liberty and its limits; the norms defining sexuality, religion, and the nature of the family, the role of art and literature in public life. In the 1980s and 90s, commentators began to imagine a way in which these various skirmishes might be linked to one another in a systematic way. Increasing cultural polarization, as well as the collapse of the distinction between politics and culture in widespread recognition of something called "cultural politics," gave birth to a conceptualization of battles over ways of life, cultural values, and beliefs, as "Culture Wars." In 1991, sociologist James Davison Hunter defined the Culture Wars as a conflict between two distinct cultural orientations in American life: those committed to a religiously-based orthodox understanding of absolute, transcendentally derived fixed belief, on the one hand, and those committed to a progressive, historically relativistic, body of beliefs, in which history exemplified an increasingly pluralistic and expansive notion of freedom. For Hunter, salient religious differences were no longer those between Protestants, Catholics, and Jews, but between the orthodox and progressive wings within those umbrella groups; Orthodox Jews and conservative evangelical Protestants, for instance, shared more with one another than Orthodox and Progressive Jews did.

The metaphor of "Culture War," derived from the German *kulturkampf*, became a way to understand the increasing polarization of public life. The political presence of evangelical Christians committed to finding political solutions to cultural issues such as the perceived secularization and liberalization of public schools, universities, media, and morality, pushed the Culture Wars to battles fought not just on the ground of culture itself, but in the formal realm of politics as well. The rise of a neo-conservative group of intellectuals deploying moral norms derived from Scottish Enlightenment philosophy dovetailed with the Religious Right in opposing what cultural conservatives regarded as the relativistic, nihilistic consequences of the 1960s counter-culture. In this sense, the Culture Wars of the late twentieth century were largely reactive, but cultural conservatives were reacting to something real—the increasing presence in mainstream institutions such as schools, universities, journalism, media, and government of a secular progressive sensibility. On a wide array of issues such as gay rights, abortion, obscenity, sexuality, feminism, patriotism, history, immigration, and religion in the schools, intellectuals were enlisted on either side of the Culture Wars. That these "wars" sometimes created odd coalitions as opposed to two fixed camps is indicative of a society that was not polarized in clear and distinct ways. Antipornography feminists could make common cause with pro-family religious conservatives; the liberal Tipper Gore could align herself with conservative critics of popular music in a common fight against obscenity in music lyrics; progressive free speech absolutists might find themselves cozying up to those who would celebrate the morality of markets against the welfare state.

The Adversary Culture and the "New Class"

The move from thinking in terms of cultural conflicts over particular issues to thinking of society involved in a polarizing Culture War came from Neo-conservative intellectuals. The rise of Neo-conservative thought in the 1970s and 1980s was a result of mid-century intellectuals of the Left and Center moving rightward, some of them gradually, others suddenly, largely in reaction to the political and intellectual upheavals of the 1960s. New Left and both liberal and radical feminist thinkers had insisted that culture—beliefs, values, forms of art, and representation—was both an object of political critique and a resource for reform or revolution. In their formulation, a battle had to be fought on the ground of culture, and not solely on the grounds of economic and political systems and structures. The rise of Black Power and the Black Arts Movement emphasized a linkage between cultural and political revolution; a culture steeped in racist ideas would have to be remade to provide the conditions in which social and political power for Blacks could flourish, on the one hand, and cultural identity could define the terms of solidarity on the other. The idea that culture and politics were not autonomous sectors or spheres of life, but were bound up with one another, meant that every work of art, every magazine cover, every form of dress, every food choice, was, at least potentially, a site of power, oppression, and potential freedom. The former Old Leftists and liberals who became Neo-conservatives—including a coterie of New York intellectuals such as Irving Kristol, Norman Podhoretz, Midge Decter, Daniel Bell, Nathan Glazer, and Gertrude Himmelfarb—took the analytical style of criticism associated with the Marxist tradition, and grafted it onto the stabilizing Cold War Liberalism in which they were steeped. They set themselves in opposition to what they imagined as a New Left and counter-culture inflected irrational and anarchic liberationist ethos, more interested in destroying cultural belief and stability than in expanding material benefits. They spoke of the ethos to which they were opposed with two terms: the adversarial culture, and the new class.

The term "adversarial culture" came from the literary critic Lionel Trilling. Long interested in the contradictions and paradoxes of modernist culture, Trilling had identified a body of modernist literature and thought—derived from Nietzsche, Freud, Marx, the cult of antimodernist irrationalism, and avant-garde bohemian opposition to bourgeois norms—that saw the dark underside of Victorian paeans to progress and "civilization." One of the "controlling ideas of our epoch," said Trilling, is "the disenchantment of our culture with culture itself." The adversarial culture present in modern thought has the "clear purpose of detaching the reader from the habits and feelings the larger culture imposes, of giving him a ground and vantage point from which to judge and condemn, and perhaps revise, the culture that produced him."[1] For Trilling, the contradictions and paradox of a modern culture, of which he counted himself a part, and which he self-knowingly stepped outside of in order to critically examine its emphasis on critically examining culture, provided the characteristic mode of thought of an expanding educated middle class. The desire to criticize the adversarial culture could not but help taking part in it, since its position "beyond culture" was the very orientation of modern culture itself. Neo-conservative thought in the 1970s and beyond took Trilling's ironic ambivalence and sense of paradox and contradiction and transmuted it into a concept used to bludgeon the cultural orientation of the progressive educated elite. Instead of ambivalently identifying with the adversarial culture, as Trilling did, neo-conservatives affixed it to their ideological enemies. "Adversarial culture" often seemed to have become shorthand for "the left hates America." The adversarial culture could be socially located in what was called "the new class."

The idea of "the new class" was taken from the Marxist tradition. Irving Kristol, former Trotskyist and the editor of *The Public Interest*, the principal periodical voice of neo-conservative thought, in the mid-1970s began to use the class-based language of Marxism to argue for a cultural conservatism. Some of the main ideas associated with the resurgent right in American thought came out of the Marxist tradition: not only "new class" thought but also what came to be labeled "political correctness" in battles over free speech, and the idea of "American exceptionalism" as a way to describe a special status for American society, free of the oppressions and conflicts of modernizing European nations. In Marxist theory, the material forms of production were held to define the basis of class formation and identity. Capitalism, in this view, involved ownership of the means of production by the bourgeoisie, and the creation of an industrial working class or proletariat through the control over material production. In the period following the Russian Revolution, anti-Stalinists, following the ideas of Leon Trotsky, argued that the Soviet Union was not a worker's state, but had created a new ruling class composed of government bureaucrats and functionaries—the New Class. The new class was distinct from both the bourgeoisie and the proletariat, neither owning productive property nor suffering from labor exploitation. James Burnham, an American Trotskyist intellectual, who moved to the far right in the mid-twentieth century, authored a foundational book for New Class theory: *The Managerial Revolution* (1941). Burnham identified the managerial class—with its administrative functions—as characteristic of an advanced capitalism. Barbara and John Ehrenreich, on the Left, in the mid-1970s identified these people as the Professional Managerial Class; this group's function was administrative and intellectual; its identity was rooted in education and knowledge, rather than ownership of property. In Trotskyist thought, the term "New Class" was used to refer to the government, administrative, functionary, and ideological class. What both of these usages had in common was the notion of a class not defined directly by the material base of society, but associated with knowledge and expertise. In the hands of neo-conservatives, the "New Class" became a collection of ideologists: university professors, journalists, Hollywood filmmakers, trial lawyers, writers, education professionals, intellectuals, psychologists, and social workers, as well as government functionaries. The "New Class" was effectively what the British called "the chattering classes": the people who manipulated language and symbols for a living. These workers in the creation of the symbolic realm, said Kristol and others, were the advocates for the adversarial culture, and its contempt for ordinary cultural norms and traditions. That neo-conservative intellectuals were themselves members of the "New Class" by definition was mostly unacknowledged, since it challenged the idea that the New Class was necessarily the site of the adversarial culture.

A significant body of conservative thought through the twentieth century had been committed to affirming the value of education and intellectual life against popular forms of culture and desire; conservatives had often embraced hierarchy against mass culture, against what they imagined as a democratic leveling. The neo-conservatives inverted this relationship. The 1970s and 80s saw a turn toward a conservative populism, especially in the coalition of conservative intellectuals who supported Ronald Reagan's presidency. If Marxists had imagined that capitalist property-owning elites were the source of oppression of the working class, neo-conservatives imagined that it was culture elites—the New Class—who were at war with "ordinary" people, their values, and their practices. Drawing on a rich strain of anti-intellectualism in American life, neo-conservative intellectuals such as Kristol, Himmelfarb, James Q. Wilson, and Francis Fukuyama developed a line of thought that William F. Buckley had initiated in the 1950s—that liberal elites in universities and the media were a threat to the common sense and values of ordinary people. Instead of embracing the older conservative vision of hierarchy against the irrationality of the democratic mob and its leveling impulses, the neo-conservatives deployed a kind of populist rhetoric against the presumed radicalism of the intellectual class. Looking to eighteenth-century Scottish Common Sense philosophy—which in its American usage had been associated with a moderating anti-radicalism—Wilson and others argued that morality rested not on the civilizing process in contrast to an irrational human nature but on the universal possession of a "moral sense" or moral sentiments. The educated elite, then, appeared as the corruptors of naturally given common sense. The uneducated masses had a natural intuition of moral values, argued the neo-conservatives, against the unnatural radicalism of New Class intellectuals. What began as a battle between two groups of intellectuals was mapped by these thinkers onto a Culture War between progressive, liberal, and radical intellectuals on one side, and ordinary people on the other. The image of ordinary people was one that centered whites, evangelical Christians, people living in the middle of the country (as opposed to "coastal elites"), and non-professionals—industrial workers, but also small business owners, clerical workers, and women who identified primarily as wives and mothers.

The University and the Battle Over the Canon

One of the major centers in the Culture Wars of the late twentieth century was the university, now imagined as the breeding ground of the adversarial culture and the New Class. Some Leftists saw the university as a place where radicalism went to be domesticated, defanged, and made safe. Such was the view, for instance, of Russell Jacoby's *The Last Intellectuals: American Culture in the Age of Academe* (1987) and Todd Gitlin's *The Twilight of Common Dreams: Why American is Wracked by Culture Wars* (1996). The decline of the public intellectual, thinkers who spoke critically to public issues and a general audience and made their living writing for newspapers and magazines, said Jacoby, was coincident with the expansion of the university; those who once spoke to the public now had academic appointments and spoke only to one another in the arcane argot of the academic disciplines. In Gitlin's words, the Left had been "Marching on the English Department, while the right took the White House."[2] Jacoby's tale of decline was countered by the neo-conservative view that the university had become the power base of New Class thought, dominating public discourse, socializing students into the radical worldview of the adversarial culture, and training members of the cultural elite who would take their positions in the ruling class of media, government, law, and education. The flash point for these thinkers was the transformation in the Humanities and Social Sciences, and the ways in which those disciplines were being remade from their presumed functions of authorizing tradition and mid-century modernist ideals such as the autonomy of the aesthetic and the transmission of high culture.

Jacoby's lament for the decline of radicalism had its mirror image in Roger Kimball's *Tenured Radicals* (1990). Kimball was one of a sizable set of conservative critics of the university: Allan Bloom, Dinesh D'Souza, Education Secretary William Bennet, National Endowment for the Humanities head Lynn Cheney, and Linda Chavez. The editor of the conservative arts journal, *The New Criterion* (established 1982), Kimball juxtaposed an ideal of high culture and its transmission, rooted in Matthew Arnold's conception of culture as "the best that has been said and thought," to what he saw as the politicized character of late twentieth century arts education and criticism. *The New Criterion* vision was one that sought to hold a strong polemical Neoconservative voice in tension with an imagined world of aesthetic values independent of politics. The defense of the Western tradition was to be both a political stance and an apolitical commitment to transcendent and universal standards. The polemical vision of Kimball, who instrumentalized his vision of culture and the arts as a political tool against the dominant orientation in the Arts and Humanities, meant that the right was "politicizing" culture as much as was the Left—or, as those on the left might say, culture was "always already" political. Kimball's argument was that the university students of the 1960s, who had created new forms of political and cultural radicalism in the expanding sphere of higher education, had moved through the institution and were now ensconced in powerful tenured academic positions in the Humanities, where they were remaking both the Western tradition and the principles of criticism and historical understanding. The title of his manifesto displayed the characteristic neo-conservative yoking of radicalism as a destructive force, with a critique of the comfortable privilege of a class of elites. The New Class was both radical and establishment, a challenge to, and an affirmation of, privilege at the same time. What Kimball called "the war against Western culture," undertaken by academic deconstructionists, Marxists, feminists, and other associated radicals had as its goal "nothing less than the destruction of the values, methods, and goals of traditional humanistic study."[3] The image of the mid-century university as bastion of tradition and advocacy for the values of the West, a conservative stronghold, rather than as a site of the destabilizing criticism and debate that modern thought had created, made the late twentieth-century academic Left appear to be a much greater departure than it was. For Kimball, the professors' attack on the humanities took a number of forms: elevating popular and mass culture as equivalent in value to high culture; using categories such as gender and race as analytical lenses through which to examine art and literature; claiming that the commitment to standards of aesthetic merit was an ideological expression of power.

One of the principal areas of contestation was over the "canon"—the body of literary, philosophical, and artistic works that were held to be worthy of study and that formed the basis for a curriculum in the Humanities. Courses in Western Civilization and the "Great Books" had been instituted in American higher education over the course of the twentieth century, often to provide a core curriculum to prevent the perceived fragmenting specialization endemic to the research university. The tendency of conservatives was to view the literary and philosophical canon—from Ancient Greek philosophy and drama through Chaucer, Dante, Shakespeare, the philosophy of Descartes, Locke, and Kant, and on to the nineteenth-century novels of Dickens, Balzac, and Flaubert, and the modernist poets of the first half of the twentieth century—as both a transcendent body of thought and art, free of politics and ideology, and at the same time, the bastion of Western values of individual liberty, ordered morality, and civilization. The criticism of the canon from the academic Left, then, was portrayed as both an attack on art and aesthetic standards and as an attack on Western values; it was both philistine and ideologically nihilistic in the imagination of Kimball and his peers.

The critics of the canon, however, were not all of one mind. A significant group of academics sought to transform the canon of literary works by making it more inclusive; they responded to the rise of African-American and Women's Studies in the 1970s, offshoots of Black Power and feminist movements, by seeking to make works written by women, Black, Chicano, Asian, and American Indian authors part of the curriculum and objects of scholarly study. Their argument was that these works had been excluded from the canon, not on grounds of aesthetic merit but on assumptions of white and European supremacy. Their vision was expansive; they argued not only the so-called identity politics line that non-whites and women had to "see themselves" in the literature they were assigned, but also that a multicultural approach to literature and the arts meant an art that was broader and more universalistic than the faux universalism of the European tradition and its assumptions. They took up the pluralistic and cosmopolitan line of earlier modernist thinkers such as Horace Kallen and Alain Locke. They were not enemies of the idea of aesthetic merit, but sought to rethink the conception of art in a multicultural sense, as a way to fulfill the traditional liberal arts goal of producing individuals capable of imagining and critically evaluating the world in which they lived. The point was not to throw out Shakespeare, but to refuse the equation of Shakespeare with humanity itself, to refuse the notion that the Western Tradition was the sole expression of the highest cultural achievement of humanity. As the literary critic Henry Louis Gates, Jr., put it

> To reform core curricula, to account for the comparable eloquence of the African, the Asian, and the Middle Eastern traditions, is to begin to prepare our students for their roles as citizens of a world culture, educated through a truly human notion of 'the humanities,' rather than... as guardians at the last frontier outpost of white male Western culture, the Keepers of the Master's Pieces.[4]

The novelist Saul Bellow responded to critics arguing for expansion in an interview, infamously doubling down on the conservative equation of aesthetic merit and European culture: "Who is the Tolstoy of the Zulus? The Proust of the Papuans?"

But Gates and others who were busy creating literary anthologies (*The Norton Anthology of African-American Literature* was published in 1996) and new courses and areas of study to expand the canon found themselves defending the very idea of a canon against critics who saw the commitment to any kind of canon as an embrace of hierarchy. There were more than two sides in the canon war, and the Left had an internal battle as well as a battle with the Allan Blooms and Roger Kimballs on their right. More radical thinkers looked to the history of canon formation, the ways in which the canon was not a stable or fixed body of texts, but an ever-changing one, and saw it as always exclusionary, always an expression of power. If Gates and his allies, such as Houston Baker and Nellie McKay, were reformers and architects of a new canon, the radicals appeared to imply abolition or rejection of canons entirely. The reformers thought that the very fact that canons were not fixed and stable provided an opening for changing those canons, for building new priorities. The abolitionists suggested that the notion of aesthetic value as different in kind from economic or social value was mistaken, and that literary canon formation was all about the expression of social distinction. "Taste," as the French sociologist Pierre Bourdieu suggested, was nothing more than a marker of social standing. The result of these canon battles on the left was to make issues of social and political representation more salient in the teaching and study of art and literature and to squeeze questions of literary form, structure, and language into a supporting role for ideologies. "[T]hose with cultural power tend to be members of socially, economically, and politically established classes," said the literary theorist Barbara Herrnstein Smith in 1988. Long-enduring literary texts "will tend to be those that appear to reflect and reinforce establishment ideologies."[5] The reformers and abolitionists might agree that canons were historically constructed pillars of exclusion; Gates and others found it troubling, however, that just at the moment previously excluded groups were attaining the cultural capital to construct a canon of their own, they were being told by erstwhile allies that canons had to go.

The Meaning of History

A second front in the battle over the humanities in the university and public life was a battle over the meaning, purpose, and value of the study of history, particularly the history of the United States. Changes in the academic study of history—a move away from the study of elites, and the emergence of a new social history that took as its object the experiences of workers, women, immigrants, local communities, and ordinary everyday life and cultural practices—challenged the notion of a singular national narrative of American history. As we have seen, the academic study of American history from the time of Progressive historians such as Frederick Jackson Turner and Charles Beard, through the critical "consensus historians" of the post-World War II era had sought to use social scientific methods and concepts, and had cast shadows on any simple celebratory national narrative; the new social and cultural history of the 1970s and 80s was not entirely new in its critical spirit. It did take some new radical directions, shaped by Black Power, feminism, and a New Left analysis of class and culture. But in many ways, especially compared to literary study, academic history was epistemically conservative. It insisted on empirical methods, documentation of claims with primary sources, and a craft tradition, reigning in some of the more destabilizing claims of historiographical relativism. Relatively few historians embraced the "linguistic turn" and the attractions of what was increasingly referred to as "theory," and when they did, they were quick to be called back by suspicious colleagues to the presumed realities of economic and social conditions. Historians frequently warned about the perils of presentism and anachronism and insisted that the past be understood "as a foreign country," even while acknowledging that all history is a view of the past shaped by the needs of the present. Most historians believed that history, for many reasons, could not be a simple record of the events of the past as they really happened, but, even if history could not achieve the goal of "objectivity," it should aspire to approximate it as best as it could. The historian Thomas Haskell argued that "objectivity is not neutrality"; one could both have a point of view *and* adhere to the rules of scholarship: no cherry-picking sources, no unearned generalizations, no ignoring inconvenient facts, no claims without empirical support. From inside the academy, the field of history appeared to be the least radical of the humanities in its epistemology and methods, if not the objects it now chose to study.

When history stepped into the public sphere, however, it encountered resistance from cultural conservatives who had a very different understanding of what the purpose and meaning of history was. Two events, in particular, are revealing. The first was a conflict over a set of National History Standards for K-12 public education, a major project initiated by the conservative head of the National Endowment for the Humanities under George H.W. Bush. Lynne Cheney. Under the direction of the UCLA social historian Gary Nash, and incorporating perspectives from a variety of educators and interest groups, the National History Standards were published in 1994 and immediately became a flashpoint in the battle over the meaning of history and history education. Cheney—no longer at the NEH—and other conservatives denounced the standards, particularly in their treatment of U.S. history, as a dismal foregrounding of oppressed victim groups, and a downplaying of what they believed to be the central features of American history—the exemplary founding and fulfillment of a nation founded on principles of liberty and individual opportunity. Complaints that the heroes of American history—George Washington, Benjamin Franklin, Abraham Lincoln—were marginalized, and that "insignificant" representatives of Black, American Indian, Chicano, working class, and immigrant groups were foregrounded, and that the standards portrayed the United States as marked by systematic forms of oppression rather than the embodiment of freedom, were made by politicians, media figures, and a small number of scholars (most academics saw the standards as positive developments based on the scholarship of the previous decades).

Although both left and right agreed that US history should play an important role in civic education, they saw that role in fundamentally different ways. The academic Left thought of history as providing critical thinking skills, a sense of the complexity of the past, a preparation for students in a society that was multicultural and increasingly diverse; their goal was to expand history and to move away from the idea that the study of the past should be primarily celebratory. The critics of the National History Standards, on the other hand, tended to see civic education as a matter of heritage, pride, and identification with the nation. Political leadership and the heroism of great individuals were at the center of this vision. Just as the opening of the literary canon to non-canonical works appeared an act of denigration, so the embrace of ordinary people's experience as central to history appeared to be a critique of national identity, and an attempt to inculcate values hostile to the Constitution and the capitalist economic system. The term that conservatives used to describe what they saw as a radical displacement of the meaning of the American past was something they called "revisionist history." What they meant by that term was that an objective past was fixed and knowable, and "revisionists" were ideologues trying to distort and change this fixed past. But academic historians were of the mind that all history is revisionist, in a positive sense—as historians examined new sources and looked at different aspects of the past through new lenses, they changed what they had to say about it. The past didn't change, but history was interpretive, and so the understanding of the past was always changing. Some conservatives accused academics of essentially inventing a preferred history out of whole cloth. What is interesting is that a similar kind of claim was coming from a more radical epistemic perspective; the historian Hayden White was arguing in the 1970s and 1980s that the form of narrative was a superimposition on the past, and that written history looked more like fictional forms such as comedy, tragedy, and romance, than the empiricist tradition could acknowledge. The difference is that White saw the fictive narrative character of history as something inescapable, while conservative thinkers thought there was a stable past that could be recovered by stripping off the narrative distortions of "revisionist" historians.

Another prominent clash over the meaning of history came in the Smithsonian National Air and Space Museum's proposed 1995 exhibit marking the fiftieth anniversary of the World War II use of the atomic bomb on Hiroshima, and centered around the display of the plane that was used in the bombing, the *Enola Gay*. The failed exhibit brought the stark difference between history as commemoration and history as critical understanding to the fore. Veteran's groups wanted a commemoration that emphasized the ways in which American technology, heroism, and military sacrifice brought the war to a close, avoiding an invasion that would have resulted in significant injury and death of American troops. Academic consultants and museum professionals, on the other hand, wanted to look at the event from a number of different angles, including the political decision to use the bomb, the horrific destruction of human life, display of Japanese artifacts from the explosion, and the initiation of a nuclear age of weapons of mass destruction. When veterans' groups such as the American Legion and the Air Force Association got hold of the script for the exhibit, they angrily denounced and criticized it for elevating Japanese victims over the sacrifices and valor of American troops and airmen, and questioning the motives behind the decision to use the bomb. Critics of the proposed exhibit pointed to the mission statement of the museum—with its commitment to portraying "the valor and sacrificial service" of the military as "as inspiration to the present and future generations of Americans."[6] The notion that history should be a record of heroism and valor offered in a patriotic frame, as much as it drew on older nineteenth-century forms of romantic history writing, was at odds with the disciplinary, political, and epistemic goals of museum professionals and academic historians. Political and media figures aligned themselves with veterans, denouncing the exhibit. Under political pressure, the Smithsonian canceled the exhibit. For Neo-conservatives, both the battle over the National History Standards and the Enola Gay exhibit were evidence that New Class intellectuals and scholars and their adversarial culture ethos were contemptuous of the meaning of history for ordinary people.

Deconstruction and Its Discontents

One of the most surprising conflicts of the Culture War surrounded a school of literary criticism that virtually no one outside of its hermetic confines understood: something called Deconstruction. If the concerns of cultural conservatives and those committed to an orthodox world view identified the cultural and intellectual offshoots of Marxism, Black Power, feminism, and gay liberation as radical and disquieting challenges that had to be met head on, it was a lot less clear why a form of literary thought that foregrounded ways of reading, rather than the obvious social change agenda of radical ideologies, should be a source of discord. New Left thinkers in the academy did target the mid-century "New Criticism" of John Crowe Ransom and Cleanth Brooks for its presumably apolitical attempts to emphasize the autonomy of literature and its covert conservativism. But this was largely an internal battle between schools of literary interpretation and took place in the pages of scholarly journals; the conservative defenders of the canon and the "Western tradition," such as Roger Kimball and Hilton Kramer, were not defending the methods of close reading, formalism, and the focus on irony and paradox that had been pioneered by the New Critics. They did share with New Critics a commitment to a notion of aesthetic evaluation, but no one was writing Culture War defenses of New Critical methods. Given just how much continuity in some respects there was between New Criticism and Deconstruction (both looked to close reading and textualism, rather than authorial intent, for instance), it's a fact of some interest that cultural conservatives in the public sphere did come to identify Deconstruction with an amoral nihilism and a threat to moral order in ways that suggested far more was at stake than a theory of how to analyze literature. On this, some Left critics, such as historian Jon Weiner, could concur with conservatives: there was something about the style and philosophical outlook of Deconstruction that destroyed ideas of social justice and equality that rested on notions of material reality, as much as it did ideas of hierarchy and order. Some Marxists and others on the Left made common cause with cultural conservatives against the threat of Deconstruction, albeit for very different reasons. Others on the Left found Deconstruction to be a tool of radical criticism.

Deconstruction was a slippery target for cultural warriors; the difficulty in pinning it down was, in part, what was troubling about it, since its mode of identifying textual contradictions allowed it to subvert any claims made about it. The key figures associated with this philosophically and linguistically-based theoretical outlook in the late 1960s, the 1970s and 80s were the members of the so-called Yale School of criticism: Paul de Man, J. Hillis Miller, Harold Bloom, Geoffrey Hartman, and Jacques Derrida. As Deconstruction was increasingly adapted by those interested in political and ideological critique in the 1980s and 90s, it helped to shape feminist theory, post-colonial theory, and queer theory. Deconstruction was commonly conflated with two other terms that received widespread use and attention during this period, both of which also had multiple and shifting meanings: postmodernism and post-structuralism.

Deconstruction, under the guiding sensibility of Derrida and de Man, ironically rested on a long tradition of Western thought, even as it declared a departure from the "logocentric" orientation of that tradition. Various forms of modernist thought, in particular, had questioned a kind of epistemic foundationalism and a notion that the categories in the mind aligned themselves with a previously existing metaphysical order. Although its advocates frequently found it difficult to define what Deconstruction was, they tended to share an outlook: an ironic sense of detachment, a hermeneutic sensibility that suggested textual meaning was always not what it appeared to be, a commitment to the artificial world of language with no fixed referent. When the queer theorist Judith Butler undercut the feminist distinction between sex and gender, for instance, she was drawing on this critical deconstructive sensibility. What Deconstruction did was to emphasize not only the arbitrariness of the relationship between words and things but also the way in which texts destabilize the very objects that claim to be stabilizing, and create a chain of reference in which closed or fixed meaning is always deferred. The use of language to stabilize order always foundered on the instability of language itself. The critics of Deconstruction, if not always conversant in the philosophical and linguistic thought at play, knew enough to recognize that Deconstruction denied the possibility of objectivity, any kind of absolute truths, and the existence of a reality beyond and outside of language. Of course, many forms of modern philosophy from the Pragmatists forward did that. But Deconstruction could be imagined as a foreign import (the term "French theory" was tossed around with disdain), and a quasi-mystical form that upended every hierarchy, every institution, every relationship. A mistranslation of a line from Derrida—"il n'y a pas de hors-texte"—as "there is nothing outside the text," became, for his critics, a kind of summation of the absurdity and danger of his philosophy. Were violence and war, bodies and physical objects, physical suffering and death, "texts"? The claim seemed to be that Derrida denied reality in favor of textuality—right could be wrong, black could be white, up could be down.

The crisis over Deconstruction came to a head in 1987, with the discovery that Paul de Man had contributed articles to a Belgian pro-Nazi newspaper, *Le Soir*, and had covered up his affiliation as he reinvented himself as a literary theorist in the United States. While his writings covered a wide terrain, some of them were explicitly supportive of Nazi policies, and at least one article was explicitly anti-Semitic. The national media seized on "the de Man affair" as evidence that the forms of interpretation and reading that de Man advocated were linked to the specific horrors of history; that his theories were expressions on the intellectual level of his willingness to serve the perverse instrumentalities of power that produced the Holocaust. The near-simultaneous revelation of the German philosopher Martin Heidegger's engagement with Nazism, and Derrida's association with the German philosophical tradition of which Heidegger was the greatest twentieth-century representative, poured oil on the flame. The take on Derrida and de Man was that textual reading of the deconstructive kind was less a philosophically based practice and more a kind of psychological expression of avoidance and amoral careerism. Derrida did not help the case when he wrote a long defense of de Man conducted through a deconstructive reading of his wartime writings. The sad irony of Deconstruction was that the term itself became widespread, but used in a way that was at odds with the theory and practice of the Yale school—in popular culture "Deconstruction" came to mean something like "analyze," "break down," or "take apart"; it was an engineer's vision rather than a literary theorist's.

The New Black Intellectuals

Henry Louis Gates, Jr., one of the architects of a new African-American canon of literature, was also one of a number of Black public intellectuals—radical, liberal, and conservative—who came to prominence in the last decades of the twentieth century: the Black feminist bell hooks, the philosopher Cornel West, the economist Glenn Loury, the political scientist Adolph Reed, the author Shelby Steele, law school professors Derek Bell, Randall Kennedy, and Steven Carter, the neo-conservative economist Thomas Sowell, the feminist sociologist Patricia Hill Collins, the religion scholar and minister Michael Eric Dyson, among many others. The diversity of Black thought meant that, while most Black Americans leaned politically left, the Culture War of the 1980s and 90s also created an internal battle among Black intellectuals, particularly over how to define the legacy of the Civil Rights movement. Conservative commentators such as Shelby Steele created a Martin Luther King, Jr. in the image of what was called a "color-blind" conservatism; those on the Left, such as Michael Eric Dyson, interpreted King as a radical calling for structural changes that merged Black rights and economic justice. The questions of affirmative action in employment and education, welfare statism, drugs and criminality in de-industrialized urban communities, and the role of continuing racism and/or economic oppression in American society, divided these figures. At the heart of the difference were irreconcilable ideas of culture. The right, following the neo-conservative line, argued that the failure to achieve Black equality was a problem of Black culture and its moral disorganization; the Left argued that pervasive inequality was a problem of an American culture that continued to sanction racism, and an unwillingness to create policies that would overcome that racism. At Harvard Law School, Derek Bell initiated an influential body of thought that came to be identified as Critical Race Theory, a theory that analyzed the American legal system as an expression of white supremacy.

One of the most significant intellectual figures of the late twentieth century was Cornel West. West was able both to be deeply committed to a left social vision, and at the same time to straddle the divides that animated the Culture Wars. Deeply immersed in both theology and philosophy, West synthesized the tradition of philosophical Pragmatism with the theological vision of Black religion. In *The American Evasion of Philosophy* (1989), West constructed what he called a "prophetic Pragmatism" from elements of an American intellectual tradition whose key figures included Ralph Waldo Emerson, W.E.B. Du Bois, and John Dewey. "The tradition of pragmatism," said West,

> is in need of an explicit political mode of cultural criticism that refines and revives Emerson's concerns with power, provocation, and personality in light of Dewey's stress on historical consciousness and Du Bois' focus on the plight of the wretched of the earth.[7]

Taking the Jamesian pragmatic injunction to sink philosophy into life and society, West argued for a recreation of a philosophy that could provide the basis for a deep and penetrating cultural criticism, a religious vision taken from liberationist theology, and a Deweyan commitment to social democracy and economic justice. As West moved his critical vision from the depths of a dense philosophical tradition to the extended crisis of race in American life, he pivoted toward a popular audience. In *Race Matters* (1993), he sought to transcend a polarization in American ideologies between liberals, who saw structural and economic problems and solutions to racial inequality, and conservatives, who saw racial inequality as tied to Black behavior and moral failures. For West, race and inequality were both material and moral, structural and spiritual, issues. The double project of undoing white supremacy and ending what he called the moral "nihilism" and hopelessness endemic in Black communities, meant that he was continuing the prophetic vision he outlined as the vocation of the philosopher/cultural critic/preacher.

Conclusion: The End of the Century

Intellectual history, like all history, does not fall into discrete containers and periods. The modernist bodies of thought that have been created since Darwin's *On the Origin of Species* landed in American thought in the mid-nineteenth century have had varied outcomes—some were entirely of their moment, others went into hibernation and were reborn in altered forms to fit new contexts, and others have had lasting consequences in shaping subsequent thought, in effect becoming historical contexts for new ideas. In one way or another, modern thinkers have all had to grapple with a world in which fixed categories and orders have continuously revealed themselves to be inadequate to the changing world that Americans have faced. The optimistic, progressive sensibility of some moderns, who saw in the unmooring of fixed foundations only the conditions of utopian possibility, was countered by those who only saw modern liberation from the past as new ways to mobilize power and to use knowledge to reaffirm the absence of freedom and equality. Between the optimists and the pessimists, the utopians and the dystopians, was a third sensibility—that of the dialectical thinkers whose vision was tragic. The tragic sensibility affirmed the contradictory nature of modernity, that loss and gain went together, that progressive liberation and epistemic and moral anxiety were yoked, that one person's freedom was another's limitation.

The Culture Wars did not end when the events of 2001 and the responses to them called forth another rethinking of the world. Modern thought perhaps opened a new chapter, but it was a chapter in the same book, beset by many of the same contradictions that thought had struggled with and shaped over the previous century and a half. This book ends at the end of the twentieth century not because we can imagine closure, a world set off from a present 25 years later, self-contained and in some sense complete. Modernist thought, including historical thought, knows that such a periodization is a convention, a way to organize the past in our own minds, but having no objective existence. Rather, what historical thought offers us is a kind of rule that demands distance in time, that says we cannot understand the past while we are still in it. The contemporary reader is sure to recognize elements of the thought analyzed and chronicled here as linked to, and part of, our present reality. But writing the intellectual history of the most recent quarter century since the closing date of this book—a world of smartphones, social media, the apparent decline of the humanities, neo-liberalism, transgenderism, and neo-nationalism— will have to wait another quarter century.

Notes

1 Lionel Trilling, *Beyond Culture: Essays on Literature and Learning* (New York: Viking, 1965), pp. 3, xii–xiii.
2 Todd Gitlin, *The Twilight of Common Dreams: Why America Is Wracked by Culture Wars* (New York: Metropolitan Books, 1995), p. 126.
3 Roger Kimball, *Tenured Radicals: How Politics Has Corrupted Our Higher Education* (New York: Harper & Row, 1990), pp. xi, xii.
4 Henry Louis Gates, Jr., *Loose Canons: Notes on the Culture Wars* (New York: Oxford University Press, 1992), p. 42.
5 Barbara Herrnstein Smith, *Contingencies of Value: Alternative Perspectives for Critical Theory* (Cambridge, MA: Harvard University Press, 1988), p. 51.
6 Quoted in Edward Linenthal and Tom Englehardt, eds., *History Wars: the Enola Gay and Other Battles for the American Past* (New York: Henry Holt, 1996), p. 20.
7 Cornel West, *The American Evasion of Philosophy: A Genealogy of Pragmatism* (Madison: University of Wisconsin Press, 1989), p. 212.

Bibliographical Essay

The field of American intellectual history is a rich and diverse one. This essay aims to highlight some of the important scholarships in the field, but with an understanding that no such essay could be comprehensive, and that the works identified here provide a way into that literature, rather than an attempt to signal the essential works in the field. Understanding the field also means, as one might expect, understanding something of the history of writing intellectual history, so the works identified here are not only the most current scholarship but also important works stretching back over the past century.

Debates on historiography, methods, and state of the field over the past half century are best accessed through three edited collections: Paul Conkin and John Higham, eds., *New Directions in American Intellectual History* (Baltimore, MD: Johns Hopkins University Press, 1979); Joel Isaac, James T. Kloppenberg, Michael O'Brien, and Jennifer Ratner-Rosenhagen, eds., *The Worlds of American Intellectual History* (New York: Oxford University Press, 2017); Ray Haberski, Jr. and Andrew Hartman, eds., *American Labyrinth: Intellectual History for Complicated Times* (Ithaca, NY: Cornell University Press, 2018). In addition, a roundtable on the state of the field was published as "Forum: The Present and Future of American Intellectual History," *Modern Intellectual History* 9.1 (April 2012), pp. 149–238. For a critical review, see Daniel Wickberg, "The Present and Future of American Intellectual History," *U.S. Intellectual History Blog*, April 3, 2012: https://s-usih.org/2012/04/present-and-future-of-american/. On the history of ideas, the *locus classicus* is the first chapter of Arthur Lovejoy, *The Great Chain of Being: A Study of the History of an Idea* (Cambridge, MA: Harvard University Press, 1936), where he discusses "unit-ideas," but see also Lovejoy's collection, *Essays in the History of Ideas* (Baltimore, MD: Johns Hopkins University Press, 1948). Recent reevaluations of the history of ideas tradition include Daniel Wickberg, "In the Environment of Ideas: Arthur Lovejoy and the History of Ideas as a Form of Cultural History," *Modern Intellectual History* 11.2 (August 2014), pp. 439–464, and Darren M. Mcmahon, "The Return of the History of Ideas?" in Darren M. McMahon and Samuel Moyn, eds., *Rethinking Modern European Intellectual History* (New York, 2014), pp. 13–31. For general attempts to define intellectual history, albeit from the point of view of European historiography, see Richard Whatmore, *What Is Intellectual History?* (Malden, MA: Polity, 2016). A good discussion of the relationship between historical contextualism and questions of truth in intellectual history is Martin Jay, *Genesis and Validity: The Theory and Practice of Intellectual History* (Philadelphia, PA: University of Pennsylvania Press, 2022). The classic statement of the methods associated with the Cambridge School of "contextualism" is Quentin Skinner, "Meaning and Understanding in the History of Ideas," *History & Theory* 8.1 (1969), pp. 3–53. For recent critiques and expansions of the idea of intellectual history from the viewpoint of African-American history, see Brandon Byrd, "The Rise of African-American Intellectual History," *Modern Intellectual History* 18.3 (September 2021), pp. 833–864, and Mia E. Bay, Farah J. Griffin, Martha S. Jones, and Barbara D. Savage, eds., *Toward an Intellectual History of Black Women* (Chapel Hill, NC: University of North Carolina Press, 2015).

It is a daunting challenge, rarely undertaken in the past 40 years, to attempt a comprehensive synthesis of the field. The most recent work to provide an accessible overview of American intellectual history is Jennifer Ratner-Rosenhagen, *The Ideas that Made America: A Brief History* (New York: Oxford University Press, 2019); its brevity is both one of its virtue and one of its shortcomings. A more general interpretive account of American history that gives substantial attention to ideas and intellectual history is Jill Lepore, *These Truths: A History of the United States* (New York: W.W. Norton, 2018). The earliest attempt to give a synthetic scholarly account of the history of American thought is Vernon Parrington, *Main Currents in American Thought*, 3 vols. (New York: Harcourt, Brace & Co., 1927). The third volume covers the period from 1860 to 1920. The mid-twentieth century was the heyday of synthetic overviews. The most prominent of those accounts was Merle Curti, *The Growth of American Thought* (New York: Harper & Brothers, 1943). Ralph Henry Gabriel, *The Course of American Democratic Thought: An Intellectual History Since 1815* (New York: Ronald Press, 1940) and Joseph Dorfman, *The Economic Mind in American Civilization*, 5 vols (New York: Viking Press, 1946–1959) provided comprehensive synthetic accounts of political and economic thought, while Henry Steele Commager, *The American Mind: An Interpretation of American Thought and Character Since 1880* (New Haven, CT: Yale University Press, 1959) focused on the modern era. A later work, more concerned with intellectuals and the status of thought in American life, rather than the history of thought itself, is Lewis Perry,

Intellectual Life in America: A History (Chicago, IL: University of Chicago Press, 1984). A more recent interpretive account of intellectual thought in the "long nineteenth century" is William H. Goetzmann, *Beyond the Revolution: A History of American Thought from Paine to Pragmatism* (New York: Basic Books, 2009). Three reference works are of particular value: Richard Wightman Fox and James Kloppenberg, eds., *A Companion to American Thought* (Malden, MA: Blackwell, 1995); Mary Kupiec Cayton and Peter W. Williams, eds., *Encyclopedia of American Cultural and Intellectual History*, 3 volumes (New York: Charles Scribner & Sons, 2001); Joan Shelley Rubin and Scott F. Caspar, eds., *The Oxford Encyclopedia of American Cultural and Intellectual History* (New York: Oxford University Press, 2013).

The question of Darwinism and evolutionary theory in shaping American thought is addressed in Ronald Numbers, *Darwinism Comes to America* (Cambridge, MA: Harvard University Press, 1998); Jon Roberts, *Darwinism and the Divine in America: Protestant Intellectuals and Organic Evolution, 1859–1900* (Madison, WI: University of Wisconsin Press, 1988); and David Hoeveler, *The Evolutionists: American Thinkers Confront Charles Darwin, 1860–1920* (Lanham, MD: Rowman & Littlefield, 2007). A readable account of Darwin's first reception by Northern intellectuals on the eve of the Civil War is Randall Fuller, *The Book That Changed America: How Darwin's Theory of Evolution Ignited a Nation* (New York: Viking, 2017). For a somewhat longer view of the changing status of Darwinian ideas in American thought, see Carl N. Degler, *In Search of Human Nature: The Decline and Revival of Darwinism in American Social Thought* (New York: Oxford University Press, 1991). General accounts of Darwinism and evolutionary thought include Peter Bowler, *Evolution: The History of an Idea* (Berkeley, CA and Los Angeles, CA: University of California Press, 2009) and Michael Ruse, *The Darwinian Revolution: Science Red in Tooth and Claw* (Chicago, IL: University of Chicago Press, 1979). An older, but still useful, work on the broader impact of evolutionary thought is Stow Persons, ed. *Evolutionary Thought in America* (New Haven, CT: Yale University Press, 1950). Nineteenth-century racial ideas are discussed in George Fredrickson, *The Black Image in the White Mind: The Debate on Afro-American Character and Destiny, 1817–1914* (New York: Harper & Row, 1971) and Thomas F. Gossett, *Race: The History of an Idea in America*, new ed. (New York: Oxford University Press, 1997). Ibram X. Kendi, *Stamped from the Beginning: The Definitive History of Racist Ideas in America* (New York: Bold Type Books, 2016) downplays the biological and evolutionary science conceptions of race in favor of a much broader conception of racist ideas. The debate over "Social Darwinism," and whether it is an adequate description of late nineteenth-century social thought, can be found by comparing Richard Hofstadter,

Social Darwinism in American Thought (Philadelphia, PA: University of Pennsylvania Press, 1944) with Robert Bannister, *Social Darwinism: Science and Myth in Anglo-American Social Thought* (Philadelphia, PA: University of Pennsylvania Press, 1979); Donald Bellomy, "Social Darwinism Revisited," *Perspectives in American History* 1.1 (January 1984), pp. 1–129; and Mike Hawkins, *Social Darwinism in European and American Thought, 1860–1945: Nature as Model and Nature as Threat* (New York: Cambridge University Press, 1997). For an account of Lester Frank Ward as a follower of the progressive philosophy of Auguste Comte, the French founder of positivist philosophy, see Gillis J. Harp, "Lester Ward: Comtean Whig," *Historical Reflections* 15 (1988), pp. 523–542. The most extensive work on Thorstein Veblen's thought has been done by Rick Tilman. Of his several books, *Thorstein Veblen and His Critics, 1891–1963* (Princeton, NJ: Princeton University Press, 1992) is especially relevant for understanding the extent to which Veblen, sometimes described as an American counterpart to Marx, has been resisted.

There is an extensive body of literature on philosophical Pragmatism and its history. For the larger philosophical shift and its implications for social and political thought, the best account remains James Kloppenberg, *Uncertain Victory: Social Democracy and Progressivism in European and American Thought, 1870–1920* (New York: Oxford University Press, 1988). A lucid narrative that brings analytical and contextual heft to the development and consequences of Pragmatic thought through a biographical approach is Louis Menand, *The Metaphysical Club: A Story of Ideas in America* (New York: Farrar, Strauss and Giroux, 2001). On the place of Pragmatism in the history of American philosophy, see two books by Bruce Kuklick, *The Rise of American Philosophy: Cambridge, Massachusetts, 1860–1930* (New Haven, CT: Yale University Press, 1977), and *A History of Philosophy in America, 1720–2000* (New York: Oxford University Press, 2002). A provocative interpretation that ties Pragmatism to the history of capitalism is James Livingston, *Pragmatism and the Politics of Cultural Revolution 1850–1940* (Chapel Hill, NC: University of North Carolina Press, 1997).

The history of the research university and its reorientation of American intellectual life in the late nineteenth and early twentieth centuries is discussed in an older, now classic text, Laurence R. Veysey, *The Emergence of the American University* (Chicago, IL: University of Chicago Press, 1965). More recent interpretations include Julie A. Reuben, *The Making of the Modern University: Intellectual Transformation and the Marginalization of Morality* (Chicago, IL: University of Chicago Press, 1996) and Andrew Jewett, *Science, Democracy, and the American University: From the Civil War to the Cold War* (New York: Cambridge University Press, 2014). Thomas Haskell, *The Emergence of Professional Social Science:*

The American Social Science Association and the Nineteenth-Century Crisis of Authority (Urbana, IL: University of Illinois Press, 1977) deals with the movement from an earlier conception of reform-oriented social science to the model of professional objectivity. The most important work on the early social sciences of the late nineteenth and early twentieth centuries is Dorothy Ross, *The Origins of American Social Science* (New York: Cambridge University Press, 1991); Ross argues for the distinguishing feature of American social science as its rejection of historical thinking in favor of American exceptionalism. The most significant historian of anthropology is George Stocking. Among his many publications, the most important are *Race, Culture, and Evolution: Essays in the History of Anthropology* (New York: Free Press, 1968) and *Victorian Anthropology* (New York: Free Press, 1987). On the classically-based curriculum, see Caroline Winterer, *The Culture of Classicism: Ancient Greece and Rome in American Intellectual Life, 1780–1910* (Baltimore, MD: Johns Hopkins University Press, 2002). James Turner's magisterial *Philology: The Forgotten Origins of the Modern Humanities* (Princeton, NJ: Princeton University Press, 2014) demonstrates the ways in which an older approach to language and its history was systematized into the modern humanities disciplines. On the "genteel tradition" and its conception of culture and education, see John Tomsich, *A Genteel Endeavor: American Culture and Politics in the Gilded Age* (Palo Alto, CA: Stanford University Press, 1971) and, for a revisionist account, Leslie Butler, *Critical Americans: Victorian Intellectuals and Transatlantic Liberal Reform* (Chapel Hill, NC: University of North Carolina Press, 2007). The idea of cultural hierarchy in the Matthew Arnold model is treated in Lawrence Levine, *Highbrow/Lowbrow: The Emergence of Cultural Hierarchy in America* (Cambridge, MA: Harvard University Press, 1988).

On general ideas about progress and modernity, and especially the criticism of progress, two invaluable texts should be consulted: Jackson Lears, *No Place of Grace: Antimodernism and the Transformation of American Culture, 1880–1920* (New York: Pantheon, 1981), and Christopher Lasch, *The True and Only Heaven: Progress and Its Critics* (New York: W.W. Norton, 1991). For a now dated but incisive historiographical analysis of Progressivism, see Daniel Rodgers, "In Search of Progressivism," *Reviews in American History* 10.4 (December 1982), pp. 113–132. One of the classic interpretations of Progressivism, although much battered by successive criticisms from every side, is Richard Hofstadter, *The Age of Reform: From Bryan to F.D.R.* (New York: Vintage Books, 1955). Two works, beyond Kloppenberg's *Uncertain Victory* noted above, should be consulted: Michael McGerr, *A Fierce Discontent: The Rise and Fall of the Progressive Movement in America, 1870–1920* (New York: Oxford University Press, 2003), and for a broader conception of transatlantic reform movements and ideologies, Daniel Rodgers, *Atlantic Crossings: Social Politics in a Progressive Age* (Cambridge, MA: Harvard University Press, 1998). Reconsiderations of the new liberalism and its relationship to post-Civil War reform movements can be found in Nancy Cohen, *The Reconstruction of American Liberalism, 1865–1914* (Chapel Hill, NC: University of North Carolina Press, 2002) and Kathleen Donohue, *Freedom from Want: American Liberalism and the Idea of the Consumer* (Baltimore, MD: Johns Hopkins University Press, 2003). A good discussion of the reform tradition that includes Henry George and Edward Bellamy can be found in John L. Thomas, *Alternative America: Henry George, Edward Bellamy, Henry Demarest Lloyd and the Adversary Tradition* (Cambridge, MA: Harvard University Press, 1983). On the settlement movement, see Mina Carson, *Settlement Folk: Social Thought and the American Settlement Movement, 1885–1930* (Chicago, IL: University of Chicago Press, 1990). Jane Addams, as one of the central figures of Progressivism, has been the subject of a great deal of scholarship, including a well-known interpretation of her thought in Christopher Lasch, *The New Radicalism in America, 1889–1963: The Intellectual as a Social Type* (New York: Knopf, 1965). On Addams and Chicago sociology, see Mary Jo Deegan, *Jane Addams and the Men of the Chicago School, 1892–1918* (New York: Routledge, 2017). On Taylorism and the cult of efficiency, see Samuel Haber, *Efficiency and Uplift: Scientific Management in the Progressive Era 1890–1920* (Chicago, IL: University of Chicago Press, 1964). On the Social Gospel, the many works of Gary Dorrien, the most prominent and prolific interpreter of liberal Protestantism, are of use. See, for instance, his *Social Ethics in the Making: Interpreting an American Tradition* (Malden, MA: Wiley-Blackwell, 2009).

A strong critical interpretation of the dominant elite strain of Black thought in the Progressive Era is Kevin Gaines, *Uplifting the Race: Black Leadership, Politics, and Culture in the Twentieth Century* (Chapel Hill, NC: University of North Carolina Press, 1996). Adolph Reed, Jr., *W.E.B. DuBois and American Political Thought: Fabianism and the Color Line* (New York: Oxford University Press, 1997) situates DuBois's thought within the contours of Progressive political thought. The best known account of W.E.B. DuBois's life and work is David Levering Lewis, *W.E.B. DuBois: A Biography 1868–1963* (New York: Henry Holt, 2009). A good account of the ways in which DuBois used his immersion in German thought to reflect upon the condition of race in the United States is Kwame Anthony Appiah, *Lines of Descent: W.E.B. DuBois and the Emergence of Identity* (Cambridge, MA: Harvard University Press, 2014). Robert Gooding-Williams, *In the Shadow of DuBois: Afro-Modern Political Thought in America* (Cambridge, MA: Harvard University Press, 2009) critically engages *Souls of Black Folk* as a central text in Black thought.

The historiography of feminist thought is substantial and deep. On the shift from "woman movement" to "feminism," Heterodoxy, and the paradox of equality and difference, see Nancy Cott, *The Grounding of Modern Feminism* (New Haven, CT: Yale University Press, 1987). On the academic development of egalitarian thought on sex, the best work remains Rosalind Rosenberg, *Beyond Separate Spheres: The Intellectual Roots of Modern Feminism* (New Haven, CT: Yale University Press, 1982). Ellen DuBois and Richard Candida Smith, eds., *Elizabeth Cady Stanton: Feminist as Thinker* (New York: New York University Press, 2007) compiles both primary readings and scholarship that provide a strong foundation for understanding Stanton's thought. On the reconstruction of the history of the movement for women's rights by participants in it, see Lisa Tetrault, *The Myth of Seneca Falls: Memory and the Women's Suffrage Movement, 1848–1898* (Chapel Hill, NC; University of North Carolina Press, 2014). Mari Jo Buhle, *Feminism and Its Discontents: A Century of Struggle with Psychoanalysis* (Cambridge, MA: Harvard University Press, 2000) and Kimberly A. Hamlin, *From Eve to Evolution: Darwin, Science, and Women's Rights in Gilded Age America* (Chicago, IL: University of Chicago Press, 2014) take on the influence and reception of Freud and Darwin respectively. An earlier, still useful, take on science and sex difference is Cynthia Russett, *Sexual Science: The Victorian Construction of Womanhood* (Cambridge, MA: Harvard University Press, 1991). Martha S. Jones, *All Bound Up Together: The Woman Question in African American Public Culture, 1830–1900* (Chapel Hill, NC: University of North Carolina Press, 2009) argues for the centrality of Black women in debates that emphasize the very thing often repressed by Stanton and others who have written the history of feminism in her wake: race and its relationship to gender equality. For an argument that rejects the frame of "respectability politics," see Brittney Cooper, *Beyond Respectability: The Intellectual Thought of Race Women* (Champaign, IL: University of Illinois Press, 2017). Judith A. Allen, *The Feminism of Charlotte Perkins Gilman: Sexualities, Histories, Progressivism* (Chicago, IL: University of Chicago Press, 2009) effectively situates Gilman's thought in a variety of intellectual contests. Allen's interpretation of Gilman differs remarkably from that offered by Gail Bederman, *Manliness and Civilization: A Cultural History of Race and Gender in the United States 1880–1917* (Chicago, IL: University of Illinois Press, 1996), who also focuses on the crisis of masculinity and Teddy Roosevelt's role in propagating ideas linking masculinity to race. Louise Michele Newman, *White Women's Rights: The Racial Origins of Feminism in the United States* (New York: Oxford University Press, 1999) argues that the racial and evolutionary discourses of hierarchy were foundational for modern feminist thought. Melissa N. Stein, *Measuring Manhood: Race and the Science of Masculinity, 1830–1934* (Minneapolis,

MN: University of Minnesota Press, 2015) puts the relationship between racial science, quantification, and gender ideology in a longer time frame.

The foundational text for the complicated history of the concept of culture is Raymond Williams, *Culture and Society 1780–1950* (New York: Columbia University Press, 1960). See, also, Adam Kuper, *Culture: The Anthropologists' Account* (Cambridge, MA: Harvard University Press, 1999). Boasian anthropology and the school of cultural relativism are addressed by George Stocking, Jr., as noted above, and by Richard Handler, *Critics Against Culture: Anthropological Observers of Mass Society* (Madison, WI: University of Wisconsin Press, 2005). A very accessible account of the Boas school is Charles King, *Gods of the Upper Air: How A Circle of Renegade Anthropologists Reinvented Race, Sex, and Gender in the Twentieth Century* (New York: Doubleday, 2019). For a critical reinterpretation of Boas and his school that emphasizes the continuing racialist assumptions in this body of thought, see Mark Anderson, *From Boas to Black Power: Racism, Liberalism, and American Anthropology* (Stanford, CA: Stanford University Press, 2019). A recent work on Margaret Mead, that pushes back against the vision of Mead as a thoroughly secular thinker is Elesha Coffman, *Margaret Mead: A Twentieth-Century Faith* (New York: Oxford University Press, 2021) For a good discussion of the culture and personality school with regard to unmooring race and sexuality from biological essentialism, see Joanne Meyerowitz, "'How Common Culture Shapes the Separate Lives': Sexuality, Race, and Mid-Twentieth-Century Social Constructionist Thought," *Journal of American History* 96.4 (March 2010), pp. 1057–1084. Intellectual historians, as opposed to scholars of literature, have not paid as much attention to Hurston as to figures like Mead and Benedict. See Karen Jacobs, "From 'Spy-Glass' to 'Horizon': The Anthropological Gaze in Zora Neale Hurston," *Novel: A Forum on Fiction* 30.3 (Spring 1997), pp. 329–360, and Ross Posnock, *Color and Culture: Black Writers and the Making of the Modern Intellectual* (Cambridge, MA: Harvard University Press, 2000). The starting point for any discussion of the history of the thought of professional historians in the United States remains Peter Novick, *That Noble Dream: The 'Objectivity Question and the American Historical Profession* (New York, Cambridge University Press, 1988). An important revision of the lineage of American historiography created by social and cultural historians in the late twentieth century is Ellen Fitzpatrick, *History's Memory: Writing America's Past 1880-1980* (Cambridge, MA: Harvard University Press, 2004). One of the major mid-twentieth-century critiques of Turner and Beard is Richard Hofstadter, *The Progressive Historians: Turner, Beard, Parrington* (New York: Knopf, 1968). An excellent analysis of the staying power of Frederick Jackson Turner's thought is Patricia Nelson Limerick, "Turnerians All: The Dream of a Helpful History in an Intelligible World,"

American Historical Review 100.3 (June 1995), pp. 697–716. Limerick is one of the central figures in the "New Western History" that sought to dismantle the Turnerian frontier thesis in the late twentieth century. An older, but still valuable, discussion of Chicago school sociology is Fred Matthews, *Quest for an American Sociology: Robert E. Park and the Chicago School* (Montreal, 1977). A thorough overview is Martin Bulmer, *The Chicago School of Sociology: Institutionalization, Diversity, and the Rise of Sociological Research* (Chicago, IL: University of Chicago Press, 1984). An effective treatment of the role of Asian thinkers in Chicago sociology is Henry Yu, *Thinking Orientals: Migration, Contact, and Exoticism in Modern America* (New York: Oxford University Press, 2001). The two best analyses of the Lynd's *Middletown* are in Christopher Shannon, *Conspicuous Criticism: Tradition, the Individual, and Culture in American Social Thought, from Veblen to Mills* (Baltimore, MD: Johns Hopkins University Press, 1995) and Sarah Igo, *The Averaged American: Surveys, Citizens, and the Making of a Mass Public* (Cambridge, MA: Harvard University Press, 2008).

Good discussions of science as a cultural orientation in twentieth-century thought include Andrew Jewett's, cited above; David Hollinger, *Science, Jews, and Secular Culture: Studies in Mid-Twentieth Century American Intellectual History* (Princeton, NJ: Princeton University Press, 1996); and Jamie Cohen-Cole, *The Open Mind: Cold-War Politics and the Sciences of Human Nature* (Chicago, IL: University of Chicago Press, 2014). On the reinterpretation of the so-called Lippmann–Dewey debate, there are two invaluable articles: Tom Arnold-Foster, "Democracy and Expertise in the Lippmann–Terman Controversy," *Modern Intellectual History* 16.2 (2019), pp. 561–592; and David Greenberg, "Lippmann vs. Mencken: Debating Democracy," *Raritan* 32.2 (Winter 2012), pp. 117–140. The pervasive idea of science as a source of modern disenchantment of the world is critically and historically examined as a "myth" in Jason A. Josephson-Storm, *The Myth of Disenchantment: Magic, Modernity, and the Birth of the Human Sciences* (Chicago, IL: University of Chicago Press, 2017). On Logical Empiricism/positivism and its ideological content and context, see George A. Reisch, *How the Cold War Transformed Philosophy of Science* (New York: Cambridge University Press, 2010) and John McCumber, *The Philosophy Scare: The Politics of Reason in the Early Cold War* (Chicago, IL: University of Chicago Press, 2016). A special 2-volume edition of the journal *Interdisciplinary Science Reviews* 41.2–3 (2016), pp. 107–277 discusses both the history and lasting legacy of C.P. Snow and the "two cultures" debate.

The most prominent recent philosophical discussion of secularization is the Canadian philosopher Charles Taylor's philosophical history, *A Secular Age* (Cambridge, MA, 2007). The newest account is David Sehat, *This Earthly Frame: The Making of American Secularism* (New Haven, CT: Yale

University Press, 2022). For a discussion of the secularization thesis, see David Hollinger, "Christianity and Its American Fate: Where History Interrogates Secularization Theory," in Joel Isaac, James T. Kloppenberg, Michael O'Brien, and Jennifer Ratner-Rosenhagen, eds., *The Worlds of American Intellectual History*, pp. 280–303. The two classic sources on Protestant modernism/liberalism are William R. Hutchison, *The Modernist Impulse in American Protestantism* (Cambridge, MA: Harvard University Press, 1976) and Gary Dorrien, *The Making of American Liberal Theology: Imagining Progressive Religion 1805–1900* (Lousiville, KY: Westminster John Knox Press, 2001). Susan Jacoby, *Freethinkers: A History of American Secularism* (New York: Metropolitan, 2004) covers freethought from the Revolution through the end of the twentieth century, including what she calls "the golden age" of American freethought in the time of Ingersoll. Christopher Cameron, *Black Freethinkers: A History of African-American Secularism* (Evanston, IL: Northwestern University Press, 2019) is particularly effective in challenging assumptions about the historical relationship between the Black church and reform and radical politics. James Turner, *Without God, Without Creed: The Origins of Unbelief in America* (Baltimore, MD: Johns Hopkins University Press, 1986) persuasively argues that it was those who sought to adapt theism to modern epistemic and moral standards who created the conditions for agnosticism and atheism. The more radical challenge of Nietzschean philosophy to theism is discussed in Jennifer Ratner-Rosenhagen, *American Nietzsche: A History of an Icon and His Ideas* (Chicago, IL: University of Chicago Press, 2012). Elesha Coffman, *The Christian Century and the Rise of the Protestant Mainline* (New York: Oxford University Press, 2013) shows the centrality of the magazine to the development and articulation of an elite Protestant liberalism. On the modernist-fundamentalist controversy, consult George Marsden, *Fundamentalism and American Culture*, 3rd edition (New York: Oxford University Press, 2022) and D.G. Hart, *Defending the Faith: J. Gresham Machen and the Crisis of Conservative Protestantism in Twentieth-Century America* (Phillipsburg, NJ: P & R Publishing, 2003). Cold War era religious revivalism/ecumenicalism are contextualized in Kevin M. Schultz, *Tri-Faith America: How Catholics and Jews Held Post-war America to Its Protestant Promise* (New York: Oxford University Press, 2011); K. Healan Gaston, *Imagining Judeo-Christian America: Religion, Secularism, and the Redefinition of Democracy* (Chicago, IL: University of Chicago Press, 2019); and Jason Stevens, *God-Fearing and Free: A Spiritual History of America's Cold War* (Cambridge, MA: Harvard University Press, 2010). For a discussion of Norman Vincent Peale and popular therapeutic religion, see Erin A. Smith, *What Would Jesus Read? Popular Religious Books and Everyday Life in Twentieth-Century America* (Chapel Hill, NC: University of North Carolina Press, 2015).

The best place to start on the development of a pluralistic perspective in American thought is Daniel Borus, *Twentieth-Century Multiplicity: American Thought and Culture, 1900–1920* (Lanham, MD: Rowman & Littlefield, 2009). Bourne, Kallen, and Locke and their cultural pluralist thought are analyzed in Everett Helmut Akam, *Transnational America: Cultural Pluralist Thought in the Twentieth Century* (Lanham, MD: Rowman & Littlefield, 2002). See also David Hollinger, "Ethnic Diversity, Cosmopolitanism, and the Emergence of the American Liberal Intelligentsia," in *In the American Province: Studies in the History and Historiography of Ideas* (Bloomington, IN, 1985), pp. 56–73. On nativist thought, the classic, though now dated, text is John Higham, *Strangers in the Land: Patterns of American Nativism, 1860–1925* (New Brunswick, NJ: Rutgers University Press, 1955). For the argument that cultural pluralism represents the maintenance of racialist thought rather than its replacement, see Walter Benn Michaels, *Our America: Nativism, Modernism, and Pluralism* (Duham, NC: Duke University Press, 1997). There is a large and significant body of scholarship on the Harlem Renaissance. David Levering Lewis, *When Harlem Was in Vogue* (New York: Knopf, 1981) provides a good overview. Black Nationalism, Garveyism, and internationalist thought in the mid-century have received considerable attention. See Keisha N. Blain, *Set the World on Fire: Black Nationalist Women and the Global Struggle for Freedom* (Philadelphia, PA: University of Pennsylvania Press, 2018) and Nikhil Pal Singh, *Black Is a Country: Race and the Unfinished Struggle for Democracy* (Cambridge, MA: Harvard University Press, 2005). Two good interpretive overviews of the thought and culture of the 1920s are Paul Murphy, *The New Era: American Thought and Culture in the 1920s* (Lanham, MD: Rowman & Littlefield, 2012), and Ann Douglas, *Terrible Honesty: Mongrel Manhattan in the 1920s* (New York: Farrar, Straus and Giroux, 1995). On the distinctiveness of the South as a figure in a modernizing discourse, see Natalie J. Ring, *The Problem South: Region, Empire, and the New Liberal State, 1880–1930* (Athens, GA: University of Georgia Press, 2012). The best work on the Southern agrarians is Paul Murphy, *The Rebuke of History: The Southern Agrarians and American Conservative Thought* (Chapel Hill, NC: University of North Carolina Press, 2001). American thought of the 1930s is covered in Richard Pells, *Radical Visions and American Dreams: Culture and Social Thought in the Depression Years* (New York: Harper & Row, 1973) and Michael Denning, *The Cultural Front: The Laboring of American Culture in the Twentieth Century* (New York: Verso, 1997). William Stott, *Documentary Expression and Thirties America* (Chicago, IL: University of Chicago Press, 1973) remains a good source on the FSA photographs and their cultural context. An interesting revisiting of Luce's "American Century" can be found in Andrew Bacevich, ed., *The Short American Century: A*

Postmortem (Cambridge, MA: Harvard University Press, 2013). Samuel Zipp, *The Idealist: Wendell Willkie's Wartime Quest to Build One World* (Cambridge, MA: Harvard University Press, 2020) is a good recent interpretation of Willkie's One-Worldism.

Two recent works provide very different pictures of the thought and culture of the post-World War era. Louis Menand, *The Free World: Art and Thought in the Cold War* (New York: Farrar, Straus and Giroux, 2021) situates American ideas of "freedom" in a variety of registers—although notably not in terms of standard ideas of Cold War ideology—in an international context. Casey Nelson Blake, Daniel H. Borus, and Howard Brick, *At the Center: American Thought and Culture in the Mid-Twentieth Century* (Lanham, MD: Rowman & Littlefield, 2020) emphasize notions of holism, integration, and universalism in mid-Century thought, as a counter to notions of modern disintegration, but also to older interpretations stressing a liberal consensus. Both Menand and Blake et al. supplant older interpretations, such as that put forward by Richard Pells, *The Liberal Mind in a Conservative Age: American Intellectuals in the 1940s and 50s* (New York: Harper & Row, 1985). Much recent work emphasizes the continuities between the mid-century years and the 1960s, where previous historians had seen a contrast. Two good examples are Fred Turner, *The Democratic Surround: Multimedia and American Liberalism from World War II to the Psychedelic Sixties* (Chicago, IL: University of Chicago Press, 2013) and Robert Genter, *Late Modernism: Art, Culture, and Politics in Cold War America* (Philadelphia, PA: University of Pennsylvania Press, 2010). One of the best works on ideas of self in American thought, although not focused exclusively on the mid-twentieth century, is Wilfred McClay, *The Masterless: Self and Society in Modern America* (Chapel Hill, NC: University of North Carolina Press, 1994). Mark Greif, *The Age of the Crisis of Man: Thought and Fiction in America 1933–1973* (Princeton, NJ: Princeton University Press, 2015) is a wide-ranging work that documents the emptiness of abstract and universalistic concepts of Man at mid-century. On the concept of totalitarianism as a key idea, see Abbot Gleason, *Totalitarianism: The Inner History of the Cold War* (New York: Oxford University Press, 1995), and on Arendt, Richard H. King, *Arendt and America* (Chicago, IL: University of Chicago Press, 2015). The lasting impact of Freudian thought, particularly at its mid-century high-water mark is ably discussed from a variety of perspectives in John Burnham, ed., *After Freud Left: A Century of Psychoanalysis in America* (Chicago, IL: University of Chicago Press, 2012). The vogue of existentialism in the post-war period is handled well in George Cotkin, *Existential America* (Baltimore, MD: Johns Hopkins University Press, 2003). The standard work on postwar conservatism, responsible for the idea of the three strands of conservative thought, is George Nash, *The Conservative*

Intellectual Movement in America Since 1945, 30th Anniversary edition (Wilmington, DE: ISI Books, 2006). An important treatment of Hayek, the Mont Pèlerin Society, and the international opposition to welfare state economics is Angus Burgin, *The Great Persuasion: Reinventing Free Markets Since the Depression* (Cambridge, MA: Harvard University Press, 2015).

A good general treatment of the thought of the 1960s is Howard Brick, *Age of Contradiction: American Thought and Culture in the 1960s* (Woodbridge CT: Twayne, 1998). The 50th anniversary of the publication of Kuhn's *Structure of Scientific Revolutions* in 2012 saw a spate of reconsiderations of its history, significance, and lasting consequences. One collection is Robert J. Richards and Lorraine Daston, eds., *Kuhn's Structure of Scientific Revolutions at Fifty: Reflections on a Science Classic* (Chicago, IL: University of Chicago Press, 2016). François Cusset, *French Theory: How Foucault, Derrida, Deleuze, & Co. Transformed the Intellectual Life of the United States*, trans. Jeff Fort (Minneapolis, MN: University of Minnesota Press, 2008) argues that the Americanized versions of French theory, including Foucault, are mistranslations of the French originals. A clarifying and short discussion of Foucault's thought is Paul Veyne, *Foucault: His Thought, His Character*, trans. Janet Lloyd (Malden, MA: Polity, 2010). On the centrality of discontinuity in Foucault, see Mark Poster, "Foucault, The Present and History," *Cultural Critique* 8 (Winter 1987–1988), pp. 105–121. On Quentin Skinner and his critics, the best book is Kari Palonen, *Quentin Skinner: History, Politics, Rhetoric* (Malden, MA: Polity, 2003). On SDS, the Port Huron Statement, and the New Left, see James Miller, *Democracy Is in the Streets: From Port Huron to the Siege of Chicago* (Cambridge, MA: Harvard University Press, 1994), and Doug Rossinow, *The Politics of Authenticity: Liberalism, Christianity, and the New Left in America* (New York: Columbia University Press, 1998). The preeminent historian of Black Power is Peniel Joseph. See his monograph, *Waiting 'Til the Midnight Hour: A Narrative History of Black Power in America* (New York: Henry Holt, 2006), and his edited collection, *The Black Power Movement: Rethinking the Civil-Rights-Black Power Era* (New York: Routledge, 2006). James Edward Smethurst, *The Black Arts Movement: Literary Nationalism in the 1960s and 70s* (Chapel Hill, NC: University of North Carolina Press, 2005) deals with the literary aesthetics of the movement. Jerry Watts, ed., *Harold Cruse's The Crisis of the Negro Intellectual Reconsidered* (New York: Routledge, 2004) gathers a number of important scholars for historical and critical analysis of this foundational text. On the aesthetics of "the new sensibility," including a discussion of Susan Sontag's place in the thought of the era, see George Cotkin, *Feast of Excess: A Cultural History of the New Sensibility* (New York: Oxford University Press, 2016). Transformations in the arts are chronicled in Barbara Haskell, *BLAM! The Explosion of Pop, Minimalism, and*

Performance, 1958–1964 (New York: Whitney Museum of American Art, 1984). A sharp recent discussion of Danto in the context of philosophical and artistic shifts is John Erik Hmiel, "Art and Indiscernibility: Arthur C. Danto and the Dynamics of Analytic Philosophy," *Modern Intellectual History* 19.4 (December 2022), pp. 1157–1181. On Daniel Bell and Post-Industrial society, see Howard Brick, "Optimism of the Mind: Imagining Postindustrial Society in the 1960s and 70s," *American Quarterly* 44.3 (September 1992), pp. 348–380, and more broadly, for a notion of post-capitalist society, Howard Brick, *Transcending Capitalism: Visions of a New Society in Modern American Thought* (Ithaca NY: Cornell University Press, 2006).

On social constructionism, the best place to start, although somewhat polemical rather than genealogical, is Ian Hacking, *The Social Construction of What?* (Cambridge, MA: Harvard University Press, 1999). For interpretations of late twentieth-century social thought and culture, see Daniel T. Rodgers, *Age of Fracture* (Cambridge, MA: Harvard University Press; 2011); and J. David Hoeveler, Jr., *The Postmodern Turn: American Thought and Culture in the 1970s* (Woodbridge, CT: Twayne, 1996). James Livingston, *The World Turned Inside Out: American Thought and Culture at the End of the Twentieth Century* (Lanham, MD: Rowman & Littlefield, 2009) makes late twentieth-century intellectual practice level with popular culture representations. Norman Dain, "Psychiatry and Anti-Psychiatry in the United States," in Mark S. Micale and Roy Porter, eds., *Discovering the History of Psychiatry* (New York: Oxford University Press, 1994), pp. 415–444 argues that anti-psychiatric thought has a long lineage dating to the mid-nineteenth century, and the movement of the 1960s and beyond was less a departure than often assumed. On late twentieth-century Pragmatism, as understood by both its practitioners and intellectual historians, consult the essays in Morris Dickstein, ed., *The Revival of Pragmatism: New Essays on Social Thought, Law, and Culture* (Durham, NC: Duke University Press, 1998) and James T. Kloppenberg, "Pragmatism: An Old Name for Some New Ways of Thinking?" *Journal of American History* 83.1 (June 1996), pp. 100–138. For a particularly strong critique of Rorty in relation to the Pragmatic tradition, see Susan Haack, "Introduction: Pragmatism Old and New," in Susan Haack, ed., *Pragmatism Old and New* (Amherst, NY: Prometheus Books, 2006), pp. 15–68. For a philosophical and historical discussion of the idea of the "social imaginary," Charles Taylor's *Modern Social Imaginaries* (Durham, NC: Duke University Press, 2003) is a clear and accessible work. There is a substantial body of work on race as a social construct. The history of the idea of race as a social construct has not received as much attention, but two good places to start are the writing of Kwame Anthony Appiah, especially *In My Father's House: Africa in the Philosophy of Culture* (New York: Oxford University

Press, 1992), and Karen E. Fields and Barbara J. Fields, *Racecraft: The Soul of Inequality in American Life* (New York: Verso, 2012). On the rise of "whiteness" as an idea in scholarly history and cultural studies, see Peter Kolchin, "Whiteness Studies: The New History of Race in America," *Journal of American History* 89.1 (June 2002), pp. 154–173. The intellectual history of the idea of Afrocentricity is discussed in Mia Bay, "The Historical Origins of Afrocentrism," *Amerikastudien/American Studies* 45.4 (2000), pp. 501–512; and Tunde Adeleke, "Afrocentric Intellectuals and the Burden of History," in Brian D. Behnken, Gregory D. Smithers, and Simon Wendt, eds., *Black Intellectual Thought in Modern America: A Historical Perspective* (Jackson, MS: University Press of Mississippi, 2017), pp. 206–236. An alternative conceptualization of Carol Gilligan's thought in relationship to the history of feminist theory is Cressida J. Heyes, "Anti-Essentialism in Practice: Carol Gilligan and Feminist Philosophy," *Hypatia* 12.3 (Summer 1997), pp. 142–162.

There are many popular accounts of the discovery of DNA. A recent work is Howard Merkel, *The Secret of Life: Rosalind Frank, James Watson, Francis Crick and the Discovery of DNA's Double Helix* (New York: W.W. Norton, 2021). Intellectual historians have not done as much as they might to examine the intellectual uses of DNA outside of the history of molecular biology, but the history of the broad use of DNA as a way to think about the world is adroitly analyzed in Judith Roof, *The Poetics of DNA* (Minneapolis, MN: University of Minnesota Press, 2007). For a more philosophical account, consult David Haig, *From Darwin to Derrida: Selfish Genes, Social Selves, and the Meanings of Life* (Cambridge, MA: Harvard University Press, 2000). The battles over the form of evolution and the uses of Darwinism in the late twentieth century are given in an account for a general readership: Andrew Brown, *The Darwin Wars: The Scientific Battle for the Soul of Man* (New York: Simon & Schuster, 2002). A more scholarly work on the intellectual fallout from these debates is Ullica Segerstråle, *Defenders of the Truth: The Battle for Science in the sociobiology Debate and Beyond* (New York: Oxford University Press, 2000). An effective and considered critical analysis of evolutionary psychology can be found in David J. Buller, *evolutionary psychology and the Persistent Quest for Human Nature* (Cambridge, MA: Harvard University Press, 2005). Kate O'Riordan, "The Life of the Gay Gene: From Hypothetical Genetic Marker to Social Reality," *Journal of Sex Research* 49.4 (June 2012), pp. 362–368 provides an overview of the movement from clinical study to media event in the United Kingdom. An attempt to establish a long-standing interest in transhumanism that links the past and future is provided by Nick Bostrom, one of transhumanism's advocates. See his "A History of Transhumanist Thought," *Journal of Evolution and Technology* 14.1 (2005), pp. 1–25.

For a comprehensive overview of feminism from the late eighteenth century, with a greater focus on the movement than specifically feminist thought, Christine Stansell, *The Feminist Promise: 1792 to the Present* (New York: The Modern Library, 2010). See also, Ruth Rosen, *The World Split Open: How the Modern Women's Movement Changed America* (New York: Penguin, 2000). Three important studies that address Betty Friedan are Daniel Horowitz, *Betty Friedan and the Making of The Feminine Mystique: The American Left, the Cold War, and Modern Feminism* (Amherst, MA: University of Massachusetts Press, 1998); Joanne Meyerowitz, "Beyond the Feminine Mystique: A Reassessment of Postwar Mass Culture, 1946–1958," *Journal of American History* 79.4 (March 1993), pp. 1455–1482; and Stephanie Coontz, *"A Strange Stirring": The Feminine Mystique and American Women at the Dawn of the 1960s* (New York: Basic Books, 2011). The classic accounts of Women's Liberation and radical feminism are Sara Evans, *Personal Politics: The Roots of Women's Liberation in the Civil Rights Movement and the New Left* (New York: Knopf, 1979), and Alice Echols, *Daring to Be Bad: Radical Feminism in America,1967–1975* (Minneapolis, MN: University of Minnesota Press, 1989). On sex in radical feminist thought leading up to the split over sex of the late 1970s and early 80s, an excellent study is Jane Gerhard, *Desiring Revolution: Second-Wave Feminism and the Rewriting of Twentieth-Century American Sexual Thought* (New York: Columbia University Press, 2001). For a recent reconsideration, see Lorna N. Bracewell, *Why We Lost the Sex Wars: Sexual Freedom in the #MeToo Era* (Minneapolis, MN: University of Minnesota Press, 2021). On the history of Black and multiracial feminist thought, see the introduction to Beverly Guy-Sheftall, ed., *Words of Fire: An Anthology of African-American Feminist Thought* (New York: New Press, 1995); Becky Thompson, "Multiracial Feminism: Recasting the Chronology of Second Wave Feminism," *Feminist Studies* 28.2 (June 2002), pp. 336–360; Brittney Cooper, *Beyond Respectability: The Intellectual Thought of Race Women* (New York, 2017). On the crisis of masculinity, from a feminist position, a well-received work is Susan Faludi, *Stiffed: The Betrayal of the American Man* (New York: William Morrow & Company, 1999).

The Culture Wars are handled comprehensively and clearly in Andrew Hartman, *A War for the Soul of America: A History of the Culture Wars* (Chicago, IL: University of Chicago Press, 2015). On neo-conservatism two early works were Peter Steinfels, *The Neoconservatives: The Men Who Are Changing America's Politics* (New York: Simon & Schuster, 1979), and Gary Dorrien, *The Neo-Conservative Mind: Politics, Culture, and the War of Ideology* (Philadelphia, PA: Temple University Press, 1993). A more recent study that argues for the use of Scottish moral philosophy in this body of thought is Antti Lepistö, *The Rise of Common-Sense Conservatism: The American Right and the Reinvention of the Scottish Enlightenment* (Chicago, IL: University of Chicago Press, 2021). For a recent revisiting of the battle over the canon, see Mary Jo Bona, "The Culture Wars and the Canon Debate," in D. Quentin Miller, ed., *American Literature in Transition, 1880–1890* (New York: Cambridge University Press, 2018), pp. 212–222. On the history wars and the changing epistemologies and approaches of historians, Sara Maza, *Thinking About History* (Chicago, IL: University of Chicago Press, 2017) is very comprehensive and clear, including a discussion of the Enola Gay and National History Standards controversies. On Deconstruction, see Gregory Jones-Katz, *Deconstruction: An American Institution* (Chicago, IL: University of Chicago Press, 2021). The announcement of new black intellectuals in the 1990s can be found in Robert Boynton, "The New Intellectuals," *The Atlantic Monthly* 275.3 (March 1995), pp. 53–70.

Index

abstract expressionism 212
academic professional societies 50, 110
Adams, Henry 12, 22
Adams, Herbert Baxter 110, 111
Addams, Jane: and Chicago sociology 113; and pragmatism 35; *Twenty Years at Hull House* (1910) 71–72
Adorno, Theodor 212; adversary culture 266–268, 276; *Authoritarian Personality* (1950) 181
aesthetic theory 132–133, 211–215
African-American thought 5, 217, 219, 230–231, 288; and 1960s 210–211; and Chicago sociology 114; and culture wars 278–280; and freethought 41–42; and Harlem Renaissance 156–159; and respectability politics 93; and women 93–94, 256–258; *see also* Baldwin, James; Cooper, Anna Julia; Cruse, Harold; DuBois, W.E.B.; Frazier, E. Franklin; hooks, bell; West, Cornel
Afrocentricity 230–231
Agassiz, Louis 26–27
agnosticism 141–142
agrarianism 161–162, 168
Allen, Theodore 230
Allport, Gordon: *Nature of Prejudice* (1954) 229
Alsop, Joseph 171
Alsop, Stewart 171
American exceptionalism 54–55, 268
American Mercury 191

American Psychiatric Association 225
American Social Science Association 53
American Sociological Association 58, 186
Americans for Democratic Action 171, 172
Anderson, Benedict: *Imagined Communities* (1983) 228
Anderson, Sherwood: *Winesburg, Ohio* (1919) 117, 160
Anthony, Susan B. 8
Anthropology 217; Boasian 103–110; critical 1980s 108; Victorian 59–61, 101–102; *see also* cultural relativism; social science; stadial theory
anti-essentialism 222–223, 258–259, 262, 263
anti-foundationalism 35, 40–42, 46–47
anti-naturalism 223
anti-psychiatry movement 224–226
Antonioni, Michelangelo 212
Anzaldúa, Gloria and Cherrie Moraga: *This Bridge Called My Back* (1981) 257
Appiah, Kwame Anthony 229
Ardrey, Robert: *Social Contract* (1970) 238
Arendt, Hannah: *Origins of Totalitarianism* (1951) 7, 178–179
Arnold, Matthew 102, 109; *Culture and Anarchy* (1868) 62; *see also* culture
artificial intelligence 245–246
artworld 214–215
Asante, Molefi Kete. 230–231

atheism 140–142
Atkinson, Ti-Grace: "Radical Feminism" (1970) 252–253, 255
Atlanta compromise 75–76
Auden, W.H. 149
Austin, J.L. 205, 260
authoritarian personality 177, 181

Babbitt, Irving 123
Baker, Houston 272
Baldwin, James: "Everybody's Protest Novel" (1955) 189; *Notes of a Native Son* (1955) 188
Baraka, Amiri *see* Jones, LeRoi
Barber, Bernard 130
Barnes, Djuna 160
Barnes, Hazel 190
Barrett, William 190
Barthes, Roland 199
Beard, Charles 102, 174, 189, 273; *Economic Interpretation of the Constitution* (1913) 112; historical relativism and 113; "Written History as an Act of Faith" (1934) 112–113; Beauvoir, Simone de 189
Becker, Carl: "Everyman His Own Historian" (1932) 113
Bell, Daniel 178, 267; *The Coming of Post-Industrial Society* (1973) 216; *The Cultural Contradictions of Capitalism* (1976) 216–217; *The End of Ideology in the West* (1960) 179, 207
Bell, Derek 279
Bellamy, Edward: *Looking Backward* (1888) 66–67
Bellow, Saul 272
Benedict, Ruth 103, 113, 202; *The Chrysanthemum and the Sword* (1945) 110; *Patterns of Culture* (1934) 107–108, 109
Bennet, William 270
Bentley, Gladys 159; Benton, Thomas Hart 165
Berger, Peter: and neo-conservatism 220; and Thomas Luckmann, *Social Construction of Reality* (1966) 220–221

Bergman, Ingmar 212
Bernal, Martin: *Black Athena* (1987) 231
biblical higher criticism 137–139
biblical inerrancy 139
Black Arts 210, 215
Black internationalism 157–158
Black nationalism 157–158, 168, 210, 215, 231
Black Power 210, 215, 231, 252, 255, 271, 273
Blackwell, Antoinette Brown 88–89
Bloom, Allan 270, 272
Bloom, Harold 277
Bly, Robert: *Iron John* (1990) 262
Boas, Franz 103–105, 143, 219; *see also* anthropology; cultural relativism
Boorstin, Daniel 175
Bourdieu, Pierre 272
Bourne, Randolph: "Transnational America" (1916) 155–156, 160
Bozell, Brent 191
Brand, Stewart 245
Briggs, Charles Augustus 138–139
Bronowski, Jacob 130
Brooks, Cleanth 132
Brownmiller, Susan: *Against Our Will* (1975) 252
Bryan, William Jennings 117, 146–147
Buckley, William F. 191–193, 269; *God and Man at Yale* (1951) 191, 193, 194
Burgess, Ernest 113
Burke, Edmund 193
Burnham, James 192; *Managerial Revolution* (1941) 268
Bush, George H.W. 274
Buss, David 239
Butler, Judith 277; *Gender Trouble* (1990) 258–259

Caldwell, Erskine 161
Calvinism 139
Cambridge school of political thought 205–207
Camus, Albert 190
canon wars 271–273
Carmichael, Stokely 210
Carnap, Rudolph 127–128, 201
Carter, Steven 278

Cash, W.J.: *Mind of the South* (1941) 162–163
Cayton, Horace 114
Chambers, Whittaker 192
Chavez, Linda 270
Cheney, Lynn 270, 274
Chicago school of sociology 113–115, 118, 163
Christian Century 145
Christianity Today 148
Cincore, David 142
civil rights 252, 260, 261, 279; and antinaturalism 234; cold war liberalism 172–173; and new left 208, 210–211; *see also* African-American thought; Black Power
civilization, discourse of 59–61, 95, 102
Clarke, Edward: *Sex Education: or, a Fair Chance for Girls* (1872) 88
Cold War 169, 187, 207, 211, 238, 294
Cold War liberalism 169–174, 188–189, 190–191, 194, 267
Combahee River Collective Statement (1977) 256–257, 259
Commanger, Henry Steele 176
Commentary 172, 188
Committee on Social Thought, University of Chicago 192
Comte, Auguste 54, 56
consensus history 174–177
conservatism 190–194; *see also* neo-conservatism
conservative populism 268–269
Cooley, Charles Horton 55, 58
Cooper, Anna Julia: *A Voice from the South* (1892) 94
Cornell University 49–50
Cosmides, Leda *see* Tooby, John
cosmopolitanism 152–157, 271–272
Coughlin, Father Charles 163
Cowley, Malcolm: *Exiles's Return* (1934) 160
Cram, Ralph Adams 123
Crenshaw, Kimberlé 256–257
Crick, Francis 234
critical race theory 279
Croly, Herbert: *The Promise of American Life* 68–69

Cruse, Harold: *The Crisis of the Negro Intellectual* (1967) 210–211
cultural criticism 169; and middle class 182–185; and neo-Freudianism 181; and social constructionism 221–224
cultural pluralism 152–159, 168, 237, 271–272, 293
cultural populism 163–165, 168
cultural relativism 103–110, 152, 176, 206; compared to epistemological and moral relativism 103–104; defined 103; opposed to naturalism 237
culture: anthropological concept of 60, 102–103, 117–118, 227; Arnoldian concept of 61–63, 94, 102–103, 270; definition of 61; W.E.B. DuBois and Arnoldian concept 76; secondary sources on 290; in social constructionist thought 219; *see also* Benedict, Ruth; Boas, Franz; Mead, Margaret
culture and personality school 109–110, 159, 162, 176, 181
Culture Wars 11, 49, 135–136, 221, 234, 265–281, 298
Curry, John Steuart 165
Curtis, George William 63
cybernetics 245

Daly, Martin 239, 241
Daly, Mary 257
Danto, Arthur: "The Artworld" (1964) 211, 214–215
Darwin, Charles 219, 234; *Descent of Man* (1871) 22, 33, 86–87, 239, 243; *Expression of the Emotions in Man and Animals* (1872) 22, 239; *On the Origin of Species* (1859) 17–28, 138, 280
Darwin wars 236–239
Darwinian feminism 86–90
Darwinism 11, 17–24, 103, 136, 203, 223, 233; American reception of 24–28; and DNA 236; and political economy 24; and pragmatism 42; and Scopes Trial 117; and

secondary sources on 285–286;
and sociobiology 237; and
transhumanism 246; and
women's rights 80, 86–90
Deconstruction 227, 270, 276–278
Davis, Allison 114; Dawkins, Richard:
Selfish Gene (1976) 238–239
D'Souza, Dinesh 270
De Kooning, Willem 212
De Man, Paul 276–278
Decter, Midge 267
Delaney, Martin 157
democracy: and cold war liberalism
171–172; John Dewey on
45–46; and science 119–123;
Tocqueville on 186–187
Derrida, Jacques 199, 204, 227,
276–278
Descartes, René 36–37, 39–41
Dewey, John 45–46, 47, 71, 75, 113,
170, 227, 246, 279; debate
on democracy 119–123;
The Public and Its Problems
(1927) 120; *Reconstruction in
Philosophy* (1920) 45
discourse, concept of 3, 203–205
Dissent 172
DNA 229, 233, 234–236, 239, 243–
244, 247, 297
Dobson, James 261
doctor of philosophy degree (Ph.D)
50–52
Dollard, John: *Caste and Class in a
Southern Town* (1937) 116,
162
Dos Passos, John 160
double consciousness *see* DuBois,
W.E.B.
Douglass, Frederick 74, 93, 141–142
Drake, St. Clair 114
Dreiser, Theodore 189
DuBois, W.E.B.: "Conservation of
Races" (1897) 156–157;
Cornel West on 279; double
consciousness 5; idea of the
talented tenth 94, 185; "Of
Mr. Booker T. Washington
and Others" 75–76; *The
Philadelphia Negro* (1899)
58–59; *The Souls of Black Folk*
(1903) 5, 76–77, 141

Dunn, John 205
Dworkin, Andrea 260; *Woman Hating*
(1974) 252
Dylan, Bob 212
Dyson, Michael Eric 279

Eastman, Crystal 91
Eastman, Max 163
Eisenhower, Dwight D. 147, 191
Ehrenreich, Barbara 268
Ehrenreich, John 268
Eliot, Charles W. 49
Eliot, T.S. (Thomas Stearns) 132, 160
Ellis, Havelock 92
Ellison, Ralph: *Invisible Man* (1952)
190; *Shadow and Act* (1964)
188
Emerson, Ralph Waldo 37, 45, 81,
170, 279
empiricism 36–37; *see also* Logical
Empiricism
end of Ideology 179–180, 207, 213
Engels, Frederick 17; *Origin of Private
Property, Family, and the State*
(1884) 60
Enola Gay Exhibit 275–276
episteme 203–205
epistemology 36–37, 39–41, 119, 121
Erikson, Erik: *Childhood and Society*
(1950) 181–182; and culture
and personality school 109; and
neo-Freudianism 181; *Young
Man Luther* (1958) 182
Essays and Reviews (1860) 137–138
essentialism: and DNA 236; and
feminism 249, 253, 254;
Frederick Jackson Turner
opposed to 112; racial 158,
228–230, 241–243; and social
constructionism 219–220,
222–223, 228–232
eugenics 33, 73, 92, 233, 244
evangelicalism 148, 149, 234, 249,
261, 265–266
evolutionary psychology 234, 239–241
existentialism 189–190, 250

Fairchild, Henry Pratt: *The Melting
Pot Mistake* (1926) 154
Falwell, Jerry 261
Fanon, Franz 210

Farm Security Administration
  photography 165
Farrell, Warren: *Myth of Male Power*
  (1993) 262
Faulkner, William 161
Felton, Rebecca Latimer 73
feminism 219, 248–263, 270, 271,
  273; and anti-psychiatry
  movement 225; and Black
  women 93–94; and cold war
  liberalism 173; critique of the
  family 60; and deconstruction
  277; and eugenics 92; and
  Freud 90–92, 225; and
  middle-class cultural criticism
  186–187; origin of concept of
  90; radical 252–259; secondary
  sources on 289–290, 298;
  and sex 90–92, 259–261; and
  transhumanism 246; varieties
  of 248–249; vocabulary of
  250; wave metaphor 249; and
  women of color 256–268;
  see also Darwinian feminism,
  Woman Movement
Fiedler, Leslie 188, 213
Fields, Barbara Jeanne 229–230
Firestone, Shulamith 255; *Dialectic of
  Sex* (1970) 252, 253–254
Fitzgerald, F. Scott 160
formalism: revolt against 103; in
  aesthetics 132–133, 213
Fosdick, Harry Emerson: "Shall the
  Fundamentalists Win?" (1922)
  145
Foucault, Michel 36, 199; *History
  of Sexuality, vol. I* (1976)
  226, 243, 258; *Madness and
  Civilization* (1961) 224–225;
  Order of Things (1966)
  203–205
Fox, Robin and Lionel Tiger: *Imperial
  Animal* (1971) 238
Frankfurt School 181, 210
Frazer, James: *Golden Bough* (1890)
  143
Frazier, E. Franklin: *Black Bourgeoisie*
  (1957) 185–186; and Chicago
  sociology 114
Freidan, Betty: *Feminine Mystique*
  (1963) 186–187, 250–251

Freud, Sigmund 219, and adolescence
  106; and atheism 140;
  Civilization and Its Discontents
  (1930) 180; and cold war
  thought 170, 190; *Complete
  Psychological Works* (1953-)
  181; and cultural criticism
  46, 180–181, 267; and
  feminism 90–92, 187, 251; and
  homosexuality 243; "narcissism
  of small differences" 194
Freudianism 80, 106, 170, 180–181,
  213, 228, 253; *see also*
  neo-Freudianism
Friedman, Milton 193
Fromm, Erich: *Escape from Freedom*
  (1941) 181
frontier thesis *see* Turner, Frederick
  Jackson
Fukuyama, Francis 269
Fuller, Margaret: and feminist theory
  81; and Transcendentalism
  37; *Woman in the Nineteenth
  Century* (1845) 82–83
fundamentalism/modernism
  controversy 144–147, 265

Galbraith, John Kenneth 171
Gamble, Eliza Burt: *The Evolution of
  Women* (1894) 88–89
Gans, Herbert: *Levittowners* (1967)
  183
Garvey, Amy Ashwood 158
Garvey, Amy Jacques 158
Garvey, Marcus 157–158, 211
Gates, Henry Louis, Jr. 272–273, 278
gay gene 243–244
gay liberation 225, 244, 248, 252,
  255, 276
Geertz, Clifford 117
gender/sex distinction 96, 254–255,
  258–259
genteel tradition 38, 63
George, Henry: *Progress and Poverty*
  (1878) 66–67
Giddings, Franklin 55, 58
Gilder, Richard Watson 63
Gilligan, Carol: *In a Different Voice*
  (1982) 231–232
Gilman, Charlotte Perkins 88; *Women
  and Economics* (1898) 89–90

Gilman, Daniel Coit 49, 52
Ginsberg, Allan: *Howl* (1955) 224
Giovanni, Nikki 215
Gitlin, Todd: *Twilight of Common Dreams* (1996) 269–270
Glazer, Nathan 267
Gliddon, George 27
Godard, Jean-Luc 212
Godkin, E.L. 63
Gold, Mike 163
Goldberg, Herbert: *Hazards of Being Male* (1976) 262
Goldberg, Steven *Inevitability of Patriarchy* (1973) 238
Goldman, Emma 91, 92
Goodman, Paul 186; *Growing Up Absurd* (1960) 182
Gordon, Caroline 161
Gordon, Mittie Maude Lena 158
Gordon, Richard *Split-Level Trap* (1961) 183
Gore, Tipper 266
Gorer, Geoffrey 110
Gould, Stephen Jay 237, 242
Grady, Henry 160
Graham, Billy 148
Grant, Madison: *Passing of the Great Race* (1915) 73, 154
Gray, Asa 20, 24–26
Gray, John: *Men Are from Mars, Women Are from Venus* (1992) 232
Greenberg, Clement 133, 199, 213; "Avant Garde and Kitsch" (1939) 164, 211
Greer, Germaine *Female Eunuch* (1970) 252
Grice, Paul 205
Grimké, Sarah: *Letters on the Equality of the Sexes* (1838) 81

Hall, G. Stanley 106
Hamer, Dean 243–244; *The God Gene* (2004) 244
Hanisch, Carole: "The Personal is Political" (1970) 252
Haraway, Donna: *Cyborg Manifesto* (1985) 246
Harlem Renaissance 156, 158–159, 211, 215
Harris, William Torrey 37
Harrison, Hubert 142
Hartman, Geoffrey 277
Hartz, Louis: *Liberal Tradition in America* (1955) 174–176
Harvard University 49–50
Haskell, Thomas 273–274
Hayden, Tom: "Port Huron Statement" (1962) 208–210
Hayek, Friedrich von 192, 194; *Road to Serfdom* (1944) 193; "Why I am Not a Conservative" (1957) 193
Hegel, G.W.F. 5, 11–12, 45
Heidegger, Martin 36, 189, 278
Hemingway, Ernest 160
Henry, Carl F.H.: *The Uneasy Conscience of Fundamentalism* (1947) 148
Herberg, Will: *Protestant-Catholic-Jew* (1955) 147
Herder, Johann 155
Herrnstein, Richard *see* Charles Murray
Herskovits, Melville 103, 109
Hicks, Granville 163, 189
Higginson, Thomas Wentworth 63; "Sympathy of Religions" (1870) 149
Himmelfarb, Gertrude 267, 269
historiographical ideas 102; and consensus historians 174–177; and culture wars 273–276; and intellectual history 283–284; and progressive historians 110–113, 118, 174, 273
history of ideas 8
Hobsbawm, Eric 228
Hodge, Archibald 139
Hodge, Charles: *What is Darwinism?* (1874) 28
Hofstadter, Richard: *Age of Reform* (1954) 177, 191; *American Political Tradition and the Men Who Made It* (1948) 174–176; paranoid style 177
Hollingworth, Leta 88
Hook, Sidney 178
hooks, bell 278; *Ain't I A Woman* (1981) 257; *Feminist Theory: from Margin to Center* (1984) 257

Horney, Karen 181
Howe, Irving 188
Howerth, Ira 65–66
Hughes, Langston: "The Racial Mountain" (1926) 158–159; sexuality 159
Hull House 66
Hunter, James Davison 221, 265
Hurston, Zora Neale 103, 108–109, 158; *Of Mules and Men* (1935) 108
Huxley, T.H. 25; and agnosticism 141; *Evolution and Ethics* (1893) 31–32

I'll Take My Stand [Twelve Southerners] (1930) 161–162
identity, concept of 181–182
identity politics 256, 259
ideology 170, 177, 179
Ignatiev, Noel 230
imperialism 61, 95, 108, 167
Ingersoll, Robert: "Why I Am an Agnostic" (1889–1890) 141
intellectual history 2–10, 283–284; overviews of 284–285
intellectuals 3, 8–10
Intelligence Quotient (IQ)—Stanford-Binet Scale 122–123, 241–243
internationalism 165–167
intersectionality 256–257

Jacoby, Russell: *Last Intellectuals* (1987) 269–270
James, Henry 189
James, William 5, 47, 76, 104, 117, 152, 155, 203, 219, 279; "The Ph.D. Octopus" (1903) 51; *Pragmatism* (1907) 42–44; *Principles of Psychology* (1890) 42; *Varieties of Religious Experience* (1902) 6–7, 43, 143–144; "Will to Believe" (1897) 43, 143
Jaspers, Karl 189
Jensen, Arthur 242
Johns Hopkins University 49–50, 52
Johns, Jasper 214
Johnson, Charles 114
Johnston, Jill: *Lesbian Nation* (1973) 252

Jones, LeRoi 215
Judeo-Christian tradition 147

Kallen, Horace: and cultural pluralism 154–155, 172; "Democracy vs. the Melting Pot" (1915) 154–155; and pragmatism 35
Kaprow, Allan 212
Kardiner, Abram 109
Karenga, Maulana 215
Kaufmann, Walter 190
Kazin, Alfred 188
Keats, John: *Crack in the Picture Window* (1956) 183
Keen, Sam: *Fire in the Belly* (1992) 262
Kelley, Florence 86
Kennedy, Randall 278
Keynes, John Maynard 193
Kimball, Roger: *Tenured Radicals* (1990) 270–271, 272
Kimmel, Michael: *Manhood in America* (1996) 262–263
King, Martin Luther, Jr. 210, 279
King, R.S. 142
Kinsey, Alfred 243
Kirk, Russell: *Conservative Mind* (1955) 193–194
Koedt, Anne: *Myth of the Vaginal Orgasm* (1970) 252
Knight, Frank 192
Kristol, Irving 267–268, 269
Kroeber, A.L. 103
Krutch, Joseph Wood: *Modern Temper* (1929) 125
Kuhn, Thomas: *Structure of Scientific Revolutions* (1962) 200–203, 204, 206, 214, 227
Kurzweil, Ray: *Age of Spiritual Machines* (1999) 246

Lacan, Jacques 228
Laing, R.D.: *Divided Self* (1960) 224–225
Larsen, Nella 158
Lasch, Christopher 216
Laslett, Peter 205
Lee, Rose Hum 114
Leibman, Joshua: *Peace of Mind* (1946) 150
Levi-Strauss, Claude 199
Levin, Harry 188

Lewis, Sinclair 164
Lewontin, Richard 237; *Not in Our Genes* (1984) 238, 243
liberalism 249; classical 179, 193; conservative view of 192–194; laissez-faire and 66; Lockean, idea of 175–176, 209; Reinhold Niebuhr on 149; and science 129; sexual 106; Tocqueville on 188–189; view of conservatism 190–191; and women's rights 83–84; *see also* cold war liberalism; new liberalism
Lichtenstein, Roy 212, 214
linguistic turn 199, 204–205, 219, 226, 276
Lippmann, Walter 46, 68–69, 125; and democracy 120–123; *Drift and Mastery* (1914) 70–71, 119; *The Phantom Public* (1925) 120; *A Preface for Morals* (1929) 79; *Public Opinion* (1922) 120–122
literary criticism 132–133, 188–189, 276–278
Locke, Alain: and cultural pluralism 156–157, 172; *New Negro* (1925) 156; pragmatism 35; and sexuality 159
Locke, John 36–37, 175–176, 193, 206
logical empiricism 126–129, 200–201
logical positivism *see* logical empiricism
Lorde, Audre 215, 257
lost generation 159–160
Loury, Glenn 279
Lowell, James Russell 63
Lowie, Robert 103
Luce, Henry: "The American Century" (1940) 166
Luckmann, Thomas *see* Berger, Peter
Luhan, Mabel Dodge 91
Lynd, Helen Merrill and Robert Lynd: *Middletown: A Study in Modern American Culture* (1929) 115–117, 118, 160
Lynd, Robert *see* Lynd, Helen Merrill
Lysenko affair 130

McCarthy, Mary 188
McCarthyism 169–170, 173, 177, 192, 207
Macdonald, Dwight 164, 178
Machen, J. Gresham: *Christianity and Liberalism* (1923) 146
McKay, Claude 158
McKay, Nellie 272
MacKinnon, Catharine: *Only Words* (1993) 260
Mailer, Norman 188, 190
Mannheim, Karl: *Ideology and Utopia* (1936) 179
Marcuse, Herbert 210
marginal man 114–115
Marshall plan 171
Marx, Karl 176; *Communist Manifesto* (1948) 17; critique of modernity 36, 46, 219, 267; "Eighteenth Brumaire of Louis Napoleon" (1852) 55; feminism on 187, 251, 253; "Theses on Feuerbach" (1845) 66; view of capitalism 217; view of history 11, 30, 112; view of religion 140
Marxism 3, 248, 176, 276; and American exceptionalism 55; concept of ideology in 221; and cultural relativism 108; Daniel Bell and 179, 207, 216; and deconstruction 276–277; and existentialism 190; and feminism 249, 253–254, 258; Frankfurt School 181, 210, 216; Harold Cruse on 210; Henry Lewis Morgan and 60–61; and neo-conservatism 267–270; and new class theory 267–269; old left 163–164, 169, 207–208; and Port Huron Statement 209; and progressivism 66, 174; and religion 140; and social constructionism 228; as social science 54–55; sociobiology against 238; Susan Sontag on 213; and Raymond Williams 61, 131
masculinity 95–96
Maslow, Abraham 186–187, 251

mass culture 170
Mead, George Herbert 35, 58, 71, 113, 115
Mead, Margaret 103, 105, 132, 187, 251; *And Keep Your Powder Dry* (1942) 110; *Coming of Age in Samoa* (1928) 106–107
melting pot 153, 168
meme, concept of 239
men's movement 261–263
men's studies 262–263
Mencken, H. L. 117, 191; and anti-democratic thought 123
Merton, Robert: on "scientific ethos" 129; sociology of knowledge 220
Meyer, Frank 192, 194
Mill, John Stuart 37, 85; "On the Subjection of Women" (1869) 84
Miller, J. Hillis 277
Miller, Perry 162
Millet, Kate: *Sexual Politics* (1970) 252
Mills, C. Wright 180; "Letter to the New Left" (1960) 207–208; *Power Elite* (1956) 185; *White Collar* (1951) 183–185
Modern Age 193
modernism 280; and relativism 103–104, 199–200, 203; theological conflict with fundamentalism 144–147
modernity 1, 10–11; acids of 46–47, 70, 79, 125; and marginal man 114–115; and moral order 119–134; and philosophical critique 36; and religious belief 77, 136; and sex distinction 95–96; and sociology 56, 65, 116; and tragic sensibility 280; Weber on 124
monogenesis 27–28
Mont Pèlerin Society 193
Montague, Ashley 103
Moraga, Cherrie *see* Anzaldúa, Gloria
Morgan, Henry Lewis 55; *Ancient Society* (1877) 59; stadial theory and 59–61, 102; *Systems of Consanguinity and Affinity of the Human Family* (1871) 60

Morgan, Robin 260; *Sisterhood is Powerful* (1970) 252
Morris, Desmond: *Naked Ape* (1966) 238
Murray, Charles: *Bell Curve* (1994) 241–243, 246; *Losing Ground* (1984) 242
Murray, Judith Sargent 81
Myrdal, Gunnar: *An American Dilemma* (1944) 173

Nash, Gary 274
National Association for the Advancement of Colored People (NAACP) 75
national character 110
National History Standards 274–275
National Organization of Women (NOW) 251, 252
National Review 191, 193, 242
nativism 116, 154, 166, 191
natural law 222, 232
naturalism 29
Neal, Larry 215
Nelson, Lorde A. 142
neo-conservatism 266–270
neo-Freudianism 181–182, 249
neo-orthodoxy 149
new Black intellectuals 278–280
new class theory 267–269, 270, 276
New Criterion 270
new criticism 132–133, 188; *see also* literary criticism
New Deal 164–165, 169, 171, 191, 194
new left 207–211, 213, 217, 267, 273
new liberalism 67–69
New Masses 163–164
New Republic 69, 145, 193, 242
Niebuhr, Reinhold 149, 171
Nietzsche Friedrich 107, 123, 223; atheism 43, 140–141; criticism of modernity 36, 46, 219, 267; and existentialism 190; and Foucault 204; on science 124–125
Nisbet, Robert 192
Norris, Frank: *McTeague* (1899) 29
Norton, Charles Eliot 63
Nott, Josiah 27

Oakeshott, Michael 191
Odets, Clifford 164
Odum, Howard 162
Okenga, Harold 148
old left 12, 207, 208, 267
Oldenburg, Claes 214
Oppenheimer, Robert 130, 133
ordinary language philosophy 205–206
Orwell, George. 131, 178

Paine, Thomas 55
pan-africanism 211; *see also* Garvey, Marcus
paradigm 200–203, 217
Park, Robert 113–115, 118
Parrington, Vernon 174, 188, 189
Parsons, Elsie Clews 92
Parsons, Talcott 12, 53, 251
Partisan Review 163–164, 172, 188, 193
Peale, Norman Vincent 150
Peirce, Charles Sanders 35, 39–42, 45, 121, 203
Phillips, William 164
Pinker, Stephen 239; *How the Mind Works* (1997) 240
Pocock, J.G.A. 205
Podhoretz, Norman 267
Polanyi, Michael 130
political economy 24, 54
politics (journal) 172
Pollack, Jackson 212
polygenesis 27–28
Popper, Karl 127–128, 201
pornography *see* Women Against Pornography (WAP)
Port Huron Statement 208–210
post-industrial society 216–217, 244
post-structuralism 199, 204–205, 227, 249, 257–259, 277
postmodernism 199–200, 212–213, 277
Potter, David 175
Pound, Ezra 160
Powdermaker, Hortense 162
Pragmatism 3, 12, 34–47; and analytic philosophy 126; and pluralism 155–157; and Progressivism 77–78, 102; prophetic 279; and Richard Rorty 227

pro-slavery theory 5; and biblical interpretation 139; and sociology 56
progressivism 64–79, 93, 102, 287–288
Promise Keepers 261
psychoanalysis 180–182; *see also* Freud; Freudianism; neo-Freudianism
Public Interest 267

queer theory 226, 243–244, 258–259, 277

race: and *Bell Curve* debate 241–243; and canon wars 271–272; cold war liberalism 172–173; and feminism 256–258; and Progressivism 73–77; and social construction 228–230; and suburban criticism 183
racialism 73, 105, 154, 228–230
racism 59, 191, 228–229, 278–280
Radicalesbians: "Woman-Identified Woman" (1970) 255
Rahv, Philip 164
Rainey, Gertrude "Ma" 159
Rand, Ayn 191
Ransom, John Crowe: and agrarianism 161–162; and new criticism 132–133
rationalism 36–37
Rauschenberg, Robert 214
Rauschenbusch, Walter 77–78
Reagan, Ronald 269
Reed, Adolph 278
regionalism 165
religion 135–150; academic study of 142–144; in the cold war 147–150; and creationism 234; ecumenical 139–140; idea of orthodoxy 136; pluralism of 136–137; secondary sources on 291–292; *see also* biblical higher criticism; evangelicalism
Reuther, Walter 171
revisionist history 275
revolt against the village 159–160
Rich, Adrienne: "Compulsory Heterosexuality" (1980) 258

Rieff, Philip: *Freud: the Mind of the Moralist* (1959) 180
Riesman, David: *Lonely Crowd* (1950) 183–184, 217
Ripley, William Z.: *Races of Europe* (1899) 154
Robinson, James Harvey 102
Roediger, David 230
Roosevelt, Eleanor 171
Roosevelt, Franklin 164
Roosevelt, Theodore: and masculinity 95–96; and melting pot 153
Rorty, Richard 46; *Philosophy and the Mirror of Nature* (1979) 227
Rosenberg, Harold 170, 199, 211–212
Ross, Edward A. 73, 154
Rossellini, Roberto 212
Rothbard, Murray 192
Rubin, Gayle: "The Traffic in Women" (1975) 252, 254
Rustin, Bayard 210
Ryle, Gilbert 205

St. Louis Hegelians 37–38
Sanger, Margaret 92
Santayana, George 38
Sapir, Edward 103, 109
Sartre, Jean-Paul 189–190, 228
Saussure, Ferdinand de 199, 204
Schapiro, Meyer 211
Schlesinger, Arthur, Jr. 178, 180; *Age of Jackson* (1945) 174; *Vital Center* (1949) 171–174
science: and biology 234; democracy 119–123; and disenchantment 124–125; history and sociology of 126, 128–131, 200–203; and modernity 119–120; and moral order 119–134; philosophy of 126–128; pragmatism 39–41, 46–47; and progressive reform 69–73; Richard Rorty on 227
Scopes Trial 117, 146, 160, 265; secondary sources on 291
Scottish Common Sense Philosophy 37–38, 57, 266, 269
secularization 135, 291–292
Sedgwick, Eve Kosofsky 258
sex-positive feminism 260–261
sexuality—idea of 226
Shaw, George Bernard 123

Sheen, Bishop Fulton J. 150
Shockley, William 242
single tax movement 66–67
Skinner, Quentin: "Meaning and Understanding in the History of Ideas" (1969) 205–206
Small, Albion 55, 57–58
Smith, Adam 57, 58
Smith, Barbara Herrnstein 273
Smith, Bessie 159
Snow, C.P. *see* two cultures debate
social constructionism 219–232, 233, 296
Social Darwinism 29–33, 47, 103, 233, 240, 247
social democracy 68–69
social gospel 77–78, 146
social imaginary 228
social question, the 65–67
social sciences 52–56, 287; *see also* anthropology; sociology
social settlements 66
sociobiology 234, 237–239
sociology 56–59, 217; of knowledge 220; and middle-class cultural criticism 182–188; *see also* Chicago school of sociology
Sontag, Susan: "Against Interpretation" (1964) 211–214
southern distinctiveness 159–163
southern renaissance 161
Spectorsky, A.C. *Exurbanites* (1955) 183
Spencer, Herbert 21, 30, 54, 66
stadial theory 54, 59–61, 102–103
Stanton, Elizabeth Cady: and racism 93; and Seneca Falls convention 83–84; "Solitude of Self" (1892) 84; *Women's Bible* (1895, 1898) 85
Steele, Shelby 279
Steichen, Edward: *Family of Man* (1955) 167
Stein, Gertrude 160
Steinbeck, John 164
Stewart, Dugald 37, 59
Stoddard, Lothrop 154
Strachey, James: translator, *Complete Psychological Works of Sigmund Freud* (1953-) 181
Strater, Henry 160

Index

stream of consciousness 42
Student Non-Violent Coordinating Committee (SNCC) 208, 210
Students for a Democratic Society (SDS) 208–210
Studies on the Left 207
Sui, Paul C.P. 114
Sullivan, Harry Stack 109, 181
Sumner, William Graham 30–31, 56, 57, 66, 104
Symons, David 239
Szasz, Thomas: *Myth of Mental Illness* (1961) 224–225

Tarde, Gabriel 57
Tate, Allan 132
Taylor, Frederick Winslow 72–73
technological utopianism 245
Terman, Lewis 122–123
Terrell, Mary Church 93
Thomas, W.I. 113, 117
Tiger, Lionel *see* Fox, Robin
Tocqueville, Alexis de: *Democracy in America* (1835, 1840) 187–188
Tönnies, Ferdinand 57
Tooby, John and Leda Cosmides: *Adapted Mind* (1992) 239, 241
Toomer, Jean 158
totalitarianism 170, 173, 177–179
Transcendentalism 37–38, 139, 187
transhumanism 244–246
tri-faith America 147–150
Trilling, Lionel 132, 213; and adversarial culture 267; on conservatism 191; "Freud and Literature" (1940) 180; *Liberal Imagination* (1950) 188–189
Trotsky, Leon 267–268
Truffaut, François 212
Ture, Kwame *see* Black Power; Carmichael, Stokely
Turner, Frederick Jackson 110–112, 273
Twain, Mark 123
two cultures debate (Snow) 131–133, 237
Tyler, E.B. 60, 102

Unitarianism 139
universities 49–63, 286–287; culture wars and 266, 269–276; German model of research and 50

Veblen, Thorstein 32–33, 56, 102
Viereck, Peter 192
Voegtlin, Walter *Stone Age Diet* (1975) 241

Waddell, Ethel 158
Wallace, Henry 170–171
Ward, Lester Frank 31–32, 56, 57
Warfield, Benjamin 139
Warhol, Andy 212
Warren, Robert Penn 161
Washington, Booker T. 5, 75–76
Waters, Ethel 159
Watson, James 234
Weaver, Richard 192
Weber, Max 5, 133; influence on C. Wright Mills 185; *Protestant Ethic and the Spirit of Capitalism* (1905) 124; "Science as a Vocation" (1917) 124
Wells-Barnett, Ida B. 94
Weltfish, Gene 103
West, Cornel 278; *American Evasion of Philosophy* (1989) 279; *Race Matters* (1993) 279–280
Weyl, Walter 68–69
White, Andrew Dickson 49
White, Hayden 275
whiteness, social construction of 230
Whyte, William: *Organization Man* (1956) 183
Wiener, Norbert 245
Willard, Frances 86
Willis, Emily 260–261
Willkie, Wendell: *One World* (1943) 167
Wilson, E. O. 237–239; *On Human Nature* (1978) 237; *Sociobiology* (1975) 237–238
Wilson, James Q. 269
Wilson, Margo 239, 241
Wirth, Louis 113
Wittgenstein, Ludwig 205
Wolfe, Thomas 161
Wollstonecraft, Mary: *A Vindication of the Rights of Women* (1792) 81
Wood, Grant 165

Woodhull, Victoria 90
Woodward, C. Vann 174; *Strange Career of Jim Crow* (1955) 163
world's parliament of religions 140
woman movement 80–96; *see also* feminism
Women Against Pornography (WAP) 261, 266
women's rights 80–96; *see also* feminism
women's studies 271
Works Progress Administration 165

Wright, Richard 189, 190
Wright, Robert: *Moral Animal* (1994) 239
Wu Ching-Chao 114

X, Malcolm 210

Yale School of Criticism 276–278

Zangwill, Israel: *Melting Pot* (1909) 153
Znaniecki, Florian 113

Made in United States
North Haven, CT
11 May 2024